The Word is Very Near You
Sundays

Also by the same author and available from Canterbury Press

The Inner-City of God: The diary of an East End parson

'This book made me laugh out loud, but it also made me cry. It is about what it means to be faithful to Christ, even if you are not successful, which is how life is for most of us.' *Nick Holtam, Vicar of St Martin-in-the-Fields*

'John Pridmore is an Anglican hero – and one of the few writers I know capable of making me a better person.' *Giles Fraser, Canon Chancellor of St Paul's Cathedral, writer and broadcaster*

'This book is and will remain unrivalled for those who wish to understand what the job of an Anglican parish priest is like.' *CR Quarterly*

www.canterburypress.co.uk

The Word is Very Near You

Sundays

Reflections on the lectionary readings
Years A, B and C

John Pridmore

CANTERBURY
PRESS
Norwich

© John Pridmore 2009

First published in 2009 by the Canterbury Press Norwich
Editorial office
13–17 Long Lane,
London, EC1A 9PN, UK

Canterbury Press is an imprint of Hymns Ancient and Modern Ltd
(a registered charity)
St Mary's Works, St Mary's Plain,
Norwich, NR3 3BH, UK

www.scm-canterburypress.co.uk

Acknowledgements of copyright material

Thomas O. Chisholm, 'Great is thy faithfulness' © 1923 Hope Publishing
Company, 380 South Main Place, Carol Stream, IL 60188, USA

'Now the green blade riseth', J. M. C. Crum (1872–1958) [altd]. Reproduced by
permission of Oxford University Press. All rights reserved.

Sydney Carter, 'One more step along the way'. Reproduced by permission of
Stainer & Bell Ltd, London, England, www.stainer.co.uk.

British Library Cataloguing in Publication data

A catalogue record for this book is available
from the British Library

978-1-85311-951-4

Printed and bound in Great Britain by
CPI Antony Rowe, Chippenham, Wiltshire

For Chris, who makes the story credible

Contents

Introduction

We are at last beginning to read the Bible together. It is the Revised Common Lectionary (RCL) that has made that possible. Whatever our denominational differences, we have always turned to the Bible when we have gone to church. Now, when we go to church, most of us are turning to the same pages of the Bible. That is because the RCL has been so widely adopted. Ecumenical progress, of which one sometimes despairs, is being made.

The Church of England's 'Principal Service Lectionary' is not a different animal from the RCL. To be sure, it tinkers with the RCL. But its sensible modifications are not substantial. The Principal Service Lectionary's readings for the Sundays of its three-year cycle are virtually identical with those of the RCL. It is those Sunday readings which I consider in these pages.

A second book is on its way. That book will contain comments on the lectionary readings for the holy days of the Christian year which do not fall on a Sunday, such as Ascension Day or Good Friday, and for the feasts which do not necessarily fall on a Sunday, such as Christmas Day and the major Saints' Days.

My focus in this book is on the figure of Jesus of Nazareth. I am haunted by a detail in the story of Jesus found only in Mark's Gospel. 'Jesus was walking ahead of them,' we are told. And Mark adds, 'they were amazed and those who followed were afraid' (Mark 10.32). The Jesus we meet in the Gospels is always ahead of us. We stumble after him, hoping to catch him up, but when we think we have done so, we find that he has moved on. That is Christian discipleship. When I was a boy in a Bible class we used to sing, 'Follow, follow, I would follow Jesus'. That determination is the perspective of these pages. I am asking one question. What do we learn from the Bible about what it means to follow Jesus?

I focus on Jesus. That focus is the reason why I have tended to concentrate, Sunday by Sunday, on the Gospel for the day. I do sometimes comment on 'the first reading' or 'the second reading', but I have not felt obliged always to do so. The sequences of readings I have chosen are those that, the lectionary claims, are 'related', but where that kinship is not immediately apparent I have not tried to establish it. Contrived connections are unpersuasive.

From time to time I have presumed to criticize some of the decisions that the compilers of our lectionary have made. Occasionally the latter seem over-anxious that we should have an easy ride. For example, 'hard sayings' are sometimes left out. (One such omission, wonderfully, is the command on the last page of the Bible never to add to or subtract from anything the text says!) Such excisions, I believe, are mistaken. The Bible is always a rugged ride. That is what makes it so challenging and exciting. But criticizing our lectionary is easy. Coming up with anything better would be difficult indeed. Our lectionary remains a tremendous achievement. Any carping comments I make about it cannot detract from that achievement.

Sometimes I propose that we look at a picture to help us see what a story in the Bible is telling us. It would have made this book prohibitively expensive to have reproduced those pictures alongside my comments. Happily, images of them are swiftly to be found on the Internet. I have not suggested each time which website to visit. The works of art I mention are famous ones and images of them are on scores of sites. A search engine will quickly locate the one you are looking for.

This book was written in two places – so we might say 'in two worlds'. It was begun in Hackney in the East End of London. It was completed in Hove on the south coast. The occasional local colour in these pieces reflects one or other of these locations.

Most of these reflections first appeared in the pages of the *Church Times*. I am deeply grateful to Rachel Boulding, the paper's deputy editor, who week by week made sure that these pieces were sufficiently presentable to appear in public.

Finally, I thank my wife Pat, not the least of whose loving gifts to me is to guard me against my inclination, endemic among clergy, to take flight into fog. Without her this book would not have been written.

John Pridmore

The First Sunday of Advent

YEAR A

Isaiah 2.1–5; Romans 13.11–14; Matthew 24.36–44

THE FAR-OFF SONG

In George MacDonald's haunting tale *At the Back of the North Wind*, the child Diamond sees the sinking of a great ship in a terrible storm. Diamond is visited by the deeply mysterious 'North Wind', the elusive and unexplained 'Wise Woman' who comes and goes in many of MacDonald's stories. Diamond asks North Wind how she can bear the piteous cries of the drowning sailors. North Wind replies, 'I will tell you how I am able to bear it, Diamond. I am always hearing through every noise the sound of a far-off song.' In Advent we strive to catch the strains of that song.

Our first reading is an anthem anticipating that far-off song. Isaiah sings of what he has seen – *seen*, notice. He rejoices in what he has witnessed, the day when the Lord will reign from his holy city and war shall be no more.

It is important to relate the rhapsody to the reality. It is not all bad news. For swords have already been turned into ploughshares. When the bitter and protracted civil war in Mozambique ceased, Goao swapped his stash of arms for sewing machines and with them started a family tailoring business. Goao was provided with his sewing machines by a Christian charity that persuaded him and hundreds of other former freedom-fighters to exchange their guns for tools.

The promise to the prophet has been fulfilled, but only in part. For nation still lifts up sword against nation and still they train for war. Still they slaughter each other in wars around the globe and still we send our princes to Sandhurst. Goao's sewing machines seem a ludicrously feeble fulfilment of the soaring vision vouchsafed to Isaiah. But lest we pooh-pooh those sewing-machines, we recall what

I

Jesus said about how God's Kingdom grows. It grows, says Jesus, from mustard seeds, 'the smallest of all the seeds on earth' (Mark 4.31).

The seeds of what we long for, of what we dare to believe will one day come to pass, must be nurtured. Advent is not a season for sitting on our hands waiting for something – or even for someone – to turn up.

The charity that offered tools for guns in Mozambique was faced with the problem of what to do with all the weaponry surrendered to it. Their brilliant solution was to cut the guns in pieces and to give them to local artists as raw material for their work. Some of the pieces they made came to London and were put on show in an exhibition held in the OXO tower on the South Bank of the Thames. The exhibition was something of a sensation. One sculpture was entitled 'Catching the Peacebird'. A critic commented: 'The peacebird of the sculptor is no gentle dove with an olive branch. It is feisty, feral creature which needs to be grasped and, perhaps, tamed.' Peace, as much as war, has to be waged.

Paul has bracing advice about the frame of mind – and the physical condition – in which we must serve our coming King. 'Not in revelling and drunkenness, not in debauchery and licentiousness, not in quarelling and jealousy.' We may congratulate ourselves that those with whom we worship this Sunday are not a conspicuously debauched lot. That sentiment is not to our credit. It reflects how far we are from the church of the New Testament which *included* the debauched – even if, to be sure, their debauchery had to be dealt with. We note too – in a Church 'by schisms rent asunder' – that St Paul sees quarrelling as just as injurious to the health of the body of Christ as the sins that the nicer class of Christian finds more objectionable.

In Advent we tend to ask what's going to happen when. Jesus turns all such questions back on ourselves. To use long words, Christian eschatology is through and through ethical. What we are told about what is to come is not to provide us with information but with motivation. Jesus does not say when it is all going to end, for the simple reason that he does not know himself. Some of the early editors of our Gospel reading, embarrassed by Jesus's admission of ignorance, left out those three little words – 'nor the Son' – that tell us so much about the humanity of Jesus. Jesus does not satisfy our curiosity. He tells us how to live.

The paradox of the coming Kingdom is that it is both a realm to which we advance one small step at a time – a sewing machine for an

AK-47, a well of fresh water instead of a two-hours' walk to a brackish river, a communion table open to children – and also a personal visitation that will overtake us unannounced, 'the coming of the Son of Man'. What the latter means is beyond us. What has to be done in the meantime is not.

YEAR B

Isaiah 64.1–9; 1 Corinthians 1.3–9; Mark 13.24–37

SOMEONE TO MEET US

There is a paradox in the teaching of Jesus about how it will all end. On the one hand he seems to be saying that there will be clear signs, both in history and in the sky, that the end is imminent. On the other hand he warns us against any attempt to forecast its date. We will be given ample warning of the end – but it will overtake us unannounced. Such paradoxes delight the 'cut and paste' critics of the Gospels. They see them as evidence of confusion in the editing of the texts. The critics may be right, but there is another way of looking at the matter. Jesus's paradoxes are the same as his parables. They are not there to make things clear. They are there to make us think.

Both elements of the paradox are true. God only knows how the story will end. But at the same time we are not left totally in the dark. We know the two things we need to know. We know what the essential nature of the end will be and we know what we must do in the meantime.

We know that at the end of the road there will be someone to meet us. We will see 'the Son of man coming in clouds with great power and glory' (Mark 13.26). Teilhard de Chardin was a priest and a palaeontologist. He wrestled all his life with the great questions of creation's destiny, its 'Omega point' as he liked to call it. He came to the conclusion that the 'Omega point' is a meeting point. 'I go forward', de Chardin said, 'to meet him who comes' (*Hymn to the Universe*, Collins, 1965).

We struggle to make sense of it all. Teilhard de Chardin says that our quest for meaning is, at its deepest level, a quest for meeting. Our need to find out reflects a still more basic need, our need to be found. That meeting may be long deferred, deferred indeed for every generation save the last beyond death, but our desire for it is anything

3

but vain. 'We will be like him, for we shall see him as he is' (1 John 3.2).

Meanwhile we must 'watch'. Here again much is left unspecified. How do we watch? Where do we look? The word which demands so much tells us so little. We must 'watch', but we are not told what exactly 'watching' requires of us in this or that situation. But that's what Jesus's 'interim ethic' is like. That's the kind of guidance he gives about how we should live in the little time left to us.

It is the same in the Sermon on the Mount. Jesus doesn't legislate for all the countless complicated situations where we have to make difficult moral decisions. Christian discipleship is life-long learning but there are no school rules. Instead Jesus calls for a certain disposition. 'Watching' is a frame of mind and heart and spirit. Perhaps we might call it 'expectant attentiveness'. As the German theologian Jürgen Moltmann put it, 'We must not drift through history with our backs to the future' (*Theology of Hope*, SCM, 1967).

We have a powerful exposition of the watchword 'watch' in the Advent parable of the sheep and the goats (Matthew 25.31–46). The parable makes it clear that the direction we must look is neither skywards nor inwards. The angels say exactly the same on Advent Sunday as they say on Ascension Day, 'Don't stand looking into heaven' (Acts 1.11). ('Or', as one of the angels might have muttered, 'don't stand contemplating your navel.')

We watch by looking around. To watch is to be alert to Jesus's 'intermediate comings' in the least of his brothers and sisters. Watchfulness then becomes a matter of imaginative openness to the significance of chance encounters. I think of the gentleman I met in church one Sunday. His clothes were threadbare and he looked ill-nourished. He had waited until after the service and until others had gone for a chance to speak to me. 'I'm Jesus,' he said. 'I've come back.' Perhaps he was. Perhaps he had.

And we mustn't forget the little fig tree. Once its first leaves appear we know that summer is on its way. That's a sign of hope for us – but it is good news for the fig tree too, and if we think that's a silly idea then we've never read St Paul. Paul was sure that in our watching and waiting we are not alone. The Advent hope is all creation's. 'For the creation waits with eager longing for revealing of the children of God' (Romans 8.20). 'Going forward to meet him who comes' isn't just what I do. Teilhard de Chardin saw that clearly. All things – fig trees included – are pressing forward towards their 'Omega point', the meeting which is their redemption too. The whole universe is watching.

4

YEAR C

Jeremiah 33.14–16; 1 Thessalonians 3.9–13; Luke 21.25–36

WHEN THE TALL TOWERS FALL

Aporia sounds like an unpleasant skin condition. It's not. It is a Greek philosophical term and it refers to a state of mind where every train of thought hits the buffers. Socrates reduced his students to *aporia*, exposing the specious grounds of their supposed certainties and leaving them unsure what to think. *Aporia* is a term popular with postmodernists. The French philosopher Derrida went on about it. *Aporia* is also a word which occurs just once in the New Testament. It turns up this Sunday in our first Gospel reading for the new church year. According to Luke, that is how Jesus describes the perplexity, triggered by terrible storms at sea, which will overtake us in the last days.

We shall be reading a lot of Luke this year. Luke has a richer vocabulary than the other evangelists. We shall be on the look-out for occasions like this when he finds an unusual but apposite turn of phrase to capture what's going on in the story of Jesus or to express the exact force of something Jesus says.

Jesus says that, as the end of the world approaches, we shall experience *aporia*. We shall no longer feel sure about all that once had seemed so certain. It is always unwise to claim that contemporary conditions fulfil something that the Bible predicts. No doubt the first readers of Luke's Gospel believed that the words of Jesus about the future were specifically about *their* time. That said, it is extraordinary, early in the twenty-first century, to hear Jesus talking about *aporia*. If the postmodernists are to be believed, we can no longer trust any 'grand narrative', any system or story which claims to give an all-encompassing account of things. We too are reduced to *aporia*.

Luke has another graphic detail, all his own, about the last act of human history: 'People will faint from fear and foreboding.' Again, wary as we are of making such connections, we recognize from our own experience the truth of the word of Jesus. People are fearful. There are the specific fears. Fear of the bomb on the bus or the plane. Fear of the boy in the hood. Fear for those dear to us who live in vulnerable places or who do dangerous jobs. Fear of financial meltdown.

But beneath lurks a deeper and more pervasive fear, the fear of what cannot be identified or named. Letty phoned me the other day. Letty rang me because she was afraid. She was not afraid of anything especially. She was simply afraid. According to Zygmunt Bauman, we are awash with anxiety, a condition he explores in his book *Liquid Fear* (Polity, 2006).

A generation ago that prescient spirit Thomas Merton felt this ultimate dread overtake him. It's his turn on fire-watch. As he pads about his sleeping monastery, he is overwhelmed by a sense of the fragility of all in which we trust.

> Lord God, the whole world tonight seems to be made out of paper. The most substantial things are ready to crumble or tear apart and blow away . . . Only man makes illuminations he conceives to be solid and eternal. But while we ask our questions and come to our decisions, God blows our decisions out, the roofs of our houses cave in upon us, the tall towers are undermined by ants, the walls crack and cave in, and the holiest buildings burn to ashes – while the watchman is composing a theory of duration. (*The Sign of Jonas*, Sheldon Press, 1976)

The tall towers fall. As the end approaches, we are perplexed and fearful.

Luke has unsparing words for the anodynes we reach for in our sick apprehension of we know not what. We must guard against 'dissipation'. That is how most of our versions translate a splendid Greek word meaning both over-familiarity with the bottle and what such intimacy leads to. Less dramatic but equally disabling are 'the anxieties of life'. We reflect on how all the modern gizmos invented to ease our daily path only multiply its pitfalls. (My wife warns me that my computer is likely to crash soon. Much as the world is.)

The prospect Luke contemplates is terrifying. It resonates with all that confuses and frightens us in our own day. Advent tells us to stay with those feelings, to address unflinchingly what awaits the universe and all of us, the 'poor, bare, forked animals' that we are. Unless we have been afraid we are not entitled to hope.

For hope is there. Just as Luke depicts more graphically than the other Gospel-writers how dark the sky grows as our little day draws to its close, so it is Luke's thrilling voice which speaks most exultantly of the light of a new day. The Son of Man will come 'in a cloud'. Not any old cloud, but *the* cloud, scarcely less glorious than the divinity from whose sight it shields our eyes.

Luke, only Luke, has the tremendous summons: 'When these things begin to take place, stand up and raise your heads, because your redemption is drawing nigh.' These are words to proclaim as our world falls apart.

The Second Sunday of Advent

YEAR A

Isaiah 11.1–10; Romans 15.4–13; Matthew 3.1–12

THE KING'S GARDEN-CITY

There are three great images in the Hebrew Bible, our 'Old Testament', of 'the best that is yet to be'. These images have enabled the Christian Church to speak, at least a little less incoherently, about the Advent hope. The prophets looked forward to 'the once and future king', to the garden, and to the city. So do we. With Isaiah, we watch and pray for the coming of 'great David's greater Son'. With him we pine for paradise. With him we long for 'the New Jerusalem'.

The coming king – here is the first startling picture – will be 'a shoot from a stump'. Matthew Henry comments, 'Both the words here used signify a weak, small, tender product, a *twig* and a *sprig* (so some render them), such as is easily broken off.' (Matthew Henry published his mighty six-volume commentary on the Bible in 1706. Evangelical students were once urged to sell their shirts to get hold of it.) A later poem, also attributed to Isaiah, will speak of one who 'grew up like a root out of dry ground' (Isaiah 53.2). 'The Messiah was thus to begin his estate of humiliation,' says Matthew Henry.

'The spirit of the Lord will rest upon him.' Again Matthew Henry – 'The Holy Spirit, in all his gifts and graces, shall not only come, but rest and abide upon him; he shall have the Spirit not by measure, but without measure, the fullness of the Godhead dwelling in him.' We duly say 'Amen' to that, but not without first noting that in the Old Testament the Spirit of God is invariably given for a specific task. So here the promised king will come with a particular mission. His royal role will be to 'judge the poor'. Judgement in the Old Testament is not the deliverance of a verdict. It is the deliverance of *people*. It is setting wrongs right. Christian readers of Isaiah's prophecy will recall words that startled the back row of the synagogue in Nazareth, 'The Spirit of the Lord is upon me, because he has anointed me to preach good news to the poor' (Luke 4.18).

Once the king comes the conditions of paradise will be restored. On that day 'the wolf shall live with the lamb'. This will come as good news for the lambs around at the time but, unless we believe in the resurrection of mutton, it will be little comfort for all those previously savaged by wolves and butchered by us. This is not a facetious point. Few issues are more troubling to the Christian conscience and to Christian faith than the pain of animals. In her novel *Peter Abelard*, Helen Waddell writes of Abelard's heart being broken by the screams of a rabbit tortured in a trap. He releases the rabbit, but it dies in his hands. 'Do you think there is a God at all?' he asks his companion Thibault. 'Whatever has come to me, I earned it. But what did this one do?' For Tennyson too, it was all too much. Nature 'shrieked against his creed'. Long before Darwin, nature's message from the fossils was clear: 'I care for nothing' (*In Memoriam*).

Now that we know something of the waste and pain that has brought us to our stage of evolution, we can perhaps begin to sense the magnitude of Isaiah's vision. Do we believe it? Paul certainly did, Paul who spoke of the whole creation obtaining 'the freedom of the glory of the children of God' (Romans 8.18–25). Are we persuaded with Paul that 'the sufferings of this present time' – the lamb's, the kid's, the calf's, the sufferings of Abelard's rabbit and of all those preyed upon by wild animals such as ourselves – are 'not worth comparing' with the glory to be revealed? The vision is beyond our imaginative grasp, and where the imagination fails faith falters too. But what we may not do is to remove Isaiah's picture of paradise and substitute one of our own. Man-made paradises have a tendency to turn into hells on earth. Better simply to stand in front of the picture and to repeat, 'Lord I believe. Help thou my unbelief.'

'A little child shall lead them.' The text means more than Isaiah meant, though surely he too rejoiced when the servant king he had seen from afar gave to a child the highest standing in his Kingdom (Mark 10.14). Isaiah pictures little children playing safely and with great *delight* (that is what the Hebrew means) in the garden of God, just as Zechariah saw them playing on the streets of the city of God (Zechariah 8.5). The boundaries of that city ('my holy mountain') in the prophet's inclusive vision are the ends of the earth, for at the last all shall know as they always have been known.

This – although we have yet to turn to our reading from Matthew – this is the gospel of the Lord.

YEAR B

Isaiah 40.1–11; 2 Peter 3.8–15a; Mark 1.1–8

GOING OUT TO GOD

Mark begins in the beginning and in the desert. Both locations are significant, for as his story unfolds it becomes clear that these are two places to which we must return.

'The beginning . . .' There's more to these words than those we sometimes hear in church – 'Here begins the first verse of the second chapter . . .' Mark isn't a churchwarden standing at a lectern. He means to ring a bell, to take us back to where the whole story starts, 'In the beginning God . . .' But the beginning is not 'the big bang', not the first moment in time when the clock started ticking. 'The beginning' *is* – not *was*. It is present tense. The beginning is the continuing spring of things, 'the love that moves the sun and the other stars'. In the pages of Mark's little book, his take on the 'good news' of Jesus, that unceasing love bids us welcome and calls us home.

'Good news' it may be, but we're quickly in the Badlands, in the desert, 'that mysterious elsewhere', as the architect Frank Lloyd Wright called the moonscapes of Dakota, 'an endless supernatural world more spiritual than earth'. Mark's desert is many places. Geographically, it is the wilderness of Judea, the arid slopes of the deepest stretch of the Great Rift Valley. Scripturally, it is the wilderness into which God entices his wayward people, where the divine lover pleads with his unfaithful bride, aching to renew his covenant with her (Hosea 2.14–15). Mystically, it is the wasteland of the spirit, the Empty Quarter of the human heart where I shall die of my thirst for God unless I find him.

Hosea had said that in the desert God would 'speak tenderly' to his people. Yet the voice we hear is far from tender. The tone of John the Baptist is as harsh as the camel's hair he wears. Who is this weird figure, munching his locusts? (Hackney Parish Church is dedicated to St John the Baptist. The Rt Revd Richard Chartres, Bishop of London, gave me an icon of John when I was instituted as Rector there. He – the Baptist, not the Bishop – is depicted preaching to his own severed head.)

Mark thinks he knows who John the Baptist is. He doesn't spell it out yet. Later he will. Here he simply scatters a few clues. John is the prophet Elijah – Elijah who dressed as John does and whose desert diet was equally unusual. But the strangest thing about Elijah was that he didn't die properly. Instead he was swept up to heaven in a chariot of fire. Prophets who ride the sky in that way may well turn up again, and so the expectation was born that, before the dread 'day of the Lord', Elijah would return. This is the warning with which the Old Testament ends (Malachi 4.5–6) and which colours the picture Mark paints of John. (Whether John the Baptist himself thought he was Elijah is quite another matter.)

John's baptism is one of 'repentance'. We are often told that 'repentance' means 'a change of mind', and in the Greek that is the root-meaning. But changes of mind come too easily. Every week I change my mind about this and that more often than I change my socks. John requires, as does Jesus, a more radical and permanent reorientation. He will warn those who flock to him, some no doubt merely to gape, that the 'space of grace' is brief. He will tell them that the axe is already raised and the time left is the merest moment before it falls (Luke 3.9). His command is that of the Old Testament prophets. It is – one blunt syllable in our Anglo-Saxon as in their Hebrew – that we 'turn'. I must prepare to meet my God.

'They went *out* to him.' The path to life is always a journey 'outside'. The people of God becomes a community of faith 'outside', whether in the wilderness of Sinai, or – where criminals are crucified – outside a city wall. We must go 'outside the camp' (Hebrews 13.13). So it is in other stories too. In Islam, for example, the faithful are those who, like the prophet, have fled, those who have left home and emigrated to God. They who go to the Buddha for refuge follow one whose path to enlightenment began with palace gates closing behind him. The test of our turning is the degree of our willingness 'to go out', to let go our individual securities and institutional privileges and to brave the desert.

John the Baptist is the last and greatest of the prophets. He is also the first of the desert fathers, those who to this day seek their Lord in remote and silent places. As Professor David Jasper has said, 'it is by these strange people that the world is truly kept in being'. (*The Sacred Desert*, Blackwells, 2004).

YEAR C

Baruch 5.1–9 or Malachi 3.1–4; Philippians 1.3–11; Luke 3.1–6

CLEARING THE ROAD

'Minimalism' dictates that your house should be free of ornament and unnecessary clutter. But 'minimalism' isn't just an approach to interior design. 'Minimalism' is a method of scholarship within biblical studies. 'Minimalism' is the house-style of the so-called 'Copenhagen School'. Those who belong to this school of thought hold that the Bible is a story book and that, as such, it sheds little light on what actually happened.

Minimalists have been a powerful force in recent years in Old Testament studies. Now they are turning to the New Testament. Thomas L. Thompson is a professor in Copenhagen University and he has written a book in which he argues that the Gospel writers are not trying to describe the life of a real person (*The Messiah Myth*, Cape, 2006). They too are telling a story. On this view it is futile to try to locate Jesus at some point in history.

You can make this claim only by ignoring the first part of Sunday's Gospel reading. Luke gives a precise date for the moment when John the Baptist came on the scene and Jesus was baptized. Certainly there are discrepancies between the details Luke gives and what is known from other sources. But that is not the point. It is clear what Luke is doing. He is setting down specific historical markers, even if they're hard to harmonize with other records. He is saying, 'This happened, and this is when it happened, and this is where it happened.' Luke's account of Jesus is certainly a story – and a rattling good story-teller Luke is too. But the story he tells is anchored in the history to which 1066 and 2066 and all of us belong. The 'quest of the historical Jesus' is far from a waste of time.

Luke says what happened. But of course he recounts these events because of what he believes they mean. To explain their significance Luke directs us to the Old Testament. That is how he makes sense of that weird figure, John the Baptist – a character crying out for explanation if ever there was one. In the later chapters of Isaiah we have a series of poems containing a message of hope for God's exiled people, those who sit by the rivers of Babylon and weep. In one of those poems 'a voice' is heard. In the version of the poem used by Luke that 'voice' is said to be 'crying in the desert' (Isaiah 40.3–5). Luke takes that 'voice' to refer to John the Baptist.

John's message was a stern one. Essentially he was telling people to turn to God before it was too late. But Luke sees the forbidding figure of John in a greater light. For Luke, the Baptist's story is part of a history whose blessed outcome John himself is not given to see. Luke reads on in Isaiah. Luke, and only Luke, gives us the prophetic vision in all its fullness. All that impedes God's purpose for humanity's total good will be swept away.

Originally the promise was that God would clear the road for the returning exiles. But the road Luke looks down is the way to glory. The stumbling blocks on that path, symbolized by what prevents earth-bound travellers getting where they want to go, impassable mountains, impenetrable valleys and the like, will all be levelled. Then, at the last, 'all shall see God's salvation'. This is Luke's hope, the Advent hope, and the Christian hope. It is grounded in the universal embrace of the love of God and it is the keynote of this Gospel, sounded on all its pages.

Luke would not agree with the definition of history offered by one of the grammar school high-fliers in Alan Bennett's *The History Boys*, 'History is just one fucking thing after another.' History, as a whole and for every individual, is what St Paul calls God's 'good work'. Once begun, this work must be – and will be – completed. Luke records the beginning of this good work. Nowhere in the Bible are we told when this good work will finally be done. No date is given for 'the day of Christ'. But of that day we can say with Thomas Traherne, 'Yet shall the end be so glorious that angels durst not hope for so great a one till they had seen it' (*Centuries of Meditations*).

That is not to say that Luke, or any other Bible writer, gives us any encouragement to believe that humanity is improving all the time. We may still be evolving, but that does not mean that we're becoming nicer to know. What a Lucan commitment to history forbids is disengagement from what is going on. This world's history is where our salvation is won. Isaac Watt's 'When I survey the wondrous cross . . .' is a great hymn. But it's right that nowadays we rarely sing the lines,

Then I am dead to all the world, And all the world is dead to me.

The Third Sunday of Advent

YEAR A

Isaiah 35; James 5.7–10; Matthew 11.2–11

WRESTLING WITH UNCERTAINTY

'Be patient,' says James. At this time of the year, they all have to be patient for their different reasons: the little children who can't wait for Christmas to come; the lonely who can't wait for Christmas to go; the unemployed who can't afford Christmas; the overworked, clergy among them, who long for life to be back to normal; the women whose men behave even worse at Christmas than at other seasons; the secularists who resent the religious festivities; the pious who deplore the pagan festivities.

James counsels patience. It is good advice, for Christmas has to be weathered as well as celebrated and only those with brains turned to tinsel would pretend otherwise. But of course James is not talking about 25 December, but of what every Christmas promises, the 'coming of the Lord', the fulfilment of our Advent hope. As models of the frame of mind he advocates, James recommends that we, 'take the prophets'. This Sunday's Gospel suggests that we look to the last and the greatest of them, John the Baptist.

The last words of John, at least the last we are allowed to hear from him, are a question, 'Are you the one?' Thomas was not the only one to have had his doubts. John's testimony to Jesus had been fearless and unwavering but now, languishing in prison, he begins to wonder. He is troubled by the possibility that his claims about Jesus ('Behold the Lamb of God') are no more substantial than the shifting sands of the desert he had made his home. We do not know the conditions under which John was being held, but Herod would not have kept his captives in a country-house hotel. Perhaps the darkness of his prison cell has invaded and possessed John's soul, so that now he fears that he has been mistaken.

Even the saints – especially the saints – know what it is to wrestle with uncertainty. Mother Teresa walked with God but in the recesses of her heart she wondered whether there was anyone there. She wrote in 1958, 'My smile is a great cloak that hides a multitude of pains. People think that my faith, my hope and my love are overflowing and that my intimacy with God and union with his will fill my heart. If only they knew.' In another letter she writes, 'I feel that God does not want me, that God is not God and that he does not really exist' (*Mother Teresa: Come Be My Light*, Brian Kolodejchuk, Doubleday, 2007).

How does Jesus deal with John's doubts? It is a timely question. Anyone with a finger on the cultural pulse will have noticed that we have now entered a new 'age of doubt', rampant fundamentalism and – its mirror image – militant atheism notwithstanding. The 'golden age of doubt' was the Victorian period. But what goes around comes around, golden ages of doubt included, and there is much evidence that we are now in a new one. One of the best of A. N. Wilson's fine books, *God's Funeral*

(John Murray, 1999), is a history of doubt. John Cornwell writes in the *Guardian* on 'The Importance of Doubt' (30 August 2007). John Humphreys' voice is heard by millions, but with his publication *In God we Doubt* (Hodder & Stoughton, 2007) he speaks for millions. Not for the first time, and probably not for the last time, Alister McGrath has written a book about doubt (*Doubt in Perspective*, IVP, 2006).

Jesus does not argue with John. He tells him what to do. John the Baptist had told people to look at Jesus. Now Jesus urges John to do the same. John too must 'behold the lamb of God'. Jesus's response to 'doubting John' is as significant and important for us as for John. For we too wonder. After all, it is two thousand years since James reassured his first readers that 'the Lord is at hand'.

Jesus does not confront John's doubts or ours with irrefutable arguments. So, far from providing support for faith, conclusive arguments – were there any – would eliminate the very possibility of faith. Instead Jesus speaks to John of what he has done, of his 'merciful ministry to the marginalized', and of those equivocal signs of his, the miracles that invite us to believe but which never force us to. Most marvellous of these miracles, more wonderful even than the raising of the dead, is that the poor have heard the good news. Jesus invites John – and we are invited too – to see what has been happening as the promise and pledge of a new day, however long delayed – the day described in the anthem appointed as our first reading, that most thrilling of visions of the end of history, chapter 35 of Isaiah.

So we look to John who tells us – and who is told – to look to Jesus. That way we'll survive Christmas and celebrate it too.

YEAR B

Isaiah 61.1–4, 8–11; 1 Thessalonians 5.16–24; John 1.6–8, 19–28

THE SOUND OF SILENCE

Mark saw John the Baptist as the prophet Elijah, his hour come again. Elijah for Mark was the promised herald of the great and terrible day of the Lord. But John himself will have none of it. He disclaims all titles, save one. He is – as they might have said in the Welsh valleys – 'John the Voice'. He is 'the voice of one crying in the wilderness'.

The desert has many voices. It is never wholly still, even when there is no breath of wind to disturb the sands. When nothing is to be heard, as all who have travelled in the desert will testify, the very silence becomes audible and eloquent. T. E. Lawrence, 'Lawrence of Arabia', was haunted by that silence. So too was Antoine de Saint-Exupéry, for whom the voice crying in the wilderness was that of a little prince, who taught him what matters and what doesn't. Elijah himself, who hid in a cave in the back of beyond, heard it. The old versions say that, after the noisy fire and earthquake, he heard 'a still small voice' (1 Kings 19.12), but the Hebrew words might just as well be translated as 'the sound of silence'.

John the Baptist is 'John the Voice'. How am I to hear that voice? Hear it I must, for I too must make straight the way of the Lord. The Lord will come to me this Christmas. He will come to me at the hour of my death. He will come – to any of us left – at the end of history. And, whether I recognize him or not, I shall run into him a dozen times today.

So how shall I hear him? I might try an 'Ignatian exercise'. That method works well with the account we have of John's preaching in, say, Luke's gospel (Luke 3.7–17). I can place myself in the story. I can imagine I am there in the crowd listening to John. In my imagination I can rub shoulders with the soldiers, the tax collectors, the common people, hanging on his words. In this way I begin to hear his voice, made hoarse by the dry desert air, addressing me personally. John now speaks directly to me as to those around me, and, like them, I too must swiftly change my ways.

But this Ignatian technique does not work with the John we meet in the Fourth Gospel. This John is too elusive. He is stripped of all distinctive features. He will allow no attention to himself. We mustn't look at him but at someone else. Even as we meet him he is passing from us. He wants to be forgotten. Notice how tersely he is introduced to us. 'There was a man sent from God.' That's all. He is no longer the hairy insect-eater of the synoptic Gospels. He has become someone altogether more mysterious. It is impossible to gain any imaginative purchase on such a figure. Like the one to whom he testifies, this John stands among us as one we do not know.

He is simply 'John the Voice', and if I am to hear him, I must cultivate a different kind of attentiveness. I must listen to him as the nomad listens to the silence of the sands. Perhaps this means finding some desert nearby. Even big cities have their Saharas. (London's most abandoned landscape, before they began to smarten it up for the Olympics, was the wasteland through which flows – with its cargo of supermarket trolleys and dead cats – the sluggish Lea.)

That voice will bear witness to the light. It is not surprising that the artist Caravaggio painted John the Baptist so many times. Caravaggio's light is violent and his darkness dense. Such light does not dispel the darkness but rather renders it, in the recesses to which it retreats, more intense. That is the light to which John testifies, not a benign and universal sunshine, but a piercing spotlight from which, in our folly, we may try to hide.

We can make two mistakes about the John the Baptist of the Fourth Gospel. Because this John wants us to forget him, we can make the error of doing so. His was a unique role in 'salvation history', and so we may conclude that, two millennia later, he has little to say to us. We could not be more wrong. There's never a day when we do not need to be told – 'There's someone coming!' The second mistake is to doubt the story, as told in this Gospel, because it has clearly been rewritten to highlight its meaning. Has John been so reinvented as to cut him loose from history? Our author anticipates that criticism. That's why he adds the footnote, as one version briskly has it, 'This all happened' (John 1.28, NIV).

YEAR C

Zephaniah 3.14–20; Philippians 4.4–7; Luke 3.7–18

FLEE FROM THE WRATH TO COME

John the Baptist must have had a loud voice. It is as 'a voice' that Luke, like the other Gospel writers, remembers him. The allusion, as we saw last week, is to the vision of the prophet who spoke of 'a voice' proclaiming God's coming salvation (Isaiah 40.3–5). But the historical John must have had a voice strong enough to raise the dead – which, in a way, was what he wanted to do. The tone of John's voice was as harsh as the arid hills of the Judean wilderness in which it echoed. That tone is set by his first words. He begins not with an engaging anecdote or a 'good to see you all here' but with an outburst of invective. His congregation, he says, is a 'brood of vipers'.

It is a striking way to start a sermon. And – lest we forget – given that these words are proclaimed in church on Sunday as 'the gospel of the Lord', we can no longer be so sure they don't apply to us. Perhaps we're the ones who should be squirming.

His opening words reveal the nature of the movement associated with John, but also the equivocal motives of those drawn to him. Those who flocked to the desert did so in the belief that only in those waste places was there any hope of escaping 'the wrath to come'. By being baptized they hoped to be spared the impending judgement. But John saw that many who sought his baptism had no intention of changing their ways. The most imperilled, those already under the axe, are the smugly pious, those who suppose that their religion will save them.

John's stentorian tones and the tenor of his message recall another who preaches that our God is a consuming fire. The former Prime Minister Jim Callaghan famously attempted to mollify Ian Paisley. 'Come, come, Mr Paisley. Are we not all the children of God?' 'No Sir!' Paisley thundered in reply, 'We are the children of wrath!'

That harsh word 'wrath' must stand. There was no mention of 'wrath' in the first edition of the New English Bible. C. H. Dodd, who chaired the translators, didn't believe that God was ever personally angry. By God's 'wrath' we are to understand, said Dodd, that there is 'an impersonal law of cause and effect in a moral universe' (*The Epistle of Paul to the Romans*, 1932). And so he insisted that the Greek word, always previously rendered as 'wrath', should be translated 'retribution' – one of those dusty donnish words which pepper the NEB. The translators of the Revised English Bible, recognizing that the sting of this word cannot be so easily drawn, and that John the Baptist was not at the time a Fellow of All Souls, restored the original. (At least they do here. Luke uses the word once more, at Luke 21.23, and in much the same context, but on that occasion, inexplicably, 'wrath' becomes 'judgement'.)

The reason why the notion of divine 'wrath' cannot be air-brushed out of Christian discourse is not because we cling to an image of an intemperate deity. We hold to the notion, for all its problems, because we believe that God has been made known to us in Jesus, and Jesus was sometimes very angry indeed.

So they ask what to do. The moral teaching of the New Testament moves giddily between the idealistic ('Be perfect', 'Love your enemies'), the axiomatic ('Be kind to one another'), the cryptic ('Pluck your eye out'), and the down-to-earth. John the Baptist's ethic belongs to the last category. He tells you what to do next and what not to do at all. Share your clothes and food. Don't fiddle the books. Don't bully. Don't demand the pay-rise you don't need.

We should pause on what John says to the soldiers, even if we're not in the army. Soldiers can be guilty of far worse crimes than extortion. Those worse crimes are all the abuse of power. Such abuse is perpetrated both in armies and by armies. NCOs sometimes bully recruits. (I know a mother whose boy was killed at the Deepcut barracks. She claims that at that base there was a culture of bullying and abuse. I believe her.) Armies sometimes fight unjust wars. But abuse of power is not confined to barracks or war zones. Every playground and every diocese has its bullies. For such is reserved 'the unquenchable fire'.

No doubt it's distasteful having to refer to such a conflagration just a few days before Christmas. But Advent is when we are meant to meditate on 'the last things', the final fire included. Now's the time for some hell-fire preaching, if only to myself. Before I listen to the sound of the angels I must hear the voice of the Baptist. In a word – in a most old-fashioned word – I must repent.

The Fourth Sunday of Advent

YEAR A

Isaiah 7.10–16; Romans 1.1–7; Matthew 1.18–25

DICTATORS' DOWNFALL

Matthew sees the birth of Jesus as the fulfilment of a remarkable prophecy of Isaiah of Jerusalem. We must go back eight centuries before the time of Jesus. The tribes that settled in Canaan are now two kingdoms, Judah in the south, and the more powerful Israel in the north. To the north of Israel lies the still more powerful Syria. Israel and Syria have forged an alliance and are now menacing Judah. The abject and lily-livered King Ahaz of Judah is quaking at the prospect of his petty little fiefdom being invaded and obliterated. Enter Isaiah. The prophet promises the pusillanimous Ahaz that God will provide a sign. A certain young woman will soon give birth to a child. Before that child is more than a few years old the kingdoms of Israel and Syria that he so dreads will be laid waste.

Isaiah's message – and Matthew's – is the same as that of Mary's *Magnificat*. God brings down the mighty from their thrones and lifts up the lowly (Luke 1.52). That is the sort of God he is and that is the sort of thing he does. He scatters the rich and arrogant and reduces proud empires to dust. He sides with the poor. He exalts the nobodies.

That was the gospel of the Lord to the contemporaries of Isaiah, king and people alike, terrorized by the armies marshalling on their

THE FOURTH SUNDAY OF ADVENT

borders. That was the gospel of the Lord to Matthew's first readers, who feared for their fate as the might of Rome bore down on them. That is the gospel of the Lord to all of us today who are aware of the imperialisms that rule our world – perhaps most menacing, that of the international money markets – and who are overwhelmed by a sense of our own inconsequence. For Matthew, 'the child to be born' is primarily a sign that God's purpose is fulfilled – as his strength is made perfect – in what the world calls weakness.

To be sure, there are other interesting aspects of Isaiah's prophecy which Matthew explores, though some of these have distracted Christian readers from what is the main thrust of the prophet's words. For example, Isaiah announces that the child is to be born to 'the young woman'. ('*The* young woman,' he says. Who was she, we wonder? Some say she was Mrs Ahaz, but we don't know.) The Hebrew word for 'young woman' implies neither virginity, nor lack of it. Hebrew has another perfectly good word for virgin which is unequivocal. Matthew, however, quotes a Greek translation of the Hebrew text. The word he uses – *parthenos* – does mean virgin. For Matthew, Isaiah's text, as well as announcing the downfall of every dictatorship – which is his main point – also predicts that the birth of Jesus will be without a human father. Luke's account of the annunciation also reflects this tradition that Jesus was born of a virgin (Luke 2.26–35). No other New Testament text makes this claim. On Sunday we shall hear Paul insisting that 'the gospel of God' was 'promised beforehand through the scriptures', but neither here nor anywhere else does he state that those promises included a prediction of the virgin birth.

Matthew will make much more of the meaning of the child's name, Emmanuel – 'God is with us' – than of the manner of his birth. Matthew's Gospel, like all the Gospels, is an extended meditation on the mystery of the Word made flesh dwelling among us (John 1.14). 'God with us' is the name Jesus is given before his birth. We are not to suppose that he forfeits that name when at the end he cries, 'My God, why have you forsaken me?' (Matthew 27.46).

Whatever his role was in the nativity of Jesus, it is good to be reminded of Joseph, that 'righteous man' as Matthew calls him. In the bewildering circumstances of his wife's pregnancy, Joseph is concerned to do what is right but also what is compassionate. The construction that censorious men would have put on Mary's situation would have sent them, licking their lips, to Deuteronomy and its fearful penalties on wanton wives (Deuteronomy 22.20–21). Law and grace do not always go hand in hand. Joseph opts for the latter.

Joseph makes one or two further fleeting appearances in the Gospel narratives. Then he passes from our story. There is no mention of him with Mary at the cross, so it is assumed that by then Mary is a widow. Pious speculation abounds. There is a strong tradition that Joseph died in the arms of Jesus and Mary. What is not a matter of speculation is that Emmanuel was born, God was with us, in a working family. According to Matthew, Jesus is 'the craftsman's son' (Matthew 13.55). Some time after Christmas most of us will have to stagger back to work. Shortly after the first Christmas Joseph had to do the same.

YEAR B

2 Samuel 7.1–11, 16; Romans 16.25–27; Luke 1.26–38

MUCH IS ASKED OF LITTLE PEOPLE

An article published in *Life* magazine estimates that two billion Hail Marys are recited daily. Perhaps Gabriel was not the first to pay Mary such attention – Joseph at least must have thought her special – but it is Gabriel's greeting which echoes down the Christian ages. '*Ave Maria* – Hail Mary, full of grace!' The familiar invocation reflects the Latin Vulgate, a version which is not such a wonky translation as some Protestant commentators have claimed. The force of Luke's Greek is to suggest that Mary, once blessed by grace, remains thus blessed.

That, however, is news to her. The encounter of the girl and the angel is inexhaustibly fascinating. Mary, unique in her destiny, is one of many. She is another of those obscure ordinary people, portrayed so vividly in the opening pages of Luke's Gospel, who wait for God to keep his promise to save his people. She belongs with Zechariah and Elisabeth, with Simeon and Anna, with all the endlessly patient and unceasingly prayerful who 'looked for the redemption of Jerusalem' – as she is one with those of every age who have lived their hidden lives faithfully.

We ponder the contrasting roles of the angel and the girl. The one who bears the message and the one who bears the Messiah; the one who carries the summons and the one who carries it out; the august being of unearthly radiance and the girl you'd not notice in the queue at the check-out; the somebody and the nobody. Paul's words are commentary on Mary's election. 'God chose what is low and despised in the world, things that are not, to reduce to nothing things that are' (1 Corinthians 1.28).

'The Lord is with you.' The bidding 'The Lord be with you' now packs all the punch of a dead battery. Not so here. The promise is not of a cosy companionship. God's company is a more mixed blessing, for it means that there is his hard work to be done. Mary 'wondered what manner of greeting this might be'. The understatement is a delicious example of Luke's little noticed dry wit.

It's a scene often painted, but artists do not always get it right. Take Tintorretto's stupendous painting of the Annunciation in Venice. His Gabriel is all wrong. Wings wide as an albatross's, he doesn't even come in to land. Much closer to the truth is Botticelli's great Annunciation in the Uffizi in Florence. Gabriel kneels, gazing up in awe on Mary. She is turning away in embarrassment and dismay. Gabriel stays kneeling. Exalted beings they may be, but angels will never know what it is to be us. God's last word is made flesh, not feathers.

Mary does raise one tiny point of order – 'I know not a man'. (The delicate euphemism is perfectly understandable. The modern translations are all equally clumsy and inept.) That concern is briskly dealt with. 'The great and mighty wonder' is not the manner of Messiah's birth, but Mary's 'Let it be.'

'Let it be.' We think of another young woman who craved anonymity, who wished to become one of 'the things that are not'. Simone Weil teaches us that all that is asked of us, as of Mary, is our consent.

Over the infinity of space and time the infinitely more infinite love of God comes to possess us. We have the power to consent, to receive him or to refuse. If we remain deaf he comes back again and again like a beggar, but also like a beggar, one day he stops coming. We can only consent. We are created for this consent and this alone. (*Waiting for God*, Harper Perennial, 1992)

Such consent is costly. In a modern myth of a world broken and remade, another who was no one accepts an unimaginable burden.

A great dread fell on Frodo, as if he was awaiting the pronouncement of some doom that he had long foreseen and vainly hoped might after all never be spoken. An overwhelming longing to rest and remain at peace filled all his heart. At last with an effort he spoke and wondered to hear his own words, as if some other will was using his small voice. 'I will take the Ring,' he said, 'though I do not know the way.' (*The Lord of the Rings*, J. R. R.Tolkien)

In Middle Earth, as among us, much is asked of little people.

Annunciations, of course, occur frequently. In her poem *Annunciation* Denise Levertov suggests that annunciations take place in most lives. 'Roads of light open', she says, but we turn away. We do so 'in dread, in a wave of weakness, in despair' – or simply in relief. Life goes on, but a gate has closed.

Mary does not turn away, as she might have done. Having delivered his message the archangel goes, and Mary takes her path, leaving angels and archangels far behind. He has delivered his message and his moment has passed. Mary is already far beyond him.

YEAR C

Micah 5.2–5a; Hebrews 10.5–10; Luke 1.39–45 (46–55)

OUR UNBORN LIFE MADE HIS

Jesus is soon to be born. While we wait, we wonder. We wonder about the world he has already made his own, the little space beneath a woman's heart. The exultation of Elizabeth is a window on that world. Her unborn son, the boy they'll call 'the Baptist', 'leaps for joy' when Mary, the mother of his Lord, greets her. There is something giddy, delirious, and irrational about such 'leaping'. Leaping is what young things do. Kittens leap. Lambs leap. Salmon leap. Little children leap. Above all, lovers leap. 'Listen! My lover! Look! Here he comes, leaping across the mountains, bounding over the hills' (Song of Solomon 2.8).

In the Bible, leaping is what you do at the last day. When that day dawns, when the sun of righteousness rises with healing in his wings, we shall 'go out leaping like calves from the stall' (Malachi 4.2). In his mother's womb, John the Baptist, the least unbuttoned of biblical characters, takes up the dance in which, at the last, all creation will join.

The Word already made flesh awaits his birth among us. Like all of us, he has been 'knit together in a mother's womb' (Psalm 139.13). Irenaeus claimed that Jesus, 'sanctifying every age', made every stage of life his own. 'He therefore passed through every age, becoming an infant for infants, thus sanctifying infants; a child for children, thus sanctifying those who are of this age' (*Against Heresies*, II xxii, 4). We dare to add that our Lord made our embryonic and foetal life his, thus 'sanctifying' too our earliest hours.

Our Lord made our unborn life his. That life, it follows, is sacred. That does not mean that there are no circumstances in which a pregnancy may be terminated. Our moral choices – we are a fallen race – are rarely between good and bad. Usually they are between what is bad and what is worse. But the principle stands. Because Christ too once waited to be born, he confers on the unborn infinite worth.

Our Lord made our unborn life his. It follows that our first church is our mother's womb and that the nurture of the child in the church must begin in that holy place. Where we lived before we were born was not some limbo from which we were delivered by our baptism, but the home where Christ first dwelled among us and where we were already known and loved.

Our Lord made our unborn life his. The late Dr Frank Lake, who so greatly influenced an earlier generation of Anglican clergy, maintained that our well-being, or lack of it, depends on how good or bad life was for us before we were born. Frank spoke, less than delicately perhaps, of the unborn child being 'marinated in the mother's emotional juices'. It is surely no longer a contentious claim that the quality of life before birth makes a difference to life after it. It follows that Christian devotion and, trailing some way behind, Christian theology, has been right all along to ascribe the honour it has to Mary. Our modern understanding of what, for good or ill, happens to us between conception and birth confirms what Christians have always believed, that in his mother – *in* his mother – our Lord was uniquely blessed.

Our Lord made our unborn life his. He too was fed by a mother's food. According to the Holy Qur'an, while Mary was carrying her boy to be born, she drank from a pure stream and fed on the dates which fell from the tree against which she rested. What his mother ate, Christ consumed. So it always is. When the sacrament of Holy Communion is administered to an expectant mother two people are fed. How curious and how sad it is it is that in the Church of England once a child is born he or she is promptly excommunicated!

Our Lord made our unborn life his. Mary magnifies the Lord who has 'lifted up the lowly', among whom are those still to be born, those of all humanity the most powerless. The very helplessness of children constitutes their claim to precedence in God's kingdom. Necessarily the most dependent and vulnerable of these little ones is the one still carried in a mother's body.

So this Christmas Eve, with an ecstatic unborn Baptist, we acclaim the mother of our Lord.

She is the great Pieta who casts her mother's cloak of mercy over our suffering humanity. She is the living womb in which, as in a second act of bodily motherhood, we are carried for the nine long months of our lives until we at last come to the glory of redemption and resurrection. (Edward Schillebeeckx, *Mary, Mother of the Redemption*, Sheed and Ward, 1964)

The First Sunday of Christmas

YEAR A

Isaiah 63.7–9; Hebrews 2.10–18; Matthew 2.13–23

BLOODSHED IN BETHLEHEM

Once again an angel appears to Joseph. It is, says a commentator with an impressive vocabulary, 'a typical angelophany'. Joseph is told to flee with Mary and Jesus to Egypt. There are others in the Bible's story who, threatened by a murderous monarch, seek asylum in Egypt (1 Kings 11.40, Jeremiah 26.21). Others in our own day look for refuge on our own shores. Some find England less hospitable that ancient Egypt. But what matters for Matthew is less the holy family's escape to Egypt than their departure from Egypt, when at last it is safe for them to return home. Matthew's first readers will have remembered, as we do, that a rabble of wretched slaves was delivered from Egypt and that by that deliverance the rabble became a people. For Matthew, a new people of God will be called into being by the mission of Jesus. Jesus's achievement will be a new exodus (Luke 9.31) and it is fitting that its architect should retrace the path of the first one. Matthew is less confident than are the other evangelists that we can put two and two together. So he spells it out. Hosea's prophecy is fulfilled. 'Out of Egypt I have called my son' (Hosea 11.1).

Was Jesus's 'exodus' from Egypt a historical event? Or is it a legend, characteristic of an author who, as we shall see as we read more of Matthew, has a taste for tales that call for a pinch of salt? Those ques-

24

tions will seem more important to some than to others. What matters is the truth which Matthew wants the Church and the world to know. As of old, God is setting captives free.

The angel warns 'the holy family' to flee from Bethlehem so as to be out of the reach of Herod. Matthew's account of what befalls the Bethlehem families unvisited by angels is not corroborated by other sources. Scholars suggest that Matthew may have included this story to allow him to bring in another Old Testament 'proof-text'. Long ago Jeremiah had witnessed the slaughter of innocent children by a merciless tyrant and he had heard the pitiful cries of their mothers. With hindsight and with the imaginative reading of the Old Testament typical of him, Matthew finds in the words of Jeremiah further evidence that the story of Jesus fulfils what the prophets had predicted.

Whether or not Herod slaughtered all of Bethlehem's under-threes, it is an action entirely characteristic of him. The man who murdered three of his own sons, not to speak of his wife and his mother-in-law, would have had no compunction in massacring a village-full of infants. But there is a more compelling reason for taking Matthew's account with the utmost seriousness. It is that Christian history is a chronicle of the slaughter of the innocent. Jesus warned that his coming was not to bring peace to the earth but a sword (Matthew 10.34). According to Matthew, that sword was first wielded in Bethlehem shortly after Jesus's birth and those that fell beneath its edge were children. From Bethlehem there runs a river of innocent blood flowing down the Christian centuries. That terrible truth does not depend on whatever did or did not take place in Bethlehem at Herod's behest.

I think of Hannah Fuchs who was born on the same day as I was. Her cheap little suitcase has her name on it. I noticed it among a mountain of similar suitcases displayed at Auschwitz, together with the teeth, the hair, the spectacles, and the prosthetic limbs of all the other victims whom that little girl joined in the slowly moving queue to the gas chamber. She would have been little more than a toddler. If Hannah's mother was still with her, she would have been holding her daughter's hand. Perhaps little Hannah wondered why her hand was being held so tightly.

Our Old Testament reading urges us join the prophet in recounting 'the gracious deeds of the Lord'. So we must. 'It is our duty and our joy.' But we remember too all the children whose suffering since the first Christmas – and because of the first Christmas – was not averted by the intervention of angels. There are those we remember individually. Every day I think of Hannah Fuchs. And there are those we think of together. We think of the little ones of Bethlehem long ago, victims of Herod. We think too of the little ones of Bethlehem today, victims of a cruel history, if not of another oppressor.

So, as the Talmud urges the Jews at Passover, 'we temper our joy'. According to some traditions, the 'celebrant' at Passover dips his finger in 'the cup of joy' and deliberately sprinkles some drops of wine away from the table. Thus he recalls that, when the Egyptians were drowning, God forbad the angels to sing. If next time I celebrate the Eucharist, I spill some wine it will not be because I am losing my grip. It will be because of Hannah.

YEAR B

Isaiah 61.10—62.3; Galatians 4.4–7; Luke 2.15–21

INCARNATION – THE MYSTERY AND THE MESS

Luke mentions the manger three times, so he must want us to notice it. The word he uses might mean a stable or, what you'd find in stable, a feeding trough for cattle. Luke's taste for sharp detail suggests that he intends the latter, that he wishes us to picture Jesus lying in a crib. My dictionary defines a 'crib' as a 'barred receptacle for fodder'. That definition will do nicely. Incarnations involve a severe curtailment of freedom. It befits this new-born child that he is put behind bars.

We had awful problems with our cribs at St Martin-in-the-Fields when I was working there. There was the huge one which went up in Trafalgar Square. This was a full-sized stable with a life-sized Holy Family. The problem was where to put it for the rest of the year. Space is precious in central London and no one would give it house-room. We asked Westminster Council if it could go in one of their redundant gents but they refused. Irony on irony, there was no room for the crib. In the end it was lodged in the dank and noisome underbelly of Church House, in what then served as a House of Lord's car park.

That was the official crib. There was also an unofficial one. This was put up in the church courtyard by rebels in the congregation who disapproved of the trade in tacky souvenirs going on there in those days. Our flat overlooked the courtyard. One Christmas morning I looked out to see that the figure of the infant Christ had been turned out of the crib and that one of London's rough-sleepers was curled up in the hay. Christ cast out of the crib – or perhaps reclaiming it.

Luke invites us to contemplate just such Christmas contradictions. If John 'unfolds the mystery of the incarnation', Luke unfolds its messiness. There are plenty of rough-sleepers in his Gospel, his first witnesses of the Nativity among them. Shepherds are poor. Not only are they poor, they are irreligious. Sheep, impious animals, do not keep the Sabbath and those who look after them don't either. The shepherds are the *anawim*, 'the last, the lost, and the least', who figure so prominently in Luke's Gospel. (When he grows up this child will claim – shockingly – to be 'the *good* shepherd', a notion as improbable to the orthodox mind as that of a good Samaritan.)

The shepherds arrive in haste. Soon they are rushing off to tell everyone about what they had heard and seen. Mary by contrast – Luke makes the contrast deliberately – stays put. 'She treasured all these words and pondered them in her heart.' Much is explained about Mary in those few words. Nowhere in the New Testament is anything like it said of anyone else.

We are told to be a 'mission-shaped Church'. We have a choice. A Church shaped for mission can be shaped by the shepherds or shaped by Mary. The shepherds suggest that we take to the streets and evangelize loquaciously. Mary suggests that we stay where we are, that we are rather more reticent. Her stillness, her silence, her deep contemplativeness, rebuke our shrillness and our hyperactivity. 'Don't just do something,' she says. 'Sit there.' Mission begins in session, in sitting – perhaps for a very long time.

St Paul has nothing to say about Mary except in his remark that God's son was 'born of a woman'. The allusion is not to the virgin birth, about which Paul knows nothing, but to Jesus's human nature. Jesus was a human being with a specific history – a Jewish male. Our salvation's story, says a commentator, 'is rooted in an almost outrageous particularity'. Jesus was physically born – not precipitated in some immaterial fashion. The heresy countered by this claim – a heresy still alive and well and preached in a church near you – is 'Docetism', that Jesus wasn't really human but only seemed to be. ('Jesus was very cross with the naughty money-changers, but remember, children, he never lost his temper.') Paul is insisting that Jesus took our nature, warts and all, not that of some demi-god.

'He was born of a woman.' But who is this woman? Is she 'the feminine face of God', 'the first disciple', 'the mother of all re-created things'? She bears many titles – Mystical Rose, Gate of Heaven, Morning Star, and countless others. (I learned to love Mary in a very beautiful place in Africa where she is honoured as 'Our Lady of the Usumbaras'.) Many of us who once refused, from fear of popery, to call her 'Mother of God' have come belatedly to our Christian senses and are now glad to call her by her best of names.

There are no such titles for the shepherds. It's back to work for them, as for us. We hear nothing more of them. Mary we shall meet again, and not only in the Gospels. We shall meet her beneath the cross of the world. Beneath that cross she is cradling the body of her son who has been shot or knifed, who has been run over by a drunk driver or who has just died from diarrhoea.

Jesus says – to us – 'Behold your mother.'

YEAR C

1 Samuel 2.18–20, 26; Colossians 3.12–17; Luke 2.41–52

JESUS WITH SPOTS?

High above Nazareth is the Basilica of Jesus the Adolescent. It is the chapel of a trade school, run by the Salesians of Don Bosco, where teenage Palestinians are trained, some to be carpenters. They say their prayers in a church that is one of the glories of the Holy Land and it is dedicated to a boy their age.

The notion of the adolescence of Jesus is one on which it is extremely difficult for the Christian imagination to gain any purchase. We can picture the baby Jesus, even if some images of his infancy ('no crying he makes') are implausible. Equally Jesus the adult is someone we can try to visualize and preachers regularly encourage us do so. But a Jesus with spots is beyond our imaginative reach.

With the one exception of this story of the twelve-year-old Jesus, the Gospels are silent about the life of Jesus between his birth and his baptism. Where the Gospels shut up, perhaps we should too. But there is one compelling reason why we must stay a little longer with this unfamiliar notion of Jesus on the cusp of adolescence. It is that we believe – or so we say this time of the year – in the incarnation. God in Christ became one of us. Unless we are 'adoptionists', we hold that the Word took human flesh from his mother at Nazareth. God, incarnate in the child and in the adult, was incarnate too in one neither child nor adult, in one both child and adult, in one sometimes child and sometimes adult. Faith in the incarnation means that we believe that there was once a gawky lad, experiencing all the startling and confusing changes that adolescence visits on us, who yet lived in abiding union with God.

Luke makes this point by placing his story of the boy Jesus in the temple within an interpretative frame. Unfortunately our lectionary rips off one side of the frame. We must replace it. Luke begins by saying that 'the child grew and became strong, filled with wisdom; and the favour of God was upon him' (Luke 2.40). And he concludes, 'Jesus increased in wisdom and in years, and in divine and human favour' (Luke 2.52). The first statement looks back across the childhood of Jesus; the second looks ahead to his teenage years.

These verses are more than dabs of glue applied between the separate 'pericopes' beloved of the form-critics. Luke's story recalls the account of the boyhood of Samuel (1 Samuel 1–3). The implication of that narrative was that a young person's physical development, as too her or his maturing human relationships, may be accompanied by a matching spiritual development. Luke's purpose is to claim that this was true of Jesus. There is a life in relationship to God appropriate to the years when the child is becoming an adult. It's good news for Year 7s.

The adolescence of Jesus confers infinite worth on a stage of life from which, we sometimes feel, all glory has departed – just as we saw last Sunday that the foetal Christ confers that worth on all yet to be born. For all young people, in these least propitious years, there is the potential of life in relation to God no less complete, no less the 'finished product', than that of the adult.

Jesus tells his parents, who have been so desperately looking for him, that he must be 'about his father's business', if that is what the notoriously cryptic Greek text means. His words leave Mary and Joseph baffled. But then not to understand what drives an adolescent – I speak with feeling – is a common enough parental experience. All parents must accept, sooner or later, with equanimity or resentment, that their children are no longer *theirs*. It is clear is that Jesus now knows himself to be commanded by a necessity which his parents cannot comprehend.

What must Mary and Joseph have felt, hearing their son speak of this necessity? A recent publication could be read as a commentary on what they went through. John Cornwell's brilliant memoir *A Seminary Boy* is a fascinating and deeply moving account both of a child's powerful sense of vocation and of the bewilderment of perplexed and sometimes angry parents failing to make sense of it (Fourth Estate, 2006).

Jesus teaches his teachers. They are all 'amazed at his understanding'. No doubt Jesus showed an insight into the things of God unusual in one of his years. Yet the Jesus we meet here is not the prodigy and freak we encounter in the apocryphal infancy Gospels. The more we trumpet his precocity, the more we risk losing him. Perhaps what this twelve-year-old is doing, more than exhibiting exceptional spiritual insight, is mounting a challenge to the structures of adult power. It won't be the last time he does so.

The Second Sunday of Christmas

YEARS A, B, AND C
(The principal readings for this Sunday are the same.)

Jeremiah 31.7–14 or Ecclesiasticus 24.1–12; Ephesians 1.3–14; John 1.(1–9) 10–18

OUR LONG EXILE

Edward Said entitled his autobiographical memoir 'Out of Place' (Vintage Books, 1999). It is an account of a life shaped by the experience of exile. Said spoke of exile as 'the unhealable rift forced between a human being and a native place, between the self and its true home: its essential sadness can never be surmounted'.

'Out of Place'– the terse words might serve as a title for the story told by the Bible. We are not far into that story before we read of human beings driven from their 'native place', albeit as a consequence of their own folly. In the pages that follow we learn of a people who, in their years of bondage in Egypt and in their long exile in Babylon, languish far from their true home. The story comes to focus on a single figure who endures exile, the one we recall as we sing: 'Thou didst leave thy throne and thy kingly crown, when thou camest to earth for me.'

It is the tale we have been telling in recent days. When we hear again this Sunday the Christmas gospel that 'the Word was made flesh and pitched his tent among us', we are hearing about a displaced person. As for those of us who try to follow this homeless king, we too know the bitterness of exile. 'For here we have no lasting city, but we are looking for the city which is to come' (Hebrews 13.14).

Said spoke of the rift of exile as unhealable and its sadness insurmountable. The Bible, while never understating the anguish of exile

THE SECOND SUNDAY OF CHRISTMAS

('By the waters of Babylon we sat down and wept') does not come to that despairing conclusion. The prophet Jeremiah has witnessed Jerusalem fall to the armies of Nebuchadnezzar and seen many of its citizens taken into captivity in a distant land. Of all the prophets, Jeremiah is the one least given to comforting pieties. Yet his message at this dark hour is not one of judgement, but one of hope. Exile shall end. Our first reading resonates with the great chapter 35 of Isaiah and its soaring vision of 'the ransomed of the Lord' returning to Zion with singing and with 'everlasting joy upon their heads' (Isaiah 35.10). Jeremiah's vision is, if possible, even larger than Isaiah's. It is more embracing and all-inclusive, for it contemplates a cosmic home-coming. They shall be brought home, not only from Babylon, but 'from the farthest parts of the earth'.

Among those who return, singing with gladness as they come, are ones who, in our cruel world, do not always make it safely back home, even when they are set free, 'the blind, the lame, those in child and those in labour'. They too, with all the others fallen by the roadside, shall be 'radiant over the goodness of the Lord'.

At Christmas, we think of the Christ of God exiled among us. By his incarnation Christ endures the affliction of the exiles of our own day. We remember the flight of the Holy Family into Egypt and we think of those who have fled from murderous regimes, especially those who have sought asylum on our own shores. But it is not only those who have fled for their lives who are exiles. For all countless multitudes across the centuries who have been driven from their homes, or who have fled their homes, exile is nevertheless a quintessentially modern phenomenon. There is a sense in which globalization has alienated us all, for when the local yields to the global, we no longer know for sure where home is. 'The experience of exile', it has been said, 'constitutes the major defining experience of the modern world.'

We are all displaced persons. We certainly are if we are baptized. That foundational fact of our Christian condition is classically argued in those closing chapters of the letter to the Hebrews from which we have already quoted (Hebrews 11–13). It is the premise of Paul's argument in our New Testament reading, although the imagery Paul uses is not of the promised homeland but of the inheritance that is ours in Christ. We have everything to look forward to. But it is not yet ours. What we enjoy now, by the gift of the Holy Spirit, is only the pledge – the initial down payment, as it were – of the inheritance promised to us.

Edward Said writes of the exile's 'crippling sorrow of estrangement'. Those who wept by the waters of Babylon would have known what he meant. Paul, longing 'that the mortal may be swallowed up in life' (2 Corinthians 5.4), would have understood too. Christmas, whatever else it does for us, should make us homesick.

The Baptism of Christ (The First Sunday of Epiphany)

YEAR A

Isaiah 42.1–9; Acts 10.34–43; Matthew 3.13–17

DEPARTING FROM THE SCRIPT

I once saw Archbishop Desmond Tutu fall to his knees before an ageing priest to seek his blessing. It was a startling departure from the script, from the order of the service over which the Archbishop was presiding. I recall how the confused and embarrassed old man protested and how the Archbishop insisted. In much the same way John the Baptist objects when he sees Jesus queuing up to be baptized, waiting his turn patiently with everyone else. For John, this is all wrong. *He* should be the one being baptized! But Jesus insists that his baptism, so far from being 'a departure from the script', is in fact a complete fulfilment of the script.

Only Matthew records this conversation between John and Jesus. Perhaps he includes it because he knows that some of those for whom he writes will be puzzled that Jesus should have been baptized. After all when you are baptized you repent of your sins. Why should Jesus need to have been baptized, if – as they had come to believe – he had no sins to repent of?

Matthew is not embarrassed by the story of Jesus's baptism. On the contrary, he gives it greater emphasis than do the other Gospel writers. According to Matthew, Jesus 'came to John to be baptized by him'. It is the first thing he does at the outset of his ministry. By his baptism Jesus announces the direction and purpose of his mission. All Jesus went on to say and to do was a working out of the implications of his initial immersion in the Jordan. Jesus's baptism is so significant in this Gospel that his first recorded words are about it. 'Let it be so now; for it is proper for us in this way to fulfil all righteousness.' ('Let it be.' Didn't his mother say much the same?) By being baptized, Jesus 'follows the script', the script written from the foundation of the world, that the Christ of God should descend into the darkest depths of our human condition, that he should let the cold waters of our sins and sorrows close over him, that he should drown in our wretchedness. And all so that we might live.

It will not be the last time that Jesus strays from the script only to keep to it. In the upper room, on the night before he dies, he once more assumes a role they suppose is far beneath him. He dresses for the part – or rather undresses for the part – they deem to be unfitting for him, taking off his outer clothing, wrapping a towel round his waist. Then he washes his disciples' feet, doing the slave's dirty work (John 13.1–17). Washing dirty feet, plunging beneath the fetid waters of the Jordan – it's all to do with what salvation costs. The disciples do not understand. Jesus says that one day they will. Perhaps one day we shall.

The Baptism of Jesus is at once a Good Friday and an Easter Day. Christ's descent into the waters is his death and his burial; his emergence from them is his rising from the dead. Other high and holy days are anticipated. The heavens open as at his Ascension; the descent of the spirit anticipates Pentecost; the voice from heaven is the same heard at the Transfiguration, 'This is my beloved Son.' Matthew delights in the multiple and bewildering scriptural allusions, scattering them as he goes, leaving us to hunt them down as best we can. The dove sends us back to the very start, to the spirit brooding on the primal waters. She is the same dove as the one that bears the promise of peace in her beak when the waters recede after the flood. At the same time, Jesus is re-enacting the exodus story, leading his chosen people to their promised land. The Spirit settling on Jesus calls to mind all the others to whom the spirit was given for a specific task, Gideon and Samson, Saul and David and the rest. Even that half-crazed seer Ezekiel, to whom the heavens opened, gets a look in.

The voice of God from Heaven announces who this Jesus is. God has a good working knowledge of the Old Testament and he quotes two texts from it. 'This is my Son, whom I love.' The words are from Psalm 2, a 'royal psalm' in which Israel's anointed king is proclaimed God's son. But a text from another source is quoted too and this additional citation makes all the difference. 'With him I am well-pleased.' The reference is to our first reading, to the song about the unnamed servant who, by his way of going about things, will contrast with most monarchs of the ancient world – and, for that matter, with some bishops of the modern one.

YEAR B

Genesis 1.1–5; Acts 19.1–7; Mark 1.4–11

BIRTH BY DROWNING

Bethlehem and the river Jordan both epitomize the conditions to which Jesus submitted. Modern Bethlehem is in a parlous state. By his birth Christ made that state – the plight of the powerless and oppressed – his own.

Today the river Jordan too is in a parlous state. Barely a few metres wide, it is heavily laden with agricultural and domestic effluents. We are told that just about the only thing that flows for large parts of the year, keeping the river alive, is sewage. Jordan today bears stinking witness to what we have done to a beautiful creation. Environmentalists say the Jordan is dying, and will soon cease to flow. This wretched river speaks of the mess we've made of things. Here at his baptism, at the outset of his ministry, Jesus made that mess his.

There is much about water in our baptismal liturgy. In 'The Prayer over the Water' we give thanks 'for gift of water to sustain, refresh and cleanse'. The words fail to capture the flavour of the river in which Jesus was baptized. The polluted and depleted waters of Jordan no longer sustain, refresh and cleanse. (I once had on display in my religious studies classroom a bottle of water which I had drawn from the Jordan. Soon the green and slimy liquid was spawning all manner of disgusting things. Clearly it was a health hazard and it had to be thrown out.)

Baptismal liturgies serve as filtration plants. Real water becomes ritual water, religious water. But Jesus was not baptized in a font, in water that had been blessed and with the chill taken off it – even if the first-century Jordan, free from modern pollutants, was fresher than it is today.

The emphasis on baptism as a kind of washing overlooks something rather important about water, a truth about it which gives baptism its primary significance. Water is lethal. People drown in it. Rivers are dangerous. (Occasionally you hear of someone being swept away by the river in which they've been baptized. A year or two ago a young man, newly-baptized in an African river, was immediately seized and consumed by a crocodile.)

Baptism in the New Testament is more about dying than cleansing. If it is about birth, it is 'birth by drowning'. For Jesus, his baptism foreshadows his crucifixion, his 'baptism on Golgotha'. We know that this is how he saw its meaning from his hard word to his disciples, 'Can you be baptized with the baptism that I am baptized with?' (Mark 10.38).

Certainly Mark saw Jesus's baptism in this light. The voice from heaven speaks of him as God's 'son'. The echoes are of the words of a psalm, understood by New Testament times to refer to one who would come as king to save God's people (Psalm 2.7). But the voice echoes too what was said by a prophet of a wholly contrasting figure, not a king but a slave, the anonymous 'servant' who would suffer and die for those who had strayed from God (Isaiah 42.1). Jesus is baptized into death, his own death. Into which death we too must be baptized (Romans 6.3). Without that death there can be no resurrection.

All of which is at some distance from what Kierkegaard deplored at the christening he attended. 'A silken priest with an elegant gesture sprinkles water three times on the dear little baby and dries his hands gracefully with the towel' (*Attack upon 'Christendom'*, 1854–55).

By his baptism Jesus accepts his immersion in our human condition. He's in the deep end with us, where we're all floundering. The confirmation to him of his identity and vocation is in the descent of the dove. Not for the first time, not for the last time, the Spirit hovers over the waters. 'With the sound of the rush of a sublime tenderness' the Spirit comes to him.

'The history of Christendom is the history of an operation,' said Charles Williams. 'It is an operation of the Holy Ghost towards Christ' (*The Descent of the Dove*, The Religious Book Club, 1939). If so, it is not only Good Friday and Easter Day which are prefigured at the baptism of Christ. Pentecost too, it seems, is anticipated and, with Pentecost, the birth of the Church. Moreover his baptism marks the end of Jesus's 'hidden years'. Now begins his public ministry. Now what he does is for all to see. So perhaps a yet more glorious day is foreshadowed when once more the heavens will be torn apart and we shall look on the one we pierced.

The multiple associations are suggestive and edifying. They are also perilously seductive, threatening to cut us adrift from history. We must get back to that river – today little better than a drainage ditch – where

Jesus was baptized. That baptism nails his story into ours, as does the bitter death it betokens.

YEAR C

Isaiah 43.1–7; Acts 8.4–17; Luke 3.15–17, 21–22

THE SILENT SERVANT

This Sunday we contradict ourselves. That is what we regularly do in church, for church is a place where truths which seem to fly against each other have to be held together in tension. (It's much the same in laboratories, of course, where the basic properties of matter are studied.) The starkest of the Christian paradoxes is that – so we say – God is all-powerful but – so it seems – we mortals can do much as we like. God's loving will, we claim, will ultimately prevail, but we insist, too, that God does not deal with us like puppets on strings. We can, in the end, refuse his love. Some say that there are only two prayers: 'Thy will be done' and 'My will be done'. The paradox is that both prayers will be answered.

The contradiction this Sunday is between the noisy God described in our appointed Psalm and the quiet God – if God he is – whose baptism by John is related in our Gospel. Psalm 29 is set each year for the Baptism of Christ. The God of Psalm 29 makes one heck of a racket. 'The voice of the Lord is a powerful voice.' So powerful is his thundering voice that it shatters the cedar trees, strips the forest of its leaves, sets Mount Hermon skipping, and makes startled goats give birth before their time. Obviously this Psalm is chosen because, in talking about 'the voice of God over the waters', it nicely anticipates 'the voice from heaven', the voice which speaks as Jesus, baptized by John, emerges from the waters of Jordan. Lectionaries love to make these neat connections.

But if those who selected Psalm 29 as the psalm for this Sunday had listened more carefully to that 'voice from heaven' they would perhaps have hesitated over their choice. Because the voice of God at the baptism of Jesus is saying who he is – and that is someone not at all noisy. Jesus is the one 'in whom God is well pleased'. The words are a direct quotation from the prophetic text (Isaiah 42.10). They speak of 'the servant', the unidentified figure, whom we meet in a series of poems in the later chapters of Isaiah, who will bear the sins of God's people. That servant will suffer – but he will suffer *silently*. He is oppressed and afflicted, we read, 'and yet he opens not his mouth' (Isaiah 53.7).

At his baptism, Jesus accepts the identity, the role, and the mission of the *silent* suffering servant of the Lord.

No doubt Psalm 29 is saying something important about the sovereignty of God, but it is not the lesson that the baptism of Christ impresses on us. The psalm speaks of the God who is 'enthroned above the flood' (Psalm 29.10). At his baptism, Jesus is not enthroned above the flood. Far from it. He is engulfed by the flood. Its dreadful waters drown him. The tide of our sins and sorrows overwhelms him. His baptism in the Jordan is one with his baptism on Golgotha, that baptism which, throughout his ministry, he knew he must finally suffer and which, until it was accomplished, so 'constrained' him (Luke 12.50). 'The God of glory thunders' says our psalm. Not the God we meet in Jesus.

The imagery of water in Holy Scripture and in Christian liturgy is rich but complex. Again we are faced with the paradoxical, if not the contradictory. Water is the means of life and the symbol of all that is spiritually life-giving. 'Everything shall live where the river runs,' says the great text (Ezekiel 47.9). Jesus is the fountain of 'living water' and the one who drinks of him shall never thirst (John 4.14). But water is also the stuff of 'waters', the primal and malign waters of chaos from which God creates an ordered world, the waters which must part if God's people are to go free, the waters which Jesus tramples underfoot, the waters which one day will be no more (Revelation 21.1).

Waters, so says our Old Testament reading, are the adversity we may be required to pass through. John, who baptized Jesus, passed through those waters. Our lectionary omits the three verses which tell us what befell him. By so doing, it leaves out a lesson that life never does and which Luke would have us learn. It is the lesson that testimony to the truth is costly.

I recently attended a baptism which, most unusually, might have conveyed something of what the sacrament signifies. The huge old font had been filled to the brim. The water was deep enough to drown in. I wondered whether the officiating Anglican priest was proposing to do what the Orthodox priest does on these occasions, to *immerse* the new Christian in the chill waters. In the event, good Anglican as he was, the priest contented himself with the usual token sprinkling.

37

If the baby I saw baptized that morning takes his baptism seriously, he is in for far worse than a splashed forehead.

The Second Sunday of Epiphany

YEAR A

Isaiah 49.1–7; 1 Corinthians 1.1–9; John 1.29–42

COME AND YOU WILL SEE

Matthew, Mark, and Luke tell us about some fishermen who left their nets to follow Jesus. John has a different account of 'the call of the disciples'. They do not leave their nets. They leave their teacher. They move from John the Baptist to Jesus. There are those who try to harmonize the conflicting records. But if the Gospels are more hymn-sheets than history books then we should be not be looking for the harmony we insist on in, say, the testimony of witnesses to a road accident. All four Gospels agree that to encounter Jesus is to be drawn to him. The evangelists, each from his own perspective, explore the nature of the extraordinary authority Jesus exercises. Their accounts of what happened differ, but there is nothing discordant in their understanding of what it means to meet Jesus for the first time.

John the Baptist has his own disciples, those who share his faith if not his diet and his wardrobe. They wait with him in the desert for the imminent judgement, for the raised axe of the wrath of God to fall. John looks for the one to come who will execute that judgement. When Jesus appears John at once recognizes him as the one he has been waiting for, even though – so he twice tells us – he did not know beforehand whom to expect. What was it, we wonder, about Jesus that leads John immediately to revise his estimate of him, to see in him mercy made flesh, 'the Lamb of God' come not to condemn but to save?

Andrew and his unnamed companion are the first to turn from John to Jesus. (Our Gospel says nothing about what their departure meant to John. As they pass from his life into the company of Jesus, does he breathe his own *Nunc Dimittis*?)

Jesus puts a question to them, a question with rather more to it than we would gather from the New International Version's lame rendering, 'What do you want?' The Revised English Bible and the more recent mutations of the Revised Standard Version have 'What are you looking for?' which is better. But, as usual, it is the older translators who register what Jesus actually says. It is they who hear the question the Lord asks of all who look to him: 'What do you *seek*?' It is not pedantry to plead for the preservation of the vocabulary of seeking and searching, a treasury with such rich associations in the Christian Bible. I look for the spectacles I have lost. I seek the meaning of life. The two activities are not the same.

The two friends reply with a question of their own. At first reading it seems an evasive inquiry. They ask where Jesus is 'staying'. But on a second reading, a reading informed by everything the Fourth Gospel says about the importance of where we stay – or, in the hallowed language we are losing – where we *abide*, we see that their response is anything but evasive. Jesus's invitation to all who would be his disciples is 'Abide in me.' Much later Jesus will expressly voice this invitation (John 15.4), but Andrew and his friend have already heard it.

'Come and see,' says Jesus – and here the New International Version, with its delicate 'Come and you will see', does catch the overtone that the other versions miss. 'To see' in the Fourth Gospel is to know who Jesus is, whom to know is to love, whom to love is to serve, whom to serve is to be free.

Andrew gets the message at once. He 'finds' his brother Simon. (Some 'find'!) Andrew tells him that they have 'found' the Messiah. (In John's Gospel Jesus is recognized as Messiah from the outset. In the synoptic Gospels it is only much later that the disciples – far slower on the uptake than the demons – recognize him for who he is.) When Andrew introduces his brother to Jesus, we read that Jesus 'looked at him'. Before our story is done Jesus will again look at him. When he does so, Peter will break down in tears (Luke 22.61).

At their first meeting Jesus says two things to Andrew's brother. 'You are Simon. You will be Peter.' Again, what Jesus says is more important than the problems of fitting his words, especially the renaming of Simon, into the story-line of the other Gospels. Jesus tells me who I am, but he also tells me who I will be. He accepts me as I am. If he does, so must I. But what I am is not his final purpose for me. He has a new name for me too. A mysterious verse at the end of the Bible refers to it. 'To everyone who conquers . . . I will give a white stone and on the white stone is written a new name that no one knows except the one who receives it' (Revelation 1.17).

YEAR B

1 Samuel 3.1–10 (11–20); Revelation 5.1–10; John 1.43–51

THE TRUE LADDER

Nathanael wonders whether anything good can come from that proverbially inconsequential place Nazareth. (It is the kind of gibe that we who were born in Sidcup are used to.) There is only one way to find out. Philip's 'Come and see!' recalls John the Baptist's 'Behold the Lamb of God!' (John 1.36) Testimony to Jesus Christ is not a matter of going on about him but of getting out of other people's line of sight so that they can see and decide for themselves.

Saint Augustine, for whom two and two sometimes made five, thought that Nathanael must have been a dreadful sinner. Why else was he lurking under a fig tree when Jesus saw him? Adam and Eve tried to hide their shame behind fig leaves. So too, said Augustine, did Nathanael. Jesus, as usual, is kinder than Augustine. For Jesus, Nathanael is a 'guiless' child of Israel, the patriarch who was formerly known as Jacob. Unlike his famously shifty forefather, Nathanael is a straightforward character, a blunt northerner in fact. Guile is primarily a sin of the tongue – saying one thing, intending or concealing another. It is a thoroughly modern vice, much exercised by spin-doctors and those who sell us what we neither need nor want. If guile is smooth-talking, perhaps an even greater compliment is being paid Nathanael. Perhaps there is an allusion here to one of whom it was said that there was 'no deceit in his mouth' (Isaiah 53.9).

What Jesus already knows about him strikes Nathanael as nothing short of a miracle. For Nathanael *this* was 'the first of signs' – not what happened next at the wedding at Cana. His response is a tad over the top, even if substantially correct. He piles on the praise, lavishing on Jesus the titles of the Messiah. Jesus is unimpressed by tributes based on his apparent powers of clairvoyance. Here is the first hint we have in John of a health warning found in all the Gospels. Miracles can be dangerously misleading.

Nathanael will see 'greater things' than displays of extrasensory perception. Like Jacob, he will see a ladder of mercy set between heaven and earth. This ladder is different from most. It is not Plato's 'Ladder of Love', by which one ascends by stages to the vision of the Beautiful and the Good. Nor is it the 'Ladder of Perfection' described by the medieval English mystic, Walter Hilton, the staircase the ardent soul must mount from the *myrknesse* of sin to union with God. It is most certainly not any rung-by-rung method of self-improvement. Images of Jacob's ladder, of heaven opened, of hurrying angels attending on the Son of Man, belong with all the other figures with which this Gospel teems. By them John unfolds the mystery of who Jesus is. As John's Jesus did not say but might have, 'I am the true ladder.'

The traffic of the angels anticipates the interplay of ascending and descending in which John so delights. At the cross, that counterpoint is at its starkest, the paradox most acute. Christ's descent to our depths becomes an ascent to his throne. The thing about ladders is that they must rest securely at both ends. The Jesus of John's Gospel is at once the Word who is God and the Word made flesh. Both ends are secure. The ladder is grounded where we are. This is good news, if where we are isn't very nice and if, as is the case, there is nowhere else to start. A weary W. B. Yeats wrote,

> I must lie down where all the ladders start
> In the foul rag and bone shop of the heart.
> ('The Circus Animals' Desertion')

We know little about Nathanael and his fig tree, except that he does not return to its shade. He reappears once in John's story, in its haunting epilogue, where he is named among the disciples to whom Jesus 'showed himself' by the Sea of Galilee (John 21.2). Why had Nathanael gone back to his fishing? At the start, his taunt about Nazareth was that of a sceptic. Now – when all seems over – there are these tales of an empty tomb. Is his scepticism once more aroused? If so, the invitation to breakfast on the beach echoes the earlier one. 'Come and see.' 'Taste and see.' There's still only the one way to find out.

Nathanael isn't the Bartholomew of Matthew, Mark and Luke, as those who feel compelled to tidy up loose ends assert. Nathanael isn't Bartholomew – he's Nathanael. He knows who he is, even if we don't. His name is one of the many references to particular places and people, otherwise unknown, against which we stub our toes in this text. Nathanael's cameo appearance is an indication that there is rather more history in the Fourth Gospel than those who see it as one long sermon allow.

41

YEAR C

Isaiah 62.1–5; 1 Corinthians 12.1–11; John 2.1–11

HE LOVES OUR GLADNESS TOO

This Sunday we're told of two marriages. The first has not lived up to expectations. The context of our first reading is the experience of those who have returned to Jerusalem after decades of exile in Babylon. They had set off home with high hopes. The very desert, they believed, would burst into blossom before them (Isaiah 35). But it has turned out very differently. Their wretched life in their own land bears no relation to what they thought they'd been promised. A grim account of their woe-begone state is given by the not-so-minor prophet Haggai.

> Consider how you have fared.
> You have sown much and harvested little;
> you eat, but you never have enough;
> you drink, but you never have your fill;
> you clothe yourselves, but no one is warm;
> you that earn wages earn wages to put them in a bag with holes.
> (Haggai 1.5–6)

'You have looked for much,' says Haggai, 'and, lo, it came to little' (Haggai 1.9). In Haggai's view the returned exiles have only themselves to blame for their wretched situation. They have forgotten the God who had set them free. They have built fine houses for themselves but have not restored God's temple. Their plight is the punishment they deserve.

The prophet whom we hear on Sunday explains things differently. (We need to read on a couple of verses to catch his drift.) He believes that it's not the fault of the returnees that life is bad for them. It's God's fault. God has neither kept his word nor answered his people's prayers. No doubt there are those who suggest our prophet should keep such impious opinions to himself. But he isn't to be silenced. Instead of shutting up, he mounts a campaign of preaching and prayer on behalf of Jerusalem.

Not to mince words, God's memory has to be jolted. He has to be reminded of his commitment to his people. Those who join this round-the-clock campaign are urged 'to give God no rest' – and to take no rest themselves – until God fulfils his promise to his people, and Jerusalem is established as a light to the nations.

God speaks. He repeats his promise to Jerusalem. 'The nations *shall* see your vindication, and all the kings your glory.' God's marriage to Jerusalem – and indeed to the whole Promised Land – will be remade. This renewed marriage will be lasting, loving, and joyful. Jerusalem will be renamed 'Hephzibah' – 'the bride in whom her husband delights'. With a little licence, the land's new name, 'Beulah', might be translated 'Just married!'

God is wedded to Jerusalem. The prophet means the earthly Jerusalem, not the 'heavenly Jerusalem', whatever and wherever that is. How has this marriage turned out? The city, for whose sake the prophet will not keep silent, is the same city that today three monotheistic faiths deem holy, that two nation-states claim as their capital, and that, so far from being a light to the nations, remains a focus of international conflict. The time has not yet come, it seems, for those who 'remind the Lord' to take a rest.

Our Gospel is a happier wedding story. At Cana Jesus turns water, there for 'rites of purification', into wine. Water into wine. It's what Jesus does with religion, if he's allowed to. It is what Jesus does for Alyosha Karamazov.

A central chapter in Dostoevsky's novel *The Brothers Karamazov* is entitled 'Cana of Galilee'. The young Alyosha is praying in the cell where the body of the venerated monk Zossima is lying. One other monk is there, reading aloud John's account of the wedding at Cana. Alyosha dreams that he is there at the marriage, along with Christ and the other guests. In his dream, he responds to the story. 'I love that passage. It's Cana of Galilee, the first miracle . . . Ah, that sweet miracle! It was not men's grief, but their joy Christ visited. He worked His first miracle to help men's gladness . . . He who loves men loves their gladness too.'

Alyosha ponders Mary's peremptory word: 'They have no wine.' 'His mother,' he reflects, 'knew that he had come not only to make his great terrible sacrifice. She knew that his heart was open even to the simple, artless merrymaking of some obscure and unlearned people, who had warmly bidden him to their poor wedding.' In his (Alyosha's) dream, Zossima, risen from the dead, appears and calls to Alyosha to join the feast. Alyosha wakes, and his eyes are filled with tears of joy. He goes outside and flings himself on the earth, kissing and embracing it.

For our Old Testament prophet, God's commitment in marriage to Jerusalem is binding, even if God has to be reminded of it. For Alyosha, as for the author of the Fourth Gospel, the wedding at Cana promises joy to the world, even if our sorrows are far from over. Marriages, it seems, must be worked at. The marriage of heaven and earth is no different from that of husband and wife. It too has to be worked at – and by both parties.

The Third Sunday of Epiphany

YEAR A

Isaiah 9.1–4; 1 Corinthians 1.10–18; Matthew 4.12–23

NORTH AND SOUTH

One of Mrs Gaskell's best novels offers instructive background reading for Sunday's Gospel. *North and South* depicts the deep divide between two Victorian worlds. One world is 'the south', the polite and refined society of the minor gentry of rural Hampshire. The other world is 'the north', specifically the brutal insalubrious world of the newly-industrialized northern city. (The grim Milton of the novel, where the sun is quenched by the smoke, is a fictionalized Manchester.) Mrs Gaskell graphically describes the contrasting social conditions of north and south – the grime and the green – but what interests the novelist still more is the mutual incomprehension and mistrust between these two worlds. Betwixt north and south a great gulf is fixed, a gulf of entrenched ignorance and suspicion.

For 'the south' of first-century Palestine, for Jerusalem and for its political and religious elite, Galilee is 'the north'. It is, in the contemptuous parlance, 'Galilee of the Gentiles'. The opprobrious term is that of the southern prophet, writing centuries earlier, whom we hear in our first reading. That such a slur was already common currency in his day is some indication of how ancient was the antipathy between north and south in the 'promised land'. We hear that God had long ago humiliated those northern territories, 'the land of Zebulun and the land of Naphtali'. The allusion is to the fall of the northern kingdom of Israel to the Assyrians in 721 BC, to the exile of its inhabitants, and to the resettlement in their homelands of people – as the southerners saw them – from 'heathen lands afar'.

Just how Jewish and just how Gentile the towns and villages of the hills around Lake Galilee were by the time of Jesus is not the issue.

The doctoral theses on the topic need not detain us. The point is that the 'northerners' – the Galileans – were perceived by the more sophisticated south as a deplorably mixed bunch, hopelessly compromised in their religious allegiance. That is how they were seen by those who – their minds made up – were never going to be confused by facts.

And it is to this 'Galilee of the Gentiles', to despised Zebulun and Naphtali, that Jesus comes at the start of his public ministry. Such is the priority of his mission. The matter of the location of Jesus is important to Matthew. Later we learn from him that Jesus is to be found in all sorts of unlikely places – in prison or on sickbeds, among the destitute or with those whom today we would call 'immigrants' (Matthew 25). This idea will prove unwelcome to the church Matthew addresses. Many of us would confess the same reluctance to seek the Lord where, in our hearts, we know he is to be found.

At the end Matthew will have one last word about where to look for Jesus. On Easter Day the women are told to tell the disciples, 'He is going ahead of you to Galilee. There you will see him' (Matthew 28.7). The disciples' last meeting with Jesus is where it all began, in 'Galilee of the Gentiles', in the lands allotted to the sons and daughters of Zebulun and Naphtali. (The four fishermen surely came from Zebulun where, we read, 'they suck the affluence of the sea', Deuteronomy 33.19.) By birth Jesus, 'Lion of Judah', may have belonged to the mainstream, but he begins his earthly mission in a backwater and there, for Matthew, he draws it to a close. Throughout that mission those he meets are mostly 'backwater people', folk far from the centres of power, those of little account but whose company he prefers. If on our own journeys we have lost touch with the him, that may be because we have dropped 'Galilee of the Gentiles' from our itinerary. When we find ourselves consorting with powerful people in high places, there is sometimes an angel whispering in our ear, 'He is not here. Go to Galilee!'

'The people who sat in darkness saw a great light.' The darkness is the primal darkness, the darkness that prevailed before God says, 'Let there be light!' (Genesis 1.3) It is the darkness of the enslaved (Exodus 10.21–22) and of the exiled (Isaiah 42.7). It is our darkness too, we who imagine that we can make our way by the guttering candlelight of our own wits.

As we shall see in weeks to come, the irony is here in Matthew's Gospel, as much as in the Fourth Gospel, that 'the enlightened' embrace darkness and 'the benighted' see the light. Matthew will record Jesus's indictment of those he calls 'blind guides', the clergymen who make everything impossibly difficult and complicated for simple people so that they can hang on to their own prestigious positions (Matthew 15.14; 23.16). But he will tell too, as do all the Gospel writers, of those who, despite being 'in the dark', find their way to him. Matthew's magi (Matthew 2.1–12) were the first of many.

YEAR B

Genesis 14.17–20; Revelation 19. 6–10; John 2.1–11

THE FIRST LIGHT BREAKING

The poet is on a 'pilgrimage'. He is one of a group being hurtled round the Holy Land by tourist bus from one dubious site to the next. The bus halts somewhere in the heat of the day. The pilgrims spill out into the fierce sun. In a herd they stumble after their tour guide. Worn-out by it all, the poet leans against a wall at the roadside. Nearby steps lead down to a well. He describes how two children approach him. They offer him a cup of cold water drawn from the well. The poet asks for the name of this place where they have stopped. The children tell him that it is the village of Kfar Kana.

The pilgrims return with their tawdry souvenirs and climb back on the bus. For them this brief stop will merge with all the others. But the poet will not forget the place where, for him, children turned water into wine.

For Charles Causley, what happened that day at Kfar Kana, the biblical Cana, was a very private miracle. But then, of course, so was that 'first of signs'. Only the kitchen staff had any idea what had actually happened. It is usually so in the upstairs–downstairs world in which the Gospel story is played out. Water into wine. It is the first sign, the first light breaking. Glory has dawned. The old is over and done with, the new is here and now. The utter newness of it all is the meaning of the miracle. That is the blazing light in which the two problems the story poses must be seen. The first problem is the pottery. The second is the demanding mother.

The six huge water jars certainly are a stumbling-block. (Some of us still insist, with the King James Bible, that they contain 'two or three firkins apiece'.) They're there, we're told, for the purifying rites of 'the Jews'. Most modern translations, apart from the NIV, tone down this terse – if not hostile – reference to 'the Jews'. For modern readers, conscious of what Christians have done to Jews across the centuries, there are too many such remarks in this Gospel. Clearly the Fourth Gospel was written and first read in a Church already at a distance from Judaism. Today we seek to reduce that distance. This means hearing how John's talk about 'the Jews' sounds to Jewish readers. Some bits of the Bible have to be read in penitence.

If there is a pooh-poohing of ceremonial cleansing in this story, the Christian response is not to nod in smug agreement but to try on the cap ourselves. We shall find it fits. Religions of every stripe, not least Christianity, prefer the ritual to the radical. We who like our purificators nicely laundered have no right to be sniffy about pots for the same purpose.

Mary's blunt remark 'The wine's run out' is an intercession of sorts. It has much in common with the chummy and proprietorial 'Jesus, we do just pray for fine weather for the fete.' When, in reply, Jesus calls his mother 'Woman' he is being stern but not rude. What he says next is more shocking. As we shall see next week, 'What's it got to do with you and me?' is how demons talk (Mark 1.24). But here it is the response of a divinity which is at no one's beck and call. Jesus says, 'My hour has not yet come.' That hour will be the hour of his 'lifting up from the earth', the one exaltation, as John sees it, of his dying, rising, and ascending. Not that Mary's prayer is ignored. The sign that saves the day promises a better day still, 'when the mountains shall drip sweet wine, and the hills shall flow with it' (Amos 9.13).

The sign is about Jesus. It is also about weddings and what can still happen at them. Glory dawned at a village wedding. I find this story poignant reading. Glory rarely dawns at church weddings these days. There are too few of them. (In the big parish church where I was Rector there were once fifteen weddings a week. Now there are one or two a year.) Couples who get married in a stately home (or in a hot-air balloon or underwater) no longer hear sublime words about that 'holy estate' which 'Christ adorned and beautified with his presence and first miracle that he wrought, in Cana of Galilee'. Our Stalinist marriage legislation forbids religious references in civil wedding ceremonies. Christ cannot adorn and beautify by his presence a wedding in a hot air balloon. He's banned by law from the basket.

The point about weddings in church, by contrast to weddings in the sky, is that Christ can be a guest. And where he is a guest there can be glory. My friend Andrew Body, who has written so well about getting married (*Growing Together*, Church House Publishing, 2005) suggests that I should stop lamenting the decline in church weddings and start promoting them.

YEAR C

Nehemiah 8.1–3, 5–6, 8–10; 1 Corinthians 12.12–31a; Luke 4.41–21

THE UNDESERVING POOR

We're told that, at the time of Jesus, Nazareth was only a tiny village, home to a couple of hundred at the most. Here Jesus spends his 'hidden years'. His emergence from obscurity is dramatic. Jesus goes to the synagogue as he usually does on the Sabbath. He takes part in the service, as perhaps he did frequently. He reads from the prophet Isaiah. Then he preaches. So far nothing exceptional has happened. Anyone versed in the Scriptures could be asked to give the sermon and we have no reason to suppose that Jesus hadn't done so previously. We get the picture of a sleepy morning service, unfolding in much the way it has always done. Pleasant memories come to mind of Sunday mattins long ago, where one's daydreams were rarely disturbed.

But today the sleepers awake. Jesus reads about one to come who would set God's poor people free. They've heard that before. It's what follows which is so electrifying. The gist of his sermon is simple. 'These words are about me and today they have come true.'

Jesus announces the purpose of his mission. He comes, 'his spirit yet streaming from the waters of baptism', to bring 'good news to the poor'. The rest of Luke's story is the account of how Jesus fulfils that mission.

Who are the poor and why are they poor? There's much talk today about the difference between 'absolute poverty' and 'relative poverty'. Jesus doesn't talk like that. His understanding of poverty is not shaped by economic theory but by Scripture and suffering, by reading his Bible and by making the pain of the afflicted his.

Not that Jesus agrees with everything the Old Testament says about poverty. Swathes of it reflect the view that the poor are poor as a punishment. Deuteronomy teaches that it's the godless that end up in the gutter. That is not how Jesus sees the poor. Later in the Bible we have a different view of poverty. Poverty comes to be spiritualized.

'The poor will eat and be satisfied,' sings the Psalmist, 'and they who seek the Lord will praise him' (Psalm 22.26). The parallelism implies that the poor are pious and the pious are poor. This is not a connection Jesus makes. Jesus may advocate selling up and giving everything away, but he never suggests that being poor of itself makes you a better person. The scriptural tradition in which Jesus stands is that of the prophets. For them the poor are the materially destitute and socially oppressed. Whether godly or ungodly, it makes no difference. They are equally victims of the rapacity of the rich.

The poor whom God loves are not just 'the deserving poor'. Alfred Dolittle of Bernard Shaw's *Pygmalion* was proud to be one of the 'undeserving poor'. In answer to Professor Higgins' question: 'Have you no morals, man?' Dolittle replies, 'Can't afford them. Neither could you if you were as poor as me.' Jesus's 'good news to the poor' is as much good news to Alfred Dolittle as it is to rather more pious dustmen.

So, does God care for the poor more than he does for the rich? It seems so, though we find it hard to say so. Instead we resort to coy circumlocutions, such as God's 'preferential option for the poor'. When we turn to Isaiah, as Jesus does, we meet a God who takes sides. Just how far he does so becomes clear in a striking text which loses in translation. God warns those who deny the poor justice that they will be punished. These poor, says the Lord, are 'the poor, my people', or 'the poor who are my people' (10.2) The usual translations, 'the poor *of* my people' and the like, mask the extent to which God identifies himself specifically with 'the least, the last, and the lost' – the kind of people we meet on many pages of Luke's Gospel.

Some have seen Jesus's sermon as an announcement of the 'jubilee year', the year – every fifty years – in which, in an ideal Israel which never was, all debts would be cancelled and all slaves set free (Leviticus 25.10–18). The vision of the jubilee year was the inspiration of the remarkable Jubilee 2000 campaign, which pressed for the cancellation of the debts which cripple the poorest countries, as does its successor, the Jubilee Debt Campaign.

How far the idea of 'jubilee' was in Luke's – or Jesus's mind – is a moot point. Jesus does not campaign for the abolition of slavery in the Roman Empire, and his treatment of indebtedness, at least as expressed in 'the parable of the unjust steward', was eccentric (Luke 16.1–8). What we witness in Luke's Gospel is not the overthrow of an unjust social and economic order. Instead we see someone going about doing good. One by one he sets us free.

The Fourth Sunday of Epiphany

YEAR A

1 Kings 17.8–16; 1 Corinthians 1.18–31; John 2.1–11

CHRIST, THE CLOWN OF GOD

'God chose by the folly of the gospel to save those who have faith.' The Revised English Bible's translation is bold, clear, and, for once, exactly right. It is important that we hear precisely what St Paul is saying. We are still misled by the echoes in our ears of the Authorized Version's uncharacteristically slack translation. The AV makes Paul talk about 'the foolishness of preaching' – as if Paul is saying that that there is something essentially ridiculous about climbing into pulpits and delivering sermons.

Had Paul said that, we would not have disagreed. But that is not Paul's point. For the apostle, the folly lies not in preaching, but in *what is preached*. What is preached is the cross. It is the cross that is mad, not our homilies about it, however blundering and inept they are.

That is how the cross was originally perceived. Famously, the earliest known depiction of the cross is a mockery of it. Originally scratched into the wall of a Roman guardroom, it shows, attached to a cross, a figure with an ass's head. To the left of the cross stands a young man, gesturing towards it. Beneath is the inscription, 'Alaxamenos worships God'.

That is how the cross is still perceived. When, a year or two ago, the Bolzano Museum of Modern Art in Northern Italy opened, its inaugural exhibition included Martin Kippenberger's notorious crucified frog. The frog is bright green. Its tongue hangs out. It is afflicted with warts. It is depicted, impaled on a cross, with a mug in one hand and an egg in the other. Local Catholics, including the Pope on holiday in the neighbourhood, were upset.

That is how the cross will always be perceived. No doubt explanations will still be forthcoming. No doubt the traditional 'theories of the atonement' – 'penal substitution' and the rest – will continue to be aired. No doubt it will still be argued that all God could do in our sinful circumstances was to suffer shameful execution in our flesh.

But so long as the original stark story is told – free from our chattering commentary – the cross will still be seen as contradictory and absurd.

That is how the cross – dare one say it? – is rightly perceived. To be sure, Paul initially distances himself from those – 'those who are perishing' – to whom the cross is folly. He places himself among those who are 'being saved', the Christian *cognoscenti* for whom the cross is not foolish at all, but 'the power of God'. But as his thought races on – and it is one of the most dazzling and breathtaking passages in the New Testament – Paul seems to recognize that 'the folly of the gospel' is not simply a misconception of the darkened minds of the unsaved. So far beyond our grasp are the ways of God, so weak are our words to speak of them, that all we say of them are misrepresentations. Better then to speak, if speak we must, of the gospel's folly than of its wisdom. For if I presume to call God's ways 'wise', it might be supposed that I claim to understand them.

We have been made to think again about the folly of God's ways by Archbishop Rowan William's study of Dostoevsky (*Dostoevsky: Language, faith, and fiction.* Continuum, 2008). (Some might say that we have been called to consider the nature of divine folly by the achbishop's own choices, most of all by the *kenosis*, the self-emptying, required by his acceptance of the primacy.) Rowan Williams sends us back to Dostoevsky's great novels. We ponder the fact that Dostoevsky's study of a man so good that he might be deemed Christlike is entitled *The Idiot*.

To take up the cross is to share in God's foolishness. Paul returns to the theme of supposed wisdom and supposed folly later in his letter. His Corinthian readers think that they are a clever lot. Paul's sarcasm is biting. 'We are fools for Christ's sake, but you are wise' (1 Corinthians 4.10). His tone may be sarcastic, but he speaks truly. They called Christ mad (John 10.20). If they say the same about us, we should not deny the charge.

Round the corner from where I worked in Hackney is the Church of All Saints, Dalston. It is known as 'the clowns' church'. Once a year it hosts a special service attended by clowns from all over the country. But every church is a clowns' church, for the one we stumble after is a clown too. Christ is the clown of God in this world's sad circus. The clown embodies, as Christ does, the love that 'bears all things, believes all things, hopes all things, endures all things' (1 Corinthians 13.7).

The Eastern Orthodox Church has always understood those who are fools for Christ's sake. I think with special gratitude and affection of Blessed John the Hairy, whose feast day is 12 November.

YEAR B

Deuteronomy 18.15–20; Revelation 12.1–5a; Mark 1.21–28

THE SECRET MISSION

Here for the first time in Mark we meet a demon. We shall meet many more before Mark is done. Secularism has not banished fears of the demonic. Parish priests are still often asked to exorcize spooky houses. Whether or not demons exist, it is wise pastorally to act on the assumption that they just might.

In Mark's Gospel we face an unholy trinity, the ugly threesome of demons, disease and death. Jesus is seen as confronting and overcoming each of them in turn. They're interconnected, of course, as trinities usually are. As Professor Alan Richardson used to say, someone in the Gospels who is possessed or ill is simply suffering from 'a mild attack of death'. Demons, disease, and death. The terrible triplets are all children of one father, named in a text which exactly summarizes the role of Jesus as Mark sees it. 'The Son of God was revealed for this purpose, to destroy the works of the devil' (1 John 3.8).

The demoniac doesn't know what's got into him. But 'what's got into him' knows that it has met its match. The first to confess Christ as Lord – 'the devils also believe and tremble' (James 2.19) – is not Peter at Caesarea Philippi but this malign thing that had made some poor soul in Capernaum its squat.

Jesus does not welcome such acknowledgement. The demand 'Be silent' is very strong indeed. Literally, Jesus is saying that the man's mouth should be muzzled. In Mark it's not just the demons who are told to shut up. Those miraculously cured, indeed the disciples themselves, are repeatedly told to keep quiet about who Jesus is and what he is doing. 'Be silent!' Such a command could not have been made up and ascribed to Jesus by a church which, within a generation, was going into all the world garrulously preaching the gospel. Here for sure we touch the rock of history.

'Be silent!' The repeated rubric has embarrassed the evangelically minded. It is a text rarely quoted in 'Mission Action Plans'. Christianity is a missionary religion. So what are we to make of this call to secrecy?

Mark is a theologian. If his Gospel is punctuated by injunctions to secrecy it is because, for him, they tell us something essential about the nature of God's self-revelation in Jesus. Mark will have us understand this about Jesus: that the man's a mystery. It is not obvious who Jesus is. That is both a fact of the history Mark records and an article of the faith he shares. (It is our experience too, we who, two millennia later, stumble after this itinerant exorcist of Galilee.) There is hiddenness about the man, this strange figure who seeks to escape the crowds, who speaks of the coming reign of God as a secret, who here urges silence on a demon as later he will on the disciples.

If God is truly one of us and not merely stealing our clothes, his identity can neither immediately be apparent nor lightly disclosed. How could it be otherwise? How could an incarnation be other than obscure and enigmatic?

'Be silent!' As our numbers decline, we raise our voices. We are rebuked by the reticence of Jesus in Mark's Gospel. There's a dusty old title which could perhaps be added to the long list of modern publications about mission – Isaac Williams's 1837 'Tract for the Times', his *Reserve in the Communication of Religious Knowledge*. Williams, peaceable disciple of the belligerent John Henry Newman, pointed out in his mild and gentle way that we do not serve the gospel by speaking too soon.

The purpose of evangelism is not to dispel the mystery surrounding the figure of Jesus, not to answer questions but – exactly as happens here – to provoke them. The sequel to Jesus's first sermon is not a mindless rendition of the closing hymn, but intense discussion. The response is not 'So now we know' but a bewildered 'What is this?'

Back to the man with the 'unclean spirit'. Our accounts of his plight will be constrained by our differing cultures. Some will dismiss talk of demons as superstitious clap-trap. Others – most of the human race – will take the existence of demons for granted. But however we explain this man's affliction, it has its equally destructive equivalents about which there is no need for metaphysical speculation.

Possession has much in common with addiction, for example. The possessed and the addicted both suffer an invasion of the self. Drink takes time in destroying my liver, but it doesn't delay in undermining my sense of identity. Canon David Williams, who has done such fine work among the drug-dependent and alcoholics of the Rochester diocese, writes of the healing of the addicted. 'It is not the addict in them that is recovering but the person that they lost in their addiction to whom they are now returning.'

Demon-possessed, addicted, or just an average boring sinner, my healing is always Christ's restoration to me of the one I truly am.

YEAR C

Ezekiel 43.27—44.4; 1 Corinthians 13.1–13; Luke 2.22–40

OLDER AND WISER

Simeon looks for 'the consolation of Israel'. So, too, must we who sing Simeon's song. The babe in his arms betokens Israel's salvation, but, as Simeon foresees, the birth of this child will only exacerbate Israel's sorrows. The infant who is the pledge of Israel's redemption will multiply Israel's suffering. Across the centuries since Simeon's day, the afflictions of the Jewish people, culminating in the Holocaust, have mounted beyond the mind's capacity to measure or comprehend. The Lord let his servant Simeon depart in peace. We who are left, aware of horrors that Simeon did not live to see, must not sing our own *Nunc Dimittis* too soon. The promise of salvation is certain, but its fulfilment is still far distant.

Simeon is better at growing older than most of us are. He does not 'rage against the dying of the light'. Rather than bewailing light's departure, he awaits its dawn. He knows what we have forgotten, how to wait.

Simeon – and still more Anna – are getting on in years. One way of reading the celebrated thirteenth chapter of Paul's first letter to the Corinthians is as an expression of the insights of ageing. The passage comes to us framed in a letter in which Paul has had to deal with a series of tiresome problems posed for him by the troublesome church at Corinth. To be sure, the hymn makes perfect sense in its present context. It can be read as Paul's rejoinder to all those in the Christian family who fall out with one another over this or that contentious issue. 'Let love be the rule,' he implies. 'Let love decide.' Famously – or notoriously – Joseph Fletcher in his *Situation Ethics* understood this to be the sole basis of Christian ethics.

So 1 Corinthians 13 sits happily where we find it. But it has often been pointed out that the chapter, soaring as it does above the spats which preoccupy Paul in most of this letter, can be read independently of its context. The chapter could well have been an originally independent composition, a hymn which Paul had come across and which he recognized as saying exactly what the feuding Christians of Corinth needed to hear.

The great hymn to love is a statement about what matters and what does not. To know the difference between these two is not universally granted to the young. Nor, of course, is such discernment necessarily acquired by the old. But more often it is the old, those versed in waiting, such as Simeon, who have won the wisdom ('that precarious gait some call experience') voiced in this great text. It is more often the old who recognize that most of our achievements are ephemeral. It is more often the old who, having finally forsaken the folly of their youthful certainties, realize that the most we can claim is to 'see through a glass darkly'. It is more often the old who know what it means 'to bear all things, believe all things, hope all things, endure all things'.

Anna is even older than Simeon. She represents those in her day who were 'looking for the redemption of Jerusalem', as she stands too in our day for all who love Jerusalem and seek its peace. There is, it seems, some connection between the fate of this child and the destiny of the city. That connection – I write as yet again Christian monks of different persuasions come to blows in the Church of the Holy Sepulchre – is hard to see. We can only make sure that, looking to Anna, our love for the city does not burn low and that our prayers for the city do not falter – however unmoved by them the Almighty seems.

Love 'bears all things, believes all things, hopes all things, endures all things'. Love even puts up with religion. This Sunday's Gospel is remarkable for the attention it pays to details of religious ceremonial. Later in his Gospel, Luke seems less enthused about such matters. Here he is at pains to stress that Mary and Joseph at every point punctiliously comply with what was 'customary under the law'.

Luke, like Paul, is concerned to stress that Jesus is born 'under the law'. From his birth Christ endures, as he will endure at his death, what religion and what religious people do to him. We are much in the same boat. Most branches of the Christian Church have their rules, 'canon law' and the like. The advance of God's kingdom is not always served by defying them, even if the purpose of the more piffling of them is not immediately apparent. Lonely stands against the system do not always achieve much. Systemic shortcomings and institutional idiocies are best addressed from within. That, amongst much else, is a lesson of the law of love – whether or not Paul was himself the author of 1 Corinthians 13.

ORDINARY TIME

Proper 1

The Sunday between 3 and 9 February (if earlier than the second Sunday before Lent)

YEAR A

Isaiah 58.1–9a (9b–12); 1 Corinthians 2.1–12 (13–16); Matthew 5.13–20

SALT OR LIGHT?

Are we salt or light? Sunday's Gospel asks us to decide. Before glibly pronouncing that we must be both, it would be wise to stop and think. Salt and light function very differently. Salt works when it is not noticed. We say that the Lancashire hot-pot is delicious, not that the salt that has enhanced its flavour is delicious. If we notice the salt, that is only because there is too much of it.

By contrast, light has to be seen. If it is hidden, as Jesus himself points out, it is no use to anyone. If the three blasts of light every sixty seconds from the Eddystone lighthouse were invisible, there would be an awful lot of shipwrecks on that nasty little outcrop of rock.

'You are the salt of the earth.' 'You are the light of the world.' The two images represent two ways of 'being church'. The metaphor of salt suggests that the role of the Church is to be a hidden – but nevertheless vital – *presence* in the world. The symbol of light speaks of the *prophetic* role of the church. And of course the notion of hidden prophets – Elijahs permanently concealed in caves – is nonsense.

The symbol of salt has a bewildering range of allusions in the Bible. Salt destroys and salt preserves. King Abimelech 'sowed salt' in the ruins of Shechem (Judges 9.45). Lot's unfortunate wife, turned to salt on the road from Sodom, is no doubt still there (Genesis 19.26). Salt purifies. Elijah throws salt into a poisoned spring and at once its water is clean (2 Kings 2. 19–22). Salt brings out the taste of a dish. Job says – and we can only agree – that 'the slime of the purslane' is inedible without it (Job 6.6).

Salt is associated with God's bond with his people. The salt with which offerings are to be seasoned is 'the salt of the covenant' (Leviticus 2.13). Paul, whose own talk was anything but bland, tells us to ensure that our conversations are 'seasoned with salt' (Colossians 4.6).

The image of light is more familiar. From the creator's 'Let there be light' (Genesis 1.3) to the city, whose light is the glory of God and whose lamp is the Lamb (Revelation 21.23), light is the supreme symbol of the divine. God 'dwells in unapproachable light' (1 Timothy 6.16) In Christ the unapproachable light approaches us. In John's 'gospel of light', Jesus says, 'I am the light of the world' (John 8.12). Jesus, the light lifted high, draws all people to himself (John 12.32).

Jesus, who claimed to be 'the light of the world', says his disciples too are 'the light of the world'. But theirs is not an independent light. Their light is his. There is only one source of light. 'This little light of mine, I'm going to let it shine.' If I let it shine for my glorification, it will be swiftly shattered.

'You are the light of the world.' 'I am the light of the world.' 'You are the salt of the earth.' Was the pattern of these sayings once complete? Did Jesus say as well, in an unrecorded utterance, 'I am the salt of the earth'? Some scholars suggest that he did. If so, there are terrible resonances in what is said of the salt that is deemed tasteless. That salt is 'thrown out and trodden under foot by men'. We think of the one who, it might be said, was not to everyone's taste and who was 'despised and rejected' (Isaiah 53.3).

Salt suggests those who are a transformative presence. Brother Lawrence 'practised the presence of God' in the kitchen of his priory, content to do the most menial of tasks for the glory of God. 'We can do little things for God,' he said. 'I turn the cake that is frying on the pan for love of him.' We have all known the likes of Brother Lawrence, those whose presence has lent a savour to our days. I think of the Little Sisters of Jesus, who live in a council flat on the 13th floor of a tower block in Hackney where I worked as a parish priest. They do not preach, but they are an eloquent presence.

Light suggests those whose role is prophetic. Prophecy does not necessarily require a pulpit or a platform. Prophecy is action as much as proclamation. Jesus said, as we hear in our Gospel, that he did not come to abolish the law and the prophets but to fulfil them. It follows that the law and the prophets are to mean for us what they meant for Jesus –

the love of God and the love of one's neighbour (Matthew 22.34–40). Prophecy takes place when this law of love is proclaimed, but still more when it is practised. 'Light shall break forth like the dawn,' says the prophet we hear in our Old Testament reading, when justice is done.

YEAR B

Isaiah 40.21–31; 1 Corinthians 9.16–23; Mark 1.29–39

HIDE AND SEEK

'Immediately.' New Testament scholars, as a breed, prefer not to be rushed. Many wish to airbrush out of Mark's story all his many 'immediatelys'. They tell us that Mark is not much of a stylist and his repeated use of 'immediately' means nothing. It's merely a verbal tic, they say. Church leaders are equally averse to the adverb 'immediately'. It rarely occurs in reports published by the General Synod. The public ministry of the Son of God took far less time than the Church of England needed to revise its ordinal. And yet 'immediately' is an evangelical word, that's to say it characterizes the Christian gospel. There is an immediacy about the impact of Jesus on his contemporaries, an urgency about his words and works. The Christian understanding of time is that there is little of it left. So Mark's narrative – 'immediately' overtaking 'immediately' – races to its terrible and mysterious conclusion.

Jesus heals Peter's mother-in law. We describe what he did as a 'miracle'. We moderns (or post-moderns) wonder what happened. We ask complicated questions about the means, natural or supernatural, by which the woman's alleged recovery was brought about. We agonize over theological significance of the miraculous in the ministry of Jesus. These questions of historicity and of meaning are important and we must return to them in weeks to come. But the risk is that, too clever by half, we miss the main point. When Jesus makes someone better he reduces the sum of human suffering. However naïve it sounds, this has to be said: most of Jesus's itinerant ministry was spent making life less miserable for people. When what we do in Jesus's name makes them *more* miserable – holding long services in cold churches, for example – it shows that we have lost the plot.

No doubt faith can move mountains but in Mark's Gospel it's usually the other way round. The mountain moves, the miracle comes

58

to pass, and then sometimes faith is kindled. There is no suggestion that Peter's delirious mother-in-law is even aware of who it is taking her hand. Once back on her feet, we read, 'she served them'. Does Mark add this comment for our edification, inviting us to reflect that we are 'saved to serve'? Such a reading belongs with the suggestion that, in telling Jesus about the woman's illness, the disciples teach us the importance of intercessory prayer. There is a taste of syrup about such pieties. More dangerously, they silence questions which need to be asked about what is counter-cultural and what remains culturally conditioned in the relationship of Jesus with those around him. It will raise modern eyebrows that the one woman in the story, barely recovered from a bad illness, is immediately waiting hand and foot on the men.

At sunset, when the day's work is done, they return to him with their troubles. The commonest problem presented to Jesus is demon-possession. He demands that the exorcized demons depart to their own place in silence. They know him, all right. 'Even the demons believe – and shudder' (James 2.19). But the only testimony Jesus seeks is from those who trust and love him.

Mark has Peter saying to this elusive Jesus, 'Everyone is looking for you.' (Older readers will be haunted by the evocative King James reading, 'All men seek thee.') Here Mark probably does mean more than Peter does. The vocabulary of seeking and searching in the Gospels is used to describe two complementary quests, our quest for God ('everyone is looking for you') and God's quest for us ('the Son of man came to seek and to save the lost', Luke 19.10). The two quests mirror and match each other. Zacchaeus clambers up a tree to look out for the one who climbed down from heaven to find him.

Not that Jesus allows himself to be easily found. The 'next towns' beckon. Just when we think that we have caught up with him, we find that he has already moved on. It is far from frivolous to see the story of Jesus and us as an extended game of hide-and-seek. Jerome Berryman, only begetter of Godly Play, suggests that our relationship with our Lord is one of 'Peekaboo'. If we find talk of Peekaboo childish, Berryman points out that we can use a Latin tag instead. God is *Deus absconditus atque praesens* – hidden yet also present (*The Complete Guide to Godly Play*, Vol. 1, *Living the Good News*, 2002). The game being played in these opening episodes of Mark's Gospel began a long time ago. 'Where art thou?' called the Lord God, peering through the bushes (Genesis 3.9). 'If only I knew where to find him!' Job cried, scraping his boils (Job 23.3).

Jesus is always on his way somewhere else. It's why he 'came forth' from Galilee and God (1.38). If we sometimes feel the good Lord is playing a game with us, we may well be right.

YEAR C

Isaiah 6.1–8 (9–13); 1 Corinthians 15.1–11; Luke 5.1–11

MIRACLES NOT MAGIC

The night's fishing had been a failure. They've caught nothing. But at Jesus' bidding, they lower their nets once more. This time the catch is so great that their nets are about to break. William Barclay tells us that what must have happened was that Jesus located the shoals the fishermen had missed. Like most such explanations of the miraculous, the natural account of what happened tests one's credulity as much as the supernatural one. It's as hard to believe that Jesus the carpenter was a better fisherman than Peter as it is to believe that he created fish that weren't there before. The question of where exactly the fish came from is not only unanswerable – it is wholly unnecessary. Luke himself, for all his concern for the historical, would surely have been baffled and exasperated that we should ask it. For Luke, it is the response of Peter that is crucial. Peter perceives in what has happened truth about Jesus and truth about himself. That is what the Gospel miracles – or, for that matter, any other Christian ones – are for.

We read that they were all 'amazed' at the catch of fish. More is implied here than astonishment at a display of extraordinary and inexplicable power. Astonishment of that kind is our reaction to magic. Father Roger is a magician who lives down the road from me. Forty years ago, at Ridley Hall, he astonished us all by his capacity to extract eggs from our ears. We were astounded by what he did, but we didn't drop everything and follow him. There is all the difference in all the worlds between magic and miracle. For the disciples, it was not a case of the magical blowing their minds, but of the miraculous touching their hearts. The word Luke uses to express their amazement suggests a sense of wonder as well. 'Who is this,' they wonder, 'that even the fish obey him?'

Peter sees in the one who does such things the beauty of holiness. That is what was different about the work and the works of Jesus.

What distinguished his miracles from those peddled by the hedge-exorcists and peripatetic wonder-workers of his day (not all of them charlatans) was their moral significance. For Luke, as for Mark and Matthew, miracles are signs that God's righteous reign has come near in Jesus. John will tell these stories, including one much like this one (John 21.4–8), because they reveal the glory, the overpowering goodness, of who Jesus is. Peter takes the point of what he has seen. For him, the miracle is a theophany, a glimpse of God, and he is overcome by a sense of his own unworthiness. Jesus's remedy for Peter's lack of self-esteem (or, if we're talking old-time religion, his 'conviction of sin') is to give him something to do – to fish for people instead of fishing for fish.

By setting the story of the call of Isaiah as our first reading, our lectionary editors suggest that we read the Gospel in its light. Both Isaiah and Peter 'see the Lord'; both feel deeply guilty; both of them are entrusted with a great commission. But the differences between the two stories are as striking and as important as their similarities.

The most significant difference between the two theophanies is the absence from Luke's story of altar, live coals, and tongs – all the paraphernalia of absolution. Isaiah has to be thoroughly shriven by all manner of religious mummery before he can do God's work. Jesus can't be doing with any of that. He doesn't keep Peter on his knees, stewing in his sins. Jesus doesn't contradict Peter's damning verdict on himself, but neither does he go off and leave him as Peter asks him to. Jesus requires of Peter no ritual of repentance, nor does he impose any penance on him. (Old chestnut time: was Peter ever baptized?) Instead, Jesus simply tells him what he must do. God knows the worst about me but employs me just the same. It is the surest of pardons.

A footnote for weary clergy. Peter is despairing. 'We have toiled all the night and have taken nothing.' We know the feeling. God called me to care for people, but my headache these days is the church roof. My vocation is ministry; my job is management. He called me to serve his Kingdom and I've ended up on synod. 'We've caught nothing.' But then there follows – at least in the Authorized Version – one tremendous word: 'Nevertheless'. (The Revised English Bible has the ludicrous, 'If you say so . . .') 'Nevertheless, at thy word I will let down the nets.' All of faith is in that 'nevertheless'. It's not the last time we hear that 'nevertheless' in Luke's Gospel. From Gennesaret we look to Gethsemane and to him who said, 'Nevertheless, not my will, but thine, be done' (Luke 22.42).

Proper 2

The Sunday between 10 and 16 February (if earlier than the second Sunday before Lent)

YEAR A

Deuteronomy 30.15–20 or Ecclesiasticus 15.15–20; 1 Corinthians 3.1–9; Matthew 5.21–37

CHOOSE LIFE

'See, I have set before you life and prosperity, death and adversity.'

The book of Deuteronomy is essentially three sermons. They are delivered by Moses to the people of Israel, who are encamped on the plains of Moab and about to invade Canaan. Our first reading is the conclusion of the third of these sermons. This final sermon is the shortest of the three and – as will come as no surprise to those who have suffered lots of long ones – much the most powerful. Moses's homily will call to Shakespearean minds another rousing exhortation, the famous speech with which King Henry V rallies his troops before the Battle of Agincourt.

The words of Moses we hear on Sunday are the thrilling peroration to the sermon, and encapsulate the message and challenge of the whole book. The *Guardian* newspaper has a witty feature – 'the digested read' – in which it summarizes books for readers with no time to read them. For even busier readers the column provides 'the digested read, digested'. If we subjected Deuteronomy to that treatment, just two words from our reading would suffice for a 'digested read, digested' synopsis of it. 'Choose life!' If – forgive the absurd proposal – we had to sum up the whole of Holy Scripture in the same way, perhaps we would settle for those same two words.

Moses bids us 'choose life!' Our minds race ahead to words of Jesus, 'I am come that they might have life in all its fullness' (John 10.10). But we must not be in too much of a hurry to make such a connection. When Jesus talks about 'life' he does not mean quite what Moses does. The choice Moses gives Israel is between either 'life *and prosperity*' or 'death *and adversity*'. In his previous sermon, in an extraordinary catalogue of 'blessings' and 'curses', Moses had made clear what would be the rewards for the right choice, and the dire consequences of the wrong one. Both the rewards in choosing life and the sanctions in refusing it are material ones. Obey God, and 'blessed will be your basket and your kneading bowl'. Disobey God, and 'cursed will be your basket and your kneading bowl' (Deuteronomy 28.5, 17). The inventory of curses – the most alarming of which must be 'the botch of Egypt" (Deuteronomy 28. 27 AV) – is much longer than the list of blessings.

This 'Deuteronomic' theology – that God will reward your obedience to him with health and wealth and victory in battle, and that he will punish your disobedience with disease, impoverishment, and defeat – underpins much of the Old Testament. Crude and extreme versions of this theology inform the so-called 'prosperity churches' which now proliferate and flourish throughout the poorer places of the world. The extent to which such churches exploit the impoverished and enrich their pastors is well documented.

The theology of Deuteronomy is already challenged in Holy Scripture. The experience of the saints of both Testaments is of the cost of discipleship. Unswerving faith is visited with affliction. Such is the testimony of the towering figure of Job, whose basket and kneading bowl are not blessed and who suffers the botch of Egypt and worse beside. Such is the experience of the prophets. Such is the witness of Jesus of Nazareth.

Jesus, like Moses, invites us to choose life. Like Moses, Jesus assures us that the choice of life will bring its blessings, though those blessings are not those promised by Moses. The blessings of the life which Jesus bids us choose are the blessings of his Kingdom. 'Fear not, little flock' says Jesus; 'for it is your Father's good pleasure to give you the kingdom' (Luke 12.32).

The way of that Kingdom is mapped in the Sermon on the Mount to which we return in the Gospel. The attitude of Jesus to the Mosaic law is radical. That is to say, he goes to its roots. But when my dentist goes to the root of one of my teeth it is not always to extract it. So it is with Jesus's treatment of the law. Sometimes the old must be taken out by the root. There is no place for the taking of oaths, for example, or for exacting of revenge. But more often the reason Jesus goes to the root of the law is not to be rid of it but to intensify its demands. The command against murder still stands. But now anger is condemned as amounting to murder.

Anger is equated with murder. Such is the value Jesus places on our relationships and on the necessity of reconciliation when those relationships break down. There has been a rediscovery in our time of reconciliation as a foundational principle in the ethic of Jesus. The work of Desmond Tutu's 'Truth and Reconciliation' Commission' in post-apartheid South Africa demonstrated the outworking of that principle. It also demonstrated what is demanded of the long alienated, if they elect to make peace with one another. To choose life is to take up the cross.

YEAR B

2 Kings 5.1–14; 1 Corinthians 9.24–27; Mark 1.40–45

THE ANGRY FACE OF GOD

An incensed Jesus cures a leper. The crux is Mark 1.41. Most manuscripts say that Jesus was 'moved with pity' for the man. But there's an early text which tells a different story. This is the famous 'Codex Bezae', the most treasured possession of the Cambridge University Library. In it we read that Jesus, faced with the leper's plight, was moved not with pity but with anger.

So which was it – compassion or fury? The New English Bible – now sounding so far from new – speaks of Jesus's 'warm indignation', a translation which tries but fails to get the best of both worlds. The Revised English Bible translators are more decisive. They recognize that no scribe would have had the nerve to make up a story about Jesus getting cross. The more problematic reading is the more probable and they rightly go for it. Jesus was angry.

The Revised English Bible is right too in retaining the word 'leper'. Of course the man's illness could have been some other skin complaint, rather than the specific condition modern medicine diagnoses as Hansen's disease. Of course the word with all its pejorative overtones is 'politically incorrect'. That's the very reason for staying with it, rather than resorting to some clumsy euphemism such as that of the Good News Bible ('a man suffering from a dreaded skin-disease'). If the term 'leper' has echoes of a prejudice and aversion which we like to think we've grown out of, then all to the good. We must listen to those echoes. They recall, however faintly, the revulsion which this man's presence in the synagogue would have provoked. That primal revulsion was sanctioned by the disgust with the disfigured which makes some parts of the book of Leviticus such unpleasant reading. 'He is unclean.

He shall dwell alone. Without the camp shall his dwelling be' (Leviticus 13.46). So said the clergymen, who wrote Leviticus, unaware that one day, 'without the camp', the leper will be in the best of company (Hebrews 13.13).

Not that we have altogether conquered such repugnance. Am I alone in having some repenting to do? I think of a visit, many years ago, to Lesotho and to the 'Botsabelo Leper Asylum', as it was then known. I think with shame of the feelings I felt in meeting those who languished there. The place had been built by the British in the Boer War as a concentration camp. Little had been done to it before putting it to its new use. It served its purpose. It ensured that the unclean dwelled apart.

The miracle signifies the advent of the Kingdom of God. That Kingdom embraces the ostracized. Jesus touches the untouchable. But he does so in anger. The great matter of this miracle is the wrath of God. If Jesus is 'the human face of God', then that face is not always wreathed in smiles. Jesus cannot contemplate this man's condition benevolently. Why is he angry? With whom is he angry? Not surely with the leper, even if he has transgressed Levitical injunctions by turning up at the synagogue and disregarded conventional courtesies by interrupting the sermon.

The account of the healing of the leper is an essay on the problem of suffering. His plight raises the question, 'How could it all have gone so horribly wrong?' Why should a world, made so well by one so powerful and by one who loved it so much, be so blighted? That question can be posed academically and discussed dispassionately. Books on my shelf do just that, coolly rehearsing the arguments. But Jesus's attitude to suffering isn't that of the detached scholar. It is a wholly human response, because Christ, such is our faith, is wholly human. The first reaction to innocent suffering, immediately overtaken in Christ's case by the instinct to do something about it, must always be outrage.

With whom is Jesus angry? If we start from Christian premises about the identity of Jesus of Nazareth, and if we find the courage to press that question to its theological conclusion, a possibility begins emerge which, if we allowed it, would have far-reaching implications for our understanding of the God of the afflicted. It is that Jesus is angry with himself.

The leper's need, beyond being restored to health, is to be restored to the community. To this end Jesus sends him to the priest to be signed off. Jesus's attitude to purity laws is pragmatic. To cure the leper he breaks the rules; to ensure the man is re-included in society he keeps them. Churches too, of course, have their Levitical codes, their canon laws and the like. Whether there's a principle here about applying them is a question for another time. Despite being told not to, the man went out and 'spread the word'. Isn't 'spreading the word' what we're supposed to do? Not always.

YEAR C

Jeremiah 17.5–10; 1 Corinthians 15.12–20; Luke 6.17–26

THE SICK AND THE SINFUL

Fire and brimstone preachers of the old school made much of a terrifying text we hear this Sunday: 'The heart is deceitful above all things and desperately wicked.' Those old-time evangelists believed that you had to get the bad news before the good news. You cannot properly repent and be 'soundly converted' unless first you have a genuine 'conviction of sin'. You will turn to your saviour only when you realize how badly you need to be saved.

We are deceitful and desperately wicked – thus the King James version of Jeremiah's damning indictment of us. Some modern versions radically alter the emphasis of the prophet's words. The Revised English Bible agrees that we are 'deceitful', but shies away from saying that we are 'wicked'. Jeremiah's diagnosis of our condition, according to the REB, is that we are 'desperately *sick*'.

So is our problem medical or moral? Are our misdeeds symptoms of an illness for which we need treatment or are they sins for which we deserve punishment? How far can we be held responsible for our behaviour? Our answer to these related questions will impact on every area of our lives as social beings, not least on how we deal with those who break society's rules and transgress its norms.

We would be wise to stay with the word of Jeremiah which the REB, along with most versions, does not attempt to tone down. The heart, says Jeremiah, is *deceitful*. We may or may not mislead others, but we have an infinite capacity to deceive ourselves. If I can offload the burden of responsibility for who I am on to someone else – if, say, I can attribute my selfish nature to the fact that I was an only child and a spoiled one – I may convince myself that, in the circumstances, I am really quite a nice chap. I am, I tell myself, 'more sinned against than sinning'. Equally, I can easily persuade myself that there are numerous good reasons why I should stay in my bed in the morning – or climb into someone else's at night.

It is because we are prone to such duplicity that we must be wary of watering down the principle of personal responsibility. That is why we need rules. That is why the doctrine of Joseph Fletcher's 'Situation Ethics', that the only rule is to do in every situation what is the loving thing to do, is so dangerous. I can so easily conclude that what love dictates is what coincides with my own self-interest – not to speak of my selfish appetites.

If my sins are sinful and not simply symptoms of my sickness I can do something about them. I can confess them and be forgiven and start again. Thomas Merton writes of his first confession. 'One by one, that is species by species, as best I could, I tore out all those sins, like teeth' (*The Seven Storey Mountain*, Harcourt Brace, 1948). If I commit a crime and am truly responsible for my actions, I can serve my prison sentence, which retributive justice rightly exacts, and, on my release, return to society with my debt to it discharged. If I am deemed not to be responsible for what I did, I can be locked up in Broadmoor for life.

Of course sometimes antisocial behaviour is clearly attributable to mental illness and those who thus suffer need to be treated, not punished. But the readiness to see ill behaviour as merely the behaviour of the ill is not as compassionate as it sounds. Rob me of my responsibility and you rob me of my humanity.

We turn to another prophet for light. For Jesus of Nazareth, sin and sickness both indicate that there is something fatally wrong with us. Both are a consequence of our primal estrangement, our dislocation from our home in God. Jesus both forgives and heals. In a word he brings 'salvation', the wholeness which once we enjoyed and which in the reign of God he inaugurates, will be restored to us. That is what we hear he is doing as we pick up his story this Sunday.

Jesus will not be drawn into the debate about the relationship between sin and sickness, except to distance himself from any who would see the latter as a punishment for the former (John 9.1–3). The way of Jesus was 'to make people better', to make them whole as they were created to be. But Jesus does not relax the requirement, with which he began his ministry, that people repent (Mark 1.15). He still holds us responsible. As we hear in the Gospel, many flock to him for healing. But not all who look to him for a cure for this or that ailment truly turn to him in repentance and faith. If Luke's story of the healing of the ten who suffered from leprosy is typical, only 10 per cent of them will have owned to their own complicity in the human tragedy (Luke 17.11–19).

Proper 3

The Sunday between 17 and 23 February (if earlier than the second Sunday before Lent)

YEAR A

Leviticus 19.1–2, 9–18; 1 Corinthians 3.10–11, 16–23; Matthew 5. 38–48

WHAT MORE ARE YOU DOING?

Noticing his initials, Gandhi renamed Charles Freer Andrews 'Christ's Faithful Apostle'. To many, Charlie Andrews was simply 'the Mahatma'. His students at St Stephen's College, Delhi, called him *Deenabandhu*, 'Friend of the Poor'. He died in Calcutta on the 5 April 1940. He was buried the same day in the Lower Circular Road cemetery, a stone's throw from the home of another whom the poor of India loved, Mother Teresa of the Missionaries of Charity. Rabindranath Tagore, who gave the address at his memorial service, saw in his life 'a noble embodiment of the Sermon on the Mount'.

Charlie Andrews, 'that jewel of humanity', incarnated the Sermon on the Mount, but he also wrote a book about it (*The Sermon on the Mount*, Allen & Unwin, 1942). The manuscript, found on his desk after his death, was his last work. For Andrews, the moral teaching of Jesus in the Sermon on the Mount was not, as some have seen it, an 'interim ethic', a sketch of the recklessly other-worldy lifestyle of those who believed that 'the second coming' was just round the corner. Nor, for him, was the sermon intended to make us feel guilty, a moral code purposely set unattainably high so as to drive us to our knees in repentance. Still less, for Andrews, was the sermon a prescription for Christian anarchism, some kind of Tolstoyan rejection of all authority.

C. F. Andrews saw the Sermon on the Mount as Christ's pattern for 'the good life'. The sermon is not unrealistsic and impracticable. It is the law of love by which we must live. The objection that the sermon is too idealistic and utopian ever to be implemented in a wicked world is sufficiently answered by Charlie Andrews' own shining life, by his involvement with Gandhi in the Indian civil rights struggle in South Africa, by his campaigns for the indentured Indian labourers in Fiji, and by his commitment to the Indian independence movement.

Andrews' discussion of our Gospel reading is irradiated by his own exultant vision of the Kingdom of God, in which 'human society can become God's realm'. His is an intensely personal and original interpretation of a too-familiar text. Three Greek words in particular pierced Andrews to the heart, so much so that he transcribed them and kept them on his study table. Jesus asks – we need five words in English – 'What more are you doing?' Andrews heard the resonances of that 'more', a rich word in the New Testament, 'taken up in the early church,' he wrote, 'to express that overwhelming experience of love, joy, and peace which came into men's hearts with the power of the Holy Spirit'.

Each day Charlie Andrews would look at that text on his study table, he tells us, and ask himself, 'Can I truly say that my own love for Christ has become the one main incentive of my life, causing me each day to go to the extreme limit in my devotion to him alone?'

'What more are you doing?' We debate endlessly how the Sermon on the Mount should be interpeted. We ask how far its ethic of non-violence, of non-resistance to the evildoer, can be implemented in a society that is far from a Christian theocracy. Some side with the Quakers and Mennonites and urge an uncompromising pacifism. Others insist that there is such a thing as a 'just war'. We argue, too, about the nature of such extraordinary injunctions as 'Turn the other cheek', 'Give your cloak as well', 'Go the second mile'. Should my teenage daughter, who was mugged and robbed the other day, have made no effort to defend herself? They stole her ipod. Should she have yielded up her mobile phone as well?

Such problems in making sense of the Sermon on the Mount are real enough. Perhaps we should not take Jesus's words literally. If so, we must not suppose that thereby the moral life becomes any easier. Charlie Andrews himself pointed out that by seeking the spirit of Christs's new law, instead of concentrating on its letter, we do not make his precepts any less morally exacting.

We talk and talk about such matters, sitting on our hands or stabbing our fingers in the air. But, as we do so, Christ confronts us with that same searching question, 'What more are you *doing?*'

The paradox of such an ethic, motivated by devotion to Christ alone, is that it is at the same time wholly inclusive. Andrews' understanding of our Gospel is informed by his attentiveness to other and older traditions. He reminds us how Gautama the Buddha discovered that 'the wheel of suffering' only revolves the faster with every act of retaliation, but that that same wheel begins to turn more slowly when good is returned instead of evil. He appeals too to the Jewish prophetic tradition and to the portrait of the one who, when he was oppressed and afflicted 'did not open his mouth' (Isaiah 53.7).

It does seem that there is more that we can do.

YEAR B

Isaiah 43.18–25; 2 Corinthians 1.18–22; Mark 2.1–12

LEARN TO SAY YES

What Paul says to us today is not always what he originally meant. Of course, it is important that we try to understand what he intended to say to his first readers. But we are not necessarily wrong to listen to what we hear him saying to us all these centuries later. It has always been like that with the Bible. Clever scholars may tell us what a text first meant. But they do not have the last word. The Bible speaks to me today. What it says may not be exactly what it once said. Provided my 'private interpretation' is not perverse, I am not wrong to take to heart what it is saying to me now.

Take the wonderful words we hear this week. Paul says, 'In Christ it is always "Yes".' What did he mean? Paul was defending himself against a specific charge – of not being a man of his word. He had said he would revisit the church in Corinth, but then he had changed his mind. The Corinthian Christians were much put out. They thought that Paul had been less than straight with them. Paul refuted this charge. He claimed that in all his dealings with the Corinthians he had acted in the light of the gospel and in the church's best interest. In saying that it is always 'Yes' with Jesus, Paul was appealing to the trustworthiness of God's ways in Christ, and asserting that he was just as trustworthy too. That is what Paul meant.

Forgive me, but two millennia later I am not interested in Paul's travel arrangements. 'In Christ it is always "Yes"'. Today those words tell me something that I need to know about the gospel. They tell me that Christianity is essentially *affirmative*.

That is not how Christianity is generally perceived. A more accurate summary of how it is viewed by many would be 'In Christ it is usually "No"'. Throughout its history, the Church has given the impression that God always defaults to disapproval. The God whom William Blake came to loathe was 'the Father of Jealousy' and the foe of joy. Blake rebelled against a Church that served such a censorious deity.

I went to the Garden of Love,
And saw what I never had seen;
A Chapel was built in the midst,
Where I used to play on the green.
And the gates of this Chapel were shut
And 'Thou shalt not' writ over the door;
So I turned to the Garden of Love
That so many sweet flowers bore.

A church with 'Thou shalt not' written over the door has yet to learn the mind of Christ.

Clearly Jesus does not approve of everything we get up to. If 'in Christ it is always "Yes"', that is because the Christian spirit is – or should be – to look for the good, to expect it, and to build on it. It is worth remembering that the character in the Bible who invariably finds fault and suspects the worst of motives is not one of Scripture's more exemplary figures, but someone called Satan.

The contrast between the spirit that denies and the spirit that affirms is sharply drawn in the Gospel. The story of the healing of the paralytic at Capernaum is of a clash between religious tradition and the way of Jesus. The former is swift to censure and forbid. The latter is eager to forgive and to make whole. The same contrast is drawn on page after page in all the Gospels. It is the affirmative way of Jesus, for example, to heal the sick and to feed the hungry on the Sabbath – a day rendered 'unfit for purpose' by the life-denying restrictions hedged about it.

Christianity is affirmative. Were Paul with us today, he would no doubt have supported 'Affirming Catholicism', just so long as the gatekeepers of that admirable movement did not object to his being at the same time a member of 'Affirming Evangelicalism', 'Affirming Liberalism', and 'Affirming Pentcostalism'. Paul's churchmanship – again we are being anachronistic – was at once 'High', 'Low' and 'Broad' in what those traditions positively stand for, if not in what they refute. As F. D. Maurice famously said – though he would have rephrased the sentiment had he been speaking today – 'a man is most often right in what he affirms and wrong in what he denies'.

If in Christ it is always 'Yes', then in Christ we must learn to say 'Yes' to each other. Christopher Cocksworth, Bishop of Coventry, is an 'affirmative theologian' who believes that the different schools of thought and worship in the Christian Church should not be channels that never meet but currents within one river. In his *Gospel, Church and Spirit* (Canterbury Press, 2008) he shows that Christianity is true to Christ only when the separate strands of 'biblical gospel, catholic church and powerful Spirit' become a single threefold cord. Amen to that.

Certainly we must learn to say 'No'. This week, however, we learn to say 'Yes'.

YEAR C

Genesis 45.3–11, 15; 1 Corinthians 15.35–38, 42–50; Luke 6.27–38

BETTER BODIES

'Someone will ask', says Paul, '"How can the dead be raised to life? What kind of body will they have?"' *Someone* will ask? Surely these are questions that *everyone* asks who claims to believe in 'the resurrection of the body'.

Entirely understandably, much speculation has focused on the nature of the resurrection body. The great Christian father Origen toyed with the idea that in heaven our bodies will be perfectly spherical. Medieval monks wondered whether in the life to come they would still be singled out by their tonsures.

Swarms of questions – philosophical, theological, metaphysical, moral and scientific – settle like flies on the notion of a resurrection *body*. What of those, including the countless discarded embryos, who never grew to physical maturity? What of conjoined twins? Does the teaching of Jesus that people do not marry in heaven, but are 'like angels', mean that our resurrection bodies will be androgynous? The prospect does not appeal.

We must proceed cautiously, aware that speech about the resurrection body, as about every aspect of life after death (if such there be), swiftly morphs into gobbledegook. That said, fidelity to Scripture requires us to stake out the ground where we must take our stand.

All we affirm is tempered by admission of our ignorance. We must listen to John as we try to make sense of Paul. 'What we will be has not yet been revealed,' says John (1 John 3.2). But that same text talks too of what we *do* know, that 'we shall be like him, for we will see him as he is'. Our hope is of the vision of God. But sight of God implies the seeing subject. As Job cried in his affliction, 'in my flesh I shall see God ... whom my eyes shall behold, and not another' (Job 19.26).

To see someone means that there is someone who sees as well as someone to see. So our hope is of an embodied identity. Paul speaks of this body as 'a spiritual body', contrasting it with 'the physical body'. The mistake is to suppose that 'the spiritual' is less substantial than the 'the physical', that what is restored to us is a ghostly shade of ourselves, some sort of wraith of the kind that makes spectral appearances at séances or which answers to the bidding of ouija boards.

Nothing could be further from the Christian understanding of the resurrection body. That body is more real – more *there* – than the intermittently malfunctioning carcase in which I am currently embodied. This was the conviction, none the worst for its debt to Plato as to Scripture, that C. S. Lewis argued so powerfully. If one who is still a child of this earth should stray into heaven, as Lewis has his protagonist do in *The Great Divorce* (Geoffrey Bles, 1946), he will cut his feet on the grass, so much more solid, so much sharper, are its blades.

Perhaps the boldest recent attempt to describe the resurrection body of which Paul speaks is Tom Wright's. Tom Wright, Bishop of Durham, grapples with the notion that the promised body is 'spiritual' only in the sense that it is more rather than less substantial than the physical. Bishop Tom offers us a big new word to say what he means. The resurrection body of Jesus was 'transphysical', Wright argues. Jesus was there with his disciples on Easter Day, eating and drinking with them – yet he could pass through closed doors. Again, he walks and talks and sups with the two disciples on Easter Day. Yet suddenly he vanishes from their sight (Luke 24.13–35).

Paul does not answer our questions about what we will or will not be able to do in our resurrection bodies. Such concerns are peripheral to his vision. Central to Paul's vision of the resurrected life, as to all his theology, is his hope of glory. This, above all, is what matters. What is raised is 'raised in glory'. The body put on by those raised in Christ, irrespective of its remarkably enhanced capacities, will be a supremely glorious body. Such is the Christian hope.

Once more we turn to C. S. Lewis. The supreme statement in the English language of what our frail flesh may hope for is Lewis's wartime sermon 'The Weight of Glory' (*Transposition and other Addresses*, Geoffrey Bles, 1949). The great periods of this famous sermon, in which Lewis exults in all we are promised, are often quoted. Less often cited – and less often noticed by those who deride Lewis – is what he has to say about the implications of this hope for how we treat other people. Lewis insists that, even if it is possible to dwell too much on our own future glory, it is impossible to think too much of our neighbour's future glory.

So we look to the one next to us in the pew as we sing,

'Oh, how glorious and resplendent,
Fragile body, shalt thou be . . .'

The Second Sunday before Lent

YEAR A

Genesis 1.1 – 2.3; Romans 8.18–25; Matthew 6.25–34

GENTIANS AND GUILLEMOTS

'Look at the birds of the air.' I am grateful to the missionary statesman and evangelist, Dr Michael Griffiths, for pointing out to me that the Greek behind Jesus's familiar command means 'Look *carefully* at the birds'. More is being asked of us here than that we all become twitchers, although clearly we are not going to learn much from the birds unless we sometimes stop what we foolishly suppose could be more important and go out and look at them.

More too, perhaps, is implied than that we notice characteristics of bird behaviour that illustrate aspects of the life of faith. To be sure, Jesus is saying that the birds teach us not to be anxious. If God feeds the birds, surely he will provide for his children. (We leave to one side whether Jesus could have said these words – or whether he still says these words – other than to those with reason to be confident about the arrival of their next meal.)

Jesus's memorable words continue to be understood as an invitation to turn to the living world for pictures of the Christian life. Another eminent evangelical leader, John Stott, has watched birds and photographed them all his life. In his beautiful book *The Birds our Teachers* (Candle Books, 2001), he writes of what the ravens teach us about

74

faith, on lessons in freedom from the flight of the eagle, on the joy we learn from the song of the lark. All this is well said in John Stott's inspirational book. Creation, thus observed, teems with Christian teaching aids.

But perhaps more is meant. The natural world is not simply replete with illustrations of spiritual truths. It is also in itself charged with meaning. Creation is sacramental. It is revelatory. It bears and conveys the truth of God. If that sounds like the dusty old idea of 'general revelation', so be it.

'Look at the birds of the air.' Then, 'consider the lilies of the field'. The poets, who know how to see, teach us how such a text is to be taken.

Christina Rossetti wrote about what it means to 'consider the lilies'.

Flowers preach to us if we will hear:-
The rose saith in the dewy morn:
I am most fair;
Yet all my loveliness is born
Upon a thorn.
The poppy saith amid the corn:
Let but my scarlet head appear
And I am held in scorn . . .
The lilies say: Behold how we
Preach without words of purity.
The violets whisper from the shade
Which their own leaves have made:
Men scent our fragrance on the air,
Yet take no heed
Of humble lessons we would read.
('Flowers')

Flowers 'preach without words'. For some feminist commentators, Christine Rossetti is saying that truth is not only told in the kind of propositions invariably manufactured by males. Be that as it may, flowers preach *to us*. They are more than fodder for our own sermons.

If flowers preach, what do they say? No doubt, their word – to those with already stuffed bellies and wardrobes – is not to fret about what to serve the Cartwrights for dinner or what to wear for Ascot. But their sermons today might have a further cutting edge.

The burden of their preaching might be their own plight. We read that one in five of Britain's wild flowers is now threatened with extinction. We read too that 'all human life is predicated on a small suite of plant species, no more than about thirty, from wheat to rice, without which we could not live' (The *Independent*, 9 May 2005).

Sermons from those so imperilled will carry a terrible warning. 'It is a warning', the article goes on to say, 'that if we cannot save the poppies and cornflowers, the gentians and wild orchids which have meant so much to people down the centuries, and which bloom still in the corners of our minds, we risk a spiritual impoverishment such as no generation has known before.'

This Sunday we shall hear how it was all well begun. We shall take to heart Christ's words to look to the birds and the lilies. Then, at the end of the service, we should ideally all move out into the churchyard, if our church is blessed with one, and if it still has some wild, untamed corners. There, among the expectant dead, with whatever flowers the season yields around us and with the song of the birds in our ears, we should listen once more to Paul's thrilling words about the hope of all creation. There we may at last be delivered from the breathtakingly self-centred notion that we, sinful creatures that we are, alone have something to look forward to. Gentians and guillemots are far more entitled to heaven than we are.

YEAR B

Proverbs 8.1, 22–31; Colossians 1.15–20; John 1.1–14

IS GOD A PLAYGROUP?

Our readings invite us to recover a sense of the divine as feminine, childlike, and playful.

For John, the Word made flesh is the embodiment of wisdom. The wisdom Jesus incarnates is not an abstract principle but a person, a woman with a name and a voice. She is *Hochmah* in Hebrew. She is *Sophia* in Greek. What shall we call her in English? Perhaps, as George MacDonald does, we should name her 'the Wise Woman'. (Back to MacDonald in a moment.) She speaks for herself in our reading from Proverbs. We have other glimpses of her, as she mysteriously comes and goes, elsewhere in the so-called 'Wisdom Literature' of the Old Testament and the Apocrypha. John's description of Jesus as the Word of God reflects the portrait of her in these strange texts. This week we are sent back to these sources, too rarely visited. To return to these springs is to renew our image of God.

All turns on Proverbs 8.31–32. And here we must applaud the translators who have given us the Revised English Bible. Their lyrical rendering of a tricky bit of Hebrew makes inspired sense – and this reader whoops for joy. 'Then I was at his side each day' – it's the Wise Woman speaking – 'his darling and delight, playing in his presence continually, playing over his whole world, while my delight was in mankind.' (We have to do something about that 'mankind', of course. Maybe we could change the last few words to 'finding everyone utterly delightful'.) The writer has dwelt on the Wise Woman's age. She is older than all that is, older than the earth and oceans, older than the mountains and hills, older than the springs and streams. The Wise Woman was already there when it all began.

And who is she, this woman more ancient than we can begin to comprehend? She is a child, a little girl who never stops playing. She's *playing*. The same word is used here as in a wonderful Hebrew text which, to the confusion of my visitors, I had on my study wall for years. 'The streets of the city shall be full of boys and girls playing in the streets thereof' (Zechariah 8.5).

The Wise Woman is at once both very old and very young. Apart from John's Gospel itself, the greatest literary account of her is the Wise Woman of George MacDonald's fantasies. In this figure, his supreme imaginative creation, MacDonald explores the myriad ways in which the Spirit of God relates to those whose lives she touches. She is, says MacDonald, 'a woman perfectly beautiful, neither old nor young; for hers was the old age of everlasting youth' (*The Wise Woman*, 1875).

To retrace our steps, the template John is using when he speaks of the one who was 'with God', the one who 'was God', the one 'by whom all things were made', is the personified wisdom of the biblical and apocryphal Wisdom Literature. The same figure is in Paul's mind – and he hopes in ours too – when he speaks of Christ as 'the Wisdom of God' (1 Corinthians 1.24) and, in our second reading, as 'the firstborn of creation' (Colossians 1.15). And that same proverbial figure has long fed into Christian reflection on the Holy Trinity.

In sending us back to the book of Proverbs our lectionary is urging us to reconnect, to return to the scriptural roots of the figure of Wisdom, which influenced John and Paul and the Christian fathers so powerfully. And whom do we meet there at the fountainhead of this rich tradition? A wise old woman who is also a playful child. There she is, on the steps of her house with its seven pillars (Proverbs 9.1). Perhaps, in her teasing way, she's hiding behind one of them.

We are bound to ask what it might mean for our understanding of God if we dared to allow these texts to have their full weight, if we opened our Christian minds to their astonishing imagery. Not only is there a femininity to the divine – we are at last learning that – but there is also a divine childlikeness and a godly playfulness. The one we worship and serve is 'continually playing', always up to games. There is nothing flippant in Jerome Berryman's brilliantly perceptive question 'Is God a playgroup?'

To say that the Wisdom of God is playful is not to suggest that she never settles to anything serious. For she was one with the one who 'assigned to the sea its limits'. We touch here on primal images and on primal fears reawakened in our own time. The sea was once dreaded, as around the Indian Ocean it is again, as the symbol of all that opposes the gracious purposes of God. But a line has been drawn in the sand. The darkness, as John puts it, cannot win.

YEAR C

Genesis 2.4b–9, 15–25; Revelation 4; Luke 8.22–25

THE GARDEN, THE SEA, AND THE THRONE

This Sunday we shall be inundated by images. There is a torrent of them in our reading from Revelation – trumpets, thrones, winged creatures (alarmingly, with many eyes) and more beside. But then that's what we expect in the last book of the Bible. A defining characteristic of 'apocalyptic' literature, of which the book of Revelation is an example, is an abundance of signs and symbols. The mistake is to suppose that the use of vivid imagery in the Bible is confined to such eccentric texts, or that there is something outlandish about it and that the rest of the Bible, not written by oddballs, is mercifully free from it.

In fact the Bible from first page to last (and we're not far from both this Sunday) is rich in images – one thing standing for another. Imagery is a powerful way of expressing what cannot be said otherwise. In Revelation we have an intense concentration of images, but the other 65 books of the Bible teem with them too.

Austin Farrer understood the importance of imagery in the Bible and of our responding imaginatively to Scripture. Here's what he said:

St. John's images do not mean anything you like; their sense can be determined. But they still have an astonishing multiplicity of reference. Otherwise, why write in images rather than in cold, factual prose? It has been said that the purpose of scientific statement is the elimination of ambiguity, and the purpose of symbol the inclusion of it. We write in symbol when we wish our words to present, rather than analyze or prove, their subject matter. (*A Rebirth of Images*, Dacre Press, 1949)

Some images in the Bible carry greater weight than others. There are three such images in our Sunday readings. The story in Genesis takes us to a garden; the Gospel reading bids us to look at the sea; the passage from Revelation sets us before a throne. Perhaps, breaking all the rules, we should read them in that – their logical – order. Garden, sea, and throne. These are not mere metaphors. They are primal images. They are archetypes, to use the Jungian term, of our doom, our deliverance, and our destiny.

The garden is the image of all we have lost but yet still long for. Our craving is to be again within those unbreached walls, beneath those trees, beside those waters. ('Those waters' – the lectionary inexplicably butchers the text by omitting the haunting image of the river flowing out of Eden.) This nostalgia for paradise, to be again where once we were and where we truly belong, is the inspiration of great imaginative works, such as *The Romance of the Rose*, Dante's *Divine Comedy* or Milton's *Paradise Lost*. But the same longing for our exile to end explains the appeal of more homely tales. It is what makes Francis Hodgson Burnett's *The Secret Garden* or George MacDonald's *At the Back of the North Wind* so timeless. The image of God in us is our divine discontent. We want to go home. Deep down, we know it is true – 'My soul, there *is* a country far beyond the stars.'

The sea – I hear it pounding on the beach as I write – is all that is recalcitrant to the will of God. In the Bible, the sea is the primordial chaos out of which God orders what is beautiful and good. When it all began, darkness covered the face of the deep. Boundaries – 'thus far and no further' – had to be set for the hostile sea. Creation in the Bible is pictured as the reclamation of land from water for God's children's sake. So too is redemption. At the Exodus, the waters once more retreated and slaves were set free. But the sea – 'the menace and caress of wave that breaks on water' – still threatens. Though it had been the source of their livelihood, the disciples still dreaded the sea. Hence their terror as their boat fills with water and their awe of one at whose word the sea is still. The calming of the storm is an image of salvation. It is the work of *Christus Victor*. It is a sign – exchanging image for image – of the last battle and the ultimate victory.

So we come to the throne. Monarchy may be in question as an institution, but the image in Revelation draws its force not from those who occupy earthly thrones, but from John's picture of one who reigns from a tree. In the bewildering kaleidoscope of images, he is also the lamb that has been slain (Revelation 5.6). Before the throne is 'the sea of glass'. Glass it may be, but there is yet a horror to break its surface. John will see 'a beast rising out of the sea' (Revelation 13.1). But the beast, whatever damage it still does in its death-throes, is vanquished. Its immemorial home is condemned too. One day 'there will be no more sea' (Revelation 21.1).

The Sunday next before Lent

YEAR A

Exodus 24.12–18; 2 Peter 1.16–21; Matthew 17.1–9

HEIGHTS AND DEPTHS

'Praise to the Holiest in the height, and in the depths be praise.'

The Transfiguration takes us to the heights. But life is a roller-coaster and any experience of the heights is usually swiftly followed by a sudden, sickening, plunge to the depths. So it was for Jesus. On descending from the mountain with Peter, James, and John to rejoin the rest of his disciples, he is confronted with a scene of failure and despair. He meets the father of the epileptic boy whom the disciples left below had failed to help. The exasperation of Jesus is palpable. 'How much longer must I put up with you?' he says to them – as to us.

Moses had much the same experience on his descent from Sinai. He had 'entered the cloud.' That is to say, the glory of God, of which the cloud is the scriptural symbol, had enfolded him. But when he came down from the mountain, he found the people running wild. Fresh from sacrificing to a golden calf of their own manufacture, they were 'sitting down to eat and drink and rising up to revel' (Exodus 32).

Our lectionary spares us the let-downs. But life never does, and so it is important that we read on. The sequel to the Transfiguration (Matthew 17.14–21) reflects life's pattern. Visions fade into the light of common day.

If tradition is to be believed, the Transfiguration took place on the summit of Mount Tabor, overlooking the plain of Megiddo. Those who take the last book of the Bible literally believe that it will be on this plain that 'the last battle' will be fought. Armageddon, they say, will be the final confrontation between the armies of good and evil (Revelation 16.12–16). We do not have to accept all the details of this apocalyptic scenario to recognize how appropriate it is that the chosen disciples are granted a glimpse of Christ's divine glory on a mountain commanding a view of such a battlefield.

We must always be careful with the Bible's future tenses. The lurid language of Revelation projects into the future what in fact is already taking place. That is how 'the seer of Patmos' writes. For him, the battle has already begun and the rest of the New Testament writers agree with him.

That is where we all are – at the foot of the mountain, where a war is raging. We have beheld the glory of God in the face of Jesus Christ (2 Corinthians 4.6). Now the final engagement has begun and the smoke of battle is in our eyes. The vision fades, as visions do, but we must hold on as best we can to what we glimpsed on the mountain. My own experience of the conflict – 'wretched man that I am' (Romans 7.24) – may well be of repeated defeat (Romans 7.14–21). When it comes to Armageddon, few of us have 'a good war'. But the outcome of the conflict is beyond even my sinful capacity to frustrate. 'Thanks be to God who gives us the victory through our Lord Jesus Christ' (1 Corinthians 15.57).

Back to Matthew's version of what happened on Mount Tabor. The story is in all three synoptic Gospels and, while John's Gospel does not have a separate record of the Transfiguration, his Gospel, with its stress on the glory of Christ incarnate, can be read as an extended meditation on the synoptic account. As we follow Matthew's version of the story, we look out for what he alone has to tell us.

Only he tells us that Peter, James and John fell to the ground in fear. Some say this detail is typical of an evangelist who likes melodrama and who is prone to sensationalize. Matthew, for example, has Jerusalem's saintly dead alive and well and wandering round the city on Easter Day (Matthew 27.52, 53).

We need not accuse Matthew of embroidery at this point. What Matthew adds is psychologically credible. It is impossible to glimpse God and stay on your feet. Ezekiel was flung to the floor by the experience

(Ezekiel 1.28). The word of Jesus to his prone and discombobulated disciples is striking: 'Get up, and do not be afraid.' The balance of admonition and assurance in that simple injunction is characteristic of 'Christ's way with people'. (I borrow the title of a forgotten spiritual classic, written during the Second World War, by F. Noel Palmer, *Christ's Way with People*, Marshall, Morgan & Scott, 1943.) The Lord, in his mercy, does not tell me what is going to happen – only that I must get up and face it, and that I need not fear.

I see in my mind's eye a poster that once, long ago, I had on my bedroom wall. It depicts a young girl. She is saying, 'I am afraid of the future.' Underneath are written someone's words: '"Do not be afraid. I have been there before." *Jesus of Nazareth*'

YEAR B

2 Kings 2.1–12; 2 Corinthians 4.3–6; Mark 9.2–9

A BOUNDARY BREACHED

When in church on Sunday I read Mark's account of the Transfiguration I shall begin at the beginning. I shall start at verse one of chapter nine, not at verse two as the lectionary stipulates. I'll do so, not because I sit loose to lectionaries, but simply because the 'difficult' saying of the first verse isn't really difficult at all. In the light of what transpires it makes good sense. 'Some here will not die,' says Jesus, 'until they see God's kingdom come.' Jesus is not saying that it will all be done and dusted in his disciples' lifetime – though he may have thought that – but announcing the nature of what is shortly to follow. His 'metamorphosis' – that's Mark's word for it – is a foretaste of the glorious Kingdom.

Transfiguring experiences have one thing in common. In the wake of them nothing is ever the same again. There's a small community of Franciscans living on the top of Mount Tabor, the traditional site of the Transfiguration. There used to be a friar there, who was very welcoming to pilgrims. I recall chatting with him – and after a while noticing that, nestling in the hood of his habit, was a single sparrow. That sight shifted permanently my perception of our kinship with the creatures, great and small, with whom we share a home. That's what transfigurations do, change our minds for good. So it is here.

The story of the transfiguration is of the breaching of the boundary between this world and another, as is the story of the resurrection which it anticipates. The difference between this story and other tales of the interface of different worlds – Philip Pullman's *His Dark Materials* (Scholastic Press, 1995–2000) comes to mind – is that this time the breach is not mended. Of course the mountain-top vision fades and the witnesses must return to the world as ordinarily experienced. And we know that what Peter, James, and John will encounter in the valley below will be distressing and humiliating. Nevertheless their return journey is not across a boundary which is reinstated once they're back. They've had a taste of heaven, but afterwards it's not just down to earth, for all the failures which will follow. The frontier has dissolved. The world where Christ reigns in glory has elided with their own, the world where, for a little longer, that reign is bitterly contested. A light has shone which shall not be put out.

So what does it all mean? We must be careful not to settle too contentedly for the familiar explanations. Moses and Elijah are there – and then they're gone. So the age of the law and the prophets is over. True. The tents they want to pitch recall the wilderness years when Israel travelled lighter and closer to God. True. A cloud overshadowed them, the cloud which in the Bible is not a sign of rain but of the glory of God. So here is a disclosure of who Jesus is. True. The dazzling appearance of Jesus and the voice from above, echoing what was said of him at his baptism, both confirm that in him God is with us. True.

And yet, and yet. Do we really know what is going on here any better than Peter who, like the others, was terrified and who 'did not know what to say'? There is deep wisdom in Peter's 'I do not know', as much perhaps as there was – turn back a page – in his more confident confession at Caesarea Philippi, 'You are the Messiah' (Mark 8.29). Peter will discover the meaning of what he has witnessed only as he perseveres in discipleship.

As for Peter, James and John, so for us. By our imaginative engagement with this story, the familiar boundaries between the apparent and the transcendent are breached and a better world has begun to merge with ours. And if our engagement with the story is at all serious, we too, with Peter, will not know what to say – for all the clever connections we make. Only as we follow will we find out. The account of the transfiguration contains one all-important imperative: 'Hear him.' In the language of the Bible, the command to hear is always the order to obey. There is no route to understanding the transfiguration, or any other Christian mystery, which bypasses the next thing to be done.

A footnote. Let's celebrate the transfiguration this Sunday – or indeed on any day in the year, so long as it is not the official feast of the

THE SUNDAY NEXT BEFORE LENT

Transfiguration. Pope Callistus III designated the sixth of August as the feast of the Transfiguration. He thought it would be a wonderful way for the universal Church to celebrate the butchery of thousands of 'infidel' Turks on the sixth of August 1456 at the siege of Belgrade.

YEAR C

Exodus 34.29–35; 2 Corinthians 3.12–4.2; Luke 9.28–36 (37–43)

GLORY – AND WHAT'S GOT TO BE DONE

Michael Ramsey, the one hundredth Archbishop of Canterbury, preached his last sermon to the All Saints Sisters in the chapel of their house in Cowley, near Oxford. Owen Chadwick, Ramsey's biographer, tells us that the superior was fearful that the old and frail Archbishop would not be audible. But every word was heard. 'Each time he said *glory*,' Chadwick tells us, 'it came out as a shout.' On Ramsey's memorial stone in the cloister of Canterbury Cathedral are inscribed words of Irenaeus: 'The glory of God is the living man; And the life of man is the vision of God.'

That epitaph – even if today we'd have to reword it – goes far to explain the incomparable Michael Ramsey. It also takes us to the heart of the story of the Transfiguration which meant so much to him. Ramsey loved to quote Westcott's words,

> The Transfiguration is the revelation of the potential spirituality of the earthly life in the highest outward form ... Here the Lord, as Son of Man, gives the measure of the capacity of humanity, and shows that to which he leads those who are united with him. (*The Glory of God and the Transfiguration of Christ*, Longmans, Green, 1949)

The Transfiguration is a revelation of Christ's identity and, in him, of our destiny.

The story could be said to be in all four Gospels, although John does not tell it the way Matthew, Mark and Luke do. For them, the face of Jesus shone but that once with divine light. For John, the whole story of Jesus is one of humanity transfigured, of incarnate light. 'The Word was made flesh and dwelled among us and we saw his glory' (John 1.14). 'We saw his glory,' says John. '*They* saw his glory,' says Luke, referring to Peter, James, and John. Only Luke makes plain what Matthew and Mark imply, that what the disciples saw in the face of Jesus was the glory of God. This is not the only individual imprint Luke has left on his account. Luke alone tells us – it is a characteristic touch – that it was as he was praying that Jesus's appearance changed. Most re- markably, in Luke's staging of the story, Moses and Elijah have more than walk-on – and walk-off – parts. For Luke, as for Matthew and Mark, they represent a dispensation which is done. But only Luke lets us listen to Moses and Elijah before they go. They are speaking of the 'departure' Jesus is to fulfil at Jerusalem. The word Luke uses is *exodos*. Classically, 'exodos' can be used as a euphemism for dying. In modern Greek, it's the word used for 'exit'. If you get off the train at Athens, you look for the *Exodos*. But in the Bible it immediately and obviously recalls the Exodus from Egypt. It is a great mystery why none of our translators is bold enough simply to leave the word as 'Exodus' in our English versions.

'Like Moses of old,' writes G. B. Caird, 'Jesus was standing on the brink of a great sea, the ocean of iniquity through which he must pass and in which he must accomplish another baptism' (*The Gospel of Luke*, Penguin, 1963). The Transfiguration of Jesus, which tears in two the veil between earth and heaven, looks ahead to the passion of Jesus, to the dark hour when the veil of the temple is rent apart. Fra Angelico, as so often, saw what it all meant. In his fresco of the Transfiguration in St Mark's Monastery in Florence, Christ's halo is cruciform and his arms are outstretched as at Calvary.

The disciples want to stay on the mountain. They want, as it were, to bottle the experience. The wish to cling on to such 'moments out of time' is both futile and dangerous, as William Blake – who enjoyed many such moments – knew well.

He who binds to himself a joy
Does the winged life destroy
But he who kisses the joy as it flies
Lives in Eternity's sunrise.

Saints still on earth are sometimes granted glimpses of heaven, but if they are to be of any earthly use they mustn't luxuriate in such raptures or seek to prolong them. (Once I was on retreat at a convent. The dry old Mother Superior noticed that one of the nuns was late joining us for breakfast. 'Another ecstasy,' she muttered.)

Michel Ramsey recognized that transfiguring experiences do not rescue us from the humdrum and the horrible. 'Transfiguration,' he said, 'is the transforming of suffering and circumstances.' Above all, such transports do not deliver us from the next thing to be done. For the sake of the epileptic boy at its foot – Luke tells us that he was an only child – Jesus and his disciples must not tarry on the mountain top.

Heaven beckons, but as C. S. Lewis pointed out, meanwhile there's Monday morning. The last word said on the mountain is 'Listen to him.' The Transfiguration may reveal that we shall share the divine nature. But, more immediately, it makes it clear that we had better do as we're told.

The First Sunday of Lent

YEAR A

Genesis 2.15–17, 3.1–7; Romans 5.12–19; Matthew 4.1–11

SEVEN DEADLY SINS

Graham Tomlin's *The Seven Deadly Sins and How to Overcome Them* (Lion, 2007) offers good Lenten reading.

Which, if any, of 'the seven deadly sins' is Jesus being tempted to commit by his 'inner demons' – as real and deadly as any mythological being with a forked tongue and tail – with which he wrestles in the wilderness? We can immediately rule out sloth and probably anger too, if only because Jesus did not always see anger as a sin. What about gluttony or greed? After his prolonged fasting, changing stones to bread would hardly have been an instance of either of them. To have stood up miraculously uninjured after falling from a great height would no doubt have impressed the crowds. A Manhattan window-cleaner did much the same a year or two ago, much to the astonishment of the pedestrians below. Would such a misuse of his lordship over the natural order have been a yielding to pride? Possibly, but Jesus was manifestly never tempted to that kind of exhibitionism. Was envy at work – or a lust for preferment – when, at the tempter's invitation, he contemplated the powerful and all their opportunities for doing good? Maybe.

But the more we think about it the plainer it becomes that Jesus's temptations in the wilderness cannot be explained in the ways we try to understand our own sinful inclinations. To be sure, like the rest of us, Jesus had valiantly to fight against 'sin, the world, and the devil' to his life's end – though we are led to believe that he made a better fist of it than we do. To be sure, 'he was in all points tempted like as we are', albeit 'without sin' (Hebrews 4.15). Yet something was going on there in that dreadful Judean desert, with only the lizards for company, which was unique. The battle being fought in the mind of Jesus – and for the mind of Jesus – was his alone. Graham Tomlin's admirable book would have been of little use to him.

At his baptism Jesus had accepted his fate. His destiny was Calvary. There was no other way. Except that – so the whispering voice within suggested – perhaps there was. Perhaps what is called for in a wicked world is some attempt to relieve the symptoms of evil rather than heroic but forlorn endeavours to kill its roots. And if a naughty world is to be changed perhaps its naughty ways have to be used. Hence Christ's temptations: to turn stones to bread to feed the starving; to win an audience for his message by some sensational public spectacle; for the world's good, to take the world over.

The temptation was not to commit one of the seven deadly sins, but to refuse the divine necessity, the terrible imperative of words written from the foundation of the world: 'the Son of Man must suffer'. How can we measure the weight of the choice before Jesus? A legend from another tradition comes to mind. It is said that the Buddha under the Bo tree wrestled with the demons. Having prevailed and having attained enlightenment, he pondered whether to pass at once to Nirvana or to return to an afflicted world 'to preach suffering and the end of suffering'. We are told that the 'the universe trembled, awaiting his reply'.

In the desert our Lord deliberated. Much depended on the outcome of his lonely struggle. That is what marks out his temptations from ours. Whilst it is true that every decision we make affects other people, it is also the case that most of our choices, including our miserable little sins, are not eternally consequential, despite what the hell-fire preachers may say. And we dare to hope that – 'under the Mercy' – even the far-reaching entail of our more heinous offences can be curtailed and that something good can be salvaged from the mess we make of things. By contrast, what was hanging in the balance as Jesus agonized in his 'desert Gethsemane' was the salvation of the world. Had Jesus have chosen the alternative path proposed by his adversary he would no doubt have still gone on to do a lot of good, but love's last battle, God's campaign to bring us home to himself, would already have been lost.

Why the wilderness? The present writer experiences more occasions of sin in down-town Brighton than on the bleak and bare uplands of Devil's Dyke, a ten-minute drive away. But the truth of Sunday's Gospel is that, unless I make time this Lent to be alone with God on Devil's Dyke – so aptly named! – I shall soon be making all sorts of bad choices among the bright lights below.

YEAR B

Genesis 9.8–17; 1 Peter 3.18–22; Mark 1.9–15

THE SCAPEGOAT

Jesus is a driven man. The spirit 'immediately' – again we must give the word its full weight – drives him into the wilderness. 'Casts him out' is what Mark says. Some translators, following Matthew and Luke, settle for a feebler turn of phrase, draining the story of its drama. There is a brutal contrast between the voice from heaven at his baptism and, now, the voice from hell. The temptation – it is to avoid the way of the cross – comes to Jesus as a whisper in his mind. We are not to envisage Satan as embodied, as some abomination squatting on a rock nearby, darting out its forked tongue. Yet Jesus is not alone. The desert is rarely that empty. Even if Mark had not told us so, we would have assumed that there were animals around.

In one of his witty poems, Robert Graves wonders which creatures, great or small, might have kept Jesus company in the wilderness. The pious pelican would certainly have been there. Near him, too, Graves insists, would have been the creepy-crawlies that make us shudder. Why are the wild things drawn to him? Perhaps because they sense that the Lord of creation is their saviour too. The cockroaches, as well as the more cuddly creatures, long to be set free from their 'bondage to decay' and to obtain 'the glorious liberty of the children of God' (Romans 8.21).

One other beast, Graves believes, would have been very near to Jesus, the pitiful skeletal scapegoat. In turning our attention to the scapegoat, the poet takes us to the heart of the story. In the times of the temple, as part of the ceremonies of the Day of Atonement, the High Priest would confess over 'the scapegoat' the sins of the people. The goat would then be driven out into the desert. William Holman Hunt inscribed two texts on the frame of his famous painting of the scapegoat: 'Surely he hath borne our griefs, and carried our sorrows; yet we did esteem him stricken, smitten of God, and afflicted' (Isaiah 53.4) and 'The goat shall bear upon him all their iniquities unto a land not inhabited' (Leviticus 16.22).

Christ's trial in the wilderness, as in Gethsemane, is both the temptation to escape his passion and at the same time a foreshadowing of it. And, as in Gethsemane, the angels lend him strength (Luke 22.43).

Jesus's first public word is about time. On the subject of time, as on everything else, Lewis Carroll is illuminating. We learn from him to distinguish between 'White Rabbit time' and 'Walrus time'. The former is 'clock time', time that ticks away. ('Oh my ears and whiskers, how late it's getting!' cries the White Rabbit.) The latter is the 'right time'. ('The time has come', the Walrus said, 'to talk of many things.') The right time, the *kairos*, which Jesus announces, is the *decisive* time. It is the deciding moment in the human story. ('Jesus comes' – so wrote Albert Schweitzer – 'and, in the knowledge that he is the coming Son of Man, lays hold of the wheel of the world to set it moving on that last revolution which is to bring all ordinary history to a close.') But it is also '*decision* time', the time to turn from wrong and to commit oneself in faith to the one who, supremely, is 'good news'.

This turning, this trusting, is in response to the advent of the Kingdom of God. R. T. France, formerly Principal of Wycliffe Hall, has memorably said that the expression 'Kingdom of God' is 'something of a rubber nose, capable of being twisted in any direction to suit the interests of the one who wears it' (*Divine Government*, SPCK, 1990). The endless debate is whether that Kingdom is still to come ('Thy Kingdom come') or already present ('For thine *is* the Kingdom'). The paradox in the teaching of Jesus is that the Kingdom is both 'now' and 'not yet'. So it is that the light of God's Kingdom sometimes shines from the very situations which deny his reign.

But for Mark, the point about the reign of God, come upon us in the person of Jesus, is that its coming is *hidden*, save to the eye of faith. The nature of his rule is more important for Mark than the timing of its arrival. For the contemporaries of Jesus, talk of a coming kingdom can only mean the restoration of their nation and its power. Jesus embodies and teaches a different model of monarchy. Mark's Gospel – its tragic dimension runs deep – is the chronicle of his disciples' rejection of that model.

To cling to power – the shreds of it left to us in an established Church – is to renounce his reign.

YEAR C

Deuteronomy 26.1–11; Romans 10.8b–13; Luke 4.1–13

HIS TEMPTATIONS AND OURS

'The Holy Gospel is written in the fourth chapter of the Gospel according to St Luke beginning at the first verse.' But my errant eye is caught by the last words of the previous chapter. Luke gives us the genealogy of Jesus. The long family tree ends with the words, 'son of Adam, son of God'. This conclusion is not just the record of Jesus's earliest ancestors. Luke tells us not just whom Jesus came from. He tells us who he is. Jesus *is* 'the son of Adam and the Son of God'.

But – one moment – so am I. I too am the child of Adam and the child of God.

If that is who I am, then Jesus's temptations are mine too. We tend to detach ourselves from the story of Christ's wilderness encounter with Satan. We see his solitary struggle as not touching us. The three temptations add up to one: the single temptation for Jesus to settle for some other path than the lonely way of the cross. Because his role – to 'give his life as a ransom for many' – was unique, we suppose that his temptations too must have been unique. 'There was no other good enough to pay the price of sin.' If no one else is asked to pay, no one else will be tempted not to. Anyway, most of us find the urge to jump off temples resistible.

Certainly Jesus's debate with the devil is over the nature of a Messiahship that is his alone and the priorities of a mission solely his. His temptation is to be the Messiah who would host the Messianic banquet, the 'feast of rich food and of well-aged wines' (Isaiah 25.6) that was the dream and hope of a hungry people. It is to be the Messiah who would 'slay their foes and lift them high', to deliver them from their oppressors. It is to provide some overwhelming proof of who he is and so to convince the sceptical that God has indeed visited his people.

Thus spoke the voice, the voice not from heaven, to Jesus as he pondered, and perhaps began to question, the mission that only he could fulfil.

But the same voice whispers in my ear too. 'If you are the child of God . . .' The tempter's tone is mocking and gleeful. 'You are, you say, a child of God. You read your Bible and claim its promises; you say your prayers, believing they will be answered; you go to church and seek sacramental strength to love and to serve. And yet the stones at your feet are still stones. The desert of your days is as arid as ever. The hunger in your heart, for you know not what, is unabated.' The temptation is to despair.

The same seductive voice seeks to persuade the Church, as it sought to persuade the Lord of the Church, to be a power for good – to be a *power* for good. To use power to achieve what must be done may be a necessity for the army, but for the Church to do so is always idolatry. The temptation to 'worship the devil' is not to do weird things in the woods at midnight. It is the temptation to stride the corridors of power and, ever since the conversion of Constantine, there has been little evidence of the Church attempting to resist it. The consequence has been 'Christendom', the triumph of what Kenneth Leech describes as a 'mutant of Christianity', the Church that colludes with the institutions and instruments of the world's pomp and power. (Not to speak of plundering its wardrobe.)

Perhaps these days 'the enemy of souls' no longer seduces us with crude promises of power, dangling before us the perks and peacock feathers that go with it. He is subtler in his overtures, suggesting that positions of greater 'influence' can better serve the gospel and the Christian cause. (In a recent sermon in Westminster Abbey, it was claimed that 'the establishment of the Church of England means that there is space for religious thought and action at the heart of our national life'.)

And are we tempted to jump from temples? Perhaps not. But we do still like to impress, and it is the same father of lies urging us to do so. We're not averse to stunts. We broadcast our successes, and conceal our failures. A famous church which boasts of converts born up on angels' wings stays silent about those dashed against the stones.

I am tempted as he is. Baptized child of God I may be, but I must still learn to respect the utter recalcitrance of how things are. I was signed with the sign of the cross. One day I'll exchange that cross for a crown, but meanwhile I mustn't try to swap it for a seat at the top table. I am defended and equipped by God's Holy Spirit. But I really must stop showing off.

The Second Sunday of Lent

YEAR A

Genesis 12.1–4a; Romans 4.1–5, 13–17; John 3.1–17

LOOK TO THE ROCK WHENCE YOU ARE HEWN

It all began so simply. 'The Lord said to Abram, "Go".' 'So Abram went.' He set out 'not knowing where he was going', as someone much later put it (Hebrews 11.8). It was a decision that would eventually involve an awful lot of people, including those who perished in Auschwitz, those who went to work in New York's twin towers on September 11th 2001, and those in soft raiment purchased from Wippells. Steps of faith can always be refused, and Abraham could have stayed put. His journey into the unknown was a free choice, not a forced march. He was of course offered an incentive, the promise that in him all the families of the earth would be blessed. Those of the Abrahamic faiths – Jews, Muslims, Christians – believe that, despite history's testimony to the contrary, despite the Holocaust, despite the falling towers, despite religious bloodshed and bickering, that that promise still stands. We hold to the universal hope that, because Abraham trusted and obeyed, *all* our families will be blessed.

So, this Sunday, 'We look to the rock whence we are hewn' (Isaiah 51.1). We look to Abraham because, says Paul, he teaches us to trust. Our New Testament lection has just two brief snippets from Paul's extended argument about the relationship of faith to works, of grace to law, of hope to experience. Unfortunately, bits of string don't let us follow the thread. We need to read the whole chapter, if only to register that Paul lived on the same planet as we do. Paul saw that acting in faith sometimes means doing things that to anyone in their right mind must seem daft. He recognized that Christian hope is always a 'hoping against hope'.

The example Paul gives is that of Abraham's confidence that his wife Sarah would bear a child, although both of them were extremely old.

We could multiply many examples of our own of how facts bid to destroy faith and of how the way things are mocks the Christian vision of what will be. In our own time Richard Dawkins and others have mounted fierce attacks on belief in God. Christian apologists have responded with powerful arguments for the reasonableness of Christian theism. Such apologists and their paperbacks come to our rescue when we are lost for what to say, but they risk falling out of step with St Paul. Paul liked a good argument as much as the next man, but at the same time he cheerfully concedes the dottiness – the sheer 'folly', as he calls it – of what Christians preach and believe. Indeed he glories in it. Look at Abraham, he says. Better still, look at the cross (1 Corinthians 1.18–2.16).

Nicodemus, who too liked an argument, endeavoured to start one with Jesus. Much is made of the fact that he came to Jesus 'by night'. Perhaps he did not wish to be seen in this controversial figure's company. Perhaps that 'by night' is intended to symbolize the spiritual darkness in which, for our Gospel writer, Nicodemus languished. Some brave commentators suggest that John was simply recording an inconsequential historical detail. After all, the heat of the day is not the best time for a theological discussion.

In the drama of John's Gospel Nicodemus is on stage only briefly. He says his few lines and then he is gone. The relationship being dramatized is less that of two characters – although there is no reason to suppose that someone called Jesus did not meet someone called Nicodemus – than that of two communities. The dialogue we overhear is between the young Christian church and the synagogue from which it is now emerging. The injunction is in the plural. 'You – all of you – must be born again.' It is addressed not so much to Nicodemus as to the congregation he represents.

Does the Fourth Gospel teach that Christianity fulfils – and so takes over from – Judaism? So it has usually been understood. The consequences of that interpretation are a matter of history, the terrible chronicle which makes our hope of what was promised to Abraham so hard to hold on to. But, whether or not that reading of his Gospel is true to the thought of John, it cannot be the last word in the continuing conversation between Jew and Christian.

Heythrop College has done much in our own day to counter the claim – as arrogant as it is naïve, as offensive as it is dangerous – that Christianity supersedes Judaism. John McDade, Principal of Heythrop College, has recently written, 'Old Law, New Law and Grace are not separable but dynamically contained one in another.' 'A simple linear supersessionism in which Christianity replaces Judaism', he bluntly maintains, 'is impossible.' And, he adds, 'Nothing of Torah is lost.'

'You must be born again.' Perhaps those words were indeed once said to the synagogue. What's for sure is that they are now said to the church.

YEAR B

Genesis 17.1–7, 15–16; Romans 4.13–25; Mark 8.31–38

JOINING JESUS ON DEATH ROW

Our lectionary is tempered to our limited attention span. Our readings are fun-sized fragments. Torn from their context, these snippets of Scripture often lose their force. So it is with Sunday's Gospel in which for the first time Jesus speaks openly of his passion. Without what's gone before – Peter's 'confession' at Caesarea Philippi – the impact of Jesus's prediction is diminished. At Caesarea Philippi Peter at last wakes up to what Jesus's strange signs and sayings mean. 'You're the Messiah!' he cries. It is the recognition Jesus has been waiting for. He can now speak of what awaits him. But it turns out that his understanding of Messiahship is very different from Peter's. Jesus accepts the title but reinterprets the role. Mark's Gospel has a dramatic structure and this – Peter's confession leading immediately to Jesus's stark warning – is its turning point. Alas, what Mark joins together the lectionary rends asunder.

Jesus now begins to speak 'plainly' of what previously he has only hinted at, that his mission as Messiah is not to restore the Davidic monarchy but to suffer, to die, and to rise again. Plain-speaking this may be, but puzzles remain, above all that of the title 'Son of Man.' Some years ago a conference of Bible translators took place in Colorado Springs on 'Gender-related language in Scripture'. The conference concluded that 'the phrase "Son of Man" should ordinarily be preserved to retain intracanonical connections' – which is an overblown way of saying that we must keep the phrase 'Son of Man' because of all its resonant echoes. 'What is man that thou art mindful of him and the son of man that thou visitest him?' (Psalm 8.4) 'I saw in the night visions and behold . . . one like unto a son of man' (Daniel 7.13). And, most hauntingly, 'Son of man, can these bones live?'(Ezekiel 37.3)

The phrase 'Son of Man' means many things. It can be equivalent to the personal pronoun 'I'. It can mean 'one' in the sense of 'one does

so love Sandringham'. It can mean 'humankind'. Probably it was a title of the Messiah. Perhaps its multiplicity of meanings is the reason
Jesus elects to refer to himself in this way. The title at once reveals and
conceals. Jesus defers to us the interpretation of the title he chooses for
himself, just as we must make what we will of the one who half-hides
behind it. Jesus speaks plainly – but keeps his secret still.

Peter rejects the construction Jesus places on Messiahship and meets
a stinging rebuke. 'Get behind me, Satan!' The ferocity of the reproof
is an indicator of the intensity of the temptation this 'Son of Man' is
suffering.

Jesus must 'take up his cross' – as too, when his hour comes, must
Peter.

Take up thy cross, the Saviour said,
If thou wouldst my disciple be.
Deny thyself, the world forsake,
And humbly follow after me.
(Charles William Everest)

The hymn misleads, for it turns what Jesus says on its head. It treats
'taking up the cross' as a metaphor for self-denial generally. Jesus is
much more specific. To deny oneself is – literally – to take up one's
cross. The criminal condemned to crucifixion must carry the beam, to
which he will be nailed, to the place where he will hang. This is the
'cruel and unusual punishment' which the disciple may well have to
face.

The text is not about giving up After-Eights for Lent. The context is
that of a Christian community in which martyrdom was no metaphor.
To be sure, crucifixion becomes for all time the supreme emblem of the
cost of discipleship. Paul, 'crucified with Christ' (Galatians 2.20), sees
to that. But for Mark and his first readers 'the way of the cross' could
be a death-row as real and grim as any in Texas.

Much mischief has been done at the behest of 'self-denial'. Feminist theologians have shown how pious talk – mostly on male lips –
about self-denial as a fundamental Christian virtue has tacitly served
to perpetuate the subjection of women in church and society. Those
temperamentally deferential confuse self-denial with their natural unas-
sertiveness. Years ago I was scandalized when a diocesan bishop said to
me, 'You have to compete for the top jobs in the Church.' I still wonder
whether my outrage sprang from a sensitive Christian conscience or
innate wimpishness.

To deny onself is to lose one's life for the sake of the gospel – and so to save it. In context, this may be Mark's comfort for the prospective martyr. Today a cross of real wood and nails. Tomorrow a crown. ('Die now – pie later'?) But those of us spared martyrdom must still make our peace with the Christian paradox that we must die to live – a topic for a Lent group and a task for a lifetime.

YEAR C

Genesis 15.1–12, 17–18; Philippians 3.17–4.1; Luke 13.31–35

THE FOX AND THE HEN

Images of animals are not as abundant in the New Testament as in Shakespeare, but in Sunday's Gospel we have two of them in the space of a few verses. They could not be more contrasting. We have Herod the fox and Jesus the hen. Fox and hen, like cat and dog, are ancient foes, as many a tale tells us. ('There was once a little red hen that lived in a house by herself in the wood. And over the hill, in a hole in the rocks, lived a sly, crafty old fox . . .')

It is Luke's witty way to juxtapose the two images. Herod is the fox, the creature who likes nothing better than chicken for supper. Jesus is the mother hen who loves her silly chicks and does all she can to protect them from predators.

First the fox. Although he makes few appearances in it, Herod Antipas has a pivotal place in Luke's Gospel. The purpose of Luke's Gospel and the Christian good news is to make us ask just one question, and it is Herod the fox who poses it. 'Who is this about whom I hear such things?' And Luke adds, in an understatement as weighty as it is laconic, 'He tried to see him' (Luke 9.9). Herod asks who Jesus is and seeks to see him. The business of evangelism is to invite that question and to encourage that quest – that's all. Herod had heard the gospel preached by the one he'd beheaded, the gospel of John the Baptist, who told people to look at Jesus and who then got out of their way so as not to impede their view of him (John 1.29).

Herod is still wondering who Jesus is when the latter is brought before him at his trial (Luke 23.8). It seems that he equivocates to the end. That being so, we are bound to wonder whether Herod wanted Jesus dead, as the Pharisees claim he did. Such clarity of purpose seems out of character. If so, the Pharisees' warning is not a word of friendly advice, but a much more mischievous suggestion. To use another animal image, this is the serpent talking. Luke told us that this slippery customer would be back (4.13). For Jesus the advice to clear off and lie low is the same temptation, to avoid the cross, with which he struggled in the wilderness.

The sayings which Luke alone attributes to Jesus have a haunting resonance all their own. 'Today and tomorrow' are the days when the signs of the coming Kingdom are to be seen. The day after tomorrow, 'the third day', will be the day when the work is finished. To be sure, talk of 'the third day' hints at the resurrection, but Luke is here speaking the language of St John for whom 'It is finished' is a cry from the cross, not from the empty tomb (John 19.30). Jesus's destination is Jerusalem and his doom is to suffer what Jerusalem does to its prophets.

'I must keep going – today, tomorrow, and the next day.' Such is the path Jesus took at his baptism. The path is much the same for us who stumble after him. Somehow we have to keep going. 'There remains a Sabbath rest for the people of God' (Hebrews 4.9) but we're not there yet. For George Herbert 'rest' was the one jewel God declined to bestow on his creature. So God keeps his child in 'repining restlessness'.

> Let him be rich and weary, that at least,
> If goodness lead him not, yet weariness
> May toss him to my breast.
> ('The Pulley')

God give me grace to persevere.

First the fox, then the hen. Jesus says that his feelings for Jerusalem, his longing to save its children from the judgement hanging over them, are those of the mother hen trying to shelter her chicks from danger. Why are we so embarrassed by this image? We need to probe our reluctance to admit the image of the hen alongside that of the lion and the lamb as an icon of Christ. Is it because we don't think much of chickens as role models? Yet Jesus implies that we can learn from them. Is it because we don't think them much to look at? But so they despised 'the man of sorrows', the one who had 'no form nor comeliness,' the one from whom 'we hid as it were our faces' (Isaiah 53, 2, 3). Is it their helplessness? But the hen destined for the pot is no more helpless than the lamb led to slaughter. Or are there obscure, unexamined and deeply unhealthy gender issues festering beneath the surface? Is our hang-up about this particular avian image the same hesitancy which makes us shy about thinking of God as mother? I only ask.

The Third Sunday of Lent

YEAR A

Exodus 17.1–7; Romans 5.1–11; John 4.5–42

THE TASTE OF WATER

Many have never tasted water. Someone who did was Antoine de Saint-Exupéry, the pioneer French aviator. He once had to bring his plane down in the Sahara desert. Days passed and he was close to dying of thirst. At last, out of the sands, came a solitary Bedouin. From the skin he carried, the nomad – Saint-Exupéry never learned his name – gave him water. He spoke of the water he drank as the water that is 'not necessary to life, but rather life itself'.

Later Saint-Exupéry wrote of another lonely pilot who had to crash-land his plane in the desert. There he met 'The Little Prince', who had made his way to earth from a distant star. The little prince told the pilot about the strange people he had met on his travels. He told him about the merchant who had invented a tablet to quench thirst. 'Take this tablet,' the merchant had said to him, 'and you will feel no need of anything to drink. That way you will save fifty-three minutes a week.' 'As for me,' the little prince said to himself, 'if I had fifty-three minutes to spend as I liked, I should walk at my leisure to a spring of fresh water.'

Many matters of great moment are raised by the story of Jesus's mid-day meeting with the woman at the well – the promise of eternal life, the status of the Samaritans, the fulfilment of what we misleadingly call 'the Old Testament', the relationship of Christianity and Judaism, the role of high and holy places, the nature of worship, 'the last things', the priorities of Jesus's mission. So we could go on and on. And so we do go on and on, forgetting that John was writing to those who knew what it was to be thirsty and who knew the grace of water.

Our Gospel is about the gift of 'living water'. Behind the phrase is the Hebrew expression *mayim chayim*, meaning fresh water, running water, water that has not been left standing in dirty jars and is not stale and brackish. Of course in our text the term is being used metaphorically. It stands for something else. Later John will tell us that when Jesus offers 'living water' he is promising the gift of his Holy Spirit (John 7.37).

The Samaritan woman fails at first to see that there is a 'spiritual' meaning to the 'living water' being offered her. But that is not because she is being obtuse. It is because, unlike us, she values water – ordinary wet water. So much so that she cannot imagine anything more wonderful than an unfailing supply of it. We are not to patronize the woman at the well, congratulating ourselves that we are quicker than she was to take the point Jesus makes. This woman knew how precious water is and in the end she will have understood far better than we do how great a gift was being offered her.

We stay with the sign so that we can value what is signified. If water gives life, the lack of it, or the pollution of it, spells death. Each year bacterial diarrhoea causes the death of nearly two million children under the age of five in the developing world. This illness is preventable through the provision of clean water. The 'living water', of which Jesus spoke, may mean more than water that does not kill little children. But were the lady from Sychar still with us, she would surely suggest that his words at least mean that. In Lent we take to heart the truth that we do not live by water alone, but we remember too that we die without it. 'Whoever gives even a cup of cold water to one of these little ones in the name of a disciple – truly I tell you, none of these will lose their reward' (Matthew 10.42). ('In the name of a disciple' – perhaps in the name, though we do not know it, of a certain Samaritan woman?)

Jacob's well is still there – or it was forty years ago when I last drank from it. I arrived there, exhausted, at midday. The orthodox monk, custodian of what had become a shrine, drew water from the well for me. That water was, as we say, 'life-saving' – so much so that it betokened something more. The sign partook of the signified. It is not only in baptism that water is sacramental.

The well is still there. The temple on Mount Gerizim, overlooking Sychar and holy to the Samaritans, is gone. So too is the temple in Jerusalem, thirty miles to the south. Jesus said that the hour was near when 'neither on this mountain nor in Jerusalem' would they worship. Today the two temples are no more. To that extent our Lord's word has been fulfilled. To the extent that we have built ten thousand times ten thousand others it has not.

YEAR B

Exodus 20.1–17; 1 Corinthians 1.18–25; John 2.13–22

WHERE DO WE MEET GOD?

Jesus enters the temple. In a blazing outburst of the wrath of God he takes the place apart. The story is told in all four Gospels. In Matthew, Mark and Luke the incident occurs at the end of Jesus's ministry. According to John, 'the cleansing of the temple' comes at the start. Here it is Jesus's dramatic entry on public life. So did Jesus storm through the temple, turning things upside down, *twice*? Some conservative commentators, determined to uphold the consistency of the Gospel record, claim as much. Common sense suggests otherwise. John puts the story near the beginning of his Gospel for theological reasons. For him this event says something about Jesus that must be made clear from the outset.

We must try to imagine 'the temple experience' at the time of Jesus. The temple itself, however magnificent, was relatively small. It was the colossal terrace on which it stood, the mightiest of Herod's building works, which would have overwhelmed the pilgrim by its scale – as it still does. Above all, we must remember that you did not go *into* the temple, not unless you were a priest. You went *to* the temple, not *into* it. You said your prayers and offered your sacrifices outside. We must rid our minds too of any idea that those temple courts were serene and peaceful, a tranquil retreat where you could compose yourself for pious thought and undisturbed prayer – far from it. The place would have been swimming with the blood and guts of slaughtered beasts and reeking with the stench of their carcasses. It would have had all the devotional atmosphere of an abattoir.

What of the market stalls and the money changers? Yes, there were animals on sale. That was a perfectly sensible arrangement. Pilgrims came from far afield to offer sacrifice. Supposing you came from Spain, say. It made much more sense for you to buy the sheep you wished to sacrifice when you got to the temple rather than to drag the poor bleating creature with you. Those who sold the animals were providing a necessary service. To be sure, you had to change your money first, but that you'd expect. The mark-up, we're told, was about two per cent. Hardly exorbitant.

So why does Jesus take a whip to the merchants and money changers? Here we must distinguish between what moved Jesus to act as he did and what John intends by transposing his account of the episode to near the start of his story. Jesus objected to the extent to which the temple, 'the sacrament of God's presence with his people', had become a commercial enterprise. The disciples see it that way. The other Gospel writers see it that way. They record Jesus's angry accusation that the temple authorities had turned it into 'a den of thieves' (Jeremiah 7.11). But, for John, Jesus has more on his mind than trade in pigeons. Jesus expels the merchants and money changers, so John sees it, because they are inextricably part of a system whose day is done. This must be made plain before going any further.

As John tells the story, the cleansing of the Temple is more than a protest against commercialism. Jesus is denouncing a much more dangerous enemy of the gospel. His protest is against *religion*. What took place in the courts of the Temple – the sacrifice of the animals and the transactions which made them possible – was religion. It is this that the Jesus of John's Gospel challenges, the Jesus who has one thing to say to those who cling to the old order, 'You must be born again' (John 3.7).

Although Jeremiah is not quoted, it is Jeremiah who is recalled. A double portion of the spirit of Jeremiah drives Jesus to act as he does. Jeremiah had condemned those who imagined that they could use religion as somewhere to hide from the living God. Jeremiah had denounced the Temple – the institution itself, not merely its abuses. By this prophetic sign, one greater than Jeremiah does the same.

Other interpretations cluster around this extraordinary event and they have left their imprint on John's account of it. By the time his Gospel is circulating, the incident is linked to Jesus's death and resurrection. Jesus's action is a sign that the temple is done for, but also that *he* is done for, that 'The temple of his body' will be destroyed. But, unlike a pile of Herodian bricks, the temple of his body will be 'raised up'.

For John, however, there is really only one question that matters: where do we meet God? The answer to that question must be made clear from page one. We meet him not in temples but in the one who 'pitched his tent among us' (John 1.14). What all this has to say to about our own religious institutions is yet another question for the Lent group.

YEAR C

Isaiah 55.1–9; 1 Corinthians 10.1–13; Luke 13.1–9

ABERFAN AND AN ALMIGHTY AND ALL-LOVING GOD

At 9.15 a.m. on Friday, 21 October 1966 a waste tip slid down a mountain into the mining village of Aberfan in South Wales. In its path was

Pantglas Junior School. The children had just returned to their classes after assembly, when the tide of waste engulfed their school. One hundred and sixteen children died and five of their teachers. The hymn they'd sung in assembly was 'All Things Bright and Beautiful'.

I was glad that I wasn't preaching the following Sunday. Down to do so were the other two clergy on the staff of the church where I was serving my title, one to preach at Morning Prayer, the other at Evensong. More than forty years later, I recall their sermons. Both my colleagues spoke of what had befallen the children of Aberfan, but the manner and matter of their homilies were altogether different.

The preacher in the morning took as his text words from this Sunday's Gospel, 'Unless you repent, you will all perish as they did.' He claimed that what had happened to the children of Aberfan was God's warning to us, the same warning that he gave when the tower of Siloam collapsed. God Almighty will not stay his hand forever. Judgement will surely fall on the impenitent. That terrible visitation will overtake the unrepentant unannounced, just as suddenly as Siloam's tower fell on those beneath it and a hill of slurry consumed the little boys and girls of Aberfan.

The sermon in the evening was delivered much less confidently. I can't remember much of what the preacher said, because he couldn't find much to say. He struggled for words. He struggled not to cry.

Which sermon got it right? At the time, as I do still more today, I recognized in that second sermon – in its silences, in its scarcely suppressed sobs as much as in its stumbling words – the Christian response to another's pain. Jesus wept and, very nearly, so did my fellow curate who was preaching.

And yet it was the first sermon, for all its insensitivity, which more accurately reflected the tenor of Jesus's words in the Gospel we hear this Sunday. Jesus, his face now set as a flint towards Jerusalem, is brooding on judgement, the judgement on humanity that he will suffer in his own flesh. He will not now be drawn into an academic debate about the relationship of sin and pain. He will deal with that problem in his own way, which is not to read a paper to a theological seminar on suffering.

Of course, those on whom the tower fell were no better or worse than anyone else. That is not the point. Jesus is not talking to the bereaved; he is talking to the morally careless, to those who see no connection between sowing and reaping, to the effete of spirit, to those at ease in Zion. He's talking to me. He's reminding me of the inexorable moral law, that one thing inevitably leads to another, that if I drift I'll surely shipwreck. It is appointed to me to die – and, after that, my judgement.

That is the word of the Lord to us this Sunday – just as surely as it's not the way to talk to parents who have lost their child in a road accident or under a mountain of waste.

We say that God is an all-loving and all-powerful God. Yet he permits towers in Siloam to collapse on passers-by and hills of slurry to swallow little children. What kind of a god is this? Sunday's Gospel does not answer the question. Indeed – always excepting Paul's letter to the Romans – there is little 'theodicy' in the New Testament, little that shares the purpose of Milton's *Paradise Lost*, 'to justify the ways of God to men'. Some argue that God had to make a world where such things can happen if we are to be truly free. That argument was eloquently deployed by the Archbishop of Canterbury in a broadcast head-to-head with the BBC's John Humphreys. Humphreys was unpersuaded. So were the mums of Aberfan, who could only utter the cry of another child of God on whom a weight of great darkness fell, 'Why, oh why?'

Not for the first or last time in the Gospels we learn a lesson from a fig tree. The farmhand who loves the fig tree he's been looking after, unfruitful as it is, pleads with the farmer to spare it one more year. The Authorized Version is more accurate (as it sometimes is) and less prim and prissy (as it always is) than the modern versions. 'Let it alone,' says the little fig tree's friend, 'till I shall dig about it and dung it.' God will not stay his hand forever, but there is yet 'a space of grace' before the axe falls. Climatologists say that we have less than a century.

The Fourth Sunday of Lent

YEAR A

1 Samuel 16.1–13; Ephesians 5.8–14; John 9.1–41

DO SOMETHING ABOUT IT

Alas, we start sinning very soon. Even though one's mother's womb does not offer a wide range of opportunities for wrongdoing, there have always been those who have said that we get up to mischief from the moment we are conceived. A rabbinic text taught that, when a pregnant woman worships in a heathen temple, the foetus also commits

THE FOURTH SUNDAY OF LENT

idolatry. The reason why such a farfetched notion gained a hearing was that it appeared to offer an explanation for congenital abnormalities or defects, for blindness from birth, for example. On this view, such afflictions could be seen as the punishment that the new-born had already brought upon themselves.

Another reason given for babies being born with disabilities was that they had been punished for what their parents did. This unpleasant doctrine, that God visits the iniquity of one generation on the next, is there in our Old Testament (Exodus 20.5; 34.7) and, although it was condemned by the prophets (Jeremiah 31.29–20; Ezekiel 18.1–4), there were plenty at the time of Jesus who still believed it.

Such ideas are in the minds of the disciples when they ask Jesus about the man blind from birth. (It is less likely that they entertain the idea that the man's blindness was his *karma*, the consequence of his misdeeds in a previous incarnation.)

The premise of the disciples' question is ours too as we contemplate innocent suffering. It is that someone has some explaining to do. The fact of such suffering is the weightiest objection to belief in a God who is good. The moral problem lies not in the amount of suffering, not in 'the starving millions' but in the starving individual, not in the multitude of children who die in torment but in the one child who does.

The late Derek Skeet was a poet and teacher. He taught children from a tough estate in a part of Cambridge unvisited by tourists. He wondered why so many of them had had such an unfair start in life. He wondered, but not for long. Instead he turned to the ninth chapter of John's Gospel. He had his own paraphrase of the opening exchange between Jesus and his disciples. 'Why suffering?' they ask. 'So that you will do something about it,' says Jesus – which is what Derek did.

We recall the context. Jesus has just escaped from the temple where they had tried to lynch him. Having left his home in heaven, he now forsakes his house on earth. Outside – they are all outside, those whom our blessed Lord seeks out – is the blind man, the embodiment of suffering humanity. John believes that the mission of Jesus to this one man and to all whom he represents is not to offer explanations but to do what must be done. This is no time for a philosophical discussion. The daylight is fading. The darkness is gathering. Explanations can wait.

Jesus restores the blind man's sight. What Jesus does – as throughout John's Gospel – is an enacted commentary on who he claims to be. He is 'the light of the world'. But his light only deepens the darkness of those who reject him. The latter are represented in our story by the clergymen who live by the letter of the law, who believe that the way to please God is to keep the rules. (How fair John is being to the Pharisees of Jesus's day, or to those whom he so problematically refers to as 'the Jews' is another matter.) They recognize that Jesus is threatening their power base. Too craven to vent their anger on Jesus, they turn it on the man born blind and his family. It is an instructive example of how clergy can be bullies.

'One thing I know,' he says. 'I was blind. Now I see.' John's irony, lost on many who preach from this text, is that of course he doesn't see. Not yet at least. It is only later, when he too has been 'driven out', that he recognizes Jesus for who he is. Only then does he 'see'. Only 'outside' does the fog lift.

So we have the three great themes of this chapter. First, the Christian response to the problem of suffering. It is, in the very little time left, to do something about it. Secondly, Christ is the bearer of light to the benighted, not all of whom will welcome that light. And, thirdly, John tells us that Jesus comes into this world 'for judgement' (John 9.39). He comes 'so that those who do not see might see and so that those who do see might not see'. The paradox is to shock us into thought. We must decide for ourselves what to make of this man who speaks to us so strangely. That will be our own judgement – in more senses than one.

YEAR B

Numbers 21.4–9; Ephesians 2.1–10; John 3.14–21

ALL YOU HAVE TO DO IS LOOK

We have mixed feelings about snakes. Most people loathe them. Some have suggested that the fear of snakes is hard-wired into our brains. I remember the first time I killed a snake. It was five-foot long and basking in the sun in a garden where three small children were playing. It may have been harmless, but I did not wait to find out. I grabbed a stick and beat it to death. I recall the frenzy with which I attacked it. Something primal had overtaken me which I cannot begin to explain.

Snakes are hated – but also venerated. Ophiolatreia, the worship of snakes, was widespread throughout the ancient world. Snakes shed their old skins and grow new ones, a trait that accounts for their being regarded as symbols of renewal or regeneration. The rod of Asclepius, a staff with a snake wrapped round it, reflects this image of the snake as a sign of hope and healing.

D. H. Lawrence's wonderful poem 'Snake' explores our ambivalence about snakes. The poet admires the beautiful snake in his water trough. He feels as if he has been visited by a god. But then he is seized with horror and tries to kill it.

> And immediately I regretted it.
> I thought how paltry, how vulgar, what a mean act!
> I despised myself and the voices of my accursed human education.

Our contradictory attitudes to snakes are apparent in the Bible. The serpent that tempts Adam and Eve in the Garden of Eden is cursed by God and condemned to go on its belly and to eat dust. We hear in our Old Testament reading how God inflicts the people of Israel, who had been grizzling about their disgusting diet in the wilderness, with a plague of poisonous snakes.

And yet it is a brass model of this same venomous snake, held high by Moses, which becomes the sacrament of their healing. The snake that kills is the snake that makes whole. Those who look to it live.

In time this snake, lethal but life-giving, somehow surviving the vicissitudes of early Israelite history, becomes an object of worship. Enter King Hezekiah. Hezekiah, 'who did that which was right in the eyes of the Lord', is appalled by what he regards as an idolatry and he smashes the brass snake to bits (2 Kings 18.1–8). The contradictions run deep. Moses is commanded to uphold the brazen serpent. Hezekiah, who 'kept the commandments, which the Lord commanded Moses', destroys it.

According to John, Jesus appeals to the story of the snake that kills and heals to interpret his death on the cross. 'As Moses lifted up the serpent in the wilderness, so must the Son of Man be lifted up.' When John uses the language of 'lifting up', he is referring to Christ's three-fold exaltation from the earth – at his death, his resurrection, and his ascension. But here the primary reference is to the cross. The cross is lethal but life-giving, just as was the snake that both killed and saved the disaffected Israelites.

The cross kills, just as the snake does. We are so used to the image of the cross as a religious symbol, that we forget that for the first readers of the Gospels the cross was not a symbol at all, but a ghastly reality. With its accompanying tackle of rope, hammer and nails, the cross was a killing-machine. Raised at many a roadside, the cross was part of the street-furniture of the Roman world. No one was in any doubt what it was for.

The cross kills, as snakes do. But the cross gives life, just as the snake does. Those who look to it live.

The Jesus of John's Gospel sees the story of the brazen serpent as a powerful symbol of saving faith. Belief is not assent to a series of propositions but an orientation of heart and soul. Those who believe, according to this Gospel, are those who do what John the Baptist told them to do. They are those who look and live (John 1.36).

It's a story beloved of evangelists. Charles Haddon Spurgeon preached on it at great length in a famous sermon, 'The Mysteries of the Brazen Serpent', delivered in the Music Hall of the Royal Surrey Gardens on the morning of 27 September 1857.

Spurgeon dwelt on the horrible things that poisonous snakes do to you and warned that sin does much the same. He lingered on the folly of those who despised so contemptible a means of a cure as a snake on a stick. He berated the 'namby-pamby' Puseyites who hid the instrument of salvation in clouds of incense. He bewailed the folly of those who procrastinated, those who found that when at last they turned to the serpent blindness had overtaken them.

But above all Spurgeon pleaded with his hearers to *look and live*. 'Do not take any notice whether you have got one serpent or fifty serpents, one bite or fifty bites; all you have to do is to look.'

YEAR C

Joshua 5.9–12; 2 Corinthians 5.16–21; Luke 15.1–3, 11b–32

GOD'S TWO HANDS

The parable of the Prodigal Son needs to be read in context, Luke's context and ours. The Lucan context is the opening paragraph of the chapter where the story is told. Luke makes it clear that Jesus is targeting religious people, those who profess a religion and those for whom a religion is a profession. Our context is where we read or hear the story. That is likely to be the Church we belong to – the Church of England, say – and the church down the road we go to. So our context is the same as Luke's: organized religion.

The tendency of religious people of every stripe – 'the Pharisees and scribes' were certainly no worse than the rest of us – is to erect palisades. Behind these palisades are those of whom we approve. Beyond the palisades are those of whom we disapprove. These circles, embracing the acceptable, excluding the unacceptable, are like modern gated communities, protected from intruders and undesirables by tight security.

Inside are those like us; outside are those different from us. The truth we have to learn, elder brothers all of us, is that the Kingdom of God is not such a society, an enclave to which only our sort are admitted, but a fellowship in which all are made welcome, including those we find uncongenial.

Perhaps the prodigal son came home with the wind behind him, so that 'when he was yet a great way off' there was borne on the air the faint whiff of pig. To the elder brother that smell is deeply offensive. But I cannot point my finger at him, for I have been to churches where the homeless – and bathless – are welcomed, and on a hot Sunday I have been careful where I sat and with whom I exchanged the Peace.

Earlier commentators were untroubled by the absence from this story of any reference to a mother. On 'Mothering Sunday' that silence shouts at us. Some – those perhaps who think that the woman's place is at the Aga, not the altar – suggest that the mother was preparing the fatted calf. Some say she was praying. Some wonder whether the father was a widower. If so, the once wayward son could have sung the wonderful Charles Fillmore hymn with its plaintive refrain.

When I became a prodigal, and left the old rooftree,
She almost broke her loving heart in mourning after me;
And day and night she prayed to God to keep me in His care:
O Saviour, tell my mother I'll be there!

Tell mother I'll be there, in answer to her prayer;
This message, blessed Saviour, to her bear!
Tell mother I'll be there, Heav'n's joys with her to share;
Yes, tell my darling mother I'll be there.

'Tell my mother I'll be there.' We're too sophisticated to sing such words this Sunday. Some of us, though, would like to.

One way to salvage something maternal from this androcentric story is suggested by the Dutch Catholic priest Henry Nouwen. Fr Nouwen invites us to look again at Rembrandt's famous painting of the return of the Prodigal Son and to notice the father's hands.

The two hands are quite different. The father's left hand touching the son's shoulder is strong and muscular . . . That hand seems not only to touch, but, with its strength, also to hold. How different is the father's right hand! This hand does not hold or grasp . . . It lies gently upon the son's shoulder. It wants to caress, to stroke, and to offer consolation and comfort. It is a mother's hand . . . As soon as I recognized the difference between the two hands of the father, a new world of meaning opened up for me. The Father is not simply a great patriarch. He is mother as well as father. (*The Return of the Prodigal Son*, Doubleday, 1992)

It is a reading of Rembrandt's painting and of Luke's text which would probably have surprised artist and evangelist alike. But no matter. As with the canvas, so with the Gospel, we ask what they say to us today. What we need to hear from the Bible is sometimes more than its writers meant to say.

There remains the question of how we tell the story. Most parables were originally told to shock. How can we convey their original impact to those who, frankly, are now bored by them? One way is to alter the punch-lines.

A certain Samaritan came that way and when he came to the place and saw him, he too passed by on the other side.

Later the foolish bridesmaids came also, saying, 'Lord, open to us.' He replied, 'Oh, all right then.'

But while he was still far off, his father got him on his mobile and told him to clear off back to his pigs.

A Gospeller bold enough to twist hallowed texts in this way would have to add, 'This is *not* the Gospel of the Lord – but for once you paid attention.'

The Fifth Sunday of Lent

YEAR A

Ezekiel 37.1–14; Romans 8.6–11; John 11.1–45

WHY JESUS WEPT

In the *Cappella degli Scrovegni*, 'the Arena Chapel', in Padua there is a cycle of frescoes by the fourteenth-century Italian artist Giotto. Giotto's sublime work is both an unmatched masterpiece of western art and a profound reading of the Christian story. One of the most remarkable of these frescoes depicts the raising of Lazarus, the story we turn to this Sunday.

The artist pictures Lazarus emerging from the tomb, still wrapped in grave cloths. Giotto vividly captures the range of responses that the miracle elicits. The various reactions reflect our own. We must step into the fresco and decide with whom we belong. Where are we in the picture? It is the question we must always ask when reading the Gospels. Jesus's disciples, grouped behind him, are spectators. One has an admonitory finger raised, but he himself seems unmoved by what is happening. After all, they have been trailing around after Jesus for some time and have seen this sort of thing before. They look a lukewarm lot. Some, one fears, might end up in the church in Laodicea (Revelation 3.14–22). We who have read the eleventh chapter of John's Gospel once or twice before may be in the same boat.

Most of the bystanders, the good folk of Bethany, are overwhelmed by astonishment. Giotto's treatment of them is a study of stupefaction. The response of one of them, however, is more complex. He leans towards Lazarus, staring at him, one hand to his chin, the other hand gesturing behind him towards Jesus. He is questioning what it all means. He seems poised between scepticism and a dawning awareness that perhaps something of eternal consequence is happening here. This, he feels, is more than another tuppeny wonder produced by one of the countless wandering miracle-workers who conjured a living from the credulous in the ancient world. It is as if he is almost persuaded to believe.

Two figures either ignore or simply do not notice what is going on. They are the two lads manhandling the huge stone that they have shifted from the mouth of the tomb. In his poem *Musée des Beaux Arts*, W. H. Auden drew attention to the fact that momentous events leave most of us unmoved. We simply carry on with our humdrum lives. So it is here.

The cemetery attendants have their job to do and they get on with it. In much the same way, no doubt, the gardener responsible for the plot where they buried Jesus, continued to weed and prune that Easter Day as on any other. For most of our contemporaries, neither the raising of Lazarus nor the resurrection it prefigures is of the slightest interest or importance.

'Jesus wept.' Why did he do that? Certainly he shared the grief of those lately bereaved of one dear to them. Certainly he mourned the passing of one who was his own friend too. Certainly he cried – as still he cries – for all those cruelly robbed of those they love. How things are makes Christ howl. Jesus indeed wept. But he wept not only because of what had happened. He wept because of what he had to do. He wept because he knew what would be in store for Lazarus because of the miracle he was about to perform. We look at Giotto's depiction of Lazarus and we hear the words of Lear on his cold lips – 'You do me wrong to take me out of the grave.' The raising of Lazarus signifies that Jesus is the Resurrection and the Life. The sign prefigures the raising of Jesus and of all who are his. It floods our hearts with hope. As Ezekiel learned, bones can live. But for this one obscure resident of Bethany to be restored to mortal life only to suffer yet again the tiresome business of dying is a very mixed blessing. No wonder Giotto's Lazarus looks peeved.

Sylvia Plath did not think Lazarus was glad to be back. In her poem 'Lady Lazarus', she imagines how irritated he must have been as the crowds milled round his grave, chomping on their peanuts, struggling to catch a glimpse of him.

Two other figures call for our attention in Giotto's fresco. They are the two Marys who kneel before Jesus. Are they prostrate in praise and thanksgiving for what he has done, recognizing in him the one who holds the keys of life and death, theirs as well as Lazarus's? Or has Giotto 'freeze-framed' this detail, so that what we are seeing is the sisters still pleading with Jesus for what they scarcely dare to name? Giotto is an artist and so he does not tell us. His sublime picture, like what it depicts and like the greater narrative of which it is a part, is a gift for each of us to unwrap and to make of it what we will.

In these reflections, I have drawn on a commentary on the frescoes of the Arena Chapel by my cousin, the art historian Brian Bishop, to whom I am grateful.

YEAR B

Jeremiah 31.31–34; Hebrews 5.5–10; John 12.20–33

LIFTED UP FROM THE EARTH

We need to go back to the previous verse in John's Gospel. The religious authorities have failed to rein in Jesus. They voice their anger and frustration. 'There's nothing we can do. The world has gone after him'

(John 12.19). By 'the world', they mean an awful lot of people. But in this Gospel words spoken often carry a greater weight than the speakers intend. 'The world' here is the world God so loved – the whole wide world held in wounded hands.

Even as the exasperated Pharisees speak, representatives of this wider world are on their way to Jesus. A group of 'Greeks' ask to see him. Did they get to meet him? We're not told; we can only hope so. What matters for John is that here for the first time Gentiles too are asking for Jesus. It is one of several sudden dramatic twists in John's account of Jesus by which he reveals the universality of his mission. Another such moment is when Jesus, expelled from the temple by the Dean and Chapter, goes out to suffering humanity. The light that leaves the temple comes to one born blind (John 8, 9).

The Greeks' request to see Jesus is the turning point of John's Gospel. (In the other Gospels Peter's recognition of Jesus as Messiah at Caesarea Philippi has the same pivotal significance.) 'Some Greeks', John curtly calls them. That's all. We know nothing about them, yet they are all humanity, their simple petition articulating humankind's ancient aching longing for some hope beyond the passing show of things.

The Jesus of John's Gospel has been waiting for these Greeks – perhaps, in his humanness, dreading their appearance, because their request means that his 'hour' has come. It is a crucial moment – literally 'crucial', for the hour now upon him is the hour when he must be 'glorified' by his death.

In a series of sayings familiar to us from the synoptic Gospels, John makes clear what manner of 'glory' it is which awaits both Jesus and his followers. Lest we should think too lightly of the cost, John takes us to Gethsemane. This Gethsemane is not a garden on the Mount of Olives, though John echoes what the other Gospel writers say happened there. It is, rather, the Gethsemane of the spirit, the dark night when we plead to be spared what the next day holds. The voice from heaven recalls Jesus's baptism, at which he first shouldered the cross, now so terribly near. Some bystanders hear thunder. Some hear an angel. John's account is curiously splintered. The dark night of the soul of Jesus is glimpsed as if by lightning – as if we could ever see it any more clearly.

'Now is the judgement . . .' 'Now this world's ruler is driven out . . .' The repeated 'nows' are hammer blows, as if already driving in the nails to be used at Calvary. The cross is both judgement and victory. The judgement is the sentence I pass on myself, by my embracing the cross or by my refusing it. The victory is the dethronement of the old enemy. (In the theology of the New Testament, Satan has lost an empire but not – not just yet – a role.)

So we come to what I find – forgive the personal note – the most memorable words in the New Testament. 'And I, if I am lifted up from the earth, will draw all people to myself.' If in some residual sense I am still a Christian, if I draw back from the abyss of total scepticism, it is because I believe that a certain Jesus Bar-Joseph once said something like this, and that, in doing so, he was moved, not by megalomania, but by divinity.

To be 'lifted up' in John can mean more than crucifixion. Jesus's 'lifting up' is his threefold exaltation from the earth, the single sequence of his death, resurrection, and ascension. But here, so that the contradiction will be absolute, John insists that Jesus, still in his soul's Gethsemane, sees no further than the cross.

In 1850 Søren Kierkegaard published an extended meditation on these words, entitled *Seven Christian Expositions*. He included them in his *Training in Christianity* (for which he proposed the sub-title *An Endeavour to Introduce Christianity into Christendom*). All subsequent commentary on John 12.32 is merely footnote. Kierkegaard insists that we understand who it is who speaks these words. 'This illegitimate child whom the race refused to recognise' – it is he who draws all to himself. The great paradox which moves Kierkegaard is that there should be 'such a word from one so humbled'. The one who will draw all to himself is 'the one who was despised, mocked, derided, spat upon'. That one so repugnant should be so compelling is an absurd idea. But, for Kierkegaard, the truth that compels is not an idea to be upheld by argument. Compelling truth is 'existential' truth, the truth we experience in the commitment of faith. 'Hence one sees what a monstrous error it is to impart Christianity by lecturing.'

Or by preaching?

YEAR C

Isaiah 43.16–21; Philippians 3.4b–14; John 12.1–8

CHRIST'S BODY AND THE WORLD'S POOR

Joseph Fletcher's *Situation Ethics* was first published over forty years ago (SCM, 1966). The book fired an argument that rages today as fiercely as ever. Fletcher argued that *agape* love, the only norm for Christian ethics, should be prudent and calculating. According to Fletcher, in any situation where a moral decision must be made, love asks, 'What will do the most good?' Fletcher was appalled by what we read as the Gospel this Sunday, the story of how Mary, the sister of Martha and Lazarus, lavished on Jesus a gift that would have cost a working man a year's wages. Fletcher thought that Judas Iscariot was absolutely right, that the ointment with which Mary anointed Jesus should have been sold and the proceeds given to the poor. 'Love', says Fletcher, 'must work in coalition with utilitarian distribution.' Judas was right. Jesus was wrong – if, that is, he ever said, 'You always have the poor with you,' which Fletcher doubted.

How are we to understand this story? The problem is as old as the New Testament. A sure sign that the authors and editors of the Gospels simply did not know what to make of the tradition of a woman publicly anointing Jesus with costly ointment is that their record of it is so confused and complicated. John's version of events closely reflects Matthew and Mark's account of how an unnamed woman anointed Jesus's head at the house of 'Simon the Leper' (Matthew 26.6–13; Mark 14.3–9). Luke has his own account of what happened in the house of a *Pharisee* called Simon. (Is this a quite separate incident? Who knows?) Luke writes – with an almost erotic *frisson* – of how a woman, who was 'a sinner', anointed and kissed Jesus's feet, bathing them with her tears and wiping them with her hair (Luke 7.36–50).

This week we must stay with John's version of what happened and not duck the accusation that using a year's salary to purchase perfume – even out of devotion to Jesus – is money misspent. Reginald Heber asks,

> Shall we not yield Him, in costly devotion
> Odours of Edom and offerings divine,
> Gems of the mountain and pearls of the ocean,
> Myrrh from the forest and gold from the mine?

Heber's answer to his own question is 'No, we shall not.'

> Vainly we offer each ample oblation,
> Vainly with gifts would His favor secure.
> Richer by far is the heart's adoration;
> Dearer to God are the prayers of the poor.

If we changed just two or three words of Heber's hymn and sang, 'Dearer to God are our gifts to the poor' we would have this eminent Victorian divine agreeing with Judas Iscariot and Joseph Fletcher.

No doubt Mary worshipped Jesus, but worship and how much should be spent on worship are not the issue here. Whatever else this story means, it cannot be used to sanction huge sums of money being spent on church buildings, for example. Such extravagance may or may not be justifiable, but, if it is, it must be on other grounds, not on the basis of the Gospel we read at Passiontide, as the concluding drama of the divine impoverishment begins.

Behind all these stories is another and altogether different question. 'What is to be done with the body of Jesus?' Here John echoes Matthew and Mark, though his Greek text is very difficult. (Notice the dinky little brackets in the New International Version of John 12.7 around the words the translators have to add so that the verse makes sense.) The evangelists are concerned that the body of Jesus should be treated reverently. John tells us that Jesus's body was anointed at his burial (19.39–40). It is that anointing which is foreshadowed – his death is now very near – by what Mary does.

The story, then, turns out to be all about bodies, Jesus's body and, by implication and inclusion, our bodies. We disapprove of the contemporary cult of the body beautiful, but apparently bodies do matter, not least dead ones.

And what of the poor who might have benefited from the cash spent on all that the perfume? Sydney Carter, who saw far more deeply into this story than did Joseph Fletcher, answers Judas's accusation.

Said Judas to Mary, 'Now what will you do
With your ointment so rich and so rare?'
'I'll pour it all over the feet of the Lord
And I'll wipe it away with my hair.'

Jesus does not spurn her gift. That gift anticipates not only his own anointing, but also the touch by which his wracked and emaciated body may still be tended.

'The poor of the world are my body', he said,
'To the end of the world they shall be;
The bread and the blankets you give to the poor
You'll find you have given to me,' he said,
'You'll find you have given to me.'

Palm Sunday

YEAR A

Isaiah 50.4–9a; Philippians 2.5–11; Matthew 26.14–27.66 or 27.11–54

THE SILENCE OF THE LAMB

The film opened 'to rapturous acclaim across the western world'. 'It has been a phenomenal box office smash-hit.' So says the slip-case which the DVD comes in. This is not the latest Hollywood blockbuster, nor is it the latest James Bond or Harry Potter. It is a documentary, nineteen years in the making and nearly three hours long, recording life inside the monastery of the Grande Chartreuse high in the French Alps. Here the monks pass their days, indeed their whole lives, almost entirely in silence. The film is largely silent too, apart from the chants we hear from the great abbey church. In its English version the film is entitled *Into Great Silence*.

As we approach the cross we enter, with Jesus, 'into great silence'.

Our readings interpret the passion of Jesus as a fulfilment of the role of 'the servant', about whom the anonymous prophet speaks whose oracles form the later chapters of our book of Isaiah. We hear the servant tell us that God gave him 'a teacher's tongue' and that he knows how 'to sustain the weary with a word'. From the day of his baptism to the hour of his arrest 'the common people heard Jesus gladly' (Mark 12.37) and many were the weary whom he consoled by the timely word.

But it is not in his speech but in his silence that Jesus is most like the promised servant. 'He was oppressed and afflicted, yet he did not open his mouth; he was led like a lamb to the slaughter, and as sheep before her shearers is dumb, so he did not open his mouth' (Isaiah 53.7). We recognize in this silent figure the one we know as Jesus of Nazareth.

Matthew's passion narrative, closely following that of Mark, is a study of 'the silence of the Lamb'. Jesus is silent before those who accuse him and torture him. He is silent before the orchestrated demands of the crowd for his death. And, after the briefest of exchanges, he is silent before Pontius Pilate. 'Are you the King of the Jews?' ask Pilate. 'So you say,' says Jesus. Pilate must decide for himself – as we must –

who he is. Then Jesus says no more, so that Pilate wonders, as well he might.

According to Mark, the earliest Gospel, the silence of Christ crucified is broken only by one terrible utterance, 'My God, my God, why have you forsaken me?' (Mark 15.34) So vividly is this cry recalled, that the very Aramaic in which it was uttered is remembered. Matthew too has just this one cry of dereliction. To be sure, the other Gospels record other sayings from the cross. According to Luke, Jesus prays for our forgiveness, because we didn't know what we were doing. He promises paradise to the penitent thief. As he dies, he commends his spirit to his father (Luke 23.34, 43, 46). John too has three sayings. Jesus commends his mother to his beloved disciple. He cries 'I thirst' and, at the last, triumphantly, 'It is finished' (John 19.26–7, 28, 30). We cling to these words and it is to our profit that we do so. But having said them, Jesus speaks no more. The great silence is now unbroken. And into that silence, the silence the other side of utterance, we must enter.

There are two types of Christianity – the talkative and the taciturn. There is the Christianity which goes on and on and there is the Christianity which shuts up. Talkative Christianity delights in argument. Talkative Christianity proves the existence of God. Talkative Christianity gives you reasons, reasons for believing in the virgin birth, in the resurrection, in life after death. Talkative Christianity tries to explain everything. It even tries to explain how a loving and powerful God can permit the innocent to suffer.

Taciturn Christianity respects the mystery of things. We try, as try we must, to dispel confusion, superstition, and misunderstanding. But the enigma of it all only deepens. Taciturn Christianity does not always try to explain, but simply watches and waits beneath the cross, echoing in its own heart the anguished 'Why?' of the one who hangs there. Taciturn Christianity reaches into the great silence of Christ crucified. That is the vocation of the monk and nun committed to the silent quest for God, knowing that only where words cease is God to be found. The rest of us, whose misfortune it is not to live in a monastery, must seek whatever silence we can salvage from the clamour of our days.

Where is silence to be found? Alas, rarely in church. In church we are either singing or someone is talking loudly – to us or to God. But the silence that eludes us in church can sometimes still be found in churches. It survives in the church that is locked between services. It is worth hunting down who has the key.

PALM SUNDAY

YEAR B

Isaiah 50.4–9a; Philippians 2.5–11; Mark 14.1 — 15.47 or Mark 15.1–39 (40–47)

PILATE WONDERS

At the passion of Jesus some jeer, some weep, some pass by. But Pilate wonders.

'To Pilate's astonishment, Jesus made no further reply.' Such translations miss Mark's emphasis. What Mark says is that, when Jesus stays silent, Pilate 'wondered'. There's more to Pilate's attitude than amazement that Jesus doesn't try to defend himself. We read, not that Pilate wondered *at* this or that, but simply that he *wondered* – period. Scholars who go train-spotting at weekends tell us that the word 'wonder' and its cognates (to be 'amazed' or 'astonished', and so on) occur thirty-two times in Mark's Gospel. 'Mark uses wonder with an intensity, frequency and mystery that surpasses the other synoptics' (*The Motif of Wonder in the Gospel of Mark*, Timothy Dwyer, Sheffield Academic Press, 1996).

The emphasis on wonder in Mark is not, as we're sometimes told, another example of the naïve breathlessness of his style. Nor is wonder dismissed by Mark as a response far short of faith and understanding. Wonder in Mark is a response to the breaking-in of the rule of God to save and to restore. Wonder may not amount to discipleship – not even the so-called *Acts of Pilate* claim that Pilate became a Christian – but it is nevertheless an indispensable prerequisite of it. (*The Acts of Pilate*, dating from the fourth century, is one of the many fanciful pieces of creative writing that make up what is sometimes called 'the New Testament Apocrypha'. These documents purport to tell you what the Gospels leave out. *The Acts of Pilate* is an amplified account – though its amplifications are historically worthless – of the trial, crucifixion, and resurrection of Jesus.)

Only once elsewhere in Mark are people left wondering, simply wondering, as Pilate is. A recovered demoniac tells the people of Decapolis what Jesus has done for him. And everyone, we read, 'wondered' (Mark 5.20). The point about Decapolis was that it was abroad, Gentile territory. In the Gospels, the Gentiles are seen as more responsive to the words and works of Jesus than his co-religionists. The Roman Governor Pilate is one with those of Decapolis, as he is with those of every age whose minds are not made up, whose certainties are never so settled that they cannot be called in question, who do not wear their religion like a suit of armour to ward off the wondrous.

Pilate wonders. Does he sense that he is the instrument of a necessity yet more awful than that of maintaining public order in a dangerously volatile territory? The Coptic Church commemorates Pontius Pilate as a saint. Perhaps Pilate should be the patron saint of all who, when contemplating the passion of Jesus, are stirred to wonder – even if to nothing more. To be sure, Pilate hands Jesus over to be crucified, but so do we all. So do I, a dozen times a day.

There are others from far away who, caught up in these events, sense that this is more than just another public execution. Clearly, Simon of Cyrene's sons were known to Mark's first readers, presumably because they were Christians. We do not know how they came to Christian faith. Perhaps they were moved by their father's testimony, his story of how, having once been forced to take up the cross, he chose not to lay it down.

The Roman Governor wonders. So, it seems, does the Roman centurion. The wording of his testimony is famously ambiguous. Did he say that Jesus was '*a* son of God', a turn of phrase which could mean no more than 'something of a hero'? Or was this the confession of one who, at the foot of the cross, comes to the faith proclaimed in the first verse of the Gospel, that here is *the* Son of God? Mark, like his master, leaves us to make up our own minds.

According to some Greek texts, the centurion is moved to testify as he does, by what he heard as well as by what he saw. The one 'word from the cross' which Mark and Matthew record – it's too much for Luke and John – is the cry of dereliction, 'My God, my God, why have you forsaken me?' The words are from Psalm 22. We must not tone down the offence of them by claiming that Jesus had the whole of the psalm in mind, including its triumphant ending. Nor should we milk the repeated 'My God' for evidence that Jesus's sense of relationship with God remained unbroken. It is a cry of utter, hopeless, abandonment.

What is really going on here? Once, long ago, I had to teach 'the doctrine of the atonement' to aspiring clergy. Poor things, they had to mug up – and later, under examination, cough up – the various theories by which theologians have tried to explain what is sometimes called 'the work of Christ'. Mark, in sharp contrast to those who lecture or preach about the atonement, does not tell us what it all means. His account of the death of Jesus is as sparing of homiletic commentary as it is of the grisly details of what's done to you when you're crucified. In the end the only way to find out what the story means – 'let the reader understand' (Mark 13.14) – is to read it again. And then, like Simon, to shoulder the cross.

YEAR C

Isaiah 50.4–9a; Philippians 2.5–11; Luke 22.14—23.56 or Luke 23.1–49

THE IMPENITENT THIEF

Luke's Gospel is good news for those who feel bad. His narrative is crowded with characters who are ashamed of themselves. There is the weeping sex worker (Luke 7.36–50), Zacchaeus hiding in his tree (Luke 19.1–10), and the spendthrift son (Luke 15.11–32). These and others like them, the least deserving and the last you'd expect, discover that they have been loved all along. Last in Luke's long gallery of cameo studies of those who have lost all hope for themselves is 'the penitent thief', crucified alongside Jesus. About to die, he has no time left to put his house in order or to make any reparation to those he has injured. Yet when he asks to be remembered, he is promised paradise. Heaven is promised to the undeserving. That promise is our only hope.

But just a moment. There is someone else there still less deserving. Perhaps it's because I think that Carol Reed's *The Third Man* is the greatest film ever made that that I am fascinated by 'the third man' in our story, the criminal who doesn't ask to be remembered. What about him? He too turns to Jesus and, in his own bitter and sarcastic way, prays to him. I identify with 'the third man', for I too have said to Jesus, 'If you are who you claim to be, then for all our sake's do something!' Is there any hope for him? Is there any hope for others of us whose prayers are sometimes as angry and impious as his?

If the penitent thief was promised paradise because he was penitent then there's no hope for the impenitent. You don't need a degree in theology to work that out. But if he is promised paradise, as Luke seems to believe, because God accepts the least deserving, then there's a glimmer of hope for the impenitent thief too – and for me. If God's grace, displayed on Christ's cross, is truly for the last ones you'd expect, if it is not conditional on the quality of my contrition, then there is reason for me not to despair.

It all depends on how we understand forgiveness. The dying Voltaire is famously reported to have said, 'God will forgive. It's his job.' That is not how Luke sees the divine mercy made crucified flesh. Voltaire's remark takes account neither of what forgiveness costs, nor what forgiveness demands.

It is far easier to discuss God's forgiveness than to offer forgiveness ourselves. We need to ponder what the Church of England priest Julie Nicholson said in the aftermath of the 7th July 2005 bombings in London, in which her daughter was killed. She told us that she found more comfort in literature than in liturgy. She sent us to back to Dostoevsky's *The Brothers Karamazov*, to a passage we must always turn to when we are minded to chatter lightly about forgiveness – perhaps, from a pulpit this Good Friday, with the manuscript of our meditation resting softly on its cushion. Ivan Karamazov puts to his devout brother Alyosha the case of the sadistic landowner who throws the child of one of his serfs to his dogs. 'I don't want the child's mother to embrace the torturer . . . The sufferings of her tortured child she has no right to forgive.'

Already from the cross Jesus has sought forgiveness for the undeserving. He has prayed, 'Father, forgive them; for they do not know what they are doing.' Some early Greek texts do not have these words. But the words must belong to the earliest tradition of the sayings of Jesus, not only because they are in tune with the whole tenor of Luke's theology, but because it is inconceivable that such a prayer was made up. Why did those early Christian editors leave it out? Better to ask why *we* might have left it out, why we might have preferred this word from the cross unsaid. Perhaps this prayer troubles us for the same reason that we find another prayer sticking in our throat. 'As we forgive . . .' as we say – as we find so hard to say.

'Father, into your hands I commend my spirit.' Whatever Jesus went through, at the end he found his Father there. The late Alexander Solzhenitsyn wrote of his experience as a prisoner in a Soviet labour camp. He told how everything which normally gives life meaning was taken from him. He was robbed of his name and was known only by a number. Close to starving, he was made to work as a slave. He was forbidden books or letters. He was stripped of all that lends a human being dignity and hope. Solzhenitsyn told how he was brought, as it were, to the bottom of an abyss. Then he adds, 'I felt it firm under my feet.'

'If I make my bed in hell,' says the Psalmist, 'behold thou art there' (Psalm 139.8) That was Christ's journey, his inner crucifixion. So he finds, as have countless of his crucified disciples across the centuries since, that the ground of being is firm beneath him, that 'underneath are the everlasting arms' (Deuteronomy 33.27).

Easter Day

YEAR A

Acts 10.34–43 or Jeremiah 31.1–6; Colossians 3.1–4 or Acts 10.34–43; John 20.1–18 or Matthew 28.1–10

A NEW VISION OF HUMAN DESTINY

On 16 February 1977 Archbishop Janani Luwum of Uganda had a meeting with President Idi Amin, whose murderous regime he had outspokenly opposed. After the meeting the Archbishop was driven away, along with two government ministers. Uganda Radio announced that the three of them had been arrested and the following morning it was stated that they had died in a car accident. In fact they had been shot on the orders of Amin. A funeral service planned for the following Sunday was forbidden by the government, and the Archbishop's body was not released. Nevertheless thousands gathered at the cathedral on Namirembe Hill and the service went ahead around an open grave. Standing over the empty grave, Luwum's successor, Archbishop Wani, repeated the message of the angel which we hear this Easter Day: 'He is not here. He is risen!'

'He is not here. He is risen!' And, according to Matthew, the angel adds, 'He is going ahead of you to Galilee.' It is as it was. It is as it was when they set out together, when 'Jesus went before them and they were amazed; and as they followed, they were afraid' (Mark 10.32). The risen Jesus is ahead of us and we must set out after him. The quest for the risen Jesus, like the quest of the historical Jesus, never ceases. Those who cheerfully claim to have 'found Jesus' sooner or later discover that they have found someone else. So we do not haunt his tomb, for example by dwelling endlessly on the question of 'what actually happened'. The resurrection is not proved by pick and shovel. Certainly something wonderful happened on the first Easter Day. But faith in the resurrection is not insistence on a particular account of what took place. To seek the risen Christ is 'to go ahead to Galilee'.

In a word – in the most precious of Christian words – it is to live in *hope*.

It is now over forty-five years since Jürgen Moltmann's thrilling *Theology of Hope* was published (SCM Press, new edition, 2002). It is one of the towering theological statements of the twentieth century. In this great work Moltmann argues that faith in the resurrection implies a new vision of human destiny. We know from Moltmann's autobiography that, given what he went through in the Second World War, he of all people might have been expected to cherish little hope for humanity (*A Broad Place: An Autobiography*, Fortress Press, 2007).

Yet his is not an escapist faith, the dream of 'a happy land, far, far away'. Not at all. 'Christian hope', Moltmann writes, 'sees in the resurrection of Christ not the eternity of heaven, but the future of the very earth on which his cross stands.' 'Those who hope in Christ,' he continues, 'can no longer put up with reality as it is. Peace with God means conflict with the world, for the goad of the promised future stabs inexorably into the flesh of every unfulfilled present.'

What is this 'promised future'? We stay with Moltmann a moment more. He insists that we turn to the prophets of what – using our insensitive shorthand – we call 'the Old Testament'. 'In the Gospel,' he states, 'the Old Testament history of promise finds more than a fulfillment that does away with it; it finds its future. All the promises of God in him are yea and in him Amen (2 Corinthians 1.20).' For example, not a jot or tittle of Jeremiah 31.1–6, our appointed Old Testament reading, shall pass away until all is accomplished. The resurrection of Jesus renews the prophet's specific promises and the Church is committed to their fulfilment. So by the light of Easter Day we seek the peace of Jerusalem and the Holy Land.

Whether or not Janani Luwum had read Jürgen Moltmann, he understood that belief in the risen Christ entails a commitment to a better world, to the new social order that Jesus called 'the Kingdom of God'. Such a commitment means a costly confrontation with the powers that be. For Janani Luwum it meant martyrdom.

As they gathered round the empty grave of their archbishop, crucified and risen, they sang one hymn over and over again.

Daily, daily, sing the praises
Of the city God hath made;
In the beauteous fields of Eden
Its foundation stones are laid.

O that I had wings of angels,
Here to spread and heavenward fly!
I would seek the gates of Zion,
Far beyond the starry sky.
(Sabine Baring-Gould)

This was the song 'the martyrs of Uganda' sang, the young men, commemorated in the Anglican calendar, who, some ninety years before Amin's tyrannous presidency, had borne witness before another tyrant and whose blood was the seed of the Ugandan church. They sang of another world, better than this one at its best. That world too is promised and Moltmann will forgive us for sometimes pining for it. But – one world at a time – it is in this one, this Easter, that we must seek the risen Christ.

YEAR B

Acts 10.34–43 or Isaiah 25.6–9; 1 Corinthians 15.1–11 or Acts 10.34–43; John 20.1–18 or Mark 16.1–8

THE GOSPEL FOR POST-MODERNISTS

Mark is the Gospel for post-modernists. Post-modernists are people who are suspicious of theories of everything. They say that you should live with loose ends, not try to tie them up. Post-modernists are distrustful of closure. There's always more to be said.

Mark's Gospel is open-ended. As such it is a tract for our post-modernist times. It's up to us what we make Mark, much more so than is the case with the other three Gospels. The final words of Mark's Gospel must constitute the most extraordinary last line of any sacred text ever written. 'They said nothing to anyone, for they were afraid.' Mark's little book is entitled 'the good news of Jesus Christ'. And how does it end? With a band of cheerful, enthusiastic, confident disciples, fired with a keen sense of mission and a clear strategic vision, setting off to win the world for Christ? Not at all. Instead we have a group of terrified and speechless women, fleeing for their lives. The abruptness of Mark's final words is almost impossible to capture in translation. It is as if he breaks off in mid-sentence. Many have supposed that the original ending of the Gospel must have been suppressed or lost. From an early date attempts have been made, by more or less clumsy prosthetic procedures, to supply what Mark omits, a more rounded and satisfying conclusion.

We must disregard these later postscripts and stay with Mark's original text. Mark's abrupt ending is far from accidental. By falling silent with the women, Mark maintains to the last the reticence which has been characteristic of his style throughout and which has faithfully reflected all that has been so enigmatic about the central figure of his story. But there's much more to the 'open-endedness' of Mark's Gospel. It is for the best of reasons that Mark denies us the closure his well-meaning sub-editors supply. Mark's purpose is not to *record* the resurrection but leave open to his readers the possibility of *experiencing* the resurrection.

The evidence for the resurrection in Mark's account of the sequel to the events of Good Friday is equivocal. There is the empty tomb. There is the testimony of a young man in a white robe. (To almost every commentator, it is obvious that this young man was an angel. The inference is too easy, too comforting.) There is the promise of 'seeing' the lately crucified Jesus in Galilee. But many questions remain. Loose end abound.

Mark has told an unclosed story. That story continues, but not in the dubious appendices tacked on to his text by early editors. What happens next is for the reader to find out in his or her own story. This is how Mark's deliberately open-ended account works. Mark's story becomes my story. In a sense, the next instalment of a tale, left so tantalizingly open, is for me to write. Did Jesus rise from the dead? It is for me to find out in the continuance of Mark's unclosed narrative which is the ongoing narrative of my own Christian journey. Mark's story does not end. Rather, it runs on into the life-story of his readers. The only ending of this unfinished story that matters is its fulfilment in the life of the believer, the disciple who holds Mark's strange little book in his or her hands.

Mark's Gospel is 'an open book'. 'An Open Book' is the title of a lecture by Gabriel Josipovici (*Times Literary Supplememt*, 24 February 2006). His lecture, subtitled 'How the Bible places realism above consolation', is a study of how the Bible works. What Josipovici says of the Bible as a whole applies to Mark in particular. 'The Bible recognizes that in the end the only thing that can truly heal and console us is not the voice of consolation but reality.' The women are not comforted by what they encounter at the tomb. They are confronted by an utterly unexpected development which, stunned and fearful, they cannot grasp. To apprehend the reality of the resurrection will be the business of a lifetime – and longer.

Mark's Gospel closes on a perplexing note, on a note of terror rather than triumph, not because Mark doubts the resurrection, but because for him the resurrection belongs to the 'the mystery of the Kingdom of God', a mystery which does not dissolve with the morning mist, even if the morning is of Easter Day.

The disciples must be told that Jesus is going ahead of them. Again we recall the moment that only Mark mentions. 'Jesus was walking ahead of them; they were amazed and those who followed were afraid' (Mark 10.32). At Easter there is sometimes an all-too-cheerful and possessive 'Great to have you back' tone to our worship. It is wholly inappropriate. Jesus has already moved on. Who knows where he might be leading us? It's all very scary.

YEAR C

Acts 10.34–43 or Isaiah 65.17–25; 1 Corinthians 15.19–26 or Acts 10.34–43; John 20.1–18 or Luke 24.1–12

THE NOTE AND THE NEED OF WONDER

Luke's account of what happened early on Easter Day corresponds closely to Mark's. But Luke's story still has his own signature on it. Four typically Lucan touches and the chords they strike catch our attention: the Christian quest, the role of memory, the obtuseness of the male, and the note of wonder.

The angels – if that's who they were – ask the women why they are looking for the living among the dead. That question is surely put to all who spend much of their life looking for things, whether for lost car keys or for the meaning of life. The question is rhetorical and its import is obvious. Search where you are likely to find. Hunt for your keys in the trousers you were wearing yesterday, not in those you are wearing today. Look for the living among the breathing, not among the buried. Recently there has been much media-induced froth about yet another ossuary purportedly containing the bones of Jesus. Even if *per impossibile* it were shown conclusively that these were the remains of Jesus, that identification would not mean that Jesus had been found. For Jesus is not to be found among dry bones – not even his own. Neither the archaeologist's trowel nor any other scientific tool can prove – or for that matter disprove – the resurrection. Jesus, if he's around, is among the living – some would say most evidently among the marginalized –

where he is to be discovered, not by detached and disinterested investigation, but by commitment to his cause.

Mary Magdalene and the other women – so says Luke and only Luke – are told to remember what Jesus had said. The women are bewildered by what they have seen. The stone rolled back, the body gone – these are data which elude explanation. Or rather they invite several explanations, all equally implausible. By recalling the women to the words of Jesus, the angels offer them an interpretative framework, within which they can begin to make some sense of what otherwise is so baffling.

Our reading of the different accounts of what happened after Jesus died – and we only make the Christian claims less credible by glossing over those differences – leaves us as perplexed as were those women. We too need a framework to help us see what is going on. We too are sent back to what was said in Galilee. Though what we hear there is not entirely to our comfort. The explanation of what it all means, it seems, comes with a cost. There is no accounting for Easter that avoids all that has to be done.

Luke affirms the women's apostolic role as witnesses of the resurrection – as indeed its first witnesses – as do the other Gospel writers. Luke is the most unsparing of the four of the evangelists in his account of how dense the men were. He tells us that the male response to talk of an empty tomb was that it was all stuff and nonsense. The word Luke uses is a strong one – the root of it underlies our word 'delirium'. Luke's purblind men could not have been more condescending and dismissive of what the women had told them. It will not be the last time that women's witness will be thus belittled.

Not all the early manuscripts of the Gospels have Luke's reference to Peter running to the tomb. Some say that this detail is a later borrowing from John, where we have both Peter and 'the beloved disciple' hurrying there. That is to overlook the Lucan seal on the story. Luke says that Peter was 'amazed' – literally that 'he wondered to himself'. This is pure Luke. Right at the start they had 'wondered' what was going on when Zechariah spent so long in the temple (Luke 1.21) and when he named the son of his old age John (Luke 1.63). People 'wondered' at what the shepherds said (Luke 2.18) and Joseph and Mary 'wondered' at the song of Simeon (Luke 2.33). Those at the synagogue 'wondered' at Jesus's first sermon (Luke 4.22) and his disciples 'wondered' at his power to calm the sea (Luke 8.25). So, with Luke, we could go on.

So we should go on. George MacDonald said that 'to cease to wonder is to fall plumb-down from the childlike to the commonplace. Our nature cannot be at home among things that are not wonderful to us'

(*The Hope of the Gospel*, 1892). There is a risk at Easter that by affirming as vigorously as we do our belief in the resurrection we drain this day of its mystery. 'Up from the grave,' we bellow before setting off home for a huge lunch. Perhaps Peter too, as the New Revised Standard Version has it, 'went home'. Peter, though, may have gone without lunch. After all, he had a lot on his mind.

The Second Sunday of Easter

YEAR A

Acts 2.14a, 22–32; 1 Peter 1.3–9; John 20.19–31

INDOORS AND OUTDOORS

Towards the end of his life Cardinal John Henry Newman said to Bishop William Ullathorne of Birmingham, 'I have been indoors all my life, whilst you have battled for the Church in the world.' (For a long time Bishop Ullathorne, who had been a missionary in Australia, kept a baked human head in a bandbox over his bed. He had intended to give it to the monks at Downside, but the maggots got to it first. So far as we know, the fastidious Newman kept no such trophies.) In his great book *The Convert Cardinals* (John Murray, 1993), David Newsome contrasts the lives of Newman and Henry Manning. The contrast is again between the 'indoor life' of the bookish Newman and the 'outdoor life' of a churchman engaged with the world's business and the world's needs, notably in Manning's case, with the education of the poor.

Our readings this Sunday confront us with the choice of leading 'indoor lives' or 'outdoor lives'. The disciples on Easter Day are indoors, literally indoors, locked indoors, fearful of what would face them if they stepped outside. Then Jesus appears among them. The risen Jesus can no more be kept out of a locked room than he can be contained in a sealed tomb. Jesus turns the disciples out of their 'safe house'. He sends them out of doors, just as he himself had left the safest of homes to lodge among us (John 1.14; Philippians 2.5–11). Jesus does not remove the dangers which, so the disciples fear, are awaiting them outside but he equips them to meet those dangers. John leaves it to Luke in his Acts of the Apostles to tell us how that story unfolds, a tale of 'outdoor life' if ever there was one. In his open-air sermon on the day of Pentecost – we hear a snatch of it this Sunday – Peter is already courting the danger that will accompany his every step now that his risen Lord has called him out of hiding.

The disciples are equipped for their hazardous outdoor life by the kiss of peace, by the gift of the Spirit, and by the authority entrusted to them to forgive and 'retain' sins. 'Peace' is much more than the conventional greeting that is used by Hebrew and Arabic speakers to this day. It is peace 'not as the world gives' (John 14.27; 16.33). The promise is not of a quiet life. On the contrary, it is the courage to bear what will prove anything but a quiet life. The gift of the Spirit, imparted by the Lord's breath, is a new creation (Genesis 2.7). It is the breath that animates the slain (Ezekiel 37.9). The authority to forgive is given to the Christian community as stewards of the good news entrusted to it. The Church is to embody and express the divine forgiveness. As for the 'retaining' of sins, lest grace be counted cheap, we warn – first taking it to heart ourselves – that, while we must never despair of God's mercy, it is perilous to despise it.

We do well to read Sunday's familiar Gospel in the light of the Epistle, a thrilling text from I Peter. What does the resurrection offer for the outdoor life of the Christian believer? A 'living hope', certainly, but also 'all kinds of trials'. We rightly associate the cost and pain of discipleship with the cross. But the resurrection does not set us free from suffering. As a consequence of the resurrection, says Peter, we shall be tested as intensely as metal is by fire. It was because they were driven out of doors by the risen Christ and his Spirit that the disciples and the saints ended up on their various stakes, gibbets, racks, wheels, spikes, and gridirons. Had they stayed indoors they would have enjoyed a much safer life – and, many of them, a much longer one.

There is a paradox here, as there usually is when we are talking about Christianity. Many of us who apparently live 'outside lives' dwell inwardly in our own comfort zones. We live our more or less public lives, whether on international platforms (the Lambeth Conference?), the national stage (the General Synod?) or in the tiny theatres of our localities (the PCC?), but we never risk the costly exposure to which Christ calls us. By contrast, there are those who, to all appearances, lead 'indoor lives', those for example who spend their lives in universities or monasteries, who yet embrace in their hearts the afflictions of a broken world. We think of Thomas Merton or, for that matter, of Newman himself.

Wherever we live, whether in a cave in a desert, in an Oxbridge college, or in a noisy house on a busy street, the fundamental condition of the outdoor life is the acceptance of vulnerability. It is all to do, as Jesus had said long before Easter Day, with becoming a child.

YEAR B

Acts 4.32–35; 1 John 1.1—2.2; John 20.19–31

CLINGING ON AND LETTING GO

The risen Christ's first word is 'Peace'. We are often told that the peace of the Lord is the Hebrew 'Shalom', a term and a concept meaning much more than the absence of war. No doubt. But it is sensible in reading the Bible to ask first what the words *at least* mean. Peace *at least* means not fighting, whether physically or verbally. Jesus sets us lofty and distant goals, but he also requires us to begin with modest and immediate ones. A truce in the fratricidal household of God, for example, would be a good start.

Jesus 'breathed on' his disciples. It's what God did to Adam in the Garden of Eden (Genesis 2.7) and to an army of skeletons in a valley of dry bones (Ezekiel 37.1–10). Clearly John intends to depict the first Easter as the beginning of a new creation. This, as at the start, is the kiss of life. But we risk 'taming the text' by decoding it in this way, albeit correctly. Citing the Old Testament background illuminates the text but it can at the same time defuse it. Holy Scripture is not so easily mastered. I think of the sixth-formers to whom I once taught John's Gospel. They found the idea of Jesus breathing on his disciples bizarre and distasteful, just as they found John's language about consuming flesh and blood repugnant.

Clement of Alexandria famously said that John's Gospel is a 'spiritual gospel'. We see what he means, but in fact this book has more in it about bodies and what they're made of than the rest of the Gospels put together. My students' uninformed gut reaction to the text was more perceptive than the more knowledgeable one. They sensed immediately the force of the audacious image. It's all about intimacy, the nearness of the relationship the risen Jesus claims with his disciples. It is a proximity which Thomas and many others of us do not welcome.

The psychiatrist Frank Lake, whose influence on an earlier generation of Anglican clergy was so profound, recognized how our doubts about the resurrection of Jesus arise from our dread of intimacy. Frank loved John's Gospel, where Jesus displays such acute insight into the personality patterns of those who encounter him. 'He himself knew what was in everyone' (John 2.24). Frank liked to draw a contrast between the two most prominent figures in John's account of the resurrection. There is the 'hysterical' Mary Magdalene, desperate for love, fearful of rejection. Jesus has to say to her, 'Touch me not' – literally, 'stop clinging on to me' (John 20.17). She must be set free from her need to have Jesus always within reach.

By contrast, we have the 'schizoid' Thomas, who abhors any kind of intimacy, who dreads relationships with all their potential for pain, who shuns commitment. Thomas's difficulty is not a reluctance to let go but an incapacity to come close. So Jesus has to tell Thomas to do the very thing he forbids Mary to do. The crude physicality of what Jesus asks of Thomas shocks us. 'Put your hand *into* my side.' This story is not for the squeamish.

Frank Lake urged us to look at ourselves in the light of Thomas. Our doubts are often rooted far beneath the intellectual level at which we defend them. Something has gone badly wrong long ago and deep within. My scepticism may be my futile attempt to salve early emotional wounds which are still raw. I was rejected once too often. Now I will not commit myself to anyone.

Thomas is persuaded by the evidence of his own eyes. Jesus's last and sublime beatitude is on those who come after the final eye-witness is gone, on those who cannot have tangible evidence of the bodily resurrection of Jesus. 'Blessed are those who have not seen and yet have come to believe.' Our English versions struggle to capture the force of words which might almost be translated 'and yet have decided to believe'. The disciples have no advantage over us, we who were born too late to see the signs 'written in this book'. 'Blessed are those who have not seen.' If we really believed this beatitude we would not go on trying so hard, two millennia later, to produce the kind of evidence of the historicity of the resurrection that Thomas mistakenly craved for.

Another wise pastor who loved this Gospel was Alan Ecclestone. For him it was 'the book most needed to be read and prayed in the world today' (*The Scaffolding of the Spirit*, Darton, Longman & Todd, 1987). That is because it promises what Ecclestone called 'the closeness of Jesus'. Obsessed as we are about bodies and confused as we are about commitment, we need this most physical of gospels. Like Mary and Thomas, we need to learn when to hold on and when to let go.

YEAR C

Acts 5.27–32; Revelation 1.4–8; John 20.19–31

CHRISTIAN DOUBT

Thomas doubted, but so did they all. According to last Sunday's Gospel, all the disciples dismissed the women's tale of an empty tomb as nonsense (Luke 24.11). It was just Thomas's bad luck not to have been there when Jesus appeared to the others. But even if his doubts were no deeper than those of the rest, Thomas will always remain 'doubting Thomas'. And for those of us who find it all very difficult he will always be our patron saint.

Two Christian traditions have claimed that a measure of certainty is possible in matters of faith, the Catholic and the Evangelical. 'I never have had one doubt,' wrote John Henry Newman, reflecting on the 'perfect peace and contentment' he had enjoyed since his admission into 'the one fold of Christ'. Evangelicals make much – or they did in my day – of 'assurance'. 'Blessed assurance,' they sing, 'Jesus is mine.' The same evangelical confidence rings out in Edmond Budry's great hymn, 'Thine be the glory'. 'No more we doubt thee,' we sing and while we sing it we mean it.

The evangelical scholar Oz Guinness has written sensitively about doubt. 'The world of Christian faith', he writes, 'is a world where doubt is never far from faith's shoulder.' But the thrust of Guinness's argument is that the doubt hovering at faith's shoulder is no friend of faith. 'If we constantly doubt what we believe and always believe-yet-doubt,' he warns, 'we will be in danger of undermining our personal integrity, if not our stability.' (*God in the Dark: The Assurance of Faith beyond a Shadow of Doubt*, Crossway, 1996).

In both traditions, at least in their more uncompromising manifestations, doubt is seen as deeply damaging, both to our effectiveness in Christian mission and to our personal well-being.

There is a third way. From this perspective doubt is not the enemy of faith. Certainty is the enemy. A characteristic of this position is an understanding of integrity that is more true to how most of us tick than the viewpoint which regards doubt as dangerous.

The prophets of this third way were two poets, Tennyson in the nineteenth century and R. S. Thomas in the last. The profound insight of Tennyson's *In Memoriam* is that intellectual uncertainty and religious commitment are not incompatible. Doubt and faith can and do coexist.

Today we talk of 'the two integrities', our conflicting views on the ordination of women, which hold uneasy communion with one another in our fractured church. The psychological truth for many an individual, however, is that two integrities – if not several more – have to share houseroom in a single heart and mind. Tennyson knew that 'calm despair and wild unrest' can be 'tenants of a single breast'.

They challenged his integrity, of course. 'You tell me, doubt is devil born,' they said. Famously Tennyson replied in *In Memoriam*,

> There lives more faith in honest doubt,
> Believe me, than in half the creeds.

It is impossible to be certain, but it is possible, as Job did, to turn in the right direction.

> I stretch lame hands of faith, and grope,
> And gather dust and chaff, and call
> To what I feel is Lord of all,
> And faintly trust the larger hope.

If for Brother Lawrence, prayer was 'the practice of the presence of God', for the poet R. S. Thomas it was, you might say, 'the practice of the absence of God'. Prayer, for Thomas, was a matter of letting go and waiting, but not waiting for answers, for any answer that satisfied would be wrong. To pray is to enter a void. Prayer must always be like that, for to pray to an imaginable deity would be idolatry.

Thomas – the disciple, not the poet – is granted, as were the others, the opportunity to see and touch the risen Lord. Jesus says to him, 'Be unbelieving no longer.' (Thus, correctly, the Revised English Bible. The New Revised Standard Version's 'Do not doubt' is a mistranslation.) This is an invitation to trust and obey, not a promise of certainty. Thomas's response is to worship the risen Lord. Does that conclude his doubting? Possibly, but if people are half as complicated creatures as they seem to be, maybe, on many a Monday morning, he is still 'doubting Thomas'.

What would our 'doubting Thomas' make of Richard Dawkins' book *The God Delusion*? Perhaps he'd suggest we read another book too, *God's Credentials* by Philip Blair (K. & M. Books, 2007). (Books about God are none the worse if they're not written by professional theologians. Blair is a professor of English at the University of Balamand in the Lebanon.) *God's Credentials* is an arresting title.

Credentials are what you must produce to show that you are who you claim to be. Blair's thesis is that the divine credentials are the life, death and resurrection of Jesus of Nazareth. In the light of Sunday's Gospel we can be more specific. God's credentials are the wounds of Jesus.

The Third Sunday of Easter

YEAR A

Acts 2.14a, 36–41; 1 Peter 1.17–23; Luke 24.13–35

THE THIRD WHO WALKS ALWAYS BESIDE YOU

The road to Emmaus is not on any map. It is whatever road we take today. For some it will be the 8.17 from Surbiton and the day in the City. For others it will be the trail round Tesco's, the dry-cleaners, the doctor's, and the school-gate. The Emmaus road may be the first-class flight and the conference in New York. Or it may be the slow painful path from bed to tall chair and the drawn-out hours by the window. On every Emmaus road there is the possibility of a stranger falling in step with us. We may or may not recognize him.

Sir Ernest Shackleton's Emmaus road was the wild Antarctic seas and the peaks and glaciers of the island of South Georgia. The crew of his ship *The Endurance* was stranded on Elephant Island. Shackleton set out in a small lifeboat for the coast of South Georgia, eight hundred miles away. He and his two companions traversed the island's unmapped mountains to reach a remote whaling station. There Shackleton reported the plight of his crew and mounted the expedition that would rescue them. The great explorer wrote of that journey,

When I look back at those days I have no doubt that Providence guided us, not only across those snowfields, but across the storm-white sea that separated Elephant Island from our landing-place on South Georgia. I know that during that long and racking march of thirty-six hours over the unnamed mountains and glaciers of South Georgia it seemed to me often that we were four, not three. I said nothing to my companions on the point, but afterwards Worsley said to me, 'Boss, I had a curious feeling on the march that there was another person with us.' (*South*, 1919)

T. S. Eliot, moved by Shackleton's story with its echoes of the Emmaus journey, wrote in *The Waste Land* of a mysterious stranger who sometimes keeps travellers company. There are two together on a 'white road' and a third falls in with them. 'The white road' is both the path across the polar snows and the Palestinian road, its dust dazzling white in the high sun, which the two friends walked that first Easter Day.

Shackleton himself wrote of 'the dearth of human words, the roughness of mortal speech' to speak of such an experience. The evangelists too, so exact – albeit so laconic – in their accounts of the crucifixion, struggle with that same 'dearth of human words' to account for the events of the first Easter Day and to describe the disciples' encounters with the risen Christ.

'The Emmaus experience' can be overwhelming, revelatory and life-transforming, as it was for Cleopas and his friend. They learned that day that redemption is won only at great cost, a truth written in their Scriptures as it is woven into the fabric of the human condition. They learned that the Messiah had to suffer, that – as our Epistle puts it – 'he was destined before the foundation of the world' to do so. They learned that the Lord is palpably present when bread is taken, blessed, broken, and given. Above all they learned, when 'he vanished from their sight', that he does not leave those who for 'a little while' no longer see him (John 16.16).

But the Emmaus experience can be less straightforward. In one of the most extraordinary pictures of a Gospel scene ever painted, the artist Velazquez suggests that for someone in the house at Emmaus what took place there was altogether more equivocal. Velazquez realizes – what occurs to few readers of Luke – that someone must have cooked the supper. He depicts a woman in the kitchen, pausing in her work to listen to the conversation going on at the table in the adjacent room. Through a serving hatch, or possibly in a mirror, we can just glimpse the meal in progress. The woman – so sad, so bemused, so weary – looks as if she is the kitchen-maid. (For Velazquez, a seventeenth-century Spaniard, she is a black African.) Of course it might have been the host's wife who was left out of the conversation to get on with the kitchen chores. Whoever she was, it seems unlikely that Jesus was made known to her in the breaking of the bread she had baked.

Unlikely – but not impossible. The poet Denise Levertov thinks that the woman in the kitchen is a servant. In her poem 'The Servant-girl of Emmaus', she imagines this kitchen-maid listening to the stranger – and then noticing that there is a light about him. It is an intriguing idea. If there is any truth in it, she would not have been the only woman that Easter to have been quicker on the uptake than the men around.

YEAR B

Acts 3.12–19; 1 John 3.1–7; Luke 24.36b–48

DISBELIEVING FOR JOY

The disciples 'believed not for joy'. Long ago in Latvia, long before the fall of communism, I witnessed this disbelieving joy. We were tourists from the West, attending a service at one of the few churches in town still permitted to stay open. A woman in our group had smuggled in a single copy of the Bible in Latvian. After the service she gave this Bible to a young girl in the congregation. I see her now, this girl, dancing about the church, both stunned in disbelief and weeping with delight. We gave her the Scriptures and she 'believed not for joy'.

There is much joy in Luke. His Gospel begins and ends in joy. The birth of Jesus is an occasion for rejoicing; Mary's Magnificat is echoed by shepherds and angels (Luke 2.13–20). There is rejoicing – strangely – at his departure, the disciples returning to Jerusalem 'with great joy' (Luke 24.52). So it is throughout the Gospel. There is joy on earth when the lost sheep is found and joy in heaven when the sinner repents (Luke 15.1–7). Yet here at the resurrection the note of rejoicing is curiously ambivalent. Beneath the surge of joy is a contrary current, an undertow of incredulity.

The disciples' 'disbelief for joy' is noticed only by Luke. The detail is typical of a writer sensitive to the contradictory feelings we experience. Luke recognizes that the disciples are confused. There is a war going on between heart and mind, the joy that Jesus is once more with them contending with what is beyond belief, that the dead should live again, that mortality should put on immortality, and iniquity not have the last word. The disciples' confusion is not mentioned again but, thank God, it is mentioned this once. There is affirmation and comfort here for those who sense, and in some measure share, the Easter joy but who still sometimes wonder whether it is all too good to be true.

The joy of Luke is frequently the joy of lunch. The joy is enhanced by sharing the meal with those who would otherwise go hungry (Luke 14.7–11). If there's something to celebrate there will be something to eat, as the prodigal son discovered (Luke 15.11–32). (Was he, perhaps, another, who 'disbelieved for joy'?) The resurrection calls for a meal, both because there's much to celebrate and because bodies need food – resurrected bodies too, if they are real bodies and not ghosts. That is why, when Jesus restores the twelve-year-old Jairus to life, he insists that she should be given something to eat (Luke 8.55). Luke does not entertain the notion of an immaterial resurrection. The idea that the resurrection is a subjective experience, rather than a concrete event, would have been foreign to his cast of mind as to that of his first readers.

'Thus it is written that the Messiah is to suffer and to rise.' The primary reference is to the Hebrew Bible in which an unknown poet speaks of a servant who not only suffers, bearing our iniquity, but who also is to be 'exalted and extolled and very high' (Isaiah 52.13). It belittles the Bible to see such texts as a merely predictive, foretelling the crucifixion and resurrection. The poet has seen deeper; he has seen into the heart of things, as poets do. There, at the root of it all, it is written that vicarious suffering will, at the last, be vindicated. The risen Christ at once affirms and embodies what is written both in scripture and in the scheme of things. It is 'the Deeper Magic from before the Dawn of Time', and this is not the only story to tell the same truth. 'Nothing is written!' Lawrence of Arabia famously cried. Nothing is predicted, certainly, but there is a pattern woven into the fabric of what is. In the dying and living of Jesus the pattern unfolds in history.

That truth is to be proclaimed to all nations 'beginning from Jerusalem'. The priority of Jerusalem is not only a matter of geography and history. Jerusalem is the place where the Christian mission began, but there is more to its precedence than that. Salvation, in the Bible, is always 'out of Zion', originating from a particular history and a specific location. In a sense, the Christian mission must always 'begin from Jerusalem'. We may go to 'all nations', to the ends of the earth 'to bear witness to these things', but – like Paul on his travels – we are really only commuting from Jerusalem until our mission in that city is accomplished. That mission is not to convert its citizens but to seek its peace.

Here is something else that is 'written', that my salvation and Jerusalem's are in some way connected. If my first prayer must be for forgiveness, my next must be for Jerusalem. 'Seek the peace of the city . . . for in the peace thereof shall ye have peace' (Jeremiah 29.7).

YEAR C

Acts 9.1–6 (7–20); Revelation 5.11–14; John 21.1–19

WHERE WE DO NOT WISH TO GO

We have come full circle. The story ends as it began, with the fishermen and the one they do not know. As at the beginning, so now at the close, the stranger's mysterious command is to follow him. Scissors-and-paste scholars fret about this final chapter of John's Gospel. They notice how the last verse of the previous chapter looks like a conclusion, summing up the themes and purpose of the Gospel. John 21 must be 'secondary', they say. Not necessarily. One possible and permissible way to read this chapter is as an epilogue to all four of the Gospels. Taken this way a remarkable symmetry becomes apparent in the four evangelists' testimony to Jesus of Nazareth. Whether or not the architect of this structure was John – or indeed whether this symmetry was ever intended – is immaterial. We have been here before. The disciples are back where they started. They are on the same shore, at the same task, hearing the same summons. It is the experience of all spiritual explorers – so T. S. Eliot claimed at the conclusion of his *Four Quartets* – to find at the end of their journey that they have returned to the place where their journey began – and then, but only then, to understand where they were when they set out.

Some commentators suggest that it is unthinkable that Peter and the rest could ever have contemplated taking up their old way of life after all they had experienced. On the contrary. Mondays follow Sundays, Easter Sunday included. The laconic exchange – 'I'm going fishing', 'We'll join you' – may seem a banal conversation to be having, if you have just witnessed the resurrection of the Son of God, except that it is exactly how we do talk when we have been overwhelmed by events which are more than we can handle. A child is born, a grandfather dies. 'I'll put the kettle on,' someone says.

We are told that they didn't recognize Jesus at first. Then the beloved disciple, as he had done on the first day of the week, 'sees and
believes'. 'It is the Lord!' he says. So now they know. Or do they? They
know who he is. Yet they still want to *ask* who he is. Such too is our
knowledge and our ignorance, our faith and our uncertainty. Risen
from the dead, he is still elusive, still beyond us. Ours is 'the Emmaus
experience'. The moment we recognize the stranger who joined us on
the road, he is lost to our sight. He escapes all our categories. He still
comes to us as one unknown.

They have breakfast on the beach. So too do Lucy and Edmund on
the shore of the Silver Sea. 'Come and have breakfast,' said the Lamb.
'Please Lamb,' said Lucy, 'is this the way to Aslan's country?' 'Not for
you,' said the Lamb. 'For you the door into Aslan's country is from
your own world' (*The Voyage of the Dawn Treader*, C. S. Lewis).

After breakfast, they get down to business. The conversation Jesus
has with Peter is not about the question Peter wants to ask, 'Who are
you, Lord?' What matters is Peter's relationship with Jesus and what
Jesus requires of him.

Jesus asks Peter three times whether he loves him more than the
other disciples do. Peter is gently reminded of his threefold denial
of Jesus. Now it seems that he is to receive a foundational role (to
borrow a metaphor from Matthew) in the mission of the Church,
though nothing is said about his having successors in this role. The
weight and gravity of Jesus's repeated charge to Peter, not to speak
of what he says about the fate awaiting him, suggests that Peter's
task will be uniquely his. But the substance of what is said to Peter is said to us all, 'If you love me, keep my commandments' (John
14.15).

'When you are old . . . someone else will take you where you do not
wish to go.' The primary reference is to Peter's martyrdom. The details
of the prediction suggest that, by the time this Gospel is in circulation,
Peter had already been put to death by crucifixion. But Peter died a
long time ago. If we allow the text to speak to our own time, it may
have other things to say. Many of us, in the wealthy world at least,
will grow extremely old. That will be our cross. In our final infirmities
others will take us where we do not wish to go. If we're lucky and can
afford a good nursing home, they'll no doubt look after us very nicely.
But our frail and failing flesh will be in their charge, not ours. Someone else will 'fasten my belt'. I won't even be able to do up my own
trousers.

We too are being shown by what death we are to 'glorify God'. What is said to us as we contemplate this destiny? The same that was said to Peter at the outset of the story, when Jesus first met him. Ultimately it is all that Jesus ever says to any of us. 'Follow me.'

The Fourth Sunday of Easter

YEAR A

Acts 2.42–47; 1 Peter 2.19–25; John 10.1–10

MORE THAN SHEEP

Back in the giddy sixties it was asserted that Christians, at least those who lived in built-up areas, should stop talking about shepherds and sheep. Jesus's imagery, we were told, needs to be industrialized. The tenth chapter of John's Gospel was judged to be particularly in need of a make-over. So we were invited to reflect on such reinventions as 'I am the true crankshaft. Everything revolves around me.' We shudder at the memory, overlooking the possibility that some of the ways in which we treat the Bible today will one day be deemed just as dotty.

But we do have a problem. The picture of the Lord as my shepherd is one of the great images of the Hebrew Bible. The twenty-third psalm – the song we sing this Sunday – is only the most well-known of the many texts in the Old Testament where God is portrayed as the shepherd of his people. In a passage of extraordinary beauty that has inspired Christian art across the ages, the prophet speaks of the Lord who will 'feed his flock like a shepherd' and who will 'gather the lambs in his arms' (Isaiah 40.11). The Messiah will be God's shepherd-king, the heir to David whom God 'took from the sheepfolds, from tending the nursing ewes, to be the shepherd of his people Jacob' (Psalm 78.71). However distant our own lives may be from that of a Palestinian or Cumbrian shepherd, the scriptural image retains its timeless appeal and, above all, its ancient power to sustain us as we pass into the dark.

The difficulty arises when we turn from the shepherd to the sheep. The sheep is a useful animal and, at least in its infancy, an endearing one. But its lifestyle is hardly a pattern of discipleship. The point is made seriously. Overexposure to sheep–shepherd imagery – perhaps in hymns more than in Scripture ('Loving shepherd of thy sheep, keep thy lamb in safety keep') – can inculcate a spirituality of over-dependency. The 'good sheep' always complies. It stays safe. It does not explore the unknown and the perilous. The attributes most desirable in a sheep are those least desirable in a disciple.

Here we turn to our reading from 1 Peter – or rather to the verse before the one where we are supposed to start. Peter says, 'Slaves, accept the authority of your masters with all deference, not only those who are kind and gentle but also those who are harsh.' What follows is a moving account of Christ's refusal to return evil for evil. His silent suffering proves to be the 'one abyss of destroying love' in which all our iniquities are absorbed without recoil – and so their deadly sting is drawn. But Peter's purpose in this sublime passage – one of the foundational texts for our understanding of the atonement – is to defend his initial injunction, his insistence that slaves should always do as they are told! If we read this passage on Sunday we should start where Peter does, and not where our lectionary says we should. We obey a first principle in the use of the Bible: 'Don't leave out the awkward bits.'

The first Christians did not immediately challenge the cultural assumptions and social institutions of their world. It was taken for granted that the good slave, like the good woman, always defers. After all, that is what the good sheep does. But the image that illuminates can also mislead, unless it is complemented and corrected by other images. So it is with 'sheep-talk'. To be sure, we belong to the Lords' flock, but we also belong to his family. We are his sheep, but we are also his children. Children, like sheep, are vulnerable and they need to be protected and guided, comforted and corrected. But, unlike sheep, children need to pose questions and to ask why, to challenge authority and not always to do as they are told, if ever they are to grow up. It is because we are more than sheep that we are bold enough to challenge some of the attitudes that the Bible itself seems to sanction, slavery and the subjugation of women among them. 'The more abundant life' which Jesus promises has no place for unquestioning acquiescence in how things are.

It has been well said of John that 'his thought moves in spirals rather than straight lines'. So we are invited to think of Jesus not only as our shepherd but also as 'the gate', the door to the fold where the sheep find safety and shelter. Again John's picture calls to mind Old Testament imagery. Jacob, wandering the earth, lay down with his head on a stone and dreamed of a ladder reaching to heaven. 'This is the house of God,' he said of that field under the stars, 'and this is the gate of heaven' (Genesis 28.10–22). Jesus may be claiming to be the only way to heaven, but the gate of which he speaks is in many places.

YEAR B

Acts 4.5–12; 1 John 3.16–24; John 10.11–18

LOST SHEPHERDS

This Sunday's Gospel contains one of the most beautiful sequence of words in the English Bible.

> And other sheep I have,
> which are not of this fold:
> them also I must bring,
> and they shall hear my voice;
> and there shall be one fold
> and one shepherd.

So reads John 10.16 in the Authorized Version.

The text can be read as a short blank verse poem. Each of its first five lines line is a perfect example of the classical 'iambic trimeter'. The sixth line breaks this regular pattern, a metrical rupture lending immense weight to the final words – 'and one shepherd'. (To expose a poem's mechanism in this way is, of course, to take a butterfly to bits to see how it works.) The subtle cadences of the simple words turn prose to music.

The translation also happens to be a flawless rendering of the Greek text. Just how good it is appears when we compare the lame efforts of some modern versions. The Revised English Bible inflicts 'sheep pen' on us. The King James translators knew that it matters how the Bible sounds, that to touch the ear is to reach the heart, that rhythms beneath words awaken perceptions beyond words.

We must not be too quick and clever in identifying these 'other sheep', or in locating the 'one fold' of which Jesus speaks. The language is oblique, its elusive register sensitively captured by the Authorized Version. The obvious reference is to the inclusion of the Gentiles along with Jewish believers in one fellowship of faith, but with John there's always the risk that in saying the obvious we miss the point.

'There shall be one fold.' Here, as in 'the great high-priestly prayer' of John 17, the vision is that the many shall be one. It is a mystical hope. Western minds, Church of England minds especially, are mistrustful of mystical visions. We prefer the joint-service with the Methodists, or the meeting organized by the Council of Christians and Jews. Jesus was not a westerner. His all-embracing vision is larger than the reconciliation of estranged faith-communities, lofty as such a goal may be. It is more akin to the apostle's hope that God will 'gather together in one all things in Christ' (Ephesians 1.10) or to the vision that 'all shall be well and all manner of thing shall be well'.

Today the only acquaintance some have with sheep is with the lamb they buy from Tesco. That is no reason for dropping sheep–shepherd imagery from Christian discourse. Such imagery – and there's a lot of it in our New Testament – appeals to the Hebrew Bible, much more than to the actual ways of sheep and shepherds. After all, a shepherd who is any good, whether in first-century Galilee or twenty-first century Galway, doesn't die for his sheep, any more than he abandons ninety-nine of them to chase after one that has wandered off (Luke 15.3–7). The background is not sheep-farming, ancient or modern, but the Old Testament picture of God as shepherd of his people.

One extraordinary passage in particular stands behind John's description of Jesus as the Good Shepherd. It is the prophet Ezekiel's searing indictment of the 'shepherds of Israel' (Ezekiel 34). Instead of guarding and tending the flock of God, these 'shepherds' have been content to see the sheep scattered and become prey to predators. Now, by his prophet, the Lord announces, 'I myself will be the shepherd of my sheep.' And he adds, most memorably, 'I will feed them with justice.'

Ezekiel's false shepherds reappear as the 'hired hands' of our Gospel reading. There may be an immediate reference here to the Pharisees, who have just treated the man born blind so harshly (John 9). Before trying the cap on others, however, we must see how it fits us. The hired hands are the professedly and professionally religious, not only of Ezekiel's day, not only of Jesus's day. The prophet condemns them in terrifying terms. 'You have not strengthened the weak, you have not healed the sick, you have not bound up the injured, you have not brought back the strayed, you have not sought the lost' (Ezekiel 34.4). Somehow I don't think that I shall escape the judgement of those words by pleading that I've kept up with the paperwork and repaired the church roof.

'I am the good shepherd.' There is, to be sure, much comfort in this great 'I am', above all in the assurance that I am known and loved. But these are far from soothing words. The tenth chapter of John's Gospel is not a reprise of 'The Lord's my shepherd' set to Crimond or Brother James's Air. This is throughout a confrontational discourse in which much is said to provoke, to offend, but also to bring us to our knees. Jesus is indeed the good shepherd. There is someone looking for us. But for the hired hands among us, however modest our stipends, that is not entirely good news.

YEAR C

Acts 9.36–43; Revelation 7.9–17; John 10.22–30

WHAT I DO IS WHO I AM

We begin with a prayer that wells from the heart. 'How long?' they ask. 'How long, do you hold us in suspense?' The idiom is rare, strange and powerful. Literally, their question is, 'How long do you carry our life?' Their lives are on hold. They cannot move on until Jesus stops torment-ing them by his refusal to give them a straight answer. Their question is the same as John the Baptist's, 'Are you the one who is to come?' (Matthew 11.3) In a word, 'Who on earth are you?'

It is our question too. Our 'Christology' – what we say about Jesus – may be thoroughly orthodox. Yet still he eludes us and still we wonder who he really is. Sometimes we feel, as they did and as Job did, that someone's playing games with us. Their prayer is ours. 'How long, O Lord, how long?'

The so-called 'Messianic secret', so striking a feature of Matthew, Mark and Luke, is found in John's Gospel as well. In John too, Jesus is both hidden and revealed. To be sure, in John Jesus's Messiahship is confessed at the outset (John 1.41), but still there is an ambiguity about him, the evasiveness about his status that so vexes 'the Jews' who want to pin him down.

For John, the mystery of Jesus's identity is shown in his 'works', in the signs that reveal his glory. In the other Gospels the emphasis is different. These signs, the miracles Jesus performs, are indicators that the reign of God is near. But for all the Gospel writers the meaning of what he does is made clear, and the mystery of who he is resolved, only to those who 'believe', that is to say, to those who commit themselves to him. His opponents refuse that commitment. Refusing that commit-ment, they'll never know his secret.

The context is still the discourse of Jesus as the 'good shepherd'. Its imagery is extended almost to breaking point. Those who have no allegiance to Jesus – and so can make no sense of him – are not 'his sheep'. Huge questions of predestination and free will loom here, not to speak of John's problematic language about 'the Jews'. What is clear is that there is no solving the riddle of Jesus without reaching out to him. Some of us used to sing, 'Trust and obey, trust and obey, there's no other way, to be happy in Jesus than to trust and obey.' There's 'no other way' either to decipher the enigma of who he is.

Jesus does not tell them plainly whether or not he is the Messiah. Instead he makes a more audacious claim. He asserts that he and God are one. Outraged by this blasphemy, as they see it, his enemies prepare to lynch him. They had done the same before when he'd said much the same (John 8.59). It is a dramatic moment. Alas, our lectionary editors have no taste for such theatre. We listen to Christ's tremendous claim. And there we're told to stop. We don't get to hear about the violent response his remark immediately provokes.

Worship, including the public reading of the Holy Gospel, is theatre. The drama of our story dictates that we read on. We need the whole story. We need to hear what they say as they choose their stones to hurl at him.

Jesus is on trial here. (He was on trial many times before those last hurried hearings on the night before he died.) The charge is blasphemy. 'You are claiming to be God,' they allege. Jesus's defence against this allegation is not to deny it, but to contend that what he claims is true. The evidence he submits is what he has done. 'My deeds are my credentials', he says, as one version felicitously puts it. Here once more is John's understanding of the identity of Jesus, affirmed almost monotonously throughout his Gospel. There are seven great signs in John's Gospel. The substance of them could be said in seven words: 'What I do is who I am.'

'I and the Father are one,' says Jesus. So now we know. Or do we? One is a very mysterious number, much more mysterious than pi. 'One is one and all alone and ever more shall be so' is a statement about God older perhaps than any in our creeds. 'Ever more shall be so' – no doubt that's true. But already here in John there is the dawning recognition that the one who is one is not necessarily 'all alone'. Later on, a lot of clever people will try to explain how this can be, how one who is God can talk to God or cry from a cross that he is deserted by God. No doubt they understand what they are talking about. John spares us the metaphysics. For him the unity of Son and Father is a communion of common purpose. His Father's hands are his. They will not let us go.

The Fifth Sunday of Easter

YEAR A

Acts 7.55–60; 1 Peter 2.2–10; John 14.1–14

ONE WAY – MANY MANSIONS

Six and a half million pounds, we learn, is to be spent on 'a multifaith building' for the University of Surrey. Muslims will be allocated more space for worship in the building than will be provided for any other faith community. 'Converting each other', we are told, 'will be forbidden.' The Diocese of Guildford has contributed a quarter of a million pounds towards the project. Predictably, there has been an angry response from those who believe that such an exercise is a betrayal of the Christian gospel. Those who signed the cheque are accused of ignoring words of Jesus we hear on Sunday, 'No one comes to the Father except through me.'

When that text is used to browbeat those who hold that heaven's doors are open to those of other faiths, I think of Kalpa, Shelina, and Karen. Kalpa is a Muslim, Shelina a Hindu, Karen a Christian. They were three young people whom I taught in a school at the foot of Mt Kilimanjaro. With our other older students, we had taken them away for a few days to one of Tanzania's game parks. Now we were driving back to school. In the back of my car these three good friends were singing. They were teaching each other and singing together the songs they had learned in their different communities. Their voices moved from the songs of one faith to another. Their singing shaped a symphony of the music of temple, church and mosque, and it was altogether lovely. I wondered – I still wonder. Did God stop listening when Karen, the Christian, started singing a Hindu song? Was he listening to Kalpa and Shelina, as well as to Karen, when together they sang in praise of Jesus? What did the good Lord make of it all? Had he surrounded my battered old Toyota with a firewall, so that only Christian words on Christian lips reached his ears? I think not. Jesus said, 'No one comes to the Father except through me.' But he said too, as we shall also hear on Sunday, 'In my Father's house are many mansions.'

'Many mansions.' Most modern versions have 'many rooms', making heaven sound like a hotel. The Greek word John uses here is the noun corresponding to the verb 'abide'. 'Abiding' is an important idea in John's Gospel. 'Abide in me,' says Jesus, 'as I abide in you' (John 15.4). We have the noun a little later when Jesus promises that he and his Father will 'make their home' with those who show they love him by doing what he tells them (John 14.23). Many who love Jesus do not subscribe to the religion that has often claimed a monoply of him. Many keep his word without knowing that it is his word they have kept. ('Lord, when was it that we saw you hungry?') The 'mansions' of which Jesus speaks are not for 'members only'.

'I am the way, the truth, and the life.' We sometimes approach this great text with its rich pickings in too much of a hurry, hardly glancing at what Jesus has already said about 'the way'. What he says baffled Thomas and has puzzled commentators too. 'Where I go – you know the way.' The remark is awkward, barely grammatical. It is the way of which Jesus dare not speak directly, such is its shame and ignomy. Much that John records of the teaching of Jesus is more theological reflection than verbatim record. But some sayings, such as this one, have the raw immediacy of words as they were originally uttered.

'I am the way, the truth, and the life.' The way to God is the way of Jesus. That way is both the path he trod and the path he is. It is 'the way of the cross', which for Stephen, as for so many who came after him, was no figure of speech. Christians were once simply those who belonged to 'the way' (Acts 9.2). Later on, they became 'the church'. It was then that things began to go belly-up. Somewhere, back along the line, some would say with the Constantinian settlement, we 'lost the way'. Ever since then we have been trying to find it again.

Philip, like Thomas, is bewildered by what Jesus says. His plea, 'Show us the Father', voices the longing of all who know that God made them for himself, all whose hearts are restless until they find their rest in him. Philip wants to see God. When Jesus tells him that he need look no further – 'He who has seen me has seen the Father' – he is not suggesting that Philip can now settle back and enjoy the Beatific Vision. There is far too much still to be done. Those who walk the way of Jesus must do his works – and even greater ones. 'Greater works'? What might those be? I mourn my student Mark who died so young. A cure for cancer would be a start.

YEAR B

Acts 8.26–40; 1 John 4.7–21; John 15.1–8

THE SAP OF THE VINE IS LOVE

'Blessed assurance, Jesus is mine!' How we bellowed the words at those Billy Graham rallies long ago! No doubts or misgivings troubled us. Now, after fifty years of failure and folly, and with John 15 in front of us, we're not so sure. The discourse on Jesus as 'the true vine' forbids such complacency. The fruitless branch is summarily severed. God lops it off. It is as ruthless and unsparing as the closure of Woolworths. St John, sometimes felt to be the gentler character, is far harsher than St Paul. The latter makes multiple comparisons between the Church and the human body but he never suggests that God amputates the bits that don't work.

Calvinists, who make much of 'the perseverance of the saints', the doctrine that the saved can never be lost, have problems with this talk of dead wood being cut out. John Wesley was an Arminian and he took the text to mean – as has mainstream Methodism ever since – that it is indeed possible to fall from grace. Perhaps that's why Methodists, braced by that thought, have done so much good.

Jesus is the vine. His disciples are the branches. The one absolutely fundamental point made here is that the relationship of Christ and Christians is a moral one. It's different with my relatives. My aunt is still my aunt even if I loathe her and behave badly to her. Not so my relationship with my Lord and with my siblings in Christ. Those relationships issue in love and service, or they do not exist at all.

The nature of this kinship is explored in Sunday's second reading. Christ is related to the believer, as are believers one to another, by love. The sap of the vine is love. We recall the legend of St John's last sermon. The 'beloved disciple' was the last alive to have kept company with Jesus on earth. Now he is close to death. His congregation in the little church in Ephesus leans forward to catch his last whispered words. 'Little children, love one another. It is the Lord's command and it is enough.'

The fruitless branch will be 'thrown into the fire and burned'. The poet William Cowper, haunted by this text and others like it, doubted his salvation. He believed that God had cast him off. There is desperation approaching total despair in his plea 'Return, O holy Dove, return, Sweet messenger of rest'. Anyone involved in the pastoral ministry will have met those similarly tormented. One of the finest priests I have known, and a very dear friend, feared that he was damned. As with William Cowper, my friend's dread of apostasy was associated with depressive illness.

The Puritan divine, Richard Baxter advises such troubled souls. His wise counsel is a 'pastoral commentary' on a text which still distresses many.

> A melancholy person can think of nothing with confidence and comfort: there is nothing but trouble, confusion, fears, and despair in his apprehension. He still seems to himself undone and hopeless. A person naturally timorous, cannot choose but fear, even if you show him the clearest reasons of assurance. But God will not impute our diseased misery to us as our damning sin. (*Obedient Patience*, 1683)

Useless branches will be incinerated. It's an awful thought, but the premise is that it will not come to that. The discourse as a whole is lit up not by the fires of hell but by the light of glory, by the persuasion that the love of the Father will not let us go. 'Abide in me,' says Jesus, 'as I abide in you.' As with a partner, a spouse, or a close friend, so it is with our Lord. To 'abide' in each other, to stay in love, is not a matter of maintaining a mood. It is something to be done. Love is a task as well as a gift. And it is a task which Jesus is better at than we are. That's why there's still some hope for us.

We may escape the fire. But we shall not escape the knife. The fruitful branch will be pruned. 'Whom the Lord loves, he chastens' (Hebrews 12.6).

Here we touch on the meaning, if any, of suffering – on which topic things are too lightly said and too cheerfully sung. J. Mason Neale exhorts us thus:

> The trials that beset you,
> The sorrows ye endure,
> The manifold temptations
> That death alone can cure.
>
> What are they but his jewels
> Of right celestial worth?
> What are they but the ladder
> Set up to heaven on earth?

My reply to Mr Neale is that he is free to interpret his own trials that way, but he must not dismiss the suffering of others quite so cavalierly. His is not a hymn to sing in the Horn of Africa.

YEAR C

Acts 11.1–18; Revelation 21.1–6; John 13.31–35

THE CHRISTIAN FENG SHUI

Fortunately it is only rarely that our lectionary gets it as badly wrong as it does this Sunday. It is as if we arrive late at the theatre. We slip into our seats at the play's most dramatic moment, but the drama is lost on us because we've missed what's just happened. Quite literally, the lectionary has lost the plot.

We need to know that we are at the Last Supper and that Judas Isacariot, who is to betray Jesus, has just left the room. We need to hear what John has just said, his comment – and judgement – on Judas's departure. Nowhere in the Bible is so much said in so few words. 'And it was night', is the usual English translation, but John's Greek – just three words and seven letters – is terser still.

'It was night.' The words fall like hammer blows, driving nails through flesh into wood. John is telling us what this moment means. Darkness has fallen. It is the darkness which, according to the other three Gospels, enwraps the earth when Jesus is crucified. It is the darkness we loved rather than the light – all of us, not just Judas – the darkness we preferred 'because our deeds were evil' (John 5.19).

Judas goes. All is night. Then comes John's tremendous 'now'. 'Now,' says Jesus, 'the Son of Man has been glorified.' Utter darkness descends and the glory of God shines. It is just the kind of paradox in which John delights. Either our editors didn't notice it or they felt it would be too much for us. We owe it to John and to the integrity of his Gospel to make sure this Sunday that we read the whole story.

Do they understand Jesus? No better, probably, than when he says that he will be with them only a little longer and that he will go where they cannot go. The path he has chosen is his alone. He has made it his so that it shall not be theirs – or ours.

Then the 'new commandment'. 'Love as I have loved.' Isn't this to demand the impossible? To love as he did is beyond us, and not just because we're not that nice. For to love as he did would be to do as he did. And has he not just told us that that is precisely what we cannot do? We cannot love like that because we cannot 'go where he is going'. That way is his alone.

The paradox here is not peculiar to John. It's in all the Gospels – indeed it runs throughout the New Testament – the manifest contradiction, so it seems, that Jesus died for me, but that I too must take up my cross.

The paradox is not to be resolved by thinking it through, but by living it out. The Archbishop of Canterbury has spoken of those who 'make God believable' by the kind of people they are. So it is with this impossible new commandment. Jesus died as a 'ransom for many', literally 'in the place of' many (Mark 10.45). He alone is our redeemer, yet there are some of whom we can say they live redemptively. Others save us and it is no figure of speech to say they do.

This 'new commandment' summarizes the distinctive ethic of Jesus. Like the Sermon on the Mount, it is a compass needle, not a road map. It does not yield instant answers to vexed questions. It is the Christian 'feng shui', determining the disposition and orientation of the disciple's moral life and of the household of God. It is an 'interim ethic'; it is the way to live now in the little time left before all comes to its appointed end.

The most alarming thing Jesus says about his new commandment is his assertion that you can tell whether people are his disciples by whether or not they obey it in their relationships with each other. There was a terrifying programme promoted in the diocese of London – perhaps it still is – called 'The Seven Marks of a Healthy Church'. For those of us who recognized ourselves in the church of Laodicea ('you are wretched, pitiable, poor, blind, and naked', Revelation 3.17) this schedule, with its multiple bullet points, brought little comfort. For John, there is only one criterion, just this one sign of health, that we love one another as much as he loved us. *Kyrie Eleison.*

Ubi caritas et amor, Deus ibi est. Where charity and love are, God is there. The familiar Taizé chant is sung at all seasons, but its home is the mass of the Last Supper on Holy Thursday, where in churches where they do things properly the words are sung as antiphons during the ceremony of the Washing of the Feet. We come back to the all-important context of Sunday's Gospel: what Jesus has just done, there in the upper room, and what for us and for our salvation he is about to do.

The Sixth Sunday of Easter

YEAR A

Acts 17.22–31; 1 Peter 3.13–22; John 14.15–21

GOD GOES WHERE GOD IS NOT

When Thomas Coram returned to London after forty years at sea he was appalled to see abandoned babies and children starving and dying on the city's streets. The plight of children left to perish touched his heart. He began a twenty-year campaign to obtain a Royal Charter to start the first 'Foundling Hospital' for exposed and deserted young children. Captain Coram was 71 years old when his hospital at last opened. The Foundling Museum in Brunswick Square tells the whole moving story.

The plight of his disciples, says Jesus, when he takes leave of them, will be akin to the desperate state of children with no one to care for them. But the good news this week is that they will not be left in that pitiful position indefinitely.

'I will not leave you as orphans; I will come to you.' The biblical picture of the orphan is a harrowing one. By night they shelter in ruins; by day they wander about and beg (Psalm 109.10). They are at the mercy of thugs (Job 24.2, 9). Certainly those who shaped Israel's social legislation – Thomas Coram's moral and spiritual forbears – sought protection for them. Together with the widows and with those today whom we would call the ethnic minorities, orphans were entitled to justice (Deuteronomy 27.19) The sheaves, the olives, and the grapes remaining after the harvest were to be left for them (Deuteronomy 24.19–22). In theory and in law, orphans were to be looked after, but in reality their situation must have remained precarious. The fact that the prophets had to take up their cause is sufficient indication that orphans continued to be the victims of neglect and exploitation (Isaiah 1.17; Jeremiah 7.6; Zechariah 7.10).

Jesus tells his disciples that he must 'leave' them. In John's Gospel, Jesus's 'leaving' of his disciples is code for his death. Without him, he knows that their bewilderment and pain will be that of children suddenly bereft of their parents. For a while, they will be 'as orphans'. There can be no more powerful symbol of their loss. But, he adds, 'I am coming to you.' The image of the orphan implies that this promise will be fulfilled at the resurrection, rather than at the coming of the Spirit or at 'the second coming', for orphans, unless something is done swiftly, have small hope of survival. It is Easter that ends the disciples' bereavement.

Remarkably, we meet another group of people this Sunday whose circumstances are, if possible, even more parlous than those of the disciples left as orphans by the death of Jesus. In a notoriously problematical passage, Peter – or whoever wrote the first of the two letters attributed to him – speaks of Christ preaching to 'the spirits in prison'.

Here we step into a mythological world, a world as foreign to us as it was familiar to our medieval ancestors who saw lurid paintings of 'the Harrowing of Hell' on the walls of their parish churches. The scene – though everything said about this text is contested – is the place of the departed whither, so we say we believe, Jesus descended after his crucifixion. There Jesus preaches to these imprisoned spirits.

Who were they? Many proposals have been made, some way off the medieval wall. Some suggest that they were demons, fallen angels who mated with 'the daughters of men' (Genesis 6.1–4). Others argue that they were the wicked lot who never made it into Noah's ark and so were drowned in the Flood. Yet others maintain that they were all those unfortunate enough to have lived before the time of Jesus – Noah included – and so could never have been evangelized.

We must turn to the work of the great Roman Catholic theologian, Hans Urs von Balthasar, for more sober reflection on this difficult text. Balthasar was bold enough to go were few have followed and to articulate a theology of Holy Saturday. 'In Sheol,' he wrote, 'all that reigns is the darkness of utter loneliness.' We do not have the words to speak of these things, but in some sense Holy Saturday brings the experience of 'godforsakenness' into the very inner life of the Godhead. Balthasar believed that hell is empty because of Christ's descent, that 'God goes where God is not, so that what is not God may be drawn into the eternal love' (*Mysterium Paschale*, Ignatius Press, 2000).

The hope, voiced by Peter in his foreign language, is more comprehensibly and most memorably expressed by Paul. 'For I am convinced that neither death, nor life, nor angels, nor rulers, nor things present, nor things to come, nor powers, nor height, nor depth, nor anything else in all creation, will be able to separate us from the love of God in Christ Jesus our Lord' (Romans 8.38–39).

Thanks be to God. Darkness is not where God isn't. Another poet, Henry Vaughan, dared to say that darkness is where God is. So he writes, 'There is in God, some say, a deep but dazzling darkness.'

YEAR B

Acts 10.44–48; 1 John 5.1–6; John 15.9–17

FRIENDS WAITING TO BE MADE

What is the heart of Christian ethics? It is often claimed that Jesus himself answers that question. A scribe asks him, 'Which commandment is the first of all?' Jesus replies, 'Love God whole-heartedly and love your neighbour as yourself' (Mark 12.28–34). Here then is Jesus's 'summary of the Law'. But of course it is just that, a digest of *the Law*. Jesus sums up the Jewish moral tradition in which he and the scribe have both been schooled. It is, in all conscience, enough to be going on with, but what it is not is the essence of the ethic of Jesus.

Christ's ethic – Christian ethics – is encapsulated in the 'new commandment' which Jesus gave to his disciples on the night he was betrayed. 'Love one another as I have loved you' (John 13.34). He demonstrated the nature of that love – its utter self-abandonment – in washing his disciples' feet. The maxim 'Love your neighbour as yourself', though it towers above us as a moral summit beyond our reach, is still the epitome of the old, not the quintessence of the new. 'Love as you have been loved'– that's what's new. So is the old done away? Not at all. 'The ethical demands of the law and the prophets are not cancelled,' wrote T. W. Manson. 'They have become flesh and blood and have dwelt among us in the person and work of our Lord Jesus Christ' (*Ethics and the Gospel*, SCM Press, 1960).

Amongst the novelties of this new ethic is a fresh understanding of friendship. C. S. Lewis's chapter on friendship in *The Four Loves* (Collins, 1964) is an essay which even his devotees have difficulty in defending. Lewis suggests that friendship is perfectly exemplified by a group of men sitting around a fire in a country inn after a hard day's tramp across the moors, slippers on, drinks at their elbows, talking about books. Friendship, on this view, flourishes in male enclaves. You enjoy the companionship of your friends at the golf club, in the mess, at table after dinner when the ladies have retired to the drawing-room. Lewis is so steeped in the culture of the senior combination-room that, for all his erudition and deep faith, he simply does not register how radically Jesus is refashioning the notions of friendship which dominated the ancient world, the world which Lewis himself, two millennia later, still contentedly inhabited – until wrenched out of it by a certain Joy Davidman.

Liz Carmichael is an Oxford don, as was Lewis, but, unlike Lewis, she has lived and worked among the afflicted. She writes from the heart of her own experience in the townships of apartheid South Africa about the nature and demands of friendship as reinterpreted by Jesus. 'The praxis of friendship requires that in addition to forming friendships with people close by, we should make efforts to cultivate a much wider network of deepening friendships in different continents and cultures' (*Friendship: Interpreting Christian Love*, T & T Clark, 2004). Such 'Messianic friendship' means making friends with those who are not my sort. Dr Carmichael quotes Desmond Tutu, 'An enemy is a friend waiting to be made.' It is an idea which, say the Moltmanns, 'stands on its head the whole ancient concept of friendship as being between males of equal status' (*Recovering Friendship*, Elisabeth Moltmann-Wendel and Jürgen Moltmann, SCM Press, 2000).

We are *chosen* friends. 'You did not choose me. I chose you.' Last week's Gospel, with its alarming references to dead wood being burned, appeared to contradict the doctrine of 'the Perseverance of the Saints', one of 'the five points of Calvinism'. Here one of those same five principles, it seems, is being upheld. 'Unconditional election' is the doctrine that, such is our 'total depravity' (another of Calvin's five points), we all deserve to be damned, but that God in his mercy chose certain people to be saved. (Total depravity. Unconditional election. Limited atonement. Irresistible grace. The Perseverance of the Saints. T-U-L-I-P The cheerful acronym is the name the great Calvinist scholar Dr Colin Brown once gave his motor-scooter.)

If Christ chooses his friends, is the necessary implication that there are those, enemies of the gospel, whom he rejects? The consequence seems logically inevitable, but logical inevitabilities usually misrepresent the message of Jesus. All such attempts to systematize his knight's-move teaching betray its eccentric idiom. Karl Barth clung to Paul's letter to the Romans as a drowning man to a rope. When Barth read the terrible words, 'Jacob I have loved, but Esau I have hated' (Romans 9.13), he did not despair. He saw the Church as at once both Jacob and Esau. We stand eternally condemned and we are chosen before the foundation of the world. The notion is paradoxical to the point of absurdity.

That is the Christian reason for thinking that there may be something in it.

YEAR C

Acts 16.9–15; Revelation 21.10, 22–22.5; John 14.23–29 or John 5.1–9

A SIGHT TO BLESS OUR WAKING EYES

The Bible closes with the vision that will bless our waking eyes, the holy city, new Jerusalem. Our Christian journey starts with the gates of a city shutting behind us; our journey ends with city gates opening to us as, our long exile over, we are at last welcomed home. The biblical image of the city represents both everything we must abjure and all we must seek.

Jesus died 'outside the city gate' and, if we would save our souls alive, we must flee the city to join him (Hebrews 13.12). For the writer to the Hebrews, the city of Jerusalem represents the old order. Jerusalem stands for what we know as 'religion', for the institutionalizing of our approach to God. Religion makes relating to God a matter of negotiating the road-blocks by which the powerful seek to control access to him. Jesus dismantled every such barrier. As a consequence he was crucified 'outside the city' and, if we want to join him, that's where we must regroup. We've nowhere else to go. 'Here we have no lasting city, but we are looking for the city which is to come' (Hebrews 13.14).

In the book of Revelation, which we have been reading recently, the city we must flee from is 'Babylon', a city condemned for its idolatry of wealth and for the traffic 'in human bodies and souls' which was the basis of its prosperity (Revelation 18.13). Crackpot exegetes attempt to locate John's mythical Babylon precisely on the world map and in world history. All that their conflicting suggestions have in common is that Babylon is seen as some place else, rather than the city I have helped to build and in which I am tempted to linger.

The symbol of 'the new Jerusalem' allows us some imaginative purchase on what is beyond our conceptual grasp. Our Christian hope is to see God. Of that beatific vision, unless we're Dante, we cannot speak. But if we cannot talk about who we long to see, we can at least say something about where we'd like to live.

Two features dominate the landscape of the City of God, the river and the tree.

The prophet Ezekiel, the Old Testament forerunner of William Blake, saw a river flowing from Jerusalem down into the Dead Sea, making its salty waters fresh, so that fishermen could make a living from it. Ezekiel says, 'Everything shall live where the river runs' (Ezekiel 47.9). This river's source was in the Garden of Eden. The river runs like a silver thread through the Bible. Jesus of Nazareth was bold enough to claim that he was channel of its life-giving waters (John 4.14). Rivers, of course, behave eccentrically. 'God does not send his rivers like arrows to the sea,' said John Oman. Churches often act like water boards and try to regulate God's rivers. They fail. The river of the water of life is always breaking its banks and carving new ones. The current of this river is the divine love which knows no bounds. It flows in full spate through the city of God.

On either side of the river there is 'the tree of life'. The roots of the tree of life, like the source of the river of life, are in the garden of God. The tree of life is the tree Yggdrasil of Norse mythology on which the world turns; it is the *Bodhi* tree under which Gautama Siddhartha attained enlightenment; it is the tree which stands at the heart of the Garden of the Hesperides on the Islands of the Blessed. It is the mighty tree 'whereon hangeth a Man, stretched and nailed, rejected, dying and alone'. It is the tree which grows on Calvary 'whose fruit doth make my soul to thrive, that keeps my dying faith alive'. It is Jesus Christ the Apple Tree.

To speak thus of the tree is not frivolous syncretism, for it is said of the city that 'the kings of the earth will bring their glory into it'. '*Their* glory', notice. To be sure, Christians have been given 'the light of the knowledge of the glory of God in the face of Christ' (2 Corinthians 4.6). '*Our* glory', as it were, was to have recognized God in the face of Jesus. But as we throng before the gates of the Holy City, where the myriad paths towards it meet, we shall rejoice with those who have seen the glory of God in other faces and who have known him under other names.

Charles Williams saw in the City of God the primary image of the Christian community, for it is in that city that we learn to practise 'co-inherence' or 'the way of exchange', that bearing of each other's burdens which is the fulfilment of the law of Christ (Galatians 6.2). Williams insisted that, even in heaven, we can't select our neighbours. 'The infamy with which the City cannot compromise is born precisely in the thought that we can choose by whom we shall be nourished' (*The Image of the City and Other Essays*, Oxford University Press, 1958).

The Seventh Sunday of Easter

YEAR A

Acts 1.6–14; 1 Peter 4.12–14; 5.6–11; John 17.1–11

BRINGING HUMANITY HOME TO GOD

We have the great councils of the church, Nicaea, Constantinople, and the rest. Arguably as important as any of them was the World Missionary Conference which took place in Edinburgh in 1910. That conference is widely seen as the starting point of 'the ecumenical movement', the endeavour to bring about a greater measure of unity between the separate Christian Churches. The conference delegates, it must be stressed, were not interested in Christian unity for its own sake. What brought them to Edinburgh was not a wish to patch up ancient quarrels, but a longing to win the world for Christ. They saw the reunion of the Churches, not as an end in itself, but as the necessary means to an infinitely greater goal, the bringing of humanity home to God. Their audacious watchword was 'the evangelization of the world in this generation'. The last words from the platform, before the closing prayer, were those of Jesus, 'There are some standing here, who shall not taste of death, till they see the Son of man coming in his kingdom' (Matthew 16.28).

Jesus prays that his disciples may be one. It is one of the biddings of Jesus's 'High-priestly prayer', from which we hear on Sunday. What Jesus has said previously and what he will later say make clear the nature and purpose of the unity he prays for. That unity will be a relationship of love, love like the Father's for the Son, love like Jesus's for his disciples (John 13.34; 15.9). It is a relationship which will unite, not only his first disciples, but also those who come to faith through their testimony. Above all, it is the 'unity in love' needed to make the world believe (John 17.21–23).

For 'the Edinburgh fathers', ecumenism makes straight the path for evangelism. It has no other purpose. A photograph of the delegates in session shows rows of men in black suits and high starched collars. The few women present wear huge hats. The picture is of another world – yet it is a world which got one of its Christian priorities right.

Jesus prays that we may be one. At least he did once. Is that still the prayer of his heart? After so much talk that has come to nothing, is the reassembling of the Church's scattered body-parts still heaven's will for here below? These are questions that must concentrate the Christian mind as, in 2010, we mark the centenary of the original Edinburgh conference.

A perspective on these issues is provided by a word recurring thirteen times in Jesus's prayer. The term 'world' often has negative connotations in John. It certainly does in Sunday's Gospel. Once the world did not exist. The disciples were given to Jesus 'out of the world'. Jesus prays for his own, but he does not pray for 'the world'. Anticipating his imminent passion, he says that he is no longer 'in the world'. 'The world' in all these contexts is a world adrift, a world which has taken leave of its creator and, without him, is lost, a world where we briefly lodge but which can never be our home. Moreover, it is a world, so our reading from 1 Peter suggests, often inhospitable to Christians.

Yet this is not all John says about the world. For God loves this world (John 3.16). According to the World Council of Churches, so must we. The WCC is calling for 'a reconfiguration process' of the ecumenical movement, for 'a re-articulation of the original vision of unity of humankind in the new *oikos* [household] of God'. Only by recapturing this original vision can life be restored to the dry bones of the ecumenical movement. Joint services with the local Methodists are not to be despised, but they do not set our hearts on fire.

As most conferences do, the first World Missionary Conference produced a report on its proceedings. Most conference reports are stultifyingly tedious. Temple Gairdner's 'account and interpretation' of 'Edinburgh 1910', a 280-page book written and published within four or five weeks of the conference, is a thrilling and a prophetic work.

Gairdner invites his readers to contemplate 'a vision of earth', the earth 'known as a unit in this our day; every day more and more closely and organically knit'. (And this was written nearly a century ago!) He calls on us to grieve for 'the children of that earth for the most part at enmity with each other', and to commit ourselves afresh to him 'who for our sakes once struck his being into bounds and became one flesh with our kind'.

In our Gospel, Jesus, looking to and through his imminent suffering, speaks of having 'finished his work'. Our work is not finished, a reality which explains why Temple Gairdner closes his account of the 1910 World Missionary Conference in the way he does. At the foot of the last page are one word and a question mark.

FINIS . . . ?

YEAR B

Acts 1.15–17, 21–26; 1 John 5.9–13; John 17.6–19

THE QUEST FOR THE HISTORICAL JUDAS

We are in the world and, so John implies, it's a bad place to be. 'The world', for John, is roughly what we nowadays call 'culture'. One definition of culture – it will do – is 'the sum of socially transmitted behaviour patterns, arts, beliefs, institutions, and all other products of human work and thought'. That totality, according to John, is a region of darkness. The Christian community from which John's Gospel came and to which it first spoke, saw the culture of those outside its own fellowship as an order both hostile and transitory. Christians are *from* that culture; they are not *of* that culture.

John's view of the relationship of church and culture is that they are opposed to each other. To use Richard Niebuhr's famous classification, John's is a 'Christ against culture' theology (*Christ and Culture*, Faber and Faber, 1952). That theology is most chillingly voiced in words here ascribed to Jesus, 'I am not praying for the world.' This text is not usually included in anthologies of the so-called 'hard sayings of Jesus'. It ought to be. We can live with these words only by recognizing how John holds starkly conflicting ideas in tension. The world for which Christ does not even pray is both loved by God and where he chose to live.

'I am not praying for the world, but for those you gave me.' So whom exactly is Jesus praying for? Old Bibles have at the top of the page, 'Jesus prays for the Church'. In other words, so we like to think, he's praying for us. Well, let's hope he is. But the context, the whole of this farewell discourse, should give us pause. The Church that John assures of the Lord's intercession is a Church that has renounced the world. But the church you and I go to hasn't renounced the world. Parish churches gladly and gratefully finance the repair of their roofs with the profits of gambling. The mainstream denominations have enthusiastically bought into the prevailing culture to smarten up their marketing and to streamline their management. Are such churches, tucked up in bed with a wicked world, struck off the Lord's prayer-list?

Southwark Cathedral – changing the subject – has two remarkable bosses. The first is a twenty-first century dean who speaks his mind, the second a fifteenth-century roof-boss depicting an obese Satan eating Judas Iscariot. The representation of Judas is grotesque and comic. Only his legs, waving out of Satan's mouth, remain to be consumed. Christians have always struggled to fit Judas into their scheme of things. The Southwark sculptor comes up with one solution. The so-called Gospel of Judas, about which there's been much hype, offers another. John's interpretation is altogether more sober and profound.

Our translations ('the one doomed to be lost' and the like) mask what John actually says. According to John, Judas is, literally, 'the son of perdition'. It's a phrase St Paul uses and his readers know exactly whom he means (2 Thessalonians 2.3). 'The son of perdition' is the dreadful personal embodiment of opposition to God who must appear, putting up a last-ditch fight, before the 'second coming' of Christ. For John, the Judas of history is this figure of myth.

But by 'mythologizing' Judas in this way, John is not robbing him of his historical identity. Far from it. He is highlighting his significance. John sees Judas as an 'eschatological' figure, that's to say he's someone with a decisive role in 'the last things'. The earliest Christians had their own script, their own story-line, about how it was all going to end. The mysterious 'son of perdition' was to have his big part in that drama. What John does is an extraordinarily bold piece of recasting. He hauls this dread but distant figure from the far future into the here and now. That last opponent, says John, has already appeared. Enmity has been made flesh and dwelt among us.

In truth, this foe makes many appearances. Another John comments 'many antichrists have come' (1 John 2.18). What about the in-between times in which we live? There was only one Judas, but he was not the last to play his role. Contemplating the twentieth century and the in-auspicious start of the twenty-first, is that so hard to believe?

None of this touches on the old intractable questions about Judas. If his was a necessary – even a predestined – role in the history of salvation, is there is any justice, not to speak of mercy, in the doom pronounced on him? Perhaps all hangs on how inclusive we understand words from another Gospel, 'Father, forgive them' (Luke 23.34).

And, anyway, it all happened so long ago.

In ancient shadows and twilights
Where childhood had strayed,
The world's great sorrows were born
And its heroes were made.
In the lost boyhood of Judas
Christ was betrayed.
('Germinal', A. E.)

YEAR C

Acts 16.16–34; Revelation 22.12–14, 16–17, 20–21; John 17.20–26

O CHRIST, COME QUICKLY!

What bits of the Bible should be read out in church? Our appointed New Testament reading highlights the dilemma. We are told to leave some verses out. We are supposed to skip the list of those who won't be let into the city of God. We are also told to leave out the warning never to leave anything out! Anyone adding to the prophetic word – so says the verse we're not supposed to hear – will go down with a nasty plague. Anyone deleting anything will be shut out of heaven. Pray God, the latter admonition does not apply to editors of our lectionary.

The policy of omitting from the public reading of Holy Scripture passages deemed unedifying is dangerous. The Bible says some dreadful things. But we mustn't airbrush them out. If, for example, the Bible says that women should keep silent, because it was Eve, not Adam, who was 'deceived' (1 Timothy 2, 12–15), then, appalling as they are, these are words we must hear. We must listen to them so that, interpreting the written word in the light of the incarnate Word, we may challenge and refute them. So it is with the list of those banned from the city. St John the Divine sees the City of God as an exclusive community, membership of which is a matter of moral entitlement. We must attend to what he says, but we must remember too that, although on its last page, this is not the final word the Bible has to say about heaven's hospitality.

A word which the lectionary does not leave out – thanks be to God – is '*Maranatha*', 'Come, Lord'. The original Aramaic, attesting to the prayer's antiquity, is preserved in the greeting with which Paul ends his first letter to the church in Corinth (1 Corinthians 16.22). That single word lies behind the 'Come, Lord Jesus' in our reading, the prayer with which the Bible draws to its close. It is John's response – it is the only possible response – to the tremendous vision revealed to him.

'Come, Lord Jesus.' It was possibly the first prayer of the church. In a sense, it will be the church's last prayer too, for when it is answered there will be no more need to use it. So why nowadays do we so seldom say it? Is it because we have no wish to be lumped with the literalists, those whose lurid interpretation of New Testament prophecy inspires the fundamentalist pulp-fiction that sells so well, at least in North America? Or is it – time to own up – simply because we no longer believe that Jesus 'will come again in glory to judge the living and the dead'?

A belief in 'the second coming' used to be something that united the catholic and evangelical wings of the Church. Evangelicals were given to qualifying any plans they announced with the cautious proviso 'if the Lord tarry'. 'The Guild of Prayer for the Return of our Lord' has been predominantly, if not exclusively, Anglo-Catholic in its membership. This 'blessed hope' was something which both traditions were *for*. Nowadays their united stand, so it seems, is more often on the things they are *against*.

The language of the New Testament and the Nicene Creed about our Lord's return has often been taken as symbolic. Some have said Jesus 'comes again' in the gift of his Holy Spirit; others have said that the promise of the Lord's return will be fulfilled in the coming of his kingdom, in a world where at long last peace and justice prevail. Conrad Noel of Thaxted, bless him, thought that the second coming had taken place with the Russian Revolution.

Such explanations (save the last) may satisfy our sophisticated minds but they do not answer to the deeper longings of our hearts. We cry with 'the Greeks' who came to Philip, 'Sir, we would see Jesus' (John 12.21). We cling to the promise that 'we shall see him as he is' (1 John 3.2). Believing that Jesus might one day return to this earth might well be naïve, but at least the thought encourages us to make it more beautiful.

In his book *Tokens of Trust* (Canterbury Press, 2007), Rowan Williams claims that George Herbert's 'Love bade me welcome' is the finest Christian poem in the English language. There's another poem that might deserve that accolade, Gerard Manley Hopkins's 'The Wreck of the Deutschland'. Hopkins was prompted to write this poem by the account he had read of five Franciscan nuns who had drowned when the boat carrying them to England foundered in the Thames estuary. Hopkins was particularly moved by the report of a certain 'tall nun', who was heard crying 'O Christ, come quickly' before she succumbed to the waves.

> She to the black-about air, to the breaker, the thickly
> Falling flakes, to the throng that catches and quails
> Was calling 'O Christ, Christ come quickly':
> The cross to her she calls Christ to her.

Amen. Come, Lord Jesus.

Pentecost (Whit Sunday)

YEAR A

Acts 2.1–21 or Numbers 11.24–30; 1 Corinthians 12.3b–13; or Acts 2.1–21; John 20.19–23 or John 7.37–39

THE ELEMENTAL SPIRIT

The three great scriptural images of the Holy Spirit are elemental. The Spirit is air, water and fire. He is wind, river and flame. Air, water and fire have a common attribute. They all *flow*, fire as much as air and water, as the terrified people who have fled its path through a forest or across a hillside will testify. Earth, the fourth element, can flow too, as the citizens of San Francisco found out in 1906 and the good people of Market Rasen in 2008. In Scripture, we are depicted by the same elemental imagery. We are but earth and breath, animated dust (Genesis 2.7).

On Sunday we shall try – and fail – to speak of a reality beyond words. On the Day of Pentecost, the apostles had the same problem of articulating the ineffable. They coped as best they could, as many do still, by 'speaking in tongues'. But in places where we can't resort to tongues, such as most pulpits, we must find words that will at least save us from gibberish. The concept of 'flow' helps to touch on what – like air, water and fire – is not to be grasped, the way God's Spirit works.

'Flow' is the title and theme of a widely influential book by a scholar with a far from flowing name. For Mihály Csíkszentmihályi 'flow' is 'the mental state of operation in which a person is fully immersed in what he or she is doing, characterized by a feeling of energized focus' (*Flow*, Mihály Csíkszentmihályi, Rider, 1992).

Csíkszentmihályi's work interprets what is going on whenever life is lived to the full. An expert skier knows what is meant by 'flow'. So does a master chef. So too does a child building a sand-castle. Jesus said that he came that we might have life and have it more abundantly – in a word, in Csíkszentmihályi's word – that we might experience 'flow' (John 10.10). That experience is the distinctive gift of God the Holy Spirit.

'A feeling of energized focus' is a good description of what the disciples experienced at Pentecost. They sensed the power they had been promised for the task ahead (Acts 1.8). The 'adventures of the apostles', Luke's account of the earliest Christian community, is the story of some remarkably energetic people. Aroused from their bewildered and fearful torpor, they are possessed by 'the force that drives the water through the rocks'.

The key-word is 'focus'. It is from being focused, Csíkszentmihályi maintains, that 'flow' follows. 'Flow' is impossible where there is a multiplicity of conflicting objectives. At Pentecost, Peter and his companions are taken to be drunk, so bizarre is their behaviour. In reality no group of twelve people could have been more clear-headed. Indeed it could be said that the Christian Church, such was its subsequent habit of setting off in several different directions at once, was never again as sober as it was that first Whitsunday.

Here was a wholly undistracted company. To be sure, it all unraveled soon enough. The rows started. The cracks appeared that were to become the deep fissures with us to this day. But at Pentecost 'they were all together in one place'. Theirs was the single-mindedness of which Kierkegaard spoke, 'the purity of heart which wills one thing'. The sharpness of the apostolic focus becomes clear if we to read to the end of Peter's sermon. All that Peter has previously said, including his rebuttal of the accusations of drunkenness levelled against the apostles, leads to his piercingly precise conclusion, the series of 'bullet-points' – the metaphor for once is exactly right – in which he summarizes the Christian gospel.

Peter and the rest, one in the Spirit, possessed by the wind, the river and the flame, knew briefly the flow of life to the full. What they were *not* doing was 'going with the flow'. On the contrary, the current that carried them was to take some of them to martyrdom. Peter himself will find out what Jesus meant when he said to him, 'someone will take you where you do not wish to go' (John 21.18).

Ultimately the flow of the Spirit is not about feelings. In the giddy early days of the twentieth-century charismatic movement, the Christian press frequently carried pictures of people with their eyes closed and mouths open. These were worshippers, 'lost in wonder, love, and praise'. Their ecstasies were real enough and the rest of us were put to shame. But it did look as if some of them were indeed well and truly *lost* in their wonder, love, and praise. In their seventh heaven, they seemed far from earth.

The experience we are promised and invited to share at Pentecost may or may not include such raptures. The transports are not guaranteed, the tasks are.

YEAR B

Acts 2.1–21 or Ezekiel 37.1–14; Romans 8.22–27; or Acts 2.1–21; John 15.26–27; 16.4b–15

WHEN WORDS FAIL

What noise do Christians make? They groan. So too does creation. So too does the Holy Spirit himself. Pentecost leaves us lost for words. Our snippet from Romans comes midstream in Paul's argument – mid-torrent, rather. Paul's subject is the glory to be revealed. His experience of the Holy Spirit is a foretaste of that promised glory. But the experience falls so far short of its promised fulfilment that it is a source of anguish. Paul dwells on the pain of Pentecost. The Holy Spirit hurts us, so great is the gulf between the Spirit's down-payment, bounty as it is, and the full sum of which it is the pledge. Our suffering is that of the whole created order, whose pangs are those of childbirth, a metaphor as apposite as it is audacious.

To tell why it hurts so badly is impossible. By the Spirit we have glimpsed where we're bound, and we can't be at home in this world any more. That promised land seems so far away that all we can do sometimes is either shut up or howl. Of course Paul has much more to say about the operation of the Holy Spirit. Indeed he will teach that a fruit of the spirit is joy (Galatians 5.22). But nothing can take away the primal Pentecostal pain.

There is a deeply paradoxical dimension to the New Testament understanding of the work of the Holy Spirit. On the one hand the Holy Spirit will tell you what to say when you're being persecuted (Mark 13.11) and he will enable you to stand up and speak out prophetically as Peter did. But, on the other hand, the Holy Spirit brings you to the boundaries of what may be put in words. Human speech is fine for the temporal, but ill-adapted to the eternal, to what can't be seen, save in those tantalizing glimpses the Spirit affords.

Except to God, 'speaking in tongues' is gobbledegook. 'Nobody understands them since they are speaking mysteries in the spirit' (1 Corinthians 14.2). Everyday language breaks down, especially when we try to pray. Speechless ourselves, we rely on the Spirit's intercession, although this can be expressed only 'with sighs too deep for words'.

Luke's account of the coming of the Holy Spirit records a lot of noise. To some the sounds make sense. The Phrygians hear fluent Phrygian; the Pamphylians catch the sound of Pamphylian; to those from Elam, it's all Elamite – and so on. The curse of Babel is revoked, albeit only briefly. But to others all that is audible is drunken nonsense. Our critics still suggest we're on something rather than on to something.

Paul is a maelstrom. Luke, tracing the current of Christian history, is a river. John is a deep, still pool. John's Jesus tells how he must go so that another may come. John's readers will make the connection which John himself does not articulate, that this 'Advocate' is not altogether another, but one in whom Jesus will be nearer to them than ever before. The language is indirect and allusive. Archbishop Rowan Williams has commented on John's 'circling, hovering, recapitulatory' style (a style, we might add, much like his own). That is the style, hesitating to settle on what exactly is to be said, of John's comments on how the Spirit convicts the world 'of sin and righteousness and judgement'. Some of our translators, uncertain what John really means, do some 'hovering', if not dithering, of their own. Is the spirit's role to 'prove the world wrong' or to 'convict the world'? Either way, how is that role to be played?

However softly focused John's meditation on the Holy Spirit may be, one principle stands out sharply. The sphere of the Spirit's work is not the private recesses of the soul, but the public arenas of the world. His business is not to cultivate my inner spiritual sensibilities, but to confront a world that has lost its way. The role of Spirit is ethical, that much is clear, and ethics are relational.

Both the revived interest in the Holy Spirit, which has swept through the Christian Church in the last fifty years, and the more widespread fascination for all things 'spiritual' which has developed over the same period, have focused on self rather than on society. Whether by 'baptism in the spirit' or by doing odd things with crystals, the quest has been for an enhanced personal experience of the transcendent. Meanwhile the world has gone its way. John's understanding of the mission of the Paraclete is in utter contrast to such self-absorbed spirituality. Sin, righteousness, judgement – those are the Spirit's concerns, not ecstasies in overheated services or the inner calm produced by sitting for a very long time on one buttock with your legs round your neck.

Those looking for a sermon starter might like to know that 'Paraclete' is the name of an American manufacturer of bullet-proof vests.

YEAR C

Acts 2.1–21 or Genesis 11.1–9; Romans 8.14–17; or Acts 2.1–21; John 14.8–17 (25–27)

THE BOUNDLESS SPIRIT

On the first Whit Sunday they asked, 'What does this mean?' This Sunday we shall hear the answer they were given, that what they were witnessing was the promised outpouring of God's Holy Spirit. We shall note the response many of them made – their delight in each other's company, their readiness to share their meals and everything else, their prayerfulness, their reckless generosity. Those were the days. Perhaps those would *be* the days, if ever we took our Christianity seriously.

On the first Whit Sunday they asked a question. This Sunday we come with a question of our own. It's time to ask it – and Pentecost is the best day to ask it. 'What is the relationship of the Spirit and the spiritual?' There is no question more important or more urgent that the Christian Churches should be asking.

Over recent years there has been an astonishing increase in the number of those claiming to have had significant spiritual experiences. For those who have had them, these experiences – of 'something or someone beyond' – have been both utterly real and almost impossible to describe or explain. These years, during which so many have testified to a spiritual dimension to their lives, have been the years when church-going has continued its steep decline.

Something is going on. David Hay, who has made the phenomenon of spiritual awareness the subject of a lifetime's research and reflection, has written a deeply perceptive book about what might be happening. *Something There* (Darton, Longman and Todd, 2006) is not a commentary on our readings, but there could be no better companion to them. Nor could there be a better guide than David Hay, as we press the question we are bound to ask at Pentecost. Can these 'experiences of transcendence', which many far from the Christian fold report, be accommodated within the Christian understanding of the Holy Spirit?

David Hay's sober and meticulously researched work contrasts markedly with the reaction of some Christian commentators to the reawakening to the spiritual so strikingly apparent in our times. Even Giles Fraser, who certainly does not believe that the Church has sole ownership of the spiritual, has described much modern talk of the spiritual as 'an empty form of free-floating flatulence' (*Church Times*, 30 March 2007).

It might seem that St John agrees with the Chancellor of St Paul's Cathedral. Our Gospel reading apparently rules out absolutely any possibility of an accommodation between the Spirit and 'the spiritual'. The contrast in the Fourth Gospel between the disciples and 'the world' is drawn sharply. John's Gospel comes from and speaks to a community that has already marked itself off from those outside its walls. 'The Spirit of truth' is given to those who believe, and no one else can receive him. If so, the purported spiritual experience of the unbeliever, however else it may be understood, has nothing in common with the Christian experience of the Holy Spirit.

But trace the story in the Acts of the Apostles and you may come to a different conclusion. What took place on the first Whit Sunday was the experience of those attached to a minority movement within first-century Judaism. The spokesman of that movement, one Simon Peter, claimed that the events of that day were the fulfilment of the prophecy that 'in the last days' God would pour out his Spirit 'on all flesh', that's to say on everyone. At that stage, it didn't occur to Peter that this gift was really for everyone, for Gentiles as well as for Jews. But later, when he found himself at a meeting where 'the Holy Spirit was poured out even on the Gentiles' (Acts 10.45), he was forced to change his mind and to recognize that nowhere is off-limits to the Spirit of God.

We discover from the experience of the spiritual what are the boundaries of the Spirit's activity, boundaries which will have to be constantly redrawn as our experience of the presence and activity of the Spirit of God is enlarged. We may well end up concluding that there are no boundaries at all.

So what is going on? No doubt – explore the stalls on the fringes of the Glastonbury festival – much that is spooky and very silly, if not downright dangerous. But perhaps at the same time old wine-skins of settled attitudes about the admissible and the inadmissible are being broken by the new wine of the work of God in unanticipated ways.

David Hay concludes his great study of the powerful spiritual currents of our time, waves racing like an incoming tide across our secular sands, by voicing his own conviction that God the Holy Spirit is already communicating with people, many of whom steer well clear of the institutional Church. Do they need our Christian language, our Christian metaphors, and our Christian traditions? Are we really to believe that everyone is hopelessly adrift until they drop anchor with us? David Hay has his own answer to that question. Buy his book and find out what it is.

Trinity Sunday

YEAR A

Isaiah 40.12–17, 27–31; 2 Corinthians 13.11–13; Matthew 28.16–20

I WITH YOU AM

The epilogue to Matthew's Gospel contains our Lord's command to baptize 'in the name of the Father and of the Son and of the Holy Spirit'. The traditional formula testifies to the early church's recognition that the one God is made known in more ways than one. By the same token, more recent Trinitarian formulae – 'creator, redeemer, sanctifier' or 'life-giver, pain-bearer, love-maker', for example – recognize that there are multiple ways in which to speak of the mystery of the divine nature. Metaphors for that mystery do not have to reflect and endorse the historic hegemony of men. Only men, jealous of that hegemony, would maintain otherwise.

'Father, Son, and Holy Spirit.' So powerfully and memorably does the title impact on us that we may overlook the possibility that it is not Matthew's last word about the mystery of who God is. I have been studying the Greek New Testament for many years but only now, in preparing these comments, do I notice that Matthew may be saying something more.

'I am with you,' says Jesus. He adds 'to all eternity', but we stay for the moment with those first four words. Their plain and simple meaning is that Jesus will continue to keep his disciples company. Even though he will seem to have left them, he will be as close to them as ever he was. The first disciples of Jesus found his words to be true. So to this day and to their great comfort have his subsequent followers.

'I am with you.' There are just four words in the Greek text too, but there they are in a different order. "I with you am" is the sequence of the words in Matthew. 'I AM', the name revealed at Sinai, is the divine name that the Jesus of John's Gospel makes his own (Exodus

3.14; John 8.58). Now we have a new name. 'I – with you – am,' says Jesus. It is as if the name beyond all names, expressive of the inexpressible, is broken open and the little company of Jesus and his friends is brought into its heart. The voice is Matthew's, the theology is John's. 'I in them and Thou in me, that they may be perfectly one' (John 17.23).

Such a reading of Jesus's promise could be said to be both contrived and unnecessary. The order of words in Matthew's text is the natural way to say, 'I am with you.' To be sure, there are occasional flights of Johannine language in Matthew's Gospel (cf. Matthew 11.27), but we need not suppose that Matthew has borrowed John's wings here. It is safe to say that Matthew himself did not intend to say more than he obviously does say. Surely we are making things far too complicated. Is it not enough to know that, as we used to sing, 'He walks with me and talks with me along life's narrow way'?

Yes, it is enough to know that he is at our side. In that knowledge we may make it through today. 'Tomorrow and tomorrow and tomorrow', can wait. But – 'only connect' – there is little value in having four Gospels if we do not read them 'synoptically', with all four of them open side by side. With Matthew and John both before us, we contemplate the possibility that companionship with Christ brings us into a relationship with God that only the language of Trinitarian theology is sufficient to describe. Jesus has said, echoing a voice from a burning bush, 'I AM.' So what does it imply for the nature of divinity and for our destiny if he goes on to say, 'I WITH YOU AM'? Has Matthew unwittingly left a door ajar through which we glimpse a glory beyond the horizon of our highest hopes?

Last words are often weighty. The last words of Jesus in Mathew's Gospel speak of his reign, an authority which differs radically from the political and religious regimes it challenges and to which those regimes must finally yield. His final words speak of the imperative of his coming Kingdom, the demand to cross all boundaries to 'make disciples.' And he tells us that we need never walk alone.

The last words *of* someone can be weighty. So too can the last words *about* someone. We notice Matthew's final reference to the disciples. Nothing he has said about them previously in his Gospel is more important. Most translations say that the disciples worshiped Jesus 'but some doubted'. That 'but' is too strong a rendering of a delicate little Greek particle and the 'some' is imported from nowhere. It is almost as if our translators are conspiring to keep from us what Matthew actually said. The Greek simply means, 'They knelt in worship, though they doubted.'

Even on our knees, we still have our doubts. They are a condition of our discipleship.

YEAR B

Isaiah 6.1–8; Romans 8.12–17; John 3.1–17

WHOLENESS, HOLINESS, AND THE PECKHAM HEALTH CENTRE

If we want to understand the Trinity and the meaning of everything we should study a long defunct health centre in Peckham. That is the interesting suggestion of a recent book (*Wholeness and Holiness*, J. D. Trotter, Pioneer Health Foundation, 2003).

Famous in the 1930s but now forgotten, the Peckham Health Centre in South London concentrated on building a healthy community, not on curing sick individuals. The doctors who founded it believed that it is together that we are made whole. The 'Peckham experiment' demonstrated the primacy of the communal for our identity and well-being. The common life of the Peckham Health Centre, Trotter claims, provides the key to understanding the divine nature and all that is.

Whatever we make of the book's thesis, we won't quarrel with its themes – wholeness and holiness. Add a third theme – the here and now – and we have a threefold cord running through our readings and a lifeline to hold on to as we try to talk about the Trinity without mouthing inanities.

The wholeness of the divine is relational. The one Lord speaks to Isaiah in the first person plural and is *thrice*-holy. The holiness of the Lord is ethical, not ritual or cultic. (It has nothing to do with changing altar-frontals or the laundering of corporals.) When Isaiah 'sees the Lord', it is as if he has looked through a window on how life should be lived, so much so that he must now hold his head in shame. There is a dynamic to the divine life, a 'holy wholeness'. Christians speak of this dynamic as a relationship of love.

The divine life is not so self-absorbed that it is undistracted by our plight and ills. The wholeness and the holiness engage with the here and now. The Trinity is as much about how we ought to be as about how God is. To see God better is to see my neighbour better, and to recognize more clearly my obligation to him. The here and now is my specific place and time with all its imperative demands. For Isaiah, the here and now was the kingdom of Judah in the eighth century BC, a society where the orphan was undefended and the widow's cause ignored (Isaiah 1.23). For me the here and now is twenty-first century Hackney, a neighbourhood with plenty of fatherless and single mums. That is why Trinitarian orthodoxy can never simply be measured by subscription to metaphysical propositions. (Pass the word to cathedrals which forbid services by Unitarians.)

For Paul, the dynamic of the divine relationship is more about how we should live than what is going on in God, a territory he left the church fathers to fight over. Paul's bold claim is that the life of God, however it is to be understood, is one into which we are 'adopted', a status demanding death to self. We cry 'Abba, Father.' James Barr, who for forty years has been telling us to watch our language, tells us that 'Abba isn't Daddy' (*Journal of Theological Studies* 39, 1988). Maybe not. But, as the Bishop of Stepney, the Rt Revd Stephen Oliver, has pointed out, the word with its echoes of 'Papa' and 'Dada' carries 'a warm and close relationship of trust and love' (*Guiding Stars*, SPCK, 2005). We are embraced by the wholeness and – here and now – we are to reflect the holiness.

The Gospel unites me with Nicodemus who came by night to Jesus. He was in the dark, where I am when I talk about the Trinity. I identify with Nicodemus, the patron saint of those who wonder what is going on. 'Are you a teacher of Israel,' Jesus says to Nicodemus and to me, 'and yet you do not understand?' No, I do not yet understand. But as I read of the Spirit of God moving as the wind, of one who goes to and fro between God and the world's wilderness, and of the God who loves and gives of his own, I sense a single purpose which is also a symphony. I sense too that the wholeness and the holiness sustained by such love have everything to do with what is immediately asked of me.

The Scriptures, such as those we shall read on Sunday, and the experience by which they were interpreted, are the material from which eventually a doctrine was fashioned. That doctrine is – Lord, have mercy upon us – an attempt to describe the mystery of who God is. But it is also an account of how things are. There is much debate these days about the so-called 'primary building-blocks of matter'. Trinitarian faith complements the theories of the physicists. What is primary, we hold, is relational, and the nature of that relationship, both in its inner dynamic and in its imperative claims, is an ethic of love. That is the faith they practised in Peckham in the '30s.

YEAR C

Proverbs 8.1–4, 22–31; Romans 5.1–5; John 16.12–15

HAPPY TO BE GOD

On Trinity Sunday we try to talk about God. That's very difficult. (It's much easier to talk about Jesus, although, if Christianity is to be believed, we are not changing the subject when we do so.) All our language about God is picture language. The abstract language that philosophers and theologians use to talk about God is just as much picture language as the naïve and down-to-earth illustrations that have helped ordinary people to relate to the God to whom they say their prayers. The famous theologian who tells me that 'the economic Trinity *is* the immanent Trinity, and *vice versa*' may have come no closer to the mystery of who God is than the child who looks at a cloverleaf and finds it strange and beautiful.

The doctrine of the Trinity is not found in the New Testament. It was formulated by the Church. No doubt Gregory of Nyssa and the others needed lots of paracetamol as they laboured over the definitions of the Trinity that baffle us to this day. But the doctrine was not spun out of thin air. It was the conclusion about God that Christians were driven to by their experience of mission and worship. For all the problems about one and one and one making one, they could find no other adequate explanation of their encounter with God in Christ by his Spirit. Nor, they insisted, was the formula – even if never defined in the Bible – unscriptural. A Trinitarian understanding of God, they held, is already implied by such passages as we read this Sunday.

Christians have long turned to the 'farewell discourses' of John's Gospel as a commentary on the doctrine of the Trinity. The fluidity of John's language in these discourses conveys something of the 'circulation of divine love' that – so the Church came to hold – constitutes the triune relationship of Creator, Redeemer, and Inspirer. Whoever has seen Jesus has seen the Father (John 14.9). Jesus is in the Father and the Father in him (John 14.10). Jesus is coming (John 14.3); the

Spirit is coming (John 16.13). Ideas surface, then submerge, and then, subtly modified, drift to the surface again. The strange elusiveness of the language – 'Soon you won't see me; soon you will' (John 16.16) – suggests a mystery to be expressed only in paradox. So in Sunday's short Gospel we learn from John that when the promised Spirit speaks it is the word of Jesus we hear and that all that the Father has Jesus has made his own.

The danger in talking about the Trinity is to suppose that a facility with clever forms of words – it's a skill they teach you in theological colleges – brings you a gnat's whisker nearer God. That is why we must not despise the child's cloverleaf or even the 'three-in-one' fruit salad served in some Catholic homes on Trinity Sunday. And we certainly do not despise what is the most hallowed image of the Trinity in Christian iconography. Andrei Rublev's fifteenth-century icon, depicting the three angels who visited Abraham at the Oak of Mamre (Genesis 18.1–8), has long been interpreted as an icon of the Trinity. This sublime image does not 'illustrate' the Trinity, although there is clearly more to be seen here than the meeting of three strangers at a table. The Trinitarian dimensions to the icon – the subtle interplay of the three figures, their deference to each other, the likeness of the faces – can all be pointed out. So too can the symbols of the tree, the rock, and the wine. Yet icons do not give up their secrets quickly. Reading an icon is not an exercise in decoding. I must stay with Rublev's icon, allowing it to lead me beyond itself, that is, to lead me into prayer. Only then will I perhaps come a little closer to the mysterious Reality to which it bears witness.

There is note of deep sadness to the figures in this icon. Why should that be? Isn't being God supposed to be blissful? Archbishop Rowan Williams thinks so. He has recently said that 'God is, in simple terms, sublimely and eternally happy to be God' (*Tokens of Trust*, Canterbury Press, 2007). So who is right – Rublev or Archbishop Rowan? There is a clue in our Gospel. Jesus says to his disciples, 'I still have many things to say to you, but you cannot bear them now.' It seems that if we were to be told all the truth all at once it would be more than we could cope with. This sombre remark does sound like something the historical Jesus must have said, even if its context is more of a meditation on the teaching of Jesus than a record of his actual words. The gospel is good news. In the end the three in one will be all in all. But the long sorry story of all that humankind must suffer isn't over just yet. That must make everyone in the Holy Trinity very unhappy.

Proper 4

The Sunday between 29 May and 4 June (if after Trinity Sunday)

YEAR A

Deuteronomy 11.18–21, 26–28; Romans 1.16, 17, 3.22b–28 (29–31); Matthew 7.21–29

FOUNDATION FOR FREEDOM

The houses on Beach Road, Happisburgh, Norfolk, stand close to the cliff-top and command a fine view of the sea. But that same sea is eroding the sandy soil on which they are built and, one by one, they are tumbling down the cliff into the waters below. With hindsight, it can be seen that a crumbling cliff-top was not a sensible place to have built a row of houses.

It is wise to build on rock; foolish to build on sand. This talk of 'wisdom' and 'folly' would have rung clear bells for those who first heard 'the parable of the two builders'. Jesus's first audience was of course predominantly Jewish, but so too, so the scholars tell us, was the community in which Matthew's Gospel originally circulated. The parable spoke to those who knew their Scriptures. It would have reminded them of a wonderful woman named 'Wisdom' who built a fine house – famously it had seven pillars – which was distinguished for its hospitality. To this house those who had lost their way in life were welcomed. There they were made to sit down to eat and drink and, thus refreshed, enabled to resume more responsible lives (Proverbs 9.1–6).

The parable is very brief. It is told with the utmost economy and restraint. Only in the description of the storm overtaking the two houses do the images multiply. 'The rain fell and the floods came and the winds blew . . .' The language reels, as to the successive blows of the buffeting storm.

We know nothing beyond what we can infer from his text about the circumstances of 'Matthew's church'. But one thing we can be sure about. His was a suffering church, a community increasingly threatened as – so those of 'the Way' believed – the end drew near. Little as we know about Matthew's church, there is much in his Gospel to suggest that it was a minority church, small in numbers and existing precariously on the margins.

How does such a church survive adversity? How does it maintain its witness unswervingly? No doubt the church prevails by faith, by trusting in the grace of God to see it through. But that is not the emphasis here. The church that cherished the Sermon on the Mount survived by its obedience, by doing what Jesus had said, by loving its enemies, by not retaliating, by doing what is unfairly demanded – and then by doing as much again. That is the rock on which this church rests.

With this parable, Jesus concludes his sermon. The crowds, we read, 'were astounded at his teaching'. Where did these crowds come from, we wonder? It seems they were not there at the start, for apparently it was in order to get away from the crowds that Jesus had ascended 'the mountain' where his disciples then joined him (Matthew 5.1). We can, if we like, picture lots of people clambering up the hillside to hear Jesus, much as on another occasion, when he wanted to be alone with his disciples, they had hurried round the lakeside to meet him (Mark 6.30–34). But there is a more important question. Do the crowds overhear a discourse intended only for the disciples? Or is that discourse as much addressed to them, as it is to those who have already given themselves to the cause of Christ's coming Kingdom? The question focuses the fundamental issue: is the ethic of the Sermon on the Mount intended as a universal law or is it applicable only to relationships within the Christian community? Who, in a word, is Jesus talking to?

What is most striking in the epilogue to the Sermon on the Mount is that it is the crowds, not the disciples, who draw the right conclusion from what they have heard. The crowds recognize that he teaches 'as one having authority'. Whether the sermon was meant for them or not, it is they who put two and two together, who recognize the all-important implication of the sermon, that by teaching with such distinctive and unparalleled authority Jesus is making a claim about his identity. Who else but one from God would claim that such eternal consequences hang on whether or not we obey his words?

On the night I am jotting down these thoughts, the Jews are celebrating Passover. Passover is both a celebration of the freedom of God's people and also a prayer for all who suffer oppression. The Sermon on the Mount is also a freedom text. We do not achieve freedom by building lives on sand, however compliant and accommodating a substance sand is. Freedom is found by building on rock, that least tractable of materials. A text from John's Gospel, not usually associated with the

Sermon on the Mount, provides a commentary on it. 'You will know the truth and the truth will set you free.' (John 8.32). The most exacting moral code known to humankind is also the most liberating.

YEAR B

Deuteronomy 5.12–15; 2 Corinthians 4.5–12; Mark 2.23–3.6

THE E=MC² OF CHRISTIAN DISCIPLESHIP

The congregation hung on his whispered words as he announced his text. 'We have this treasure in earthen vessels.' He could only whisper because he had just come out of hospital, where they had done awful things to his throat. Canon George Sandfield, for twenty years Rector of Camborne in the west of Cornwall, knew only too well that we are clay – 'common clay pots', as the Good News Bible has it. He was often ill, but his bodily infirmities only served to make his spiritual strength the more manifest. He was my Rector. I was his curate. I thank God for him.

George Sandfield was a living commentary on our New Testament reading, an extract from Paul's correspondence with the church at Corinth. Our eight verses belong to a passage, continuing well into the next chapter, which constitutes Paul's supreme statement of what it means to bear witness to Jesus Christ.

Paul's extraordinary testimony – and there is none more profound or more moving in the literature of Christianity – is that what he has suffered in his many afflictions has been the death of Jesus. His actual words take one's breath away, so astonishing is the claim he makes. Paul speaks of himself 'always carrying around the *necrosis* of Jesus'. He has poured out his life – and his life poured out has proved life for others. Paul is saying much more than that his experience resembles that of Jesus. He dares to claim that the dying of Jesus and his own are one.

Albert Schweitzer wrote of the 'mysticism of Paul the Apostle'. Certainly Paul's vision, that in dying the death of Jesus he yields life to others, can be seen as deeply mystical. But it may also be seen as recognition of a truth that is not in the least mystical, but rather a fact about the nature of things. When matter is destroyed – what goes to the making of stars or clay pots, say – immense amounts of energy are released. Paul's theology complies with the fundamental laws of physics. 'Death is at work in us, life in you.' It is the $e=mc^2$ of Christian discipleship. If Einstein and Paul have now met, they will have had a lot to talk about.

Paul sees his afflictions as those that put Jesus to death. But not all of those afflictions were nails or thorns. When Paul tells the Corinthians that he is 'often troubled', he will surely be thinking ruefully of the raft of problems, some petty enough, which the Corinthians presented to him. He will have been wounded by their endless schisms and scandals. He will have been hurt that they have been so slow to learn the way of Christ. He could have said to them what he said to the Galatians, 'My dear children, I am again in the pains of childbirth until Christ is formed in you' (Galatians 4.19).

Jesus too is wounded well before Good Friday. The Jesus of Mark's Gospel is a man being watched. They watch him eating, watching especially those he chooses as his company. They watch him walking through the fields. They watch him in the synagogue. Every inch of the way he is under observation. One step out of line – the line drawn by those in whom interpretation of the law is vested – and he is immediately attacked.

Our Gospel records two such perceived transgressions. Jesus permits his followers to harvest the corn, albeit only a few heads of grain, on the Sabbath. What they do is regarded by his opponents as work and thus as a breach of the fourth commandment. On a subsequent Sabbath day, Jesus heals a disabled man. Treatment of the sick, like plucking an ear of corn, is seen as work Again, those watching are swift to condemn.

Jesus's answers to his critics are a window on his mind on how the Mosaic law should be interpreted, although what exactly those answers assert remains debatable. Whether or not Jesus or his disciples were in fact breaking the law is a nice question which we leave to the big commentaries. Suffice it to say, that the views of Jesus on such matters were – to use a modern ecclesiastical term – liberal.

But in the light of our reading from Paul, we leave aside how Jesus counters the arguments of his adversaries and reflect instead on what such unremitting opposition is doing to him. We read that Jesus is angered and distressed by the hardness of his opponents' hearts. Not to use the word lightly, the intransigence Jesus encountered must have been 'crucifying' for him. The thorns, the nails, and the spear are still to come. But in the meantime we must not minimize the pain which the professionally pious inflict on Jesus by their wilful refusal to recognize that one from God is doing a new thing among them.

YEAR C

1 Kings 8.22–23, 41–43; Galatians 1.1–12; Luke 7.1–10

UNDER AUTHORITY

Here are four assumptions which we regularly bring to our reading of the Gospels and to our retelling of the story of Jesus:

1 The Romans despised the Jews.
2 The Jews hated the Romans.
3 The Romans were a brutal lot.
4 The Jewish religious leaders were opposed to Jesus and wanted to be rid of him.

The fascinating tale we hear this Sunday obliges us to question each of these assumptions. It seems that some of the things said to us since our Sunday-School days need to be qualified.

The Roman centurion does not despise the people of the remote region of the Empire to which he has been posted. On the contrary, he respects them and is drawn to them. Indeed he has come to love them. He is attracted by the 'ethical monotheism' of Judaism, by its austere and lofty vision of the divine, contrasting so strongly with the Roman pantheon of fickle, bellicose and lascivious deities insatiably demanding propitiation. The house of prayer he has built for his Jewish neighbours will not resemble those where he was taught to pray, for it will contain no image of the one worshipped there.

The respect the centurion feels for the Jews is reciprocated. He is of the company honoured by the Jews as 'righteous Gentiles', those 'of the nations' who have declined to play the role of persecutor. The centurion's kindly disposition to his Jewish neighbours is matched by his devotion to his sick slave and his determination to do something for him. (This detail will not surprise those who have been in the army, a world in many ways far more humane in its relationships than that of 'civvy street'.)

The most startling detail of the story – to those settled in conclusions to which they have too swiftly jumped – is the cordial relationship between the Jewish elders and Jesus. The elders recognize the authenticity of Jesus's miracles and, by implication, that of his mission.

'He loves our people,' they say. We must stay with these words until all they imply at last dawns on us. The basis and power of the elders' appeal to Jesus is that he is one of the Jewish people as they are. 'Our people,' they say. That 'our' includes Jesus. They count him as one of their own. Jesus was not a Christian. Christianity had not been invented. Jesus was a Jew. It is because he belongs with them to the same community of faith that the elders can appeal to Jesus on their Roman benefactor's behalf.

Jesus has not ceased to belong to that community. The Jews are still his people. It follows that if we are Christ's people – and, as the *laos* of God, we claim to be just that – then that community is our kindred too. Christianity and Judaism, as Rabbi Tony Bayfield has repeatedly argued, are siblings. 'We now understand that we are the siblings of a Parent who has no favourites,' Rabbi Bayfield has written. 'That alone should cause us to revise the truth claims that we make for ourselves and the light in which we regard the other. It should lead us to take much more seriously the different routes that each sibling has taken on their particular journey, respecting the other and allowing the other to be' (*Church Times*, 13 February 2009).

Luke tells this story with an acute ear to its internal echoes. 'He is worthy,' they say of the centurion. 'I am not worthy,' says the centurion. The echo of these echoes sounds in our liturgy: 'Lord, I am not worthy . . . but speak the word only and I shall be healed.' The message the centurion sends to Jesus reflects his experience as a soldier, as an officer who is used both to giving commands and to obeying them. Again, we must try to catch the emphasis of the words Luke wants us to hear. 'I also am a man set under authority . . .' The weight of his words is as much on the authority to which he is subject as the authority which he exercises. The centurion recognizes in Jesus someone 'under authority' as well as someone 'in authority'.

To what, to whom, is Jesus under authority? Yes, to be sure, Jesus is under God's authority. The mission of Jesus is to manifest and implement the reign of God. That is true. But that is also rather too easily said and perhaps it is not all that needs to be said.

It could be said that the one in this story who commands the narrative and determines what takes place is neither the powerful soldier nor the one whose mighty works inaugurate God's Kingdom. Nor does that decisive role belong to the Jewish elders. The one whom all seek to serve in this brief story, the one who in that sense commands the greatest authority and whose claim is sovereign, is an unnamed desperately sick slave.

Proper 5

The Sunday between 5 and 11 June (if after Trinity Sunday)

YEAR A

Hosea 5.15—6.6; Romans 4.13–25; Matthew 9.9–13, 18–26

MORE LOVING-KINDNESS, LESS RELIGION

Why is there anything? The question taxes our minds, but also bids to break our hearts, for such is the scale of suffering that sometimes it seems as if it would have been better if there had been nothing at all. Why is there anything? It is a question a child can ask, for children are natural philosophers. Why is there anything? We have learned from Professor Richard Dawkins – and if we haven't yet learned, it is high time we did – that it is perilous to claim that there are questions which fall outside the province of science to investigate. But if there are any such questions, here surely is one.

Why is there anything? The Jewish mystical tradition has a one-word answer to that question. All that is exists because of an original act of *chesed*. The Jewish mystics paraphrase a text from the Psalms freely but truthfully. 'The world is built with *chesed*' (Psalm 89.2). There is no word in our Hebrew Scriptures more important than *chesed* and none more difficult to translate. Our English versions ring the changes. *Chesed* is 'loving-kindness', 'mercy', 'faithfulness', 'loyalty', 'steadfast love' – these are but some of the unavailing attempts to pin the word down.

Chesed is fundamentally pro-active love, love that acts without prior cause to do so. Why is there anything? There is something rather than nothing because God is *chesed* – preemptive, unilateral and initiatory love.

In our first reading we have one of the primary texts of the Bible and it is a text about *chesed*. The prophet Hosea speaks of *chesed* as what God desires in his people. God looks for *chesed* because *chesed* is what God is. 'I desire *chesed* and not sacrifice, the knowledge of God rather than burnt offerings.' The importance of this prophetic text is that it illuminates much else in the scriptural story that might otherwise remain baffling. For example, it goes a long way to explain that puzzling character, Jesus of Nazareth.

Hosea's ringing words –'*chesed* not sacrifice' – meant much to Matthew. They helped him make sense of what Jesus says and does. In our Gospel we hear Matthew's version of a story he took from Mark. To the astonishment and outrage of the local clergy, Jesus sits down to eat with 'tax-collectors and sinners', with those who fell scandalously short of the exacting standards of religious respectability set by the professionally pious. According to Matthew – and here he adds to the tale he has taken from Mark – Jesus justifies his action by appealing to our text from Hosea. To share a meal with those shunned by everyone else is *chesed*. It is *ex nihilo* love, 'the love that hung the sun and all the stars'. It is a love that brings into being a state of affairs which for these pariahs had not existed before, a relationship with someone who does not condemn them.

'*Chesed* not sacrifice.' Matthew loves this text and he will quote it again. When Jesus is accused of encouraging his disciples to 'break the Sabbath', by allowing them to pluck ears of corn on the day in the week when no such 'work' is permitted, he appeals once more to Hosea's words (Matthew 12.7).

'*Chesed* not sacrifice.' Why are these words so important for Matthew? If the author of the Gospel that bears his name was indeed Matthew the tax-collector, the same Matthew whose call we read about on Sunday, then it is no surprise that he twice quotes this tremendous text. For Matthew has known from his own experience what it means to be blessed by *chesed*, to have been called out of non-being into being by creative love. His job – collecting taxes for the hated oppressors and siphoning off much of the takings for himself – would have made him in most eyes a nothing, a no one. Now, called by Christ, there is, as Paul will say, 'a new creation' (2 Corinthians 5.17). Love bade him welcome, the one whom all despised.

In fact, the disciple Matthew probably did not write the Gospel attributed to him. That attribution was made much later than the original anonymous text. But we can still be sure that behind the Gospel with which our New Testament begins is the experience of someone who knew what *chesed* means, who could testify to the creative grace that makes a somebody out of a nobody.

'*Chesed* not sacrifice.' 'The knowledge of God, not burnt offerings.' We can infer, from what we shall read in weeks to come, that the author of the little book with Matthew's name on the cover had had some experience of sacrifices and burnt offerings and that those rituals had done him no good. What Hosea was saying in the eighth century BC to Israel, and what Matthew was saying to the first-century church, is what both are saying to twenty-first-century Christendom. What God wants is more *chesed* and less religion.

YEAR B

Genesis 3.8–15; 2 Corinthians 4.13–5.1; Mark 3.20–35

LORD OF THE LORD OF THE FLIES

Adam ate from the tree from which he had been commanded not to eat. That tree, we recall, was 'the tree of the knowledge of good and evil' (Genesis 2.17). Adam craved certainty, to know for sure, as all of us who are of Adam do. That longing has been our undoing, the undoing we call 'the Fall'. 'The lust for certainty,' Bishop Tom Butler of South-wark once said, 'is the original sin.' Those who presume to comment on Holy Scripture are not immune from that lust, a consideration we must have in mind as we come in a moment to the hardest of 'the hard sayings of Jesus'.

Many complain about pressure at work. The office 'lunch-hour' belongs to a past as distant as manual typewriters. Lunch these days is, at best, a snatched sandwich at one's desk. Jesus was under that kind of pressure. He experienced in the first century what many do in the twenty-first. Mark tells us that Jesus and those with him were not able to eat, such were the demands being made on him. When we work so hard that we don't stop for food, our families worry about us. They see our life-style as insane. So it was with the family of Jesus. They watch him working all hours, always yielding to the relentless demands made on him, and they wonder whether he has gone mad.

It is a rare glimpse of how Jesus was seen by those closest to him. It's too much for the other Gospel writers that Jesus's family want him sectioned and they omit this passage. No doubt it was not just his boundless availability that made them question Jesus's mental balance. Little about his conduct was conventional. Jesus came to redefine what it means to be human. Given that purpose, much of what he said and did was eccentric. Jesus continues to call in ques-tion much that passes for common sense in a world off its hinges.

Those who wish to charge Jesus with insanity will never be short of evidence.

His family say that he is out of his mind. The religious leaders say that his mind has been taken over. Already the local thought-police has sought to silence him. Now he has come to the attention of the central authorities. The fact that they send some of their own people to confront him is a measure of the threat he is seen to constitute. The charge is that Jesus is possessed by 'Beelzebul' and that by Beelzebul's power he exorcizes the demons.

Just who Beelzebul was – or is – is a debate which need not detain us. The name, which could be translated 'Lord of Dung', may be a contemptuous parody of the name of the Philistine god 'Baalzebub' (2 Kings 1.2). 'Baalzebub' was 'the Lord of the Flies' – so named, perhaps, because he was believed to have power over plagues of insects. But for readers of modern classics, 'the Lord of the Flies' will always be the figure that so terrified the children of William Golding's novel of that name. That ghastly 'fly-lord', hanging from a tree on the hill dominating the island where the choir-boys had crash-landed, was, in fact, the corpse of a dead pilot, still entangled in the cords of his parachute. Simon, the Christ-figure of Golding's story, faces the 'fly-lord' without flinching, and by doing so delivers the island from its malign presence. The price he paid was life.

Golding's famous tale is a commentary on the lonely mission of the one who – so far from driving out demons by the ruler of demons – confronts, overcomes, and banishes them to their own place by the power of sacrificial love.

So we come to the hardest of 'hard sayings', the pronouncement that whoever blasphemes against the Holy Spirit can never be forgiven. Many have been tormented by these words. But those thus troubled, those fearful that they have committed 'the unforgivable sin' are not those who Jesus had in mind, for to be so disposed is to be open to Spirit, rather than resistant or closed to the Spirit.

If ever it matters to read Jesus's words in context, it matters now. The gravest blasphemy is to attribute to Satan what is done by Jesus in the power of the Spirit. That is what the representatives of the central religious authorities in Jerusalem have done. It needs to be added that, even now, even taking account of the heinousness of what has been uttered, Jesus's saying may still be a warning, rather than a final pronouncement of condemnation.

The last word on this solemn saying belongs to the commentator C. E. B. Cranfield. 'Those who most particularly should heed the warning of this verse today are the theological teachers and the official leaders of the churches' (*The Gospel according to Mark*, Cambridge University Press, revised edition, 1972).

YEAR C

1 Kings 17.17–24; Galatians 1.11–24; Luke 7.11–17

THE DEATH-THROES OF DEATH

I think of the first child I buried. Terry too was the only son of a widowed mother. He suffered from severe cerebral palsy. He was a total paraplegic and unable to speak. His mother used to trundle him around on a huge cumbersome gurney. In many ways she was as dependent on him as he on her. As at Nain, we carried him to where he was to rest. But our sad cortege was not met by another procession coming towards us. We did not meet the Lord of Life on the road from Camborne church to the cemetery, and Terry was not returned alive to his mother.

Luke's story echoes our Old Testament reading. The scene is Zarephath, which is not that far from Nain, as it happens. The land is suffering from a drought – all God's doing, as droughts in the Bible usually are. Elijah is lodging with a widow and her son. One miracle has already happened. The widow's jar of meal and jug of oil remain full, however much is taken from them. Now the son has died. Elijah prays. Here we must go back to our older English translations that retain the force of the Hebrew text. Elijah asks God a rhetorical question. The King James Version, followed by the 1881 Revised Version, renders Elijah's prayer accurately. 'Hast thou also brought evil on the widow by slaying her son?' The answer is 'Yes'. Of course that death was a 'tragedy' (New International Version). Of course it was a 'calamity' (Revised Standard Version). But the thrust of Elijah's prayer and the weight of the word he uses is that what God has done is an *evil*.

The timid modern translations are not so much mistranslations as 'undertranslations'. They shrink from the understanding of pain and suffering that – listen to Job! – is affirmed so powerfully in the Hebrew Bible. Our afflictions are not morally neutral. They are worse than tragic and they are worse than calamitous. We must give them the name that Elijah does. And we must not shy from the prophetic conclusion about where the buck stops. God is implicated. 'Shall evil befall a city,' asks Amos, 'and the Lord has not done it?' (Amos 3.6) 'I form the light, and create darkness; I make peace, and create evil. I am the Lord, who does all these things' (Isaiah 45.7).

Elijah's prayer, which Luke expects us to recall, provides the theological background for the story of what happened at Nain. To be sure, the plight of the widow, with no one now to support her, is truly desperate. When Jesus saw her 'his heart went out to her' – thus the NIV, and this time there can be no complaints about the translation. Yet the scene that greets Jesus and his disciples as they approach the town is more than a deeply affecting human misfortune. The company coming towards them is more like a Roman 'triumph', the procession of a commander who has won a signal victory in battle. Death has conquered life and this is its V-Day parade. The death of the only son of the widow of Nain was a triumph of evil, as was the death of Terry, the child I buried all those years ago. (Indeed I remember that my prayer at the time was much the same as Elijah's: 'Dear God, did you have to do something quite as cruel?')

Jesus addresses the dead boy with a word which belongs to New Testament's resurrection vocabulary. We could translate it literally, if clumsily, as 'Be risen!' Death's triumph proves short-lived. Here is 'Christus Victor'. Death has met its match. Of course the boy is not raised immortal, any more than Lazarus was or Jairus' daughter. Sooner or later he will be taken out of the town again on the same journey he was making when Jesus met him. Today the boy is returned to his mother, but tomorrow his dust will return to the earth it was (Ecclesiastes 12.7). Signs must not be confused with what they signify. Both son and mother are still under sentence of death. When the trumpet sounds, it will be another matter.

Meanwhile every day widowed mothers lose the children on whom they depend and – we think of the AIDS pandemic in sub-Saharan Africa – countless children lose their widowed or abandoned mothers. Jesus is not there for them in the way he was for the widow of Nain. But we note the response of those who witnessed what he did. 'A great prophet has arisen,' they cried. Again Luke sends us back to the Old Testament. Moses had promised that 'the Lord will raise up a great prophet'. And Moses had added, 'Listen to what he says' (Deuteronomy 18.15).

'Listen to what he says.' We cannot return the dead child to the mother, nor the mother to the orphaned child. But we can shut up and listen. If we do, we shall not be left long in the dark about what to do.

Proper 6

The Sunday between 12 and 18 June (if after Trinity Sunday)

YEAR A

Exodus 19.2–8a; Romans 5.1–8; Matthew 9.35 – 10.8 (9–23)

LOVE IS A LONG HAUL

He was in the army and out in the field on manoeuvres. To make the best use of any spare time, he had packed a Greek New Testament into his haversack. During a pause in one of the exercises, he turned to the tenth chapter of Matthew's Gospel. There he read words of Jesus which we hear on Sunday. Jesus sends out his twelve disciples to teach and to heal. He warns them that they will experience intense persecution. Then he tells them, 'You will not have gone through the towns of Israel before the Son of Man comes.'

The young soldier – he was only nineteen – was Albert Schweitzer. He had already been studying theology at Strasbourg University, where he had been taught that the sayings of Jesus about the future coming of the Son of Man were made up by the early church. As Schweitzer read Matthew's Greek text, he found himself coming to a different conclusion about these strange words. Schweitzer realized that a prediction on the lips of Jesus that did not come true could not have been invented. We are hearing, rather, the Jesus of history. According to Schweitzer, Jesus was convinced that, before his disciples had completed their missionary tour, he would be revealed as the coming Son of Man. But it did not turn out like that. So, Schweitzer famously argued, Jesus then set out for Jerusalem to suffer and die with the intention of thereby 'forcing the hand of God' to make his Messianic identity known, to bring history to a close, and to usher in his Kingdom.

Jesus's announcement that the 'coming of the Son of Man' is imminent is just one of a number of his 'hard sayings' which we shall hear on Sunday – if, as it should be, the longer Gospel reading is used. Jesus also instructs the Twelve to 'go nowhere among the Gentiles and to enter no town of the Samaritans'. Instead they are to confine their mission to 'the lost sheep of the house of Israel'. The hardest saying of all – if, that is, we think that Jesus is talking to us too – is Jesus's terse and peremptory 'raise the dead'.

Such sayings – Schweitzer was right, they could not have been made up – anchor us in history. We believe that Jesus was much more than the leader of a dissident movement within first-century Judaism, but he was at least that. Such a figure he was and thus he spoke. If some of Jesus's sayings do not easily 'fit' – that the end of the world was weeks away, that his mission was to his own people and not to foreigners, that his followers must bring the dead back to life – then we must not erase such awkward remarks from the record, any more than Matthew did. It is more important that we live with the hard sayings of Jesus than we explain them.

To be sure, Jesus was typical of the prophet in every age for whom what is certain is bound to be soon. To be sure, his charge to the Twelve to avoid the Gentiles and Samaritans was far from his last word about the recipients of his gospel. To be sure, the mission of Jesus's disciples was – and remains – continuous with his, to 'go about doing good' as he did (Acts 10.38). But we smooth the edges of the hard sayings of the Gospels at our peril. To try to make the ways and words of Jesus conform to our prior understanding of him is an attempt to bring him under our control – and that is not at all a Christian thing to do. At my baptism I submit to Christ. I am using my Bible in the wrong way if I try to make him submit to me.

Because I do not airbrush out the awkward texts, I have reason to cling the more confidently to those that bring me comfort. So I seize on Matthew's cameo of the 'harassed and helpless' crowd in which I am lost, one errant sheep among many. 'Harassed' is a strong word. The big dictionaries say that it can mean being 'flayed alive'. It feels like that sometimes, when the demands are multiple and incessant. It is the sensation, well known to clergy, graphically described by Kierkegaard as 'the sustained agony of being trampled to death by geese'. If I do not go under, it is because I hold to the lifeline that my Lord has 'compassion' on me.

'Compassion' on the lips of Jesus is a rich word. As the theologian, Christopher Cocksworth, Bishop of Coventry, has written, 'Behind the gentle word of our translation is a much stronger original that's about guts being stirred and wills being activated for the long haul of love.'

Love is indeed a long haul – which is one reason why, like the Twelve, we are told to travel light.

YEAR B

Ezekiel 17.22–24; 2 Corinthians 5.6–10 (11–13)14–17; Mark 4.26–34

DESPITE US, THE SEED GROWS

'The kingdom of God is as if someone would scatter seed on the ground.' By modern standards that is an absurdly inefficient method of farming. The parable of the sower highlights just how unproductive it is (Mark 4.3–9). The sower throws a handful of seed into the wind in the forlorn hope that some will land on hospitable soil and germinate. Three-quarters of the seed is wasted. As a model for mission it is ludicrous, as laughable as the efforts of the Victorian evangelists who, in the early days of the railways, disseminated the gospel by scattering tracts from the windows of speeding trains.

Yet the text stands and it is an indictment of us. Kierkegaard has taught us that the counter-cultural words of Jesus censure the Church before they judge society. Professor Richard Roberts of Lancaster University argues that we are witnessing in the contemporary Church 'the triumph of a managerial performance culture, concerned with religious product delivery'. The Church, says Dr Roberts, 'would appear to have followed contemporary trends and to be involved in the process of managerializing its mission and identity' (*Religion, Theology and the Human Sciences*, Cambridge University Press, 2002). Across this tightly managed landscape there wanders a lonely farmhand, tossing seed in the air. How ever did we get it all so wrong?

Despite us, the seed grows. We don't know how. We love to think we do. Hence the flood of publications about how to grow the church, hence all our 'mission action plans' and the like – but really we haven't a clue. It's all a great mystery. To admit that is not a cop-out. It is to heed the word of the Lord who teaches us that the Kingdom and the manner of its growth are precisely that – a mystery (Mark 4.10). I reflect gloomily on forty-five years of what might loosely be called Christian ministry and I recognize that any good that has come of it bears scant relation to anything planned.

The marvellous image of the mustard seed, 'smallest of all seeds' addresses the frail and the few – that's us – and gives us grounds for hope. Po-faced critics tell us that the middle-eastern mustard plant (*Brassica hirta*) couldn't grow into a bush big enough to accommodate flocks of birds. Such critics fail to register the sheer light-heartedness – all that is witty and whimsical – in the teaching of Jesus. After all, we are talking about the Kingdom of God where even mustard doesn't behave as everywhere else.

That Kingdom will be inclusive. Just how inclusive, just how accommodating this mustard plant will be is nicely captured – if you happen to speak English – by the Authorized Version So great will be the branches of the full-grown plant that 'the fowls of the air may lodge under the shadow of it'. The word 'fowl' has resonances, fortuitous as they are. The pun, if available only in English, hints that, come the Kingdom, there may be some strange birds nesting with us.

We do not, however, have to depend on such word-play to believe there's hope for vultures. The image of the mustard seed is drawn from the prophet Ezekiel's picture of a tree with a more capacious canopy. Unlike *Brassica hirta*, the *cedrus libani*, the cedar of Lebanon, has branches big enough for all the birds to settle in. The tree of which Ezekiel speaks is the Last Tree, surpassing in majesty all other trees, more glorious even than the tree of which it was said 'no tree in the garden of God could match its beauty' (Ezekiel 31.8). The prophet stresses that 'winged creatures of every kind' will nest in its shade. (I consult a list of 'unusual birds', all of which – such is Ezekiel's universalism – will surely be there, and I wonder with which one I most identify. I come in the list to the 'barking owl' and I read no further.)

All is 'in parables'. Only by telling parables – stories – can we speak of the things of God, even if some of the stories, as in the case of the parable of the mustard seed, are little more than one-liners. If the story doesn't contain within itself – and itself express – whatever may be its point, no explanation will make up for the failure. Faced with blank looks, the only recourse the story-teller has is to tell the story again or to tell another story. It's often said that parables are like jokes, that either you 'see' them or you don't. True, but perhaps it would be more accurate to say that the parables *are* jokes.

That is why we're bound to puzzled by Mark's footnote, that Jesus explained everything in private to his disciples, both because parables are essentially inexplicable – they speak for themselves or not at all – and because the notion of an inner coterie of those 'in the know' is worrying. There's no place for such charmed circles in the Church.

YEAR C

2 Samuel 11.26–12.10, 13–15; Galatians 2.15–21; Luke 7.36–8.3

CENSORIOUS MEN

Gallery-goers of refined sensibility and nervous disposition often hurry past the steamy works of Peter Paul Rubens. For delicate tastes, there is far too much flesh in his huge canvases. Certainly his voluptuous brushwork is sometimes gratuitous. But that is not true of a painting by him – it hangs in the Hermitage in St Petersburg – entitled *Christ in the house of Simon the Pharisee.* This altogether extraordinary picture provides a powerful commentary on Sunday's Gospel.

Our eye is at once drawn to the weeping woman. Her dress is slipping from her shoulder. She is nuzzling the leg of Jesus. With her loosened hair, she is wiping his foot, which at the same time she is drawing to her breast.

We may well be uneasy with these sensuous details – though why we should be, we who claim that 'the Word became flesh', is a great mystery. If we are uneasy, our disquiet is nothing to that of the men at the table. One of them peers down at the woman through his spectacles like a pathologist studying a corpse. Another is apparently about to be sick. Most avert their gaze in disgust.

Jesus is gesturing towards the woman. It is as if Rubens is asking us the same penetrating question that Jesus asks Simon, 'Do you see this woman?'

In one way, Simon sees her very clearly. It is part of his job as a clergyman to pass judgement on people, about where they stand before God and in the religious community in which he holds his important office. In her case, he has no difficulty in discerning her status. She is an unclean thing, not to be touched. In a word, she is a 'sinner'.

Jesus sees her differently. She is one of the 'poor' who in Luke's Gospel are seen as the recipients of God's salvation. Her poverty may not be material – she has her alabaster jar of ointment – but she is one of the excluded, one of the many treated by the professionally pious as pariahs because of their moral lapses and their failure to keep a hundred and one religious rules.

We look at Rubens' masterpiece again and we notice something else about it. We see this circle of censorious men, confident of their tenure of the moral high ground, united in their abhorrence of this 'fallen' woman – and we realize we have been here before. For these men are surely next-of-kin to those encircling 'the woman taken in adultery' and who are so eager to stone her (John 7.53 – 8.12). That story is no part of the original text of John's Gospel, certainly, but Jesus's words 'neither do I condemn you' locates the story at the heart of John's good news.

It is instructive to compare the two stories. In John's account, Jesus is relatively gentle with these appalling men. 'Let him who is without sin among you be the first to throw a stone at her,' he says. And they slink off one by one. (The context demands that the masculine pronoun 'him' be retained. Modern translators, eager to eliminate linguistic sexism, forget that it was a group of *men* who were so looking forward to putting this woman to a horrible death.)

In Luke's story the men are not let off so lightly. At least Simon is not. His reception of Jesus had been cold and perfunctory, lacking in any of the little gestures which would have made a weary footsore guest feel truly welcome and at home. Jesus does not condemn Simon. It is not only those whose sins are sins of the flesh who are not condemned. Jesus does not condemn Simon, but he does tell him straight. Simon needs to learn that those who refuse to love or to be loved are further from God than those whose loves are excessive and misdirected.

'Do you see this woman?' Jesus asked. In the end *does* Simon see the woman? Does he see her as Jesus does? Does he see her, no longer as a moral and religious outcast but as one whom God loves and has forgiven? We are not told.

In the end does Simon see himself as Jesus does? Does he cease to see himself as the proud custodian and arbiter of the law of God? Does he recognize himself at last as one who needs God's forgiveness as much as any of those he was so swift to condemn? We are not told.

We are not told, because we do not need to know. Far more important is that we hear the same question ourselves – 'Do you see this woman?' And as we sit with Simon the Pharisee at his table, do we go on to ask how far our own lack of love is rooted in our own refusal to be forgiven?

There is of course one further question put to us by this story and Rubens magisterial depiction of it. 'Do you see this man?'

Proper 7

The Sunday between 19 and 25 June (if after Trinity Sunday)

YEAR A

Jeremiah 20.7–13; Romans 6.1b–11; Matthew 10.24–39

THE COST OF PROPHETIC DISCIPLESHIP

Jesus warns his disciples, as they are about to set out on their mission to 'the lost sheep of the house of Israel', that people will speak ill of them. Indeed, they will be derided even more then he has been. If we are followers of Jesus, we too must expect to 'bear the abuse he endured' (Hebrews 13.13). In reality that may not be our experience. We live in an easy-going age and, most of us, in societies where the worst verbal assaults we are likely to suffer are the mild ribbing of one's mates or accusations of inanity by a Richard Dawkins. But in the light of our readings this Sunday we would be foolish to pooh-pooh the possibility that times may change and that we may yet be mercilessly mocked for the sake of whose we are.

What does it feel like – what does it *feel* like, as the interviewers always ask – to be hated and vilified for the message one brings? There is someone in the Bible who tells us and we hear him on Sunday. Jeremiah was active throughout the most turbulent period of biblical history. He witnessed the invasion of the kingdom of Judah by the Babylonians, the siege and the sacking of Jerusalem, the destruction of the Temple, and the deportation of the community's leading citizens into exile. Jeremiah saw the hand of God in this unfolding history. He proclaimed that the Babylonian armies were instruments of God's judgement on his faithless people and he bluntly declared that the best thing to do was to surrender to them. It was no way to make friends.

Jeremiah's public witness, despite the obloquy it brought on him, was fearless and unwavering. But that outward confidence masked a very different inward experience, as – day on day, decade on decade – there was only disdain for what he was divinely driven to say. Jesus was in Gethsemane for a few hours. Jeremiah was there for upwards of forty years. We would know nothing of that long night, were it not for a series of extraordinary soliloquies in the book in the Bible that bears his name, in which the prophet bares his anguished soul and berates the Almighty for what he has made him go through.

These so-called 'confessions' of Jeremiah – our first reading is an extract from one of them – reveal the personal cost of 'prophetic discipleship'. Such was the path the Twelve were called to tread and it is the way we may yet have to walk.

The prophet begins with a bitter outburst. 'Lord, you have deceived me' – or 'duped' me, or 'tricked' me, or 'enticed' me'. Jeremiah, shaking his fist in the face of God, would not have split hairs over niceties of translation. He complains that when he speaks he is ridiculed, but that when he stays silent the word of the Lord becomes – in his memorable image – 'a fire in his bones' that he cannot contain. To be sure, God is with him, but – 'dread warrior' that he is – the Almighty is not the most comforting of companions. Just how bitter is the cup, which Jeremiah must drain to the dregs, becomes apparent if we read on a few verses – if we dare – from where the lectionary tells us to stop. The prophet bewails the day he was born. Then he utters a yet more terrible imprecation. Jeremiah curses the messenger who brought the news of his birth to his father. And why? 'Because he did not kill me in the womb; so my mother would have been my grave and her womb forever great.' (Jeremiah 20.15–17). 'So my mother would have been my grave.' No text in the Bible is more terrible.

A skilful curator will hang pictures next to each other in an exhibition so that they may throw light on each other. Sometimes, as this week, our lectionary succeeds in doing much the same. The disciples, sent out to teach and heal, will suffer contempt and scorn. The juxtaposed confession of Jeremiah suggests something of what such 'prophetic discipleship' – to stay with that idea – can do to you. No wonder our tender Lord is solicitous for his friends. 'Do not be afraid,' he says. He knows better than they do that they have every reason to fear. Jeremiah's cup will be theirs, as it was his, as it may be ours. We may be more valuable than sparrows, but we are vulnerable to sorrows that sparrows will never know.

It is now over eighty years since John Skinner published his magisterial work on Jeremiah entitled *Prophecy and Religion* (Cambridge University Press, 1922). Skinner, writing of 'the inner life of Jeremiah', comments, 'Out of the Hebrew prophet, there is created in Jeremiah a new spiritual type – the Old Testament saint.' And he concludes, 'Jesus Christ would have said that, though among those born of women there has not arisen a greater than Jeremiah, yet whoever is least in the kingdom of heaven is greater than he.'

Greater than Jeremiah? Is that possible?

YEAR B

Job 38.1–11; 2 Corinthians 6.1–13; Mark 4.35–41

AT SEA IN A SMALL BOAT

Once a week, Hackney baths are taken over by men and boys from the ultra-orthodox Jewish community in Stamford Hill. That is because the Talmud tells Jewish fathers to teach their sons to swim (*Kiddushin 29a*). The background to the rabbinic injunction, and to the regular booking of our local baths by observant Jews, is the visceral dread of the sea which characterizes almost every reference to the sea in the Bible. That dread underlies this Sunday's Gospel.

The Bible story starts with a sea battle, with the triumph of the Lord over the hostile waters. The sea is what's left of the primordial chaos, the *tohu-wa-bohu*, the maelstrom of menacing water which the Almighty divides so that dry land appears (Genesis 1.1–8). The terms of the divine peace settlement with the sea are strict and clear and are promulgated – at least in the Authorized Version – in language of surpassing splendour. 'Hitherto shalt thou come but no further: and here shall thy proud waves be stayed' (Job 38.11).

What terrified Jonah was not so much being swallowed by a fish but the prospect of being strangled by seaweed and drowning (Jonah 2). The sea is home to Leviathan, the beast of the abyss (Job 41.11; Psalm 74.14). When Job cries, 'Am I a sea, or a whale, that thou settest a watch over me?' he couldn't have uttered his outrage against God more angrily (Job 7.12). In the Bible, deliverance from servitude is salvation from the sea. So it was at the Exodus. So it will be, says the prophet, at the liberation from bondage in Babylon, when the desert highway by which the exiles return will be as 'a way in the sea, a path in the mighty waters'(Isaiah 43.16) So it will be at the last. The promise we cling to 'while the nearer waters roll' is that one day 'there shall be no more sea' (Revelation 21.1).

Many myths circulated in the ancient world about the sea and its monsters. The difference in the Bible is that myth becomes history. The waters part and a people is born. The Word made flesh silences the sea – as on another occasion he will trample it underfoot (Mark 6.47–52).

So here is a story with many resonances for those who know their Bibles. But we don't have to be experts in ancient Near-Eastern mythology to be moved by it. Nor do we need to be told – though we will be in many a sermon this Sunday – that the Sea of Galilee is prone to sudden storms. The story taps into scriptural imagery, but it's not necessary to read the book of Jonah to dislike drowning. Mark tells us what we need to know and he does so in vivid detail. Here is eye-witness testimony, probably Peter's, to an unforgettable incident. Only here in Mark do the disciples reprimand Jesus for his apparent indifference to their plight. Their reproach is toned down by both Matthew and Luke. By the time the latter tell the story the belief – or is it the heresy? – prevails that Jesus is someone you must talk to politely.

The question posed by the story, but not answered by it, is voiced by the disciples. 'Who is this man?' Miracles, like parables, do not make things any easier for us. They do not dispel the mystery of things – far from it – but they do take us to the mystery's heart. It is as if the miracles say to us, 'Find out who this man is and all will become clear.' That will take some time.

The story is usually read where it was written, on dry land, but it speaks to circumstances which only the imagery of storms at sea can adequately describe. Commentators tell us that the story reflects and addresses a church suffering persecution. But storms are the stuff of life at any time, even when we're not being fed to lions. Outward circumstances in the brief intermissions between crises may be calm, but they do not bring inner peace. There is always the wretched restlessness of the unquiet mind, memorably compared by Buddhists to 'the elephant Dhanapalaka which is hard to control in rut' (*Dhammapada*, 324).

Our good Lord wakens from his untroubled sleep. He raises his head from his cushion (mentioned only by Mark). He tells Leviathan, as he had told the unclean spirit, 'Be muzzled' (Mark 1.25). On this occasion the storm at once ceases. On other occasions – Calvary, Rwanda, chronic mental illness come to mind – the storm doesn't stop quite so soon. Rather 'the sky grows darker yet and the sea rises higher'. 'Have you no still no faith?' Jesus asks. To which I can only reply, 'Lord, I believe. Help thou my unbelief' (Mark 9.24).

Only short prayers are possible in storms and so I say, 'Dear Lord, be good to me. The sea is so wide and my boat is so small.'

YEAR C

Isaiah 65.1–9; Galatians 3.23–29; Luke 8.26–39

PRAYERS OF THE POSSESSED

There are three disturbing prayers in this Sunday's Gospel. First, the Gerasene demoniac pleads with Jesus: 'Do not torment me!' Secondly, the demons beg Jesus not to order them back into the abyss. Thirdly, those in the region – it is Gentile territory – to whom word of Jesus's mighty work has reached, ask but one thing of him, that he clear off somewhere else.

These prayers – as much prayers as the more pious effusions we dignify by that name – resonate with the desires of our own hearts, even if they are not voiced in our liturgies.

'Do not torment me' is the first prayer. I do not always welcome the love that will not let me go. That love, if I resist it, will resort to severe measures to win my heart and mind and will. In many of George Mac-Donald's fantasies and fairy tales there appears the mysterious figure of 'The Wise Woman'. As for who she is, 'let the reader understand'. Suffice to say that she embodies the love that will not rest until those whose lives she touches themselves learn to live in love. Her love is relentless and unsparing. She subjects those she loves to terrifying trials. Such was the tormenting love that the Gerasene demoniac experienced. Such is the love we often wish would leave us alone.

The second prayer: The demons repeatedly implore Jesus not to send them back to the 'abyss'. 'The abyss' is the abode of 'the beast', the mythical malignity that lurks in the waters which God sundered and confined to their appointed bounds when he made the world (Job 38.8–11). The author of the Revelation to St John peers into this abyss. He sees the beast emerging from it in the last days to terrorize the saints (Revelation 11.7). The beast's final destruction is certain (Revelation 17.8), but his day is not yet done. Cryptically and alarmingly, 'he once was, now is not, and yet will come' (Revelation 17.11). It is hardly surprising that the demons prefer their present lodging in the mind of a crazed denizen of the tombs to the place where they belong.

Whether or not demons exist is the least thing we have to worry about. Talk of demons may be figurative. Or it may be of supposedly existent realities. Where we stand on the question may depend on where we've been. I remember a missionary, recently returned from Africa, remarking, 'The trouble with Dr Nineham is that he's never met a demon.' What matters are not the metaphysical questions, but what we do about what possess us – our obsessions, our embedded resentments, our unhealed memories, and our sedulously nurtured antipathies. What matters is whether we are prepared to let our demons go.

The demons entreat to be allowed to stay where they are. It's much the same as my prayer – for that is what my longing amounts too – that God will let me retain houseroom in my head for what rightly belongs in the abyss.

They beg Jesus to go. Is this third prayer so strange? It is not the first time in this Gospel that Jesus is asked to go away. 'Depart from me, Lord,' says Peter, 'I am a sinful man' (Luke 5.8).

In public and private prayer we frequently ask the Lord to be with us. But do we mean what we pray? Do we really want that awkward, unsettling, threatening figure around? We may not burn people at the stake these days, but we might not welcome having Jesus on General Synod or the PCC – any more than did the Grand Inquisitor who was about to set light to a hundred heretics when Jesus mysteriously appeared before him. Perhaps we too would wish our Lord elsewhere.

We recall the Grand Inquisitor's words – it is the most famous passage in Dostoevsky's *The Brothers Karamazov* – 'Why hast thou come now to hinder us? And why dost thou look silently and searchingly at me with thy mild eyes? Be angry. I don't want thy love, for I love thee not . . .' We recall, too, the final plea of the Inquisitor when, at the conclusion of his tirade, Jesus does not speak to him but simply kisses him 'on his bloodless, aged lips': 'Go, and come no more . . . come not at all, never, never!'

There is, of course, a fourth prayer. The exorcized demoniac asks to stay with Jesus. This prayer is one we would expect. But the answer to it is unexpected. Jesus sends him home – it's good to hear he has one – and commands him to tell everyone what God has done for him. The odd thing is that Jesus does not enjoin secrecy on the man, as he often does on those he has healed. The Gentiles, it seems, are to be let in on the secret of who Jesus is before his own people.

Proper 8

The Sunday between 26 June and 2 July

YEAR A

Jeremiah 28.5–9; Romans 6.12–23; Matthew 10.40–42

GIVE THE CHILD A DRINK

Some say that the quest to identify exactly what Jesus originally said – and where he said it and to whom he said it – is futile. Rarely can we catch the accents of the Aramaic in which he spoke. The record of what he said and did was preserved by word of mouth long before it was written down. No doubt people in those days were better at remembering things than we are. No doubt they were deeply respectful to the sacred tradition of the master's words and works. Nevertheless, that process of 'oral transmission' could never have been totally secure. The temptation for the first Christians to add what they wished Jesus had said to the record of what he actually did say will have been powerful. Moreover, sayings of Jesus will have drifted free from their original moorings. Such sayings, coming into land far from where they originally took off, may no longer mean what once they meant.

How then can we ever be sure that we are hearing what Jesus really said? How can be certain that the occasion on which we are told he spoke as he did has been correctly recalled? We cannot always be sure, but sometimes detective work yields some clues.

A few words in our brief Gospel this Sunday concentrate our minds on these questions. The passage we hear concludes Jesus's instructions to 'the Twelve' when he sends them out to teach and to heal. They will be his representatives. Their mission will be continuous with his own. Jesus identifies himself totally with this brave little band, setting out 'like sheep among wolves'. 'Where you are welcomed,' he says, 'I am welcomed.'

Jesus has told his disciples that they are to take nothing with them on their mission. As they wander from place to place, they are to be totally reliant on people's hospitality and generosity. He promises that those who receive them will not go unrewarded.

Then we come to the closing words of Jesus's 'missionary charge' –
the words that make us wonder. The New Revised Standard Version is one of the few English versions to translate the text correctly.
'Whoever gives even a cup of cold water to one of these little ones
in the name of a disciple – truly I tell you, none of these will lose
their reward.' Most of our versions have 'because he is my disciple',
or a similar turn of phrase, rather than 'in the name of a disciple'.
The subtle spin these versions place on the saying settle it more
smoothly into its present context. Jesus is made to say that anyone
who quenches the thirst of these weary missionaries will be rewarded.
After all, that amounts to what Jesus has already said elsewhere (Mark
9.41).

The 'little ones', on this reading, becomes an affectionate reference
to the disciples. Now the whole passage reads much more easily. But
at a price. We have sacrificed accuracy for a comfortable ride. It is as
if we had translated the Old High Norse for 'Give Jones a muffin in
the name of Smith' to mean 'Give Jones a muffin because he is Smith.'
No Old High Norseman would suppose the two admonitions were
equivalent.

Where any saying of Jesus sits awkwardly in its present context, it is
wiser to look for a situation in the ministry of Jesus where, without any
dodgy translating, we can see it makes better sense.

After some detective work, we discover just such a context for Jesus's
saying about giving 'little ones' a drink. On an earlier occasion the
disciples had been bickering among themselves about which of them
was the greatest. Jesus silenced this absurd argument by placing a child
among them. Jesus then says, 'Whoever welcomes one of these children
in my name receives me' (Mark 9.33–37).

When we hear Jesus talking about children we touch the bedrock
of history. Jesus may well have referred to his disciples as 'little ones'
and have identified himself with them. What is certain is that Jesus
identified himself with actual 'little ones' – real live Galilean kids. How
we treat them, these children who in their thousands die unnecessar-
ily every day, is how we treat him. Here is the most likely original
context for Jesus's saying about giving one 'little one' a cup of cold
water.

We still resist the notion that Jesus could have aligned himself so
uncompromisingly with children, irrespective of their faith, their understanding, or their virtue. We still conscript them as symbols into an
adult discourse preoccupied with adult concerns. That development –
discussed in a fine book by James Francis (*Adults as Children*, Peter

Lang, 2006) – is already well under way in the New Testament. What we hear on Sunday suggests that Matthew may have been party to that process.

YEAR B

Wisdom of Solomon 1.13–15; 2.23, 24; 2 Corinthians 8.7–15; Mark 5.21–43

BE CAREFUL WHAT YOU SAY

The first child we meet in Mark is Jairus's daughter. She is much loved. That needs to be said to counter the claims – still common currency – of Philip Ariès' fascinating but flawed *Centuries of Childhood* (Jonathan Cape, 1962). Ariès claimed that childhood is a modern invention and that in earlier centuries parents were less attached to their children than they are today. So many children died young, Ariès argued, that parents became inured, if not indifferent, to their passing. Ariès was mistaken, as subsequent studies have amply demonstrated, but it is always difficult to nail a nonsense once it has caught on. Jairus and his wife, and indeed their daughter, will surely stand at the last day and tell Ariès that he got it wrong.

We don't know the child's name. All we know is that her dad was some sort of churchwarden. (The 'ruler of the synagogue' was a lay-person who looked after the synagogue building and arranged the services.) For me, this little girl will always be Louise, a twelve-year-old I once taught. Louise fell gravely ill, apparently fatally. I knelt with her parents in the exquisite little chapel of the Great Ormond Street Hospital for Sick Children. Mother and father were, in effect, giving their little girl back to God. A day or two later Louise sat up in bed. And someone gave her something to eat.

How do we know about the raising of Jairus's daughter from the dead? We know the story because it was leaked. Either Peter, James, or John, or someone in the family, disobeyed Jesus's instruction that no one should be told what had happened. Mark too ignored Jesus's explicit command and published an account of the miracle in the little booklet which bears his name. Our congregations will get to know the story this Sunday because – obeying the lectionary rather than the Lord – we shall read aloud the record of it. We shall proclaim as 'the gospel of the Lord' something we've been expressly told to shut up about.

The way we use the Bible in church is really very strange.

Why the injunction to secrecy? The secrecy belongs to the enigma of who this man is. But perhaps there is another and more straightforward reason why Jesus did not wish this miracle publicized. For Jairus and his wife will not have been the only parents in their community to have lost a child. Perhaps Jesus is thinking of those who would have asked, 'Why was Jesus there for Jairus and not for me?' It is what any parent bereaved of a child will ask. It is the cry once heard in Rama and heard today when a child is run over, 'a voice of lamentation and weeping and great mourning'. It is Rachel's cry, Rachel who is 'weeping for her children and who will not be comforted because they are not' (Jeremiah 31.15; Matthew 2.18).

Of course, we cannot now hide these events away again behind the closed doors of Jairus's house where Jesus meant them to stay. But we can be a little more sensitive about how we speak of one who brought a dead child back. Many who come to church this Sunday will walk past clusters of flowers at the roadside marking the spot where a child was killed. Some perhaps will themselves be mourning the loss of a child. Rachel may well be in the congregation. Yes, there is the hope. We look to the day, to which the raising of Jairus's daughter points, when 'death is swallowed up in victory' (1 Corinthians 15.54). But if I chatter about heaven to someone whose child has died I only show that I do not understand. Good news, quite as much as bad news, must sometimes be broken gently. For pity's sake, for Rachel's sake, we must be careful how we tell this story.

The account of the raising of Jairus's daughter frames another problematical story requiring sensitive handling. We find the presupposition of the story, that a medical condition can make someone ritually unclean, both bizarre and repugnant. That assumption goes unchallenged here, but we are not to suppose that Jesus shared it. At other times, when he deliberately 'touched the untouchables with love' his healing of a sick body was judgement on a sick system.

More puzzling is the suggestion that Jesus heals the woman *inadvertently*. Jesus becomes aware that 'power had gone forth from him'. Someone serving as an unwitting medium for a force beyond him – even if that force was divine – is not the Jesus we know from the rest of his story. But there is another and more Christian perspective on this incident. Power drains from Jesus because his ministry is the self-emptying of the Son of God. We tend to see the miracles as displays of power. Perhaps the point of them, in a sense, is the very opposite. The story of Jesus is not of power exhibited but of power exhausted. Hence the cross.

YEAR C

1 Kings 19.5–16, 19–21; Galatians 5.1, 13–25; Luke 9.51–62

FOR THE LOVE OF SAMARIA

Paddy Ashdown knows about divided cities. That experience lent great authority to his television documentary *Battle for the Holy Land*. Lord Ashdown believes that building peace in the Middle East is a process and that there are some simple steps that could start that process. Step one must be to put Jerusalem first. The wounds of Jerusalem must be treated first, if ever the Holy Land is to be healed.

Luke agrees with Lord Ashdown about the pre-eminent importance of Jerusalem. For Luke, the mission of Jesus is a prophet's progress to the City of God. Sunday's Gospel announces the start of the last stage of that journey. Soon Jesus will be 'received up'. Luke, as he often does, is speaking the same language as John. John saw the 'lifting up' of Jesus as a triple exaltation from the earth, at once his death, his resurrection, and his ascension. So for Luke the culmination of Christ's journey to Jerusalem is his threefold 'reception'. He will be embraced by the cross, taken from the tomb, received into his father's hands.

Jesus 'sets his face' towards the city. The image is powerful and prophetic. Ezekiel too was told to 'set his face' towards Jerusalem (Ezekiel 21.2). We learn that the Lord toughened him up for his task. 'As an adamant harder than flint have I made thy forehead' (Ezekiel 3.9). Ezekiel's confrontation with Jerusalem was a bruising head-to-head encounter. Jesus's mission to Jerusalem is equally unflinching and unswerving, but, whereas Ezekiel was called to preach 'against' the city, Jesus is *for* Jerusalem – so much so that, when he has to pronounce judgement on the city, it breaks his heart (Luke 19.41–44).

Luke will soon be telling us about 'the good Samaritan' (Luke 10.25–37). This Sunday we meet Samaritans who are not so good. Their lack of hospitality is uncharacteristic, if the Samaritans' present-day tolerance of tourists and of spectators of their gory Passover celebrations is anything to go by. Lack of manners, however, is not the issue here. The Samaritans snub Jesus because he is heading for Mt Zion, not for Mt Gerizim, the mountain where, to this day, Samaritans say God is to be worshipped. And we know from the woman at the well how contentious this dispute was (John 4.9).

The Samaritans refuse to 'receive' Jesus. We wonder how much Luke is saying here, for yet again echoes of the Fourth Gospel sound in our ears. 'He came unto his own and his own received him not.' Is Luke hinting that the Samaritans too are 'his own'?

James and John certainly don't think so. Always wanting to help, they suggest they do as the hairy Elijah did and call down fire from heaven to consume those who have the temerity to rebuff a mighty prophet (2 Kings 1.10–12). Is the urge in our hearts to incinerate those who disagree with us altogether extinguished? These days we draw the line at torching those who see things differently. Yet the inflammatory exchanges between the polarized parties in some of the controversies tearing us apart are fierce enough to make one wonder. 'See how these Christians loathe one another.'

Most modern versions consign to a footnote the poorly attested but haunting words ascribed to Jesus at this point, 'You do not know of what spirit you are.' The words may not record what Jesus actually said, but surely they tell us what he thinks of our fratricidal antipathies.

'The Son of Man has nowhere to lay his head.' There is no evidence in the Gospels that during his public ministry Jesus went home each night to a wife and children. But we make too much of this famous saying if we infer from it that Jesus was unmarried. That conclusion ignores what Jesus says here and everywhere else about the priorities of his mission.

The hard word of Jesus is that the disciple must forego all lesser loyalties for the sake of the Kingdom of God. Jesus is not advising his followers merely to be careful about the attachments they contemplate. (It is Jesus talking, not St Paul.) The overriding claims of the Kingdom mean that *existing* ties must be broken off. The would-be disciple must not even go back and say good-bye to his family. It is Luke who puts the matter at its starkest. 'Whoever comes to me and does not hate father and mother, wife and children, brothers and sisters . . . cannot be my disciple' (Luke 14.26).

The disciples who left their nets left their wives and families too (Mark 10.28). We are not involving ourselves in asinine speculation about the bloodline of Jesus to allow that he might have done the same. Nor is it wholly frivolous to wonder what happened to the women who were left behind.

Least of all is it flippant to ask how we find the path of discipleship through the forest of our own entanglements. On that question, serious enquirers are referred to T. S. Eliot's *The Cocktail Party*.

Proper 9

The Sunday between 3 and 9 July

YEAR A

Zechariah 9.9–12; Romans 7.15–25a; Matthew 11.16–19, 25–30

SLUGS AND SNAILS – AND SUGAR AND SPICE

Broadly speaking, there are two 'theologies of childhood'. There is the 'slugs and snails and puppy-dogs tails' theology that holds that all children – little girls just as much as little boys – are 'lost'. On this view, the child is born a guilty sinner and his or her spiritual plight is as desperate as that of the unrepentant adult. Every child is born at enmity to God. Accordingly, 'the breaking of the child's will betimes', as the Puritans used to say, is a parental duty.

Then there is the 'sugar and spice and all things nice' theology. Those of this school of thought are sure that all children – little boys too – are innocent. They agree with Wordsworth. Children come 'trailing clouds of glory' and 'heaven lies about them in their infancy'. So far from being a depraved state, from which the child must swiftly be saved, childhood is emblematic of what the adult, who has strayed far from this early paradise, must recover.

On a selective reading of Sunday's Gospel, both parties might claim that Jesus is on their side. Jesus compares his opponents to ill-tempered street urchins, bloody-minded little brats who are impossible to please. John the Baptist leads a life of extreme austerity – and they say he's mad. 'The Son of Man' enjoys a meal and a drink with his iffy friends – and they call him 'a glutton and a drunk'. Such critics are behaving exactly as children do.

That, however, is not Jesus's last word this week about children. He goes on to say that children – the very children who can be so stubborn and wilful – are quicker to see some things than most grown-ups. There are things God has hidden from the supposedly knowledgeable but which he has revealed to infants.

In context, the primary reference is probably to the disciples, to that little band of untutored odd-bods who have stumbled after Jesus long enough to catch a glimpse of who he is. But Jesus is not talking just about grown-ups and it is only adult chauvinism that disposes us to suppose so. Wordsworth was right. Children are born with a sense of transcendence, with an awareness of 'the other and the beyond'. Rigorous empirical research has shown this to be so. Alas, this spiritual acuity tends to fade as children grow up. (Schools don't help. Required by law to 'promote spiritual development', they usually throttle it.)

Remarkably, within the space of just a few sentences, Jesus has deployed the same imagery of what children are like both negatively and positively. The same imagery illustrates both the wilful refusal of the religious elite to see the hand of God in what Jesus does and the spiritual awareness granted to the contemptible band of little ones who have fallen in step with him.

The way in which Jesus uses the imagery of childhood shows that he neither romanticizes childhood nor condemns it. We who seek the mind of Christ about our children must likewise eschew comforting simplicities that relieve us from the strain of thought. Neither a 'slugs and snails and puppy-dogs tails' understanding of childhood, nor a 'sugar and spice and all things nice' estimate of our earliest days, gives a Christian account of what it means to be a child. Neither the doctrine of 'original sin' nor the notion of 'original innocence' help me to understand Alex, aged four, and Max, aged two, the grandchildren romping round me as I write.

There is a third way – and a more Christian way – of seeing the status of the child. The child is neither innocent nor sinful, but nevertheless from birth – indeed from before birth – he or she is inescapably bound up in a web of life shot through with sin and tragedy. Children may or may not be culpable. What is certain is that they are vulnerable.

Jesus invites the heavy-laden to come to him. A wisdom-writer, telling the timeless truth as all the wisdom writers do, observes, 'Hard work is the lot of every mortal, and a heavy yoke is laid on the children of Adam' (Ecclesiasticus 40.1). What is promised to the overworked is not so much peace of mind as deliverance from oppression and exploitation.

'Come to me,' says Jesus to the oppressed. On another occasion he says just the same to children (Mark 10.14) and, with the imagery of childhood so conspicuous this week, we stay with them a moment more. Our culture is confused about children. Concern for the rights of the child and for the protection of children from abuse is intense. Yet we continue to exploit them mercilessly. Children are ever more relentlessly exposed to commercial, social, and educational pressures. They are the helpless victims of our sinful structures. When Jesus invites our oppressed children to come to him it is not so that they can be 'saved'. He is inviting them to come out and play. A dreadful fate awaits those who try to stop them (Matthew 18.6).

YEAR B

Ezekiel 2.1–5; 2 Corinthians 12.2–10; Mark 6.1–13

MASTER CARPENTER

Was Jesus a carpenter? Mark doesn't say so. He says that they said he was. And the word Mark uses – our word 'technician' has the same root – doesn't specifically mean someone working with wood. It could be used of a craftsman in some other material. Jesus might have been a mason. It's interesting that Jesus talks more about building houses than making tables.

The one word on which it all turns comes only here in Mark and in Matthew's version of the story, where Jesus is said to be 'the son of the carpenter'. It boggles the mind to contemplate the vast devotional superstructure which has been erected on this, the flimsiest of foundations – the kitsch art, the speculations about the boy Jesus in the carpenter's shop, the millions of words from the one word spun by parsons from pulpits, the prayer 'Jesus, Master-carpenter of Nazareth', and so on and on.

Should we then stop talking – and preaching – about 'Jesus the carpenter'? No. Tradition mustn't always yield to pedantry. If it did, all sorts of claims about Jesus would collapse, claims far more central to Christian faith than that he was a wood-worker. Not that there is any hope of successfully introducing a new tradition – starting, let's say, at half-past-nine this Sunday morning – to the effect that Jesus worked in bricks and mortar rather than wood and nails. That Jesus was a carpenter is as ineradicable from the Christian imagination as the equally ill-supported assumption that he died on a hill-top.

So, in my mind's eye, I still return from time to time to Israel's oldest hospital, the Edinburgh Medical Missionary Society's hospital in Nazareth. The communion table in the hospital chapel is a carpenter's bench. On it stands a small lectern made from a carpenter's tool box. And I still pray that, coming rough-hewn to the Carpenter's bench, I shall be fashioned to a truer beauty by his hand.

Not that it matters how Jesus worked for his living. What matters is the fact he did, and what we make of that fact. There are important things to say, albeit too easily said, about 'Jesus the workman', and some rather less easy questions to ask. Jesus got his hands dirty. He knew what it was to be tired out after a day's work. He experienced the anxiety – notwithstanding Matthew 6.25 – of having to make ends meet. The Word was not made pampered flesh.

There is a harder question to ask. If Jesus made 'the world of work' his own, he would have had to face the moral dilemmas of a working life. Doctors are not the only people who sometimes have to make difficult moral decisions. The point is powerfully made by Nikos Kazantzakis in his controversial novel *The Last Temptation of Christ* (Simon and Schuster, 1951) from which came the still more controversial film. Kazantzakis notoriously revives the old canard that Jesus had a relationship with Mary Magdalene. But the book raises a more plausible and more disturbing possibility. The Romans used great quantities of crosses, which presumably they ordered from local carpenters. Kazantzakis wonders whether Jesus found himself making one of these gibbets for some other condemned prisoner long before his own fate was sealed.

The notion is speculative, but not absurd. The question posed by Jesus's working life is how he dealt with the morally compromising choices which, in this naughty world, every job involves. Carpenters and stonemasons, surgeons and parish priests – all of us sometimes have to choose between what's bad and what's worse. Faced by such a choice we ask – the question isn't so naïve – 'What would Jesus do?'

Nazareth's synagogue-goers think that Jesus has got above himself. He comes unto his own and his own receive him not. There is unwitting irony in their question – literally, '*Whence* these things?' – an irony more characteristic of John's Gospel than of Mark. There is little Jesus can do in Nazareth. 'He could do no deed of power there.' It is a moral impossibility. Miracles are meaningless in such a climate of unbelief. They are merely signs which no one is willing to read. In the Gospels faith is neither the cause of healing, nor even its precondition. Miracles invite discipleship; they do not presuppose it. But where there is a wilful refusal to believe, as in Nazareth, miracles cease to be signs of the Kingdom of God. They are no more than displays of supernatural power, the stock-in-trade of the countless wandering wonder-workers who roamed the ancient world.

The call and the commission of the twelve disciples contrast interestingly with the service of Installation and Induction of an incumbent in the Church of England. Jesus tells the Twelve 'to take nothing for their journey'. Our new incumbent, by contrast, is inducted into 'the real, actual and corporeal possession of the parish church'. And he or she is given a bunch of keys to prove it. *Kyrie eleison*

YEAR C

Isaiah 66.10–14; Galatians 6. (1–6), 7–16; Luke 10.1–11, 16–20

TRAVELLING LIGHT

Jesus tells 'the seventy' (or 'the seventy-two' – the readings are equally well-attested) to 'travel light'. It is the same demand to relinquish material possessions and earthly attachments made on us in last Sunday's Gospel. It is the same demand – and the same dilemma. Yes, we must 'travel light' – but how light is light? Does 'travelling light' merely mean 'sitting light'? Is that all I am asked to do – to sit lightly to the things I have? Or am I being told to get rid of them?

I am moved by the witness of those who have taken Jesus at his word. I am moved by the monks I know – cheerful, level-headed, kindly, competent people who make Christianity both credible and attractive. (Talking of monks, there is a striking parallel to the sending of the seventy or the seventy-two in the Buddha's charge to his first disciples. 'Go forth, O monks, on your journey for the weal and the welfare of much people, out of compassion for the world, and for the weal and the welfare of angels and mortals.')

I am moved too by those who, even without the structure and discipline of the religious life, still significantly disencumber themselves. To this day, I am rebuked by the testimony of David, a fellow student at my theological college. David was reading for the Cambridge theological Tripos. The rest of us avidly accumulated lots of books. (Lust takes unlovely forms.) David renounced books. He had none at all. If he needed a Bible, he borrowed one from the college library. (He gained a good degree, incidentally, and he abstained from idolatry in the getting of it.)

That said, it is clear that some are called to travel more lightly than others. The seventy (or seventy-two) are told to treat the bed and board provided by their hosts as the payment they are entitled to. But to be in a position to offer that kind of hospitality those hosts had to earn a living. They certainly had to 'carry a purse' – and a well-filled one too – if they were to be ready to accommodate any passing missionary. So there were farmers who went on farming, fishermen who went on fishing, builders who went on building, while our bare-foot disciples moved from village to village telling people of the coming Kingdom. The latter had the luxury of travelling as lightly as they did only because others were prepared to travel a good deal less lightly.

Were there seventy or seventy-two of them? For Luke, as for all the Gospel writers, Jesus is a second Moses. He may well want us to remember that Moses was told to appoint seventy elders 'to bear the burden of the people' with him (Numbers 11.16–17). Or, if there were 'seventy-two others', Luke may be emphasizing once more the universality of the gospel for, according to the Greek version of the Old Testament, there were seventy-two nations on earth (Genesis 10–11). Seventy or seventy-two? Luke is not around to tell us. As elsewhere, what the Bible says here is what we hear it saying. (The 'we' is important. Crackpot private interpretations are out.) 'Heal the sick,' says Jesus. The global AIDS pandemic suggests that it is the seventy-two – and a few more – we need.

While they were away on their mission, Jesus sees a vision. 'I watched Satan fall from heaven like a flash of lightning.' Half a dozen images are woven into this one short sentence. It is possible, but not helpful, to un-pick them – and then to pick over them – one by one. Risking cerebral seizure, we can ask who this 'Satan' is, where has he been, and what has he been up to. We can enquire what and where 'heaven' is and what it might mean to 'fall' from it. (Such questions are addressed in a recent lively 'biography' of Satan by Henry Ansgar Kelly of the University of California (*Satan*, Cambridge University Press, 2006).)

We can tease out these threads, but only at a price. For once unrav-elled, the mystery ceases to move us. The myth of Satan and his fall re-tains its tremendous imaginative and moral power only by remaining a myth. Jesus sees in the success of his disciples' mission the sign and the promise of his own victory. His exultant cry, as he rejoices with them, amounts to a triumphant 'Yes!' There is no need to demythologize that cry of jubilation.

Luke, like most of us, does not like snakes or scorpions. They reappear together very soon (Luke 11.11–12). The seventy-two enjoy supernatural protection from them. So did St Paul, apparently (Acts 28.1–6). So do the snake-handling members of the Appalachian 'Church of God with Signs Following'. The rest of us do not.

Nor, at Calvary, did Jesus.

Proper 10

The Sunday between 10 and 16 July

YEAR A

Isaiah 55.10–13; Romans 8.1–11; Matthew 13.1–9, 18–23

STORIES TO MAKE US THINK

This year our lectionary provides for a sequence of Sunday readings from Matthew's Gospel. But we don't hear all Matthew has to say. Mindful of our short attention span, the lectionary is selective. Matthew is the longest of the four Gospels and some of his story is left out. How do our lectionary-makers decide what to include and what not to? Sometimes it seems as if they are mainly concerned to give us an easy ride. They want to make the prophet's words come true: 'The rough country will become smooth' (Isaiah 40.5).

In reality, reading the Bible is always a rugged ride. That is what makes it so challenging and exciting. Removing the humps and bumps from the Bible may make for easy listening, but if what we are left with suggests that we are in for an easy life the process has done us no service. This Sunday and the next two Sundays we hear from Matthew chapter 13. To ease us gently through this long chapter, the lectionary tinkers with the order of verses and leaves out two substantial sections. The verses omitted this week tell us why Jesus taught in parables. What he says is difficult and unpalatable. Like 'sleeping policemen' in a suburban side street, his words make us slow down and go more carefully.

Given that the chapter is an anthology of parables and not much else, the decision to omit the very verses, problematical as they are, that tell us what parables are for was eccentric, to say the least.

Jesus talks about an impoverished peasant-farmer, for whom his recalcitrant land at last yields a harvest. Jesus addresses 'the crowds', that's to say anyone who cares to listen. People must decide for themselves what the parable means, for Jesus does not explain it to them – not that you would know that from the lectionary's abridged version of Matthew's account. 'Let anyone with ears, listen!' Jesus curtly concludes.

Jesus then explains to his disciples – and only to his disciples – why he teaches in parables. (We are now looking at the passage the lectionary tells us to skip.) Here Matthew tones down what he has taken from Mark. According to Mark 4.11–12, Jesus taught in parables *so that* people would not understand him! According to Matthew, Jesus used parables *because* people did not understand him.

Much turns on what we make of a couple of tricky Greek words. By leaving this section out, our lectionary editors no doubt wanted to spare us Sunday morning headaches. Their kindness was misplaced. However we interpret this thorny passage, it makes one essential point clear. Jesus's parables are not the verbal equivalent of visual aids. They are not just illustrations, homely stories for simple folk intended to help them understand his teaching. Typically, the parables of Jesus are as enigmatic as his miracles. The purpose of parables is not to make things easy for us, but to make us think.

The 'sleeping policeman' removed from our path by the lectionary will break the axles of any reader careering through this chapter at too great a speed. We have words of Jesus that are perhaps best not read by those in dark places. 'The one who has will be given more; from the one who has not even what they have will be taken away' (Matthew 13.12). Commentators coat these words with sugar by telling us that they express the truth that those who welcome the reign of Jesus are blessed increasingly, but that those who refuse his reign find that whatever else they cling to for security turns to dust. The pious comment is unexceptionable, though it brings little comfort to those who wonder what more their Lord, in his 'severe mercy', will require of them before he is done.

Jesus then explains in detail to the disciples what the parable of the sower means. No doubt that explanation will have encouraged the churches, where Matthew's Gospel was first read, to go on 'spreading the word', especially when their endeavours seemed unrewarding.

But what of 'the crowds', those who were left with Jesus's dismissive 'Let anyone with ears, listen!' There was no line-by-line explanation of the parable for them. Yet among them there were those 'with ears to hear'. They will have brooded on this puzzling tale. They will have been troubled by how commonplace – even banal – Jesus's simple anecdote is. They will have worried away at the parable, doggedly trying to tease out its significance. Above all, they will have wondered and wondered who this strange story-teller was. They will have persevered, just as the sower did. And their perseverance, like the sower's, will finally have been rewarded. Jesus's seminal words will have taken root, germinated, and come to harvest.

They too will have known joy at the last – a greater joy, perhaps, than of those who had to have everything explained.

YEAR B

Amos 7.7–15; Ephesians 1.3–14; Mark 6.14–29

THE PASSION OF THE BAPTIST

Enoch Powell's view of John the Baptist has not enjoyed wide support among students of the New Testament. Years ago, in a lecture Powell gave to a conference of the Modern Churchman's Union, as it was then called, I heard him argue that Jesus and John the Baptist were one and the same person. Over lunch I asked Mr Powell how it was that this fact had escaped the notice of so many scholars. His response was that most people's reading of the Bible is undistracted by the obvious.

We don't have to go as far as Enoch Powell on this matter – still less on some other matters – to grant that he saw something significant about John and Jesus which is often overlooked. Powell recognized that there was more to the kinship of John and Jesus than the fact that they were cousins. We stress the distinction between John and Jesus, the line drawn in the sands of time which John may never cross. John appears in the Gospels as the last of the old order, and the least in the new order is greater than he (Matthew 11.11). In his great book *Jesus of Nazareth* (Harper & Row, 1960), Günther Bornkamm memorably spoke of John the Baptist as 'the sentinel at the frontier between the aeons'.

Indeed so. But Mark sees that what joins John with Jesus is more important than what divides them. John is united in his death with the very one who stands beyond the boundary he cannot pass. There are two passion narratives in Mark's Gospel, that of Jesus and that of John. John's death both anticipates the dying of Jesus and participates in it. United with Christ in his death and – as Herod unwittingly suggests – in his resurrection, the baptizer becomes the baptized. 'I need to be baptized by you,' John had said to Jesus (Matthew 3.14). Now he is.

We mustn't get our Herods muddled. This is not 'Herod the Great' who indifferently slaughtered his wives, his offspring and Bethlehem's babies, but his son Herod Antipas, 'tetrarch' of Galilee – Herod 'the fox', according to Jesus (Luke 13.32). His sin was to have married someone too closely related to him, a woman who was both his sister-in-law and his niece. In the old days every English parish church displayed in its porch 'A Table of Kindred and Affinity wherein whosoever are related are forbidden by the Church of England to marry together'. Herod and Herodias would not have got past the door.

The parallels between the passion of John and the passion of Jesus are not so slight as to be insignificant. Herod's recognition of John as 'a righteous and holy man' anticipates Pilate's insistence on Jesus's innocence (Mark 15.14). Both Herod and Pilate yield to pressure. There is a foreshadowing of Good Friday in the sombre reference to John's disciples seeing to his burial. But correspondence is at a deeper level than that of incidental detail. John 'becomes like Jesus in his death'. He belongs to those who 'overcame by the blood of the Lamb' (Revelation 12.11).

We dare to ask what their passion means, those whose sharing of the sufferings of Christ is as intimate as this. What they endured is more than admirable and exemplary. The martyrs, those who witness to Christ by their death, merge with the one to whom they testify. In some sense – perhaps it is best not to define it too closely – their death too is redemptive. Calvary is many places. Calvary is Auschwitz, where the frail Franciscan Maximilian Kolbe offered his life for another prisoner. Calvary is the cellar in Kampala where Archbishop Janani Luwum perished at the behest of the tyrant he had challenged. Calvary is the altar of the hospital chapel in San Salvador at which Oscar Romero was assassinated. Calvary is the dungeon beneath the Machaerus fortress where the Baptist was beheaded. These are famous Calvarys, but there are countless others where those, who will never be canonized, died so that 'what is lacking in Christ's afflictions' might be completed (Colossians 1.24).

There is a renewed interest in John the Baptist's role in the story of Jesus. A recent and much hyped book by James Tabor argues that John the Baptist and Jesus were *both* Messiahs, that John – descended from

Aaron – was the priestly Messiah, and that Jesus – 'son of David' – was the royal Messiah (*The Jesus Dynasty*, Simon & Schuster, 2006).

It seems unlikely. To be sure, John was of priestly descent. But if, as Jesus said, John despised the soft robes worn in palaces (Matthew 11.8), he surely would have been equally disdainful of those worn in sanctuaries. It's hard to picture John the Baptist being kitted out at Wippells. For those willing to see it, John was neither prince nor priest, but Elijah who was to come (Matthew 11.14). Like the first Elijah, he confronted kings. But at far greater cost. Fiery chariots don't call at Calvary.

YEAR C

Deuteronomy 30.9–14; Colossians 1.1–14; Luke 10.25–37

THE WOUNDED ON THE WAYSIDE

Our Old Testament reading, so says our lectionary, is 'related' to our Gospel. Indeed it is – as chalk is to cheese. God's promise to his people, given through Moses as they are about to take possession of their promised land, is that they will 'abundantly prosper' – if, that is, they do as they are told. The prosperity promised is material. God will bless you with a big family and with fertile flocks and fields, if you love him and keep his commandments.

Such an ethic is prudential. Attached to it are rewards and penalties. It is in your interest to comply with it. An earlier chapter in Deuteronomy gives a list of the good things that will come your way if you keep the rules ('blessed shall be your basket and your kneading bowl') and is terrifyingly specific about the disasters that will overtake you, including 'the boils of Egypt', if you do not (Deuteronomy 28). Obey God, and you will do well for yourself. That is the gist of Deuteronomy and of the passage from it appointed for our edification this Sunday. It is also the gist of the 'good news' preached by the many so-called 'prosperity churches'.

To be sure, motives for keeping such a prudential ethic can never be wholly selfish and calculating. The command is to turn to God and to obey him *wholeheartedly*. I cannot do that if I am constantly checking my bank balance or my body for boils. Moreover, there is a prudential aspect – 'Great shall be your reward in heaven' – to the moral teaching of Jesus.

Nevertheless, when we turn from Deuteronomy and its threats and promises to the parable of 'the good Samaritan' we are entering a different moral universe. Whatever we make of the story, it is certainly not an illustration of prudential ethics. The Samaritan is out of pocket to the tune of two denarii, not to speak of the cost of the oil, wine and bandages, by the time he rides off out the story. The Samaritan acts as he does because it is right to go to the aid of someone injured, not because to do so brings a reward in this life or the next, nor because failure to do so means being punished.

'Who is my neighbour?' The lawyer wants to know the limits of his liability. The premise of his question is that there are categories of people who have no claim on him. Jesus's parable blows that 'us and them' premise out of the water.

The parable radically reinterprets what being a neighbour means. But there is more to it than that. There are really only two ways of making a moral decision. You can decide what to do in any situation on the basis of what you judge will have the best outcome. Utilitarians, who believe that 'the end justifies the means', make their moral decisions on that basis. Or you can maintain that some things are always right and others always wrong, regardless of the consequences. The 'good Samaritan' acts as he does on that basis. The parable attests that there is an absolute moral law – a law that even God himself cannot rewrite – that I must cross the road to go to help the wounded stranger.

Most commentators suggest that the priest and the Levite 'passed by on the other side' so as to avoid contact with what might have been a dead body. They feared defilement. The comment is illuminating, but before we let the two of them hurry on their way we should notice something else. These two gentlemen were both clergymen.

I picture the two of them as men with full diaries. They ignore the injured figure by the road because they have things to do. They have other plans – possibly, each of them, a detailed 'Mission Action Plan'. Before speculation becomes frivolous, the substantial point must be made. All our ministerial plans must be provisional. We must be prepared to postpone them, to alter them, or to jettison them, when what awaits us around the next corner on our wilderness journey comes into view.

Many years ago I was staying at St George's College, Jerusalem. At breakfast one morning the man sitting next to me, a total stranger, turned to me and asked if I had any plans for the day. If not, would I like to walk to Jericho with him? I did have other plans, but I abandoned them. So we helped ourselves to a couple of oranges and set out.

I am glad that I went with the flow that day, rather than sticking to my plans. My companion on the old Jericho road turned out to be the late Hugh Pilkington, scholar and saint. Hugh Pilkington's commitment to the education of Africa's children was a shining light. And as for the wounded he found on Africa's waysides, he brought them, not to an inn, but into his own home.

Proper II

The Sunday between 17 and 23 July

YEAR A

Wisdom of Solomon 12.13, 16–19 or Isaiah 44.6–8; Romans 8.12–25; Matthew 13.24–30, 36–43

A CIRCLE WITH NO CIRCUMFERENCE

Unlike some sectarian movements within first-century Judaism, the Augusta National Golf Club and many twenty-first century Christian churches, the circle round Jesus was truly open. To be sure, some in that circle, such as 'the Twelve', were invited to join it, but not because they had already shown any aptitude or inclination for the kind of life they would subsequently lead. Others, having met Jesus in dramatic circumstances, decided to stay with him. We think of Bartimaeus who 'followed Jesus in the way' (Mark 10.46–52). Others out of curiosity simply tagged along with him. Because he got on rather well with them, there seems to have been a disproportionate number of reprobates and rejects in his entourage.

Even to speak of that group as 'a circle' is misleading, for a circle has a circumference and to draw a circumference you have to draw a line. Jesus's refusal to draw lines was one of the things about him that infuriated his opponents. Needless to say, you did not have to attend a course of preparation classes or take part in some 'rite of passage' before joining Jesus. The group around Jesus of Nazareth had no name, no organization, and no hierarchy. It was all wonderfully ad hoc and unsystematic and light years distant from the ever more obsessively managed institutions which today make their competing claims to represent him.

'The parable of the wheat and the weeds' is about how God puts up with us all. It certainly does not tell you how to run a farm or – I write with feeling and a stiff back – an allotment. What the farmer does, letting the weeds flourish alongside the wheat, is about as absurd as a shepherd abandoning the rest of his flock for the sake of a single sheep that has wandered off (Luke 15.3–7). But the parable is not about farming but about 'the kingdom of heaven'. The expression 'kingdom of heaven' in Matthew's Gospel means the same as 'the kingdom of God' in Mark. It means 'how God works' here and now, not where you go when you die. And the way God works is not the way we do.

Sensible farmers weed out the weeds. Our farmer doesn't. What he does is an example of what Paul will call 'God's foolishness' (1 Corinthians 1.25). The mad way God works is not to weed out anyone. That is how crazily hospitable the company of Jesus is.

The gist of it all is in very few words: 'Let them grow together.' It is a maxim the followers of Jesus have always found hard to stomach. Repeatedly, sickeningly, across the centuries the Church, wonderfully confident that it knows which are the weeds and which is the wheat, has sought to incinerate the former in order to maintain the purity of the latter.

The same St Paul, who rejoiced in the divine folly of welcoming all and sundry – especially the sinfully sundry – could default to a much harder line. 'Come out from among them and be ye separate,' he said (2 Corinthians 6.17). We have been coming out from among each other and being separate ever since. There is of course a judgement. In the vivid imagery of the parable, there will be a bonfire and there will be a barn. But it is not down to us to decide who is for the flames.

Is it necessary to add that the imagery of 'binding bundles to be burned' is not to be taken literally? Perhaps it is, if only because we have in Matthew's Gospel, as we shall hear on Sunday, a later allegorizing interpretation of the parable of the wheat and the weeds which does just that. But, whatever else they are, the parables of Jesus are not allegories. In an allegory, every detail stands for something else and has to be decoded. ('The reapers are angels,' and so on.) The parables of Jesus are winged creatures and we must take imaginative flight ourselves if we are to catch their drift. You don't need wings to allegorize, only an anorak.

The great New Testament scholar Joachim Jeremias argued that parables make one point, rather than umpteen as allegories do. If so, then this parable is surely about the all-embracing inclusivity of the Kingdom of God. That it is a tale for our times hardly needs to be stressed.

The parable contains two questions. The first goes unanswered. 'Where did these weeds come from?' the servants ask. I ask this question about my allotment and I ask it about my world, fashioned so beautifully and so well. 'An enemy has done this,' I learn. Yes, but how did that weed of enmity come to take root in his heart? We do not know. 'The mystery of iniquity' (2 Thessalonians 2.7) is just that – a mystery.

But the servants have a second question – not 'Why is it a wicked world?' but 'What should we do about it?' That question can be answered.

YEAR B

Jeremiah 23.1–6; Ephesians 2.11–22; Mark 6:30–34, 53–56

IN PRAISE OF CROWDS

The Gospel calls for a Christian reappraisal of crowds. Jesus saw a great crowd 'and he had compassion on them because they were like sheep without a shepherd'. Jesus singles out the individual from the crowd – Zacchaeus in his tree (Luke 19.1–10), the woman who touches the hem of his garment (Mark 5.24–34), and the others – but he also takes the multitude to his heart.

It's hard to love a crowd. T. S. Eliot did not like crowds. He writes in *The Waste Land* of the commuters he sees, making their way to work across London Bridge. They seem to him like a crowd of corpses. But sometimes the sight of a crowd can be strangely touching. Early newsreel footage of tides of people can move us almost to tears – crowds cheering long-dead dictators, soldiers marching to old wars, packed terraces at some distant cup-final. Who were all these people, we wonder, and what became of them? Sometimes we'll wonder about the crowds we end up in ourselves, on a busy street, say, or in a crowded tube. Just occasionally, such curiosity will briefly yield to a more Christ-like sentiment as we sense, however swiftly the moment passes, a surge of compassion for those swathes of our kindred about whom we know nothing.

In the New Testament the word translated 'compassion' is used only of Jesus and by Jesus. The English word means 'suffering with'. The

Greek is much more visceral, locating the seat of compassion in the entrails. It is a gut-feeling, but a gut-feeling that gets things done. Jesus has compassion on the crowds, but then he taught them, fed them (mysteriously, the lectionary leaves out the feeding of the four thousand), and heals them.

Here, for the only time in Mark, the disciples are called 'apostles'. Jesus's invitation to them to 'rest a while' calls attention to an essential part of the apostolic ministry. The apostolate to which they are appointed is, periodically at least, an apostolate of doing nothing. The Twelve are told to stop. To do so belongs to their apostolic vocation.

The roots of such an understanding of what it means to slow down and come to rest are deep in the Hebrew Bible, primarily in its opening creation narrative. Here the Sabbath rest is not the divine 'day off', but the day when creation reaches its goal, when work passes into worship. In the imagery of the New Testament, it is the next best thing to heaven. 'There remains a Sabbath rest for the people of God' (Hebrews 4.9). It is the day for being what we were made for, rather than for doing what we have to. This exalted understanding of stopping is no doubt light years distant from our experience of Sunday. All the more reason for returning to it.

A writer who has done just that is Graham Neville. In a book which, sadly, many seem to have missed, *Free Time: A Theology of Leisure* (University of Birmingham, 2004), he explores the significance of life other than work. For Neville, the enquiry 'Anyone for tennis?' is a theological question. It asks about the meaning of what we do and who we are when we are not earning our living.

'Teach us, good Lord,' we pray, 'to serve thee as thou deservest.' St Ignatius Loyola, whose prayer this is, is sure he knows what it means to serve God as he deserves. It means 'to give and not to count the cost; to fight and not to heed the wounds'. So far, so good. But it also means, Ignatius says, 'to toil and not to seek for rest'. That is a line too far. To toil and not to seek for rest is both psychologically damaging and plainly unscriptural. I know several clergy who toil and do not seek for rest, and they give me the heebie-jeebies. By contrast, I think of a saint of God, long at rest, who served a busy inner-city parish. To the irritation of his colleagues, he spent most of his time painting water-colours. Yet people loved him, if only because he did not display symptoms of terminal exhaustion.

We need to rest, not primarily to recuperate, but to meet God. Stressed-out clergy don't need managers to control their work load. They simply need to read their Bibles. 'It is in vain that you rise up early and go late to rest, eating the bread of anxious toil, for he gives to his beloved sleep'(Psalm 127. 2). Thus the RSV. What the Hebrew actually says is 'he giveth to his beloved *in* sleep'. It is an admirable attribute of Almighty God that he 'neither slumbers nor sleeps' (Psalm121.4), but it is not a desirable trait in a parish priest.

YEAR C

Genesis 18.1–10a; Colossians 1.15–28; Luke 10.38–42

OUR NEED TO HEAR SARAH

Composing lectionaries must be exquisitely difficult – far harder than finding fault with them. Nevertheless we still have to point out the howlers. We have one this week. Our reading from Genesis concludes halfway through a verse. The angel of the Lord tells Abraham that his aged wife Sarah will bear a son. Had we been allowed to hear what comes next we would have learned that Sarah overhears what the angel says and starts laughing.

The lectionary breaks off at the precise point when a woman emerges from the shadows, comes out of the kitchen, and takes centre stage. Such moments are rare in the Bible. They need to be highlighted, not left out. We must hear Sarah's stifled laughter, not because she is a doubting Thomasina and a warning to us that we should not question the Lord's promises. Not at all. We need to hear Sarah's laughter because we need to hear *Sarah*. So far in the story she has been there simply as the dutiful wife, who does what her husband tells her. She has been making cakes as good wives do.

Today we ask questions about this vivid and fascinating story that once would not have occurred to us. We wonder why this annunciation is to Abraham and not to his wife who, we would have supposed, had some interest in what the divine messenger had to say. A modern Sarah would have been as much outraged as incredulous. For today's Sarah, what would be beyond belief – and laughable – would not be the news that she was going to have a baby but that she should not be the first to hear it. A subsequent and more celebrated annunciation is managed more equitably.

Apart from our blessed Lord, the Gospel reading is blessedly free from men. Traditionally, Jesus's mild reprimand of Martha has been taken as the dominical seal of approval on the contemplative life. If

Mary has 'chosen the better part', then so too have monks and nuns. The fourteenth-century author of the spiritual classic *The Cloud of Unknowing* saw Martha as typical of those in his – or her – day who were scathing of 'the religious life'. 'And right as Martha complained then on Mary her sister, right so yet unto this day all actives complain of contemplatives.' The author defends the perfection of the contemplative life, though conceding that some religious, 'have turned either to hypocrites or heretics, or have fallen into frenzies and many other mischiefs, in slander of Holy Church'.

Few today would claim that monasteries and convents are hotbeds of hypocrisy and heresy. If such houses are closing it is not because of 'mischiefs' uncovered in them, but because there is a catastrophic decline in vocations to 'the religious life', at least in the west. That decline is not rooted in disapproval of the religious life but – the occasional TV series notwithstanding – in a total incomprehension of it.

Today we are all activists, even if we have no idea what we are doing. Like Martha, we are 'distracted by our many tasks'. We need to ask ourselves what makes us so resistant to the traditional interpretation of the story. Do we dread the inner emptiness we might find if we stopped all we are doing long enough to look within? What is it about Jesus of Nazareth that makes us unwilling to be alone with him?

It is significant that today we have far more problems with the story of Mary and Martha than with the story which immediately precedes it in Luke's Gospel, the parable of 'the good Samaritan' (Luke 10.25–36). The punchline of the parable is 'Go and do'. Whether or not we obey that injunction, its bracing tone is congenial to the hyperactive temper of contemporary church life. We applaud the church where 'there is a lot going on'. The church next door, where the only sign of life is a tiny congregation saying its prayers, will not fare well at the dread day of the archdeacon's visitation.

To be sure, there is likely to have been more to Martha's angry outburst than resentment that her sister had left to her all the work of preparing a meal. Mary has usurped what traditionally was a male role. Men, not women, sat at the teacher's feet studying Torah. A famous rabbi was supposed to have said, 'If a man gives his daughter knowledge of the law, it as though he taught her lechery.'

Such was not Jesus's view. As Leonard Swidler has well said, 'Jesus made it abundantly clear that the supposedly exclusively male role of the intellectual, of the "theologian", was for women as well as for men . . . How this story must have buoyed up those Jewish women

whose horizons and desires stretched beyond the kitchen threshold!'
(*Jesus Was A Feminist*, Catholic World, 1979).

Sarah will have rejoiced to see Mary's day.

Proper 12

The Sunday between 24 and 30 July

YEAR A

1 Kings 3.5–12; Romans 8.26–39; Matthew 13.31–33, 44–52

TEACHERS MUST BE LEARNERS

Most of Matthew 13 is a picture gallery. There are two big pictures and
several small ones. The first big picture is of a peasant farmer whose
land is so intractable that you'd have thought he would have done better to have found somewhere more fertile to farm. But he stays with
the patch he's got and in the end there's a good harvest. (For 'patch',
read 'parish'?) The second large canvas depicts a field which is as much
weeds as wheat. That is what the Church is like – no better than most
other places and often much worse. The other pictures in Matthew's
gallery are cameo studies. A bush with birds in it; a housewife making
bread; a stash of coins hidden in the ground; a jewel in the junk; fishermen sorting their catch. Make of them what you will.

The Jerusalem Bible calls this collection of pictures Jesus's 'Sermon
of Parables'. If it is a sermon, it is a very puzzling one and nowhere
more so than in its conclusion. Jesus abruptly asks whether the disciples
have understood what he has been saying. They say that they do understand – and so reveal how little they have learned. They are unlike King
Solomon, whom we heard in our first reading. Solomon admits to not
knowing 'how to come out or go in' – and so shows that his prayer for
wisdom is already well on the way to being answered.

Jesus's concluding comment is as cryptic as any of his teasing 'parables of the Kingdom'. We sense that he is saying something very important, if we could only catch his drift. Of our various translations,
all trying to capture the elusive, that of the Revised English Bible is the

best. 'When a teacher of the law has become a learner in the kingdom of heaven, he is like . . .' – then there follows about the briefest of all the parables Jesus ever told – 'a householder who can produce from his store things both new and old.'

Teachers must become learners. Two roles are being contrasted here, as they often are in Matthew's Gospel. The first role is that of the religious professional, the person who presumes to tell other people what they must believe and how they must behave to please God. The second role is that of the disciple of Jesus of Nazareth. All the Gospels, but especially Matthew's, make it clear that these two roles conflict. It is almost impossible to be both at once. The terrifying 23rd chapter of Matthew leaves us in no doubt about that. Needless to say, a Christian reading of the New Testament does not allow us to redirect such texts, whatever their original context, away from ourselves on to this or that sect or party in first-century Palestine.

Teachers must become learners. The premise of Jesus's remark is that the transition is possible. Here is good news for those in what are curiously called 'holy orders'. Popes, precentors and prebendaries; archdeacons and archbishops; abbots and archimandrites; canons and curates; bishops, priests and deacons – all can become disciples. It is never too late. I, too, after a lifetime clambering in and out of pulpits, can become a disciple. But conversion of one's life is not like the conversion of one's loft. It is not a once-for-all event. Becoming a disciple is like becoming a child (Matthew 18.1–5). The process required is a constant conversion, a continuous emptying of one's mind – and in some cases one's vestry – of all the paraphernalia with which religion clutters up the way of Jesus.

What does this 'cleric-turned-disciple' have to offer? The tiny sketch that is the last on display in our picture gallery allows space to the imagination. The disciple is like the householder in whose home both old and new are valued. The disciple hears what the prophet says about the old. 'Thus says the Lord, "Stand ye in the ways, and see, and ask for the old paths, where is the good way, and walk therein"' (Jeremiah 6.16). But the disciple hears too what the same prophet says about the new. 'For the Lord has created a new thing on the earth' (Jeremiah 31.22). (Jeremiah is looking ahead to 'the new covenant', the time when long-hallowed traditions will be turned upside-down. The example he gives of a bad tradition that will have to go is that of the subordination of women.)

The temptation of the professionally religious is to go overboard for either the old or the new, to refuse ever to touch the ark, or to be forever

tinkering with it. The Christian disciple, by contrast, is committed neither to the old nor to the new, but to the one who transcends both. So,
with Sydney Carter, we pray:

> You are older than the world can be,
> You are younger than the life in me;
> Ever old and ever new,
> Keep me travelling along with you.

YEAR B

2 Kings 4.42–44; Ephesians 3.14–21; John 6.1–21

THERE IS A CHILD HERE

The story of the feeding of the five thousand is in all four Gospels, but
John's account is no mere reprise of the other three.

Only John mentions the child with his loaves and fishes. Much of the
commentary on this detail is disappointing. The word translated 'boy'
occurs just this once in the New Testament. In the Greek it is a 'double
diminutive'. Here we have not 'a little boy', but rather 'a very little
boy'. (Not that we can be certain that the child was male. My seriously
unreconstructed dictionary tells me that the word can refer to 'even a
female'.) Scholars are quick to point out that the word can be used for
a young man rather than a child. Perhaps, they say, John had in mind
the servant who helped Elisha miraculously feed a hundred hungry men
at Gilgal (2 Kings 4.38). Or perhaps the detail reflects what happened
at the Eucharist in the early church; the 'boy' is then some sort of server
or sub-deacon.

Maybe. But what is sad about such commentary is the failure even to
consider the possibility that when John talks about a child he might have
meant a child and that the reference to the child is more than a charming
pictorial detail. Theologians work in clinically child-free zones. Their la-
bours are undistracted by children and so the books they write – glance
at the index to any of them – have little to say about children.

We need a rubber stamp with Andrew's words on it in huge capitals:
'THERE IS A CHILD HERE!' (We might add, 'In case you hadn't noticed.') This admonition then needs to be imprinted across this page of
the Bible, as across many another where children have been written out
of the story.

The 'Child Theology' movement is still quite new. The movement is as much concerned with theological method as with our estimate of children and childhood. It urges us to ask what it might mean for the way we do theology if we allowed the child to be 'in our midst' where Jesus set him or her (Mark 9.36). What would be the consequences, Child Theology asks, for our understanding of Christian doctrine, if the child 'in the midst' informed our reflection about it?

The child in our story this week invites us to reconsider the Eucharist from his or her perspective. John has no account of 'the institution of the Eucharist'. Instead he portrays the feeding of the five thousand as a dramatic sign of Jesus as 'the bread of life', the theme of the great discourse which will shortly follow. For John, past and future meet in the sharing of this meal. At this repast, manna in the wilderness is recalled and the final Messianic banquet is anticipated, the feast in heaven when all God's children will eat at his table, and the long promised party at last begins.

And it all starts with the child. With the gift of a child the hungry are fed. This wonder takes place, John tells us, at Passover. We are bound to recall the role of the child at Passover, at least as it later developed. Without the child's contribution, without the questions the child asks, the feast cannot even begin. So here with the miracle of the loaves and fish. Nothing happens until the child's presence is acknowledged and the child's gift received. What one child offers then becomes bread for all.

The interesting question arises as to whether this little Galilean child himself, herself, gets a bit of the bread so marvellously multiplied. I like to think so. Fortunately regulations about 'The Admission of Baptized Persons to Holy Communion', as set out in paragraph 1(c) of Canon B15A of the Canons of the Church of England had not yet come into force.

Another detail told only by John is the sequel to the story. The crowd, mistaking Jesus's sign, try to 'make him king'. Jesus's response to this attempted coup is not the stately departure most English versions suggest, but flight – so at least some early texts tell us. The only enthronement Jesus accepts is his crucifixion. His renunciation of power, his rejection of 'the kingdoms of this world and the glory of them' (Matthew 4.8), is unconditional.

Jesus refuses to be conscripted for a role he has repudiated from the outset of his ministry. His disciples have always been less reluctant to seize and exercise power. The traditional site of the feeding of the five thousand is today the setting for an absurd example of such impenitent triumphalism. Here a consortium of Christian groups, led by the egregious evangelist Pat Robertson, is planning to build a biblical theme park. The venture is expected to bring up to one million extra tourists a year but, we read, 'an undeclared benefit will be the cementing of a political alliance between the Israeli right-wing and the American Christian right'.

YEAR C

Genesis 18.20–32; Colossians 2.6–15 (16–19); Luke 11.1–13

THE AUDACITY OF PRAYER

Sunday's Gospel has one story which only Luke tells and lots of little details besides that are solely and characteristically his.

The little details first. Unlike Matthew, Luke contextualizes the teaching of Jesus. He relates Jesus's precepts about prayer to Jesus's practice. We know from Luke that Jesus prayed on special occasions – at his baptism and transfiguration, for example (Luke 3.21; 9.28,29). But Luke's casual comment that 'he was praying in a certain place' makes it clear that Jesus, unlike many of us, did not turn to prayer only at critical moments.

'Lord, teach us to pray.' The request is itself a prayer. By asking to be taught to pray the disciples have already started to pray. Prayer is a conversation and this request begins it. John the Baptist, so they remind Jesus, taught his disciples to pray. The passing comment makes us revise our image of John. We do not usually think of this eccentrically dressed and fiercely confrontational figure as a man of prayer. And yet Luke has told us that where he grew up and where he grew spiritually strong was 'in the wilderness' (Luke 1.80). What else is there to do in that desolate landscape – apart from foraging for locusts and wild honey – except to pray?

Luke's version of the Lord's Prayer begins with the direct address to God as 'Father', rather than as 'Our Father' (Matthew 6.9). Behind the Greek *pater* is the Aramaic 'Abba', the term Jesus himself used in prayer to God (Mark 14.36). Some commentators and many preachers have made too much of this word. It was not a word only used by tiny children in talking to God. Jesus does not tell us to call God 'Daddy'. A more serious criticism for some is that by approaching God as 'Abba' we allow the concept of God as male to continue unchallenged.

Nevertheless, having noted all the theological health warnings the word 'Abba' carries, we are still bound to register just how remarkable Jesus's use of it is. The word is a rare window into the consciousness of the historical Jesus. It is an unparalleled way of talking to God. Jesus's contemporaries did not call God by this name. The German theologian Joachim Jeremias, who himself admitted that he may have built more on this one word than it can properly support, was still right to conclude, 'Abba expresses the heart of Jesus' relationship to God. He spoke to God as a child to its father: confidently and securely, and yet at the same time reverently and obediently' (*New Testament Theology*, Scribner, 1971). Into that relationship we too are called (Romans 8.15; Galatians 4.6). In that spirit we boldly say, 'Abba, Father, hallowed be your name.'

The fascinating little story, usually referred to as 'The Friend at Midnight', is found only here in Luke. We would gather from some translations that the parable is teaching us to keep on praying without being discouraged, the attitude urged on us in the familiar sayings (found also in Matthew) which shortly follow, 'Go on asking . . . Go on seeking . . . Go on knocking . . .'. The householder, who is so reluctant to stir from his bed, eventually gets up because of his friend's 'persistence'. Thus the New Revised English Bible and the New English Bible – and thus many a sermon. But 'persistence' is a virtue. The Greek word used, however, denotes a vice. A more accurate translation would be 'shameless audacity'.

Something other than – or at least more than – persistence in prayer is being taught here. There is an inescapable effrontery in the business of prayer, which this tale brilliantly captures. (We shall meet another story making much the same point a little later in Luke 18.1–8). In prayer we ask for what we need, our 'daily bread' for example. Or we ask for another's needs, healing for a sick child perhaps, or the end of some dreadful war. Jesus encourages us to believe that the one we address as 'Abba' knows our needs, that the world where we suffer our privations is not out of his control, and that he is a loving God who likes to give. If God is indeed all-knowing, all-powerful, and all-loving then every prayer – the instant 'arrow prayer' as much as the prayer that beats on heaven's door until the knuckles bleed – has an element of impertinence. That is no reason whatsoever for ceasing to pray.

All prayer is audacious. If intercessory prayer is a conversation, we should expect to hear an incensed voice from heaven answering our petitions with a sharp, 'You've got a nerve!' That is certainly what Abraham expected to hear as he tried to persuade God to spare Sodom.

PROPER 13

Our first reading this Sunday – an Oscar this week to our lectionary editors – lets us listen in on the conversation between the patriarch and the Almighty. 'Oh do not let the Lord be angry if I speak just once more,' says Abraham.

So say we all.

Proper 13

The Sunday between 31 July and 6 August

YEAR A

Isaiah 55.1–5; Romans 9.1–5; Matthew 14.13–21

SLEEPWALKING INTO A CRISIS

Jesus 'withdrew to a deserted place by himself'. Why did he do that? We are not told, but we do not have to speculate. We don't have to speculate, because we can imagine. St Ignatius Loyola taught us that, if we are Christians, our imagination, along with everything else about us, is baptized. It is a baptized imagination, exercised within the community of faith, which must be brought to bear on a terse text such as this.

Jesus has just had bad news. John the Baptist, his kinsman and kindred spirit, has been butchered by Herod. We have hints and more than hints that there was a special bond between Jesus and the one who went before him on the path of history. It was not only at the passing of Lazarus that Jesus wept. Jesus needs to be alone with his grief. His uncomprehending disciples can offer little comfort, for they cannot begin to fathom how, for their master, the Calvary of the Baptist foreshadows his own.

Jesus longs for somewhere away from it all where he can deal with his grief in his own time and in his own way. So he sets out for the desert, where 'nature has clefts in the rocks where he may hide, and secret valleys in whose silence he may weep undisturbed'. His intention is to grieve and to pray in the terrain that John had made uniquely his. There, in the desert, the memories of the one he mourns will be intense

230

and vivid and there he will feel close to him in spirit. That, we Christianly imagine, is his intention.

But more is going on here. A more powerful compulsion draws Jesus to the desert than a desire to mourn in private. The Spirit drove our Lord into the wilderness long before the martyrdom of the Baptist, long before even those forty days and forty nights when he fasted in the wild. Jesus's first departure for the desert took place when 'he left his throne and his kingly crown'. In setting sail for 'a deserted place' Jesus follows the trajectory of the Incarnation. The orientation of Jesus's ministry is always away from the centres of power, always towards the periphery. Jesus's destination is outside because his destiny is 'outside'. To be sure, Jesus made his way to Jerusalem, but the end of his earthly journey was not the city itself, but a waste place outside its walls, a hill of skulls and bones. Such was the self-emptying of the Son of God.

Jesus sails across the lake to a deserted beach. Except that it is no longer deserted. The crowds have followed him on foot around the shore and, as soon as he disembarks, they clamour about him. The quiet uninterrupted period of mourning for John he had planned is no longer possible.

He has come to this peripheral place and here he meets peripheral people. Far from the centres of power, he finds himself among the powerless. The distant margin of the lake is emblematic of the margins of society, and the five thousand – and many more, so Matthew suggests – represent the marginalized of every age, those at the mercy of powers to whom they do not matter.

Famously, Jesus feeds them. We must read the oft-told tale of the feeding of the five thousand in context. The context is not so much what went before and what comes next in Matthew's Gospel. The context is what is going on now in our own hungry world. The context is the recent report of an Afghan father who sold his eleven-year-old daughter for $2,000 to buy food for his family. The context is the food riots occurring in places as far apart as Mexico and Morocco, Uzbekistan and Yemen, Haiti and Senegal. The context is what UNICEF tells us about the steeply rising incidence of child malnutrition in the Indian state of Madhya Pradesh. The context is the doubling of wheat prices and the mounting cost of bread.

The context are the utterances of today's prophets. For example, Tim Lang, Professor of Food Policy at the University of Leeds, lecturing in London in March 2008, warned, 'We are sleepwalking into a crisis.'

'We are sleepwalking into a crisis.' John the Baptist, whom Jesus missed so much, said much the same to his own complacent contemporaries.

He told them that swift and terrible retribution would fall on them for their careless, self-indulgent and exploitative way of life (Luke 3.7–14). Herod, having murdered John, later came to wonder whether John had been raised from the dead (Matthew 14.2). Perhaps Professor Lang is John the Baptist risen from the dead. Be that as it may, we'd better pay attention to him.

YEAR B

Exodus 16.2–4, 9–15; Ephesians 4.1–16; John 6.24–35

OUR WRONG QUESTIONS

According to John, people often misunderstand what Jesus says. They repeatedly ask the wrong questions. Some see this as simply a literary device, as John's way of telling his story. John pictures most people as getting hold of the wrong end of the stick and Jesus then putting them right. Telling it that way is John's method of keeping the story moving.

John certainly recasts the story of Jesus in his own idiom. But, however inventive his narrative, the crowd's failure to grasp what Jesus means is surely not something John makes up. There is something condescending and belittling in commentary which sees the masses as being there merely to ask more or less daft questions and to make inept comments. As if we knew any better where Jesus is, what he is doing, and what he means.

The crowd is 'lost'. They are bewildered by the miracle they have experienced, and baffled by what they've heard. So too are we. If in our pride we suppose otherwise, we're riding for a fall. That's where we are in this story, lost in the crowd – nowhere else. Two thousand years of theology, confessions, catechisms and creeds have not provided for us some exalted vantage point from which we enjoy an unimpeded view of who Jesus is, although we like to think so.

The crowd's misconceived questions are ours. One of the questions is 'What must we do to perform the works of God?' It is the Philippian jailor's question, 'What must I do to be saved?'(Acts 16.30). Jesus challenges the premise of the question, the assumption that salvation is won by what we do. So too does Paul. The 'work' of God, says Jesus, is to believe in him. 'Believe in the Lord Jesus Christ,' says Paul, 'and you will be saved' (Acts 16.31).

But we're still part of that crowd and it's the question we still ask. 'What must we do?' We ask the question because everyone in every other walk of life asks it and because we've convinced ourselves as a church that at all costs we must keep up. 'What must we do?' we ask – or, in our ghastly management-speak, 'What is good practice?' Jesus's response to the question is not to provide a wealth of advice – that is readily available from all good church bookshops – but to expose the misconceptions about his mission lurking behind it.

'What sign are you going to give us then, so that we may see and believe you?' If Jesus is claiming to be greater than Moses, then a confirmatory sign even more marvellous than manna in the wilderness is clearly called for. Again, they ask the wrong question and again, alongside them, we do the same. In a word, we demand miracles. Some are so confident of this demand being met that they count on miracles every time they meet. There are scores of little churches in the East End – and one absolutely enormous one – where miracles, or what pass for them, are commonplace. Others, more cautious, seek another sort of miracle. They look to the Lord to turn the tide running against them, to reverse the slow decline in their numbers and in the notice anyone is taking of them, to touch the hearts of funders so that holes in the roof may be mended, to give them some reason for carrying on.

But to the crowd and to us lost in it, Jesus gives no sign save himself. We have the bread, that's all. Here is John's version of Matthew's cryptic 'sign of the prophet Jonah' (Matthew 12.39), the only sign given to the 'wicked and adulterous generation' to which we belong. 'I am the bread of life. Whoever comes to me will never hunger . . .'

'I am the bread of life. Whoever comes to me will never hunger . . .' At once, without bidding, familiar images of starving children superimpose themselves on the text and we find the words shocking. Such embarrassment is not a modern problem, only arising because we can watch these terrible images while tucking into a TV supper. Jesus did not require harrowing television documentaries to tell him that this is a hungry world. The cry 'Give us this bread always', echoing the Samaritan woman's 'Give me this water!' (John 4.15), may reflect yet another misunderstanding, but it is the voice of desperation not of greed. 'I am the Bread of Life.' Those who first heard or read those words were far nearer the breadline than we are and they would have been all the more aware of the outrageous audacity of Jesus's claim.

'I am the Bread of Life.' The context of that assertion was a world where children often went hungry to bed. That world is still with us and it is still the context in which the great claim of Jesus is to be interpreted. His words are more than a statement of who he is. They are telling us what to do.

YEAR C

Ecclesiastes 1.2, 12–14; 2.18–23; Colossians 3.1–11; Luke 12.13–21

HERE TODAY, GONE TOMORROW

Wealth is not a vice. Were it a vice we would not be trying to make poverty history. The evil we are warned against is not wealth but greed. The word Luke uses – *pleonexia* – crops up regularly in the New Testament's checklists of deadly sins (Mark 7.22; Romans 1.29; Ephesians 4.19; 5.3). Take the word apart and we find its root meaning. It is simply the desire to 'have more'. The problem with *pleonexia* is that it is insatiable. Ancient writers saw *pleonexia* as the spiritual equivalent of dropsy. Those with dropsy always craved more to drink, although the water they imbibed only made them worse.

Wealth is not wicked. As we saw a few Sundays ago, it was because 'the good Samaritan' was well-off that he was able to do something for the one fallen by the roadside (Luke 10.25–37). In his book *Is there a gospel for the rich?* (Mowbray, 1997) Bishop Richard Harries argues that – notwithstanding the tale of 'the rich young ruler' (Luke 18.18–30) – the economically successful are not barred from salvation. Nor should Christians feel a paralysing sense of guilt about benefiting from a market-based capitalist system. What matters about my whopping city bonus is what I do with it.

Richard Harries writes with the sobriety which befits his purple cloth. Richard North's panegyric in praise of wealth, *Rich Is Beautiful: A very personal defence of mass affluence* (The Social Affairs Unit, 2005), is headier stuff. North believes that wealth – 'lots of it' – is lovely and good. This may not quite catch the drift of Sunday's Gospel, but it would be a bad mistake not to give North a hearing. North claims that there is a potential spiritual dimension to wealth creation. The perilous human condition is not the well-heeled life but the unexamined life. Wealth is not wrong. Private equity can do public good. What is wrong is not making the wealth more widely available.

'Wealth is not wrong.' I am sure I would find that truth comforting if I were reading 'the parable of the rich fool' on board my luxury yacht. I am worried that I find it equally reassuring, equally an endorsement of an easy lifestyle, in my more modest circumstances. In our epistle this Sunday, Paul calls *pleonexia* 'idolatry'. An idol is any-thing – or anyone – other than almighty God in which, or in whom, I find my ultimate security. That idol does not have to be a yacht. It need not be inordinately expensive. It is anything I am reluctant to let go, though let it go I must on the night – tonight, maybe – when my soul too is required. The great Congregationalist scholar George Caird has wisely commented that 'wealth is a peril to those who have it, but also to those who do not' (*Saint Luke*, Penguin Books, 1963).

Our first reading is from a book we rarely turn to. The lectionary sends us to Ecclesiastes this Sunday presumably because 'Qoheleth', the 'preacher' behind this anonymous text, is as scathing of *pleonexia* – of wanting to have more and more – as ever Jesus or Paul were. 'Vanity of vanity,' says the Preacher, 'all is vanity.' 'Qoheleth' is a pen-name. It could just as well have been Eeyore, for our author's world-view is unremittingly bleak. To capture the flavour of this extraordinary text one should read it aloud slowly, sadly, and wearily, interspersing one's delivery with the occasional deep melancholy sigh.

Ecclesiastes certainly supports our two New Testament readings in their condemnation of *pleonexia*. The trouble is that its indictment goes much further. Ecclesiastes passes the same judgement – 'all is vanity' – on all human endeavour. The sentence of death, passed on the property developer in Jesus's parable, is written across everything we do. The life of the playboy plutocrat, says the Preacher, who makes himself the wealthiest man in Jerusalem and who supposes he can take his concu-bines with him, is a striving after wind. But so, too, is a career spent in the acquisition of knowledge and wisdom.

Most commentaries on Ecclesiastes are a damage-limitation exercise. They point to the book's 'orthodox postscript' – 'Fear God and keep his commandments' (Ecclesiastes 12.13–14) – and find in it a counter-balance to the cynicism and world-weariness in which the rest of the book is steeped.

But Ecclesiastes does not have to depend on its pious conclusion to qualify as Holy Scripture. However tasteless, unfashionable and unpal-atable it is to do so, we need to remind ourselves occasionally of our mortality. Dust we are, and to dust we shall return. Our life is 'a mist that appears for a little time and then vanishes' (James 4.14). So, too, are our structures, the Church of England among them. We shall soon be forgotten. We need to read Ecclesiastes much more often. It, too, is the Word of the Lord.

Proper 14

The Sunday between 7 and 13 August

YEAR A

1 Kings 19.9–18; Romans 10.5–15; Matthew 14.22–33

MONSTERS MEET THEIR MASTER

'Thalassophobia' has been defined as 'the persistent, abnormal, and un-warranted fear of the sea'. The fishermen among the disciples certainly feared the sea, but not because they were thalassophobics. There was nothing irrational in their recognition that big seas can do bad things to small boats. Far from being a sick phobia, their fear of the sea was entirely healthy.

They had been taught by experience – by having to wrest a living from it – to dread the sea, but they had learned the same lesson from their Scriptures. In the Hebrew Bible, the sea is the primal image of all that is malign and menacing, of all that continues to resist the purpose of God. All the seas of Scripture are serpentine – not serpentine in name and shape like the lovely lake in Hyde Park, but serpentine in essence and character.

The language of the ancient myths evokes the terrors of the seas. 'You rule the raging of the sea. You crushed Rahab like a carcase' (Psalm 89.9). Rahab is not the hospitable lady whose clients included Joshua's spies (Joshua 2), but the sea-monster we meet in many an ancient Near-Eastern text. She has many names but a single malevolent purpose, to frustrate and defeat the creator God. Rahab is better known as Leviathan – 'Leviathan, the twisting serpent . . . the dragon that is in the sea' (Isaiah 27.1). If God's vision for humankind is to be achieved, Leviathan must be overcome. The New Testament is the story of how that victory was gained when, one Friday, someone stepped into Leviathan's jaws. The most eloquent and profound literary commentary on the atonement, understood in these mythological terms, remains Herman Melville's *Moby Dick*. Christ's decisive victory over Leviathan is anticipated in earlier battles which he won, when he stilled an angry sea (Mark 4.35–41) and when, as we hear this week, he came to his terrified friends, walking on the water.

Jesus walks on the water. As with all the miracles, we must ask what this story means. The question of 'what actually happened', while not wholly unimportant for those who believe that something did happen, is a distraction. (Do any of those ancient modernists survive, I wonder, who used to tell us that in fact Jesus was walking along the shore or on a sandbank?)

Jesus tramples the old enemy underfoot. He does what God does. 'It is God who by himself spread out the heavens and trod on the back of the sea monster' (Job 9.8.). Lest we fail to see the significance of his action, all three Gospels that have this story record the telling words with which Jesus reassures his terrified disciples. 'I am,' he says (Matthew 14.27; Mark 6.51; John 6.20). Having done what God does, Jesus says what God says, for these are the very same revelatory words that Moses heard from the burning bush (Exodus 3.14). (It would be impossible to imagine a translation more grotesquely mistaken than 'It's only me.')

The miracle is a divine disclosure, a 'theophany'. Matthew – and only Matthew – makes doubly clear what the story is saying by recording the disciples' response in worship to what they have witnessed. 'Truly,' they say to Jesus, 'You are the Son of God.'

Jesus does what God does. All the more the remarkable, then, that Peter asks to do the same. Peter too – with the saving help of his best of friends – does what is divine. He leaves the boat. He too confronts Leviathan. In Matthew's Gospel Peter represents the Christian community. That is to say, he represents us. Like Peter, our way to Jesus is in and through the contradictions and adversities that the sea-beasts of Scripture symbolize, not along some pleasant detour round them.

I write these notes, as is my custom, very early in the morning. In need of fresh air, I break off to walk the few yards down to the front. Nearing the beach I become aware of a torrent of raised voices mingling with the thunder of the waves. A group of some thirty men women and children, most wearing white robes with red sashes, is assembled on the otherwise deserted beach, just a few yards from the water's edge. They stand facing the sea as if to confront it and rebuke it. Each worshipper, arms raised, is making his or her own prayer, crying out across the deep. Some hold their Bibles high and shake them defiantly at the waters.

At last their prayers subside and the service ends. In two and threes they make their way back to the promenade. I ask one of the worshippers why they should choose to stand facing the sea. He tells me that, when they see the sea, they think of all their troubles. This morning they have not walked on the waters. They tell me that they come from north London where soon they will be returning. Leviathan will be waiting for them there. So too will the one who has defeated him.

YEAR B

1 Kings 19.4–8; Ephesians 4.25 – 5.2; John 6.35, 41–51

WHEN IT'S ALL TOO MUCH

Elijah, we're told, personally slaughtered several hundred prophets of a religion he disagreed with. Evidently he was not an advocate of inter-faith dialogue.

'What doest thou here, Elijah?' God asks him this question when he finds him hiding in a cave (I Kings 19.9). We might well ask Elijah the same question about his place in the lectionary. If we are to survive the twenty-first century we must learn to live at peace with one another. So why pay attention to this bellicose character? What can such a religious extremist possibly have to say to us?

We are drawn to Elijah because we know him well, warts and all. The windows we have on his life are not of stained glass. The first serious study of the Bible I read was entitled *Personalities of the Old Testament* (James Fleming, Scribner, 1939). Elijah is a personality, someone we can picture. No wonder his life has generated so many legends. We genuflect to the prophets and saints whose piety is exemplary – and swiftly move on. We stay with Elijah.

'I have had enough, Lord,' says Elijah – and when he says that we know that he's made of flesh and blood and not of plaster. Elijah teaches us how to pray. The first principle of private prayer, as almost everything else, is taught by Shakespeare. His most profound and un-sparing exploration of the tragedy of life and of the hope of redemption is *King Lear*. The play draws to its close with the line 'Speak what you feel, not what you ought to say.' Our liturgies are anthologies of public prayers, the prayers we 'ought to say'. But to 'speak what you feel' is to pray from the heart, as Elijah does, to tell God what it's really like. There are the prayers we say and the prayers we mean. Elijah's prayers are the latter.

'I have had enough, Lord.' The point on the sad scale of our sorrows when deep gut-wrenching misery descends into clinical depression is impossible to determine. Some commentators suggest that Elijah's malaise was a predictable psychological reaction to his recent exertions –

butchering false prophets takes it out of you – and to Jezebel's threat on his life. The analysis belittles Elijah. 'He's not himself,' we say of someone who is ill. But Elijah was wholly himself when he told God that he'd had enough, as was Job – another who 'spoke what he felt' – when he too told God to take his life.

Elijah's experience is best understood neither as clinical depression, nor as 'the dark night of the soul' which, we're told, those sufficiently advanced on the spiritual life pass through. His symptoms were neither of sickness nor of sanctity. He'd simply had enough. It's not uncommon. The urge to sit down under a juniper tree and to ask to die overtakes us all occasionally. Those with an intense sense of vocation seem especially vulnerable to such moods. As with Elijah, it can be the apparent successes they experience, as much as their failures, which engender self-doubt and bring them close to despair. George Herbert, best loved of pastors, prays, 'Kill me not ev'ry day, Thou Lord of Life.' We think of Gerard Manley Hopkins, 'pitched past pitch of grief', who gave glory to God for dappled things but whose last sonnets are cries of dereliction.

> I wake and feel the fell of dark, not day . . .
> I am gall, I am heartburn. God's most deep decree
> Bitter would have me taste; my taste was me;
> Bones built in me, flesh filled, blood brimmed the curse
> Selfyeast of spirit a dull dough sours. I see
> The lost are like this.

At such bleak times it's important to get lots of rest and not to stop eating. Elijah falls asleep under his juniper tree. He is awakened by the angel who tells him to get up and to get on, but first to have breakfast.

This moment has been captured in one of the masterpieces of Flemish art, the Holy Sacrament Altarpiece in the Church of St Peter in Leuven, painted by Dirk Bouts. The central panel of the altarpiece depicts the Last Supper. The surrounding panels show four Old Testament episodes prefiguring the Eucharist, of which 'the Sleep of Elijah' is one. The angel touches the sleeping prophet at whose side he has set a cup of water and a cake, looking for all the world like a chalice and paten.

The side-panel on the Leuven altarpiece directs our eye to the great central scene of the institution of the Eucharist, just as on Sunday the story will serve as prologue to the Gospel's proclamation of Jesus as the Bread of Life. Christian art and Christian liturgy assume that the Hebrew Scriptures are really *about* someone they do not mention.

That 'about' has to be unpacked carefully. Elijah's role is not that of a warm-up.

YEAR C

Genesis 15.1–6; Hebrews 11.1–3, 8–16; Luke 12.32–40

SEEKING THE CITY OF GOD

John Bunyan's last sight of Christian and his companion Hopeful is of the two pilgrims at the end of their journey as they enter the City of God. Bunyan has one glimpse of the city shining like the sun. He sees a throng of crowned figures. He glimpses 'them that had wings' and catches the sound of their singing. Then they shut up the gates. As the vision fades and he wakes to where he is, in the cramped little lock-up on Bedford bridge, Bunyan adds, 'which, when I had seen, I wished myself among them'.

'The Lord loves the gates of Zion more than all the dwellings of Jacob. Glorious things are spoken of thee, O City of God' (Psalm 87:2).

The idea of the city of God haunts the Christian imagination. It certainly has had a powerful hold on our hymnody, even if some of these songs of Zion are falling from fashion. Much to our loss, we sing less often than we did, John Mason Neale's hymn,

Blessed City, heavenly Salem,
Vision dear of peace and love

– with its thrilling lines:

Many a blow and biting sculpture
Polished well those stones elect.

Bunyan's longing for the City of God is the yearning felt by the men and women of faith whose stories are recalled in the great eleventh chapter of the letter to the Hebrews, Abel, Enoch, Noah and the rest. Our lectionary cherry-picks a niggardly few verses from the chapter. We need to hear the whole roll-call. Lunch can wait. Rahab (Rahab!) Gideon, Barak, Samson, Jepthah . . . There is, it seems, a faraway look in the eyes of these down-to-earth figures. They know themselves to be 'strangers and foreigners on the earth'. They 'seek a homeland'. They desire 'a better country'. That homesickness, shy as we are of saying much about it, is ours too. For the writer to the Hebrews, the reality that answers to that longing, theirs and ours, is the city God has prepared for those who walk by faith.

There was a time when faithful people focused their hopes and dreams on the earthly Jerusalem, the city where God had 'caused his name to dwell' (Deuteronomy 12). All roads led there and there was no greater joy than to go there. But the earthly Jerusalem failed, as all our worldly Jerusalems always will. Condemned for its idolatry and injustice, the city falls – razed to the ground by the Babylonians. But even as the man-made Jerusalem falls, the vision of a new Jerusalem is born. The prophets exult in the hope of it. 'Oh, afflicted one, storm-tossed and not comforted; behold I will set your stones in antimony and lay your foundations in sapphire. I will make your gates of jewels and all your walls of precious stones' (Isaiah 54.11). Above all, its streets will be safe for children to play in (Zechariah 8.5).

Once more the vision fades. At last one greater than the prophets comes to the city. He weeps over the city, warns of its destruction, and dies outside its gates. Some say that his death is not the end and, in that faith, they do not let go the dream of a better Jerusalem, even when the Jerusalem they know finally falls to the Romans. 'And I saw the holy city, new Jerusalem, coming down out of heaven' (Revelation 21.2).

The vision of the city of God is not some private fantasy peculiar to Christians who find the present world uncongenial. The longing for somewhere where justice is done, where joy lasts, where beauty does not wither, and where peace reigns, is a hunger of the human heart, not only of the Christian heart.

To dwell on the city where dreams come true is not escapism. The revelation to St John may be of a city that comes down from the sky, but the writer to the Hebrew sees the city of God as a goal to be pursued on earth. The quest of that city makes inexorable moral demands. The figure that dominates the great portrait gallery of Hebrews 11 is Abraham. Abraham 'looked forward to the city that has foundations whose architect and builder is God'. And how does Abraham set out on his search for that city? 'By faith,' we read, 'Abraham *obeyed.*'

Abraham obeyed. The road to the city of God is the path of obedience. For Abraham that path took him, aged 100-plus, to the summit of Mount Moriah, where he raised a knife to slay his only son. That may well have been, as Kierkegaard called it, 'divine madness' but it certainly was not escapism.

The contrast between the Jerusalem where Tony Blair now has an office, a city where the children of Abraham continue their fratricide, and the Jerusalem our hearts long for is stark, but that is the last reason for abandoning the vision. The blueprint of the city to come is given to us so that we can build better cities now.

Proper 15

The Sunday between 14 and 20 August

YEAR A

Isaiah 56.1, 6–8; Romans 11.1–2a, 29–32; Matthew 15.(10–20)21–28

PASS THE PARCEL

Much of Matthew either mirrors Mark or shares its material with Luke. That being so, we can easily miss the often brief asides and interjections with which Matthew impresses his own stamp on the story of Jesus. We must read the longer Gospel this Sunday, where we have an exchange between Jesus and his disciples which is only in Matthew and which we must not overlook.

The context is the conversation Jesus has been having with the Pharisees about 'tradition'. The Pharisees were 'traditionalists'. A 'traditionalist', in the language of the New Testament, is someone who hands on what he receives. (The custodians of the tradition were, needless to say, all men.) A traditionalist hands over what he receives without tampering with it. He 'passes the parcel' without changing its contents. When St Paul became a Christian there was much about his old way of life, both customs and convictions, which he gave up. But he did not cease to be a traditionalist. 'I handed on to you as of the first importance,' he tells the church at Corinth, 'what I in turn had received' (1 Corinthians 15.3). In this respect Paul is still the Pharisee he always was. He still passes the parcel – it is just that the package is now a new one.

The Pharisees who clashed with Jesus would have claimed, as Paul did, that they were guardians of a tradition which they were not free to change. That tradition – that 'package' – was a long schedule of 'dos and donts'. The purpose of these many rules was to 'fence the law' so that you could not come within even a gnat's whisker of breaking God's commandments. For example, the Pharisees said that you were never to help yourself to the odd head of corn as you walked through a wheat-field on a Saturday. In that way you would not risk breaking the fourth commandment (Mark 4.23–28).

Jesus has accused the Pharisees of making the fence more important than what the fence was there to protect. 'For the sake of your tradition,' he has just said, 'you make void the word of God' (Matthew 15.6). The shocked disciples reprimand Jesus. They tell him that the Pharisees have taken offence at what he's said. But Jesus does not retract his accusation. Far from it. He goes further. He says that, come the Day of Judgement, the Pharisees will be 'uprooted'. They are the 'weeds in the wheat-field' that Jesus once said will one day be bound in bundles and burned (Matthew 13.24–30). They are, in Jesus's vivid but disturbing image, 'the blind leading the blind'.

This passage is fraught with difficulties. One of those difficulties is pointed out by the educationalist Professor John Hull on the *New Statesman*'s 'Faith Column Homepage'. Professor Hull, who lost his sight in middle life, writes, 'What worried me about the sighted Jesus was the way he fell in with common assumptions and prejudices about blind people. For example, he said that the blind could not lead the blind without both of them falling into a ditch.' Professor Hull tells his sighted readers that 'these are images from your sighted world, and they have the effect of marginalizing my world' (www.newstatesman. com). Does Jesus's use of such imagery justify its acceptance today? John Hull thinks not.

The severity of Jesus's attack on the Pharisees is equally problematical. (It gets worse in Matthew 23.) Some commentators claim that the polemic ascribed to Jesus tells us more about a deepening antipathy towards mainstream Judaism in the congregations where Matthew's Gospel first circulated than it does about the mind of Jesus himself. The bad press that the Pharisees get in the Gospels, it is argued, is unwarranted. According to Anthony Harvey, reviewing Hyam Maccoby's *Jesus the Pharisee* (SCM Press, 2003), 'the Pharisees were popular, humane and conscientious; they were not necessarily the same, in all respects, as the rabbinic scholars of later generations' (*Church Times*, 22 August 2003).

So far, we have reflected on what Jesus may – or may not – have been saying about a party within first-century Judaism. But let's suppose for a moment that the Gospel, as well as talking about someone else, is talking to us. After all, that's why we read the Gospels in church. Supposing that Jesus's – or Matthew's – excoriating words about the custodians of religious tradition are applicable to any and all who are charged with 'passing the parcel'. (I write these notes, having spent two hours earlier in the day in Southwark cathedral witnessing the consecration of two bishops.)

Supposing these terrifying words apply to those who write books like this one? I search my heart – which in the end is what this Sunday's Gospel is inviting us all to do – and I do not like what I find there.

YEAR B

Proverbs 9.1–6; Ephesians 5.15–20; John 6.51–58

THE PRIEST, THE PROPHET, AND THE PRAGMATIST

Wisdom 'Wisdom has built her house'. We really should drop in on her more often. It is much to our loss that we have ignored her.

Biblical religion is expressed in three ways: the way of the priest, the way of the prophet, and the way of the pragmatist – the wise. Priestly religion is about worship, its transports and its trappings. It aspires to the sublime, but does not always rise above the ritual. Priestly religion is about services in sacred places. It flourishes in sanctuaries and at altars. Priestly people know about purificators and patens, amices and aumbries, palls and veils. Priestly literature tells you how to do things properly. The Levitical codes of the old dispensation prescribe what to do in the tabernacle; those of the new – *Common Worship*, for example – regulate what to do in church.

Prophetic religion challenges priestly religion. 'I hate, I despise your feasts,' says God (Amos 5.21) Prophetic religion takes to platforms in public places. It 'speaks out' about what God has done, what he is doing and – take cover! – what he will do. Prophets speak in the voice of thunder. Their characteristic cry is 'Thus says the Lord.'

Wisdom religion by contrast is not interested in services, nor does it dwell on the acts of God in history. Wisdom religion is about misbehaving children and mischievous gossip. It's about chronic illness and how to cope with it. It's about keeping your temper and keeping to time. It's about the perils of making money and the joys of making love. Wisdom religion is about everyday life. It is about how to keep going.

Wisdom religion is more obviously and immediately relevant to the concerns of ordinary people than priestly religion or prophetic religion. And yet it is almost left out of the life of the church. Church life is primarily the practice of priestly religion and prophetic religion. Its main business is worship and proclaiming the acts of God to save and judge. This is important business, to be sure, fraught with eternal consequence, but short on advice about how to cope with the kids.

The great canonical texts in the Wisdom tradition are Proverbs, Job, the Song of Songs, and Ecclesiastes. This week's Old Testament reading is from Proverbs. Alas, it's not there to recall us to a forgotten spring. It's there only because the clever compilers of our lectionary spotted a connection with the Gospel reading. 'Eat my bread! Drink my wine!' says Wisdom. We are meant to hear these words, not as a bidding to cultivate wisdom, but as an overture to the Gospel's invitation, with its eucharistic overtones, 'He who eats my flesh and drinks my blood has eternal life.' The lectionary has conscripted Wisdom into the service of priestly religion, not a role for which she would have volunteered.

These writings must be interpreted in their own terms, rather than as a quarry for texts to back up Christian claims. There are four good reasons for revisiting them. First, wisdom religion sets everyday duties in the context of the life of faith. Living faithfully is as much about not festering in bed all day as about being saved. Secondly, wisdom religion focuses on human relationships, on getting on with other people, as much as on getting right with God, though that is important too. Thirdly, wisdom religion draws on experience, rather than invoking revelation. Its appeal is to what we share as human beings, not to the confessions which divide us. People of all faiths want to know how to look after their children and how to live with their neighbours. Our reading urges us 'to walk in the way of understanding'. That is something we can do together, whatever our belief-systems. Fourthly – and here is a reason which makes a return to these ancient springs so urgently necessary – wisdom religion questions our current educational culture. Today's schools do not teach children how to be wise. They teach them instead how to pass exams.

The importance of the scriptural wisdom tradition is that it takes the demands of daily life as seriously as the great matters of worship and salvation. Not that we have to agree with everything the wisdom writers say. Proverbs 22.15 ('Iniquity is bound up in the heart of the child, but the cane will thrash it out of him') is a little harsh, perhaps.

When Paul moves from theology to ethics, as he does in our New Testament reading, his thought turns on the first pillar of wisdom.

'Watch how you walk, not as the unwise but as the wise.' Paul weaves the prophetic, the priestly, and the pragmatic into a threefold cord. There is the prophetic warning that 'the days are evil' and the priestly summons to worship in the Spirit. But interwoven is wise advice. Use your time well. Stay sober – but don't stop singing.

YEAR C

Jeremiah 23.23–29; Hebrews 11.29–12.2; Luke 12.49–56

THERE IS A WAR GOING ON

The Christ-child is born, says Zechariah, to guide us in the ways of peace (Luke 1.79). At his birth the night sky rings with the joy of the angels as they sing of the peace this child will bring (Luke 2.14). With the infant in his arms, Simeon declares that he can now 'depart in peace' (Luke 2.29).

The peace that the new-born Christ will impart is one of the leading themes of Luke's infancy narratives. The same theme is taken up in many of our Christmas carols. Perhaps this Sunday's Gospel should be included in our carol services as a tenth lesson tacked on to the traditional nine. It is a salutary reminder that the grown-up Jesus had his own ideas about what manner of peace he would bring to the earth.

'Did you think that I came to bring peace on the earth?' asks Jesus. Well yes, Lord, actually we did. We believed those angels with their siren songs. We remember how you blessed people with the benediction, 'Go in peace' (Luke 7.50; 8.48; 10.5–6). Peace was your bequest to us – at least that's what your beloved disciple said (John 14.27). We were led to expect that peace was a fruit of your kindly spirit (Galatians 5.22).

Yes, Lord, we did think that you came to give us peace. And now you come to us brandishing a sword!

The contradictions run deep, most starkly in Jesus's apparent claim that his intention is to undo the work of his predecessor John the Baptist. For Gabriel had said that it would be John's mission to heal family divisions (Luke 1.17). Now Jesus is saying that his purpose is the exact opposite, to foment family divisions, to set close relatives against each other.

How are we to resolve these contradictions? However can we harmonize 'the peace on earth' song of the Christmas angels and the 'fire on earth' warnings we hear in our Gospel? How do we reconcile the scriptural promises of peace, the vision of lions lying down with lambs, of swords becoming ploughshares, and the rest, with what is in fact going on in a broken world, in a fissiparous church, and – for much of the time – inside my own head?

One way of resolving the apparent conflicts in Jesus's teaching about peace is what we might call 'the Bickersteth method'. The Victorian bishop and hymn-writer Edward Bickersteth would have us believe that 'peace, perfect peace' is indeed possible 'in this dark world of sin'. 'The blood of Jesus,' he tells us, 'whispers peace *within*'. It is a feeble hymn, but it draws its inspiration from a great text. 'Thou wilt keep him in perfect peace whose mind is stayed on thee' (Isaiah 26.3).

There are skills by which the mind may find rest, and we have our schools of Christian prayer that teach them. There are, too, the techniques of other faith traditions, especially those of Buddhist meditation. Was Jesus a master of such methods? Did he practise 'right mindfulness'? He certainly slept through the storm that terrified his disciples (Mark 4.38). But, whatever the meditative techniques of Jesus, the evidence of Sunday's Gospel ('What stress I am under!') is that he never achieved the unruffled serenity of the Buddha. Beneath the Bo tree Siddhartha Gautama found enlightenment. Beneath Gethsemane's olive trees Jesus embraced the cross – and the way of the cross is not a fast track to a quiet mind.

The promised peace may be 'peace within'. Or it may be 'peace hereafter'. The good Bishop Bickersteth thought that it was both.

It is enough: earth's struggles soon shall cease,
And Jesus call us to Heaven's perfect peace.

Christian spirituality has no quarrel with the quest for 'peace within' nor with the hope of 'peace hereafter'. We are more likely to be of some use if we keep our stress levels down and we shall be less discouraged by failure if our perspective is not bounded by the transient. We return this Sunday to the great eleventh chapter of Hebrews, to those whose desire for 'a better country' only made their engagement with the one they were in more purposeful and effective.

What matters, however, is that these paths, that which seeks inner peace and that which pursues peace 'beyond the river', do not become detours to avoid the demands of the present and what's happening outside the walled garden of my own soul.

The language of Sunday's Gospel is that of the prophet, the role in which Luke casts Jesus as he approaches Jerusalem. Prophets possess a still centre and they see beyond the horizon. But their focus is on the here and now. They do not agonize over the seeming contradictions between what we are promised and what we experience. There is far too much to be done. After all, there is a war going on.

Proper 16

The Sunday between 21 and 27 August

YEAR A

Isaiah 51.1–6; Romans 12.1–8; Matthew 16.13–20

BODY-BUILDING

Our readings make us think about the one and the many.

Abraham was one, says the prophet, but God made him many. He is the rock from which we are hewn, the quarry from which we are dug. These are extraordinary images. We are carved, excavated, from Abraham. All of us – Francis of Assisi, Dietrich Bonhoeffer, and Mabel who does the flowers and cares for her demented mother – are equally 'chips off the old block'. Some chips. Some block. No wonder we should 'look to Abraham'.

Paul looked to Abraham. The significance of Abraham for the Christian believer is a major theme of his letter to the church at Rome. The experience of Abraham is that faith is essentially defiant. It is always a 'hoping against hope'. It was a forlorn hope indeed that in their extreme old age he and Sarah should produce an heir. But, wilfully and irrationally, Abraham went on believing (Romans 4).

The writer to the Hebrews looked to Abraham. For that anonymous writer, Abraham exemplifies how faith is essentially nomadic, how it contradicts the received wisdom that it is sensible to settle down. Those hewn from Abraham are forever aliens until they find 'the city with foundations' (Hebrews 11.8–19) and come home to God.

Søren Kierkegaard looked to Abraham. He brooded on the absurdity of Abraham's faith, the faith that does not falter even on Mount Moriah. God had promised Abraham, that, though but one, he should become many. Now he is commanded to slaughter the son on whose survival the fulfilment of that promise depends. Kierkegaard reflects on 'the distress and dread in the paradox of faith', on the infinite distance between true faith – the faith that must 'draw the knife before retaining Isaac' – and its caricatures (*Fear and Trembling*).

We look to Abraham. 'He is the father of us all' (Romans 4.16). If our DNA is his, so must our faith be.

Our New Testament reading develops the themes of the one and the many with its appeal to the idea of 'the body'. *The Body* (1952) is the title of an early work by the late Bishop John Robinson. Robinson wrote some startling books. Famously, he argued in *Honest to God* (SCM Press, 1963) that the notion of a God 'out there' or 'up there' is as unnecessary as it is implausible. Just as radical in its way – though this time a book for the study rather than the bus queue – was his *The Priority of John* (1985). (The title gives away the plot.) But in some ways *The Body* was his boldest book. In it Robinson asked what Paul meant when he said that Christians are 'the body of Christ'. His conclusion, shocking in its simplicity, was that Paul meant what he said.

When I say my friend Jones is a 'star', I am using a metaphor. I do not mean that Jones is fiery ball of molten matter found millions of light years away in deep space. When Paul says that we are the body of Christ, however, he is not using a metaphor – so says Robinson. The organic unity of Christ and his people in one 'body' is such that it is quite misleading to say that Paul is using a figure of speech. Robinson held that Paul came to see that Jesus and his church are one body – not *like* one body, but *really* one body – when, on his way to make life difficult for the Christians of Damascus, he heard Jesus say, 'Why are you persecuting *me*?' (Acts 9.4)

We are Christ's body – and not merely in a manner of speaking. Within that body, we are 'members one of another'. Again – if John Robinson is right – we are not speaking metaphorically. In his earlier letter to the young Christian church at Corinth, Paul had spoken graphically of the organic interdependence of Christians. He spoke of the foot and the hand, the eye and the ear, and of the nonsense it would be if these parts of us insisted on having nothing do to with each other. He alluded as well to our less presentable features. Those on the PCC whom we regard as arm-pits are also a necessary part of the Christian anatomy.

The many parts make one body. As I write these notes, a mailing from a theological college arrives. One item refers to 'a Church culture that is increasingly prone to cliques of the like-minded'. The Church is probably no more prone now to tearing itself apart limb from limb, than it was in Paul's day, even if the Anglican Church's enthusiasm for suicidal self-dismemberment has been hard to match.

For the arrest and reversal of this process, a return to the biblical understanding of the body is required. The person next to me at the communion rail, whom I happen to cordially dislike, is in fact part of me. Recognizing that reality is what Paul meant by 'discerning the body' (1 Corinthians 11.29).

YEAR B

Joshua 24.1–2a, 14–18; Ephesians 6.10–20; John 6.56–69

HARD CHOICES

When I was a boy there was a rousing chorus we used to sing in our Crusader class, whose lyric was lifted from our first reading –'Choose you this day whom you will serve'. The chorus ended with the refrain, 'As for me, as for me, as for me . . . I will serve the Lord.' We bellowed the umpteen 'as for me's louder and louder, and with the final 'I will serve the Lord' we raised he roof. It was a rollicking number, and our enjoyment of it was not reduced by the fact that we hadn't a clue what we were singing about.

Had we stopped to think, we might not have sung so loudly. The nature and role of choice in the life of faith seems to have received little study. The questions multiply. What does it mean to choose to serve the Lord? Is that ever a genuine choice? After all, didn't someone say, 'You did not chose me but I chose you' (John 15.16)? How many on the face of the earth have the possibility of choosing? Isn't the freedom to choose a peculiarly western privilege, a liberty granted only to a prosperous and educated elite? Above all, when does a choice – if the options open to us are unequal – cease to be a choice?

There are strong arguments for theism and Christian faith and in our own time apologists such as the Bishop of Durham, Dr Tom Wright, and Professor Alister McGrath have marshalled and deployed them effectively. But here lies the problem. If the case for Christianity is as overwhelming as these advocates suggest, then the decision 'to serve the Lord' becomes a good deal too easy, almost ceasing to be a choice at all. (I think not only of the bishop and the professor, but also of the loud evangelist at the bottom of my drive.) If to become a Christian is truly a choice, then, necessarily, it must be a hard choice. Easy choices are no choices.

The choice to serve the Lord is hard, not only because the claims of religion are contestable, but also because the cost of discipleship is high. There is the small matter of what you are letting yourself in for. The way is tough, as we were warned it would be. Dietrich Bonhoeffer said, 'When Christ calls someone to follow him, he calls them to die.' To choose to die. To say such a choice is 'difficult' is an understatement. If we claim that, in our experience, we found it an easy choice, then it is a choice we have never really made. We're still serving the gods of the Amorites.

How well Søren Kierkegaard understood all of this! Kierkegaard saw clearly what it means to choose. (He wrote a book of eight hundred extraordinary pages on the subject entitled *Either – Or.*) He recognized that if it is made easy for someone to become a Christian, as it was in the Denmark of his day, then what that person becomes is not a Christian at all.

The significance of choice and the essential difficulty of choosing 'to serve the Lord' is a stern theme of the Gospel. 'Many of his disciples turned back.' That was their choice. Jesus gives Peter the choice of staying with him or of joining the others in full flight to a safer life. Peter's choice is to stay. The reason he gives for doing so is as instructive as it is deeply moving. 'Lord, to whom shall we go . . . ?' Neither the arguments for or against Christian theism nor prudential calculations about the cost and rewards of Christian discipleship – such dire warnings, such glorious promises – determine the choice I make. There is only the lonely Son of God, wondering whether his last few friends will leave him.

We hear him saying to us too, 'Do you also wish to go away?' The choice is ours. And what if, having weighed the arguments and counted the cost, we're still undecided? Perhaps in the last analysis, the choice is intuitive, as some would say all our choices ultimately are. We simply fall in with him and see what happens.

The Crusaders, with whom I sang 'Choose you this day whom you will serve', aren't 'Crusaders' anymore. Sensitive to Muslim objections, they have re-branded themselves as 'Urban Saints'. They have changed their badge too. The old one depicted all the military hardware which Paul catalogues in his appeal to us to 'put on the whole armour of God'.

The Crusaders' decision to demilitarize their badge tacitly acknowledges that such symbolism is problematical. It's easy enough redesign a badge. It is less easy to rid Scripture of the images of war – not to speak of the bloody battles – which crowd its pages. Paul is unembarrassed by such imagery. Indeed he milks it for all its worth. But he puts the martial metaphors to the same use as, one day, real weaponry will serve. Paul beats swords into ploughshares, spears into pruning-hooks.

YEAR C

Isaiah 58.9b–14; Hebrews 12.18–29; Luke 13.10–17

BURNED ALIVE

Blaise Pascal died at one o'clock in the morning of Saturday 19 August 1662. Shortly after his death a servant noticed what appeared to be padding sewn into the dead man's doublet. The padding proved to be a piece of parchment and, wrapped inside the parchment, a faded piece of paper. Upon both the parchment and the paper was written, in Pascal's hand, an account of an intense experience that had overwhelmed him one night some eight years previously. The words on the paper are scribbled in agitation, a torrent poured out in the immediate aftermath of that experience. The parchment, with some alterations, omissions, and additions, is written calmly and carefully, as a confirmation of his original testimony.

The scrawled words on the scrap of paper are often quoted – 'Fire. The God of Abraham, the God of Isaac, the God of Jacob. Not of the philosophers and intellectuals.' Henceforth, for Pascal, God ceases to be merely a concept, a subject of dispassionate rational enquiry. Like Moses, he has seen the burning bush.

The words which Pascal wore on his heart for the rest of his days recall the tremendous text ending Sunday's New Testament reading, the affirmation which concludes what has been described as 'the longest sustained argument in the Bible', the first twelve chapters of the letter to the Hebrews. 'Our God is a consuming fire.'

The image of the deity as a 'consuming fire' is taken from the Old Testament where it speaks of a wrathful and avenging God. When the children of Israel pass over Jordan, God will be a 'devouring fire' to destroy the tall and terrible Anakim (Deuteronomy 9.3). 'Sinners in Zion', too, will tremble. 'Who among us can dwell with the devouring fire?' they will ask. 'Who among us can dwell with the everlasting burnings?' (Isaiah 33.14).

The description of God as 'a consuming fire' disturbs most of us. Such language makes us think of 'the lake of fire' (Revelation 21), of 'the eternal fire prepared for the devil and his angels' (Matthew 25.41), and of tormented Dives begging for a drop of water to cool his parched tongue (Luke 16.24). The picture of an angry and pitiless God, annihilating the sinful – or, still worse, preserving them alive – in the agonies of hell, is repellent.

We do well to be troubled by the picture of God as a consuming fire. We would do better still if we were terrified by it. Because we too are 'sinners in Zion'. Isaiah's warnings about those 'everlasting burnings' are for us as well. Lurid accounts of the flames of hell – not to speak of the unpleasant properties of sulphurous brimstone – may well have to be demythologized. But the moral reality behind the metaphors, the truth that what we once called 'sin' has to be dealt with, is not to be disposed of so readily. And it is for our salvation that it is so.

It is all to do with how we understand the love of God. For George MacDonald, the love of God is inexorable. It will not admit defeat. That is how he could understand God as a God of fire. The circle of fire about the Almighty is not there to prevent us, sinners that we are, from approaching him. On the contrary, the wall of fire around him is about us too. It encircles us to drive us back to him, should we stray too far from his heart of love. And so MacDonald prays,

> But at length, O God, wilt thou not cast Death and Hell into the lake of Fire – even into thine own consuming self? For then our poor brothers and sisters, every one – O God, we trust in thee, the Consuming Fire – shall have been burnt clean and brought home . . . As for us, now will we come to thee, our Consuming Fire. And thou wilt not burn us more than we can bear. But thou wilt burn us. And although thou seem to slay us, yet will we trust thee. (*Unspoken Sermons*).

So we pray, if we dare, for the touch of the Spirit's holy flame.

> O let it freely burn
> Till earthly passions turn
> To dust and ashes in its heat consuming.

'Not the God of the philosophers and intellectuals,' wrote Pascal, incandescent with the love of God. He might have added, in the light of our Old Testament reading and our Gospel, 'Not the God of religion either.' For the anonymous prophet whom we hear on Sunday, whose oracles are later attributed to Isaiah, the only 'fast' God delights in is the liberation of the oppressed. For Jesus – confronting yet again an indignant ecclesiastic incensed that he has ignored canon law – holy days are not for adding to the weight of human bondage, but for setting the imprisoned free.

Proper 17

The Sunday between 28 August and 3 September

YEAR A

Jeremiah 15.15–21; Romans 12.9–21; Matthew 16.21–28

PRAYING WITHOUT PRETENDING

Years ago the priest, doctor, and psychotherapist Anne Townsend wrote a little book that was a blessing to many. It was entitled *Prayer without Pretending* (Scripture Union, 1973). Anne Townsend argued that when we pray we should tell the truth. In our prayers we should say how it is. We should not bottle up our feelings but give vent to them, even if those feelings are not in the least bit pious – indeed, especially if they not pious.

When I was a school chaplain I used to tell my teenage confirmation candidates that there are only three rules about prayer: 'Be honest', 'Be honest', and 'Be honest.' The prayers of the Bible are honest prayers, notably those of the Psalms, of Job, and of the angry, anguished prophet, whom we hear in our first reading. Jeremiah does not tell God how wonderful he is, as we are cajoled to do in public worship. Jeremiah doesn't think God is wonderful. He does not believe that God has blessed him. He believes that God has betrayed him. 'Truly you are to me like a deceitful brook, like waters that fail.' The image is of the *wadi*, the watercourse, which the thirsty traveller reaches at the end of a weary journey in the desert, only to find that it is bone dry.

The logic of Jeremiah's bitter prayer is straightforward. 'Lord, I have done what you told me to do. You, Lord, have not done what you promised to do.' Many a parson, gloomily surveying an expanse of empty pews beneath a leaking roof, has felt the same – even if they have not had the bottle of a Jeremiah to turn their feelings into his kind of prayer.

Jeremiah 'prays without pretending'. He prays for his enemies, though not in the spirit of Paul's 'Bless those who persecute you.' (Our second reading can be heard as Paul's 'Symphony on themes from the Sermon on the Mount'.) On the contrary, Jeremiah asks to be avenged on his enemies. 'Bring down retribution for me on them,' he pleads.

My edition of the New Revised Standard Version heads this section of Jeremiah with a misleading strapline which is no part of the Hebrew text: 'Jeremiah Complains Again and is Reassured'. Is Jeremiah reassured? It is not clear. The Lord tells Jeremiah to repent – 'turn back and I shall take you back'. He tells him to continue as his spokesman – 'utter what is worthy, not worthless'. And he promises – only now is there an element of divine reassurance – to deliver him from his opponents.

Jeremiah may or may not have been reassured. That is immaterial. God's purpose is not to console or comfort Jeremiah – generally that is not his way with our wounded feelings – but to tell him what to do.

My friend David served under Archbishop Janani Luwum of Uganda. David once went to the Archbishop with a complaint about his situation. Like Jeremiah's, David's complaint was justified. Archbishop Luwum listened to David, offered him good advice, and then said a prayer for him. David tells me that he remembers the Archbishop ending his prayer with the words: 'And, Lord, save David from self-pity.'

Jeremiah prayed without pretending. So did Jesus. We think of how he prayed to be spared the cross (Mark 14.32–36). We remember too how, from the cross, his prayer is one that Jeremiah might have made: 'My God, my God, why have you forsaken me?' (Mark 15.34)

Just as Jesus does not beat about the burning bush in talking to God, so too he speaks plainly to Peter. Yesterday he called Peter 'The Rock' (Matthew 6.18). Today he calls him 'Satan'. Peter deserves the name because he is doing what that 'old enemy' has always done, suggesting that there are ways of doing what God wants without anyone getting hurt.

Peter had confessed Jesus to be Messiah, the promised king, but he cannot conceive of the possibility that sovereignty could ever be exercised through suffering. Peter does not 'think the things of God'. His mind-set, as we'd say, is all wrong. The key-word – in this context, it is only here in Matthew – is 'stumbling-block', as it is usually translated. Jesus tells Peter that he is a 'stumbling-block' to him. It is an interesting and important word that occurs quite often in the Gospels. A 'stumbling-block' is anything you fall over – such as the cat – on the way from A to B. Jesus says that anyone who puts a stumbling-block on a child's path to God deserves to be drowned (Matthew 18.6). What Peter has said is a stumbling-block for Jesus, for it is like a tripwire across his path to the cross.

Sometimes of course a stumbling-block is necessary. That is why Paul will refer to the cross itself as a stumbling-block (1 Corinthians 1.23). Such an obstacle in your path will either make you turn back or bring you to your knees.

YEAR B

Deuteronomy 4.1–2, 6–9; James 1.17–27; Mark 7.1–8, 14–15, 21–23

ORPHANS ANCIENT AND MODERN

'Don't shoot the pianist.' Editors of lectionaries need a similar sign on their desks. Theirs is an impossible task. This Sunday's readings start with the express command, 'Do not add anything to what I say and do not take anything away from it.' 'Don't take anything away' – and immediately our editors take out the next the next two verses. These describe how God destroyed those within the community who had embraced another religion. The decisions that have to be made by those compiling lectionaries reflect a deep dilemma. What are we to make of scriptural texts – not confined to the Old Testament – which we now find unedifying?

It is of the first importance that we engage with these problematical texts rather than airbrushing them out. 'Difficult' texts are usually windows on difficulties – if not demons – within ourselves. What I don't like in the Bible exposes what I don't like in me. The urge to destroy the idolater is rooted in the same soil as the desire to deport the immigrant. 'It is from within,' says our Gospel, 'from the human heart, that evil intentions come.'

The letter of James is a text which, if not exactly airbrushed out of the Christian tradition, has been sidelined within it, at least within western Protestantism. That's largely down to Martin Luther's famous indictment of it as 'an epistle full of straw, because it contains nothing evangelical' – or, as he was later to say, 'I almost feel like throwing Jimmy into the stove.' But a text which explores the relationship of faith and works, of being and doing, in Christian discipleship as profoundly as does this letter is not to be dismissed so lightly. For James, the spiritual and the moral are one. It is not the case that we must get right with God first and with our neighbour next. We find God in our neighbour and our neighbour in God.

But wait. The term 'neighbour' is too vague. James is more specific. 'Pure and undefiled religion' is to care for 'orphans and widows in their distress'. The many references to widows and orphans in the Bible reflect an understanding of 'the father's house' as the primary unit of family life. Without the father the situation of the remaining members of the household becomes both anomalous and tragic. That is why Jesus says, 'I shall not leave you as orphans' (John 14.18). James echoes the ancient codes which required that the rights of orphans and widows be upheld and their needs met. Theirs are the sheaves, the olives, and the grapes which remain after the harvest (Deuteronomy 24.17–22). This is not charity, neither in the old dispensation nor in the new. It would be better described as worship, so closely has God, the 'father of the fatherless' (Psalm 68.5), identified himself with those so utterly bereft.

There was a time when the word 'orphans' had a quaint old-fashioned ring to it. Orphans ended up as crossing sweepers or were sent up chimneys. If they were lucky – or unlucky – they were taken in by an orphanage. But do a Google today on the words 'AIDS' and 'orphans' and you hit a million websites. The first I visit tells me that a child is orphaned by AIDS every 15 seconds. So far from being a bundle of straw, the letter of James is a lash to whip me awake.

The makers of our lectionary take their scissors to Mark's Gospel too. The first chunk of chapter 7 that they cut out (vv. 9–13) contains the puzzling reference to 'Corban', which – fair enough – is too much to take in on a Sunday morning. But the second omission (vv. 16–20) is much more serious. With its talk about stomachs and sewers, you can see why it was felt it must go, but in fact the passage contains one of the most significant statements in the Gospels. Jesus is talking about food. His remarks – 'What comes in, must go out' – are less than delicate. But Mark's gloss on what Jesus says, is the lobbing of a grenade. 'Thus he declared all foods clean.' This throw-away line blows out of the water the whole elaborate system of the Levitical dietary laws. (You can eat bald locusts but not bats, grasshoppers but not geckos, and so on.)

No doubt Mark's comment was for the benefit of his readers in Rome, who were wondering whether they still had to keep such rules.

The question, which dogged the apostolic church, of what to keep and what to jettison from the Hebrew Bible has never gone away. Mark makes us face it. More fundamentally still, he forces us to re-examine the foundations of our moral judgements. Are there other matters in Leviticus – some currently hotly debated – about which we must now say with Hamlet, 'There is nothing either good or bad, but thinking makes it so'?

YEAR C

Ecclesiasticus 10.12–18 or Proverbs 25.6–7; Hebrews 13.1–8, 15–16; Luke 14.1, 7–14

THE ABOLITION OF THE EGO

A difficult query was recently put to the *Church Times* 'Out of the Question' column. What did Simone Weil mean by the word 'decreate'? Simone Weil had such a subtle and mobile mind that it is never easy to pin down exactly what she meant about anything. Capturing her thought is a binding of Ariel.

One approach to Simone Weil's concept of 'decreation' would be to see it as her attempt to trace to its roots a hard saying from Sunday's Gospel. Jesus said, 'Go and sit down in the lowest place.' Simone Weil said that the essential fact about the Christian virtues – in her words 'what lends them a special savour of their own'– is humility. She described humility as 'the freely accepted movement towards the bottom'. For Simone Weil, the heart of Christian obedience is the consent to be last, the willing acceptance of 'the lowest place'. (I contrast her mind with that of a previous Bishop of London who objected to where I'd seated him for a service I was involved with. 'Comes to something,' he growled, 'when I'm given a back seat in my own diocese.')

'Go and sit down in the lowest place.' In the parable's picture language the seat to choose is the one furthest from the top table, ideally somewhere close to a door swinging open on the din and pong of the kitchen. According to Paul, the ground and motive of this bizarre ethic – after all, for the Greeks humility was a vice not a virtue – is the incarnation and passion of Jesus. God 'emptied himself' both by assuming our sinful nature and by suffering on the cross our nature's awful entail. Henceforth that self-emptying determines the character and direction of the Christian ethic. 'Let his mind be yours,' says Paul (Philippians 2.5–11).

Simone Weil's audacious claim – St Paul never went as far as this – was that God 'emptied himself' in creation too. God's creation, so Simone Weil argued, is an act of abdication. By allowing the existence of other creatures, God refuses to be everything. 'My very existence is like a laceration of God,' she says. The Christian response to the God who abdicates – the 'decreation' required of each of us – reflects that initial divine sacrifice. 'Decreation' is the extinction of the autonomous self. By the grace of God I must utterly destroy the 'I' in me. As Weil famously remarked, 'To say "I" is to lie.'

Rowan Williams has pondered long on Simone Weil's 'decreation'. He writes, 'I must enter the process of decreation so that between the world and unconditional love no barrier is set up in the shape of an ego with plural and specific needs and projects' (*Simone Weil's Philosophy of Culture*, ed. Richard Bell, Cambridge, 1993). Many mighty egos, with their clamorous demands, bid for power in the Church. They need the Archbishop's reminder of this wraith of a woman who saw that the repudiation of power, rather than the assertion of power, is the way of Christ.

Such was Simone Weil's understanding of the Gospel we hear this Sunday. Such too was her own renunciation. Such was the witness of her frail and wasted figure, the anorexic carcase on which she visited such affliction. 'She was a saint,' an archdeacon remarked to me recently. 'Totally barking, of course,' he added.

Simone Weil was one of those very rare Christians indeed who, believing that what Jesus teaches is true, did what he said. My friend the archdeacon was only voicing aloud what most of us tacitly acknowledge: that you would need to be sectioned if you took Jesus at his word and lived the way he said we should. In many a church and cathedral this Sunday there will be a discussion in the vestry about who should process in front of whom when the service starts. It is safe to assume that this discussion will be uninformed by the Gospel that someone proudly placed in the procession will shortly be reading.

For the author of the letter to the Hebrews, 'the lowest place' is 'outside the city', the killing-field where Christ died. The radical renunciation required of the Christian believer is the abandonment of all the security, all the material comforts and institutional privileges symbolized by the city from which he or she has fled. The 'lowest place' – the only place for the disciple of Jesus whose faith is more than a frivolous posture – is 'outside' beneath the cross. There are some biblical texts which speak with special and devastating power to a specific era or particular situation in the life of the church. The tremendous peroration to the letter to the Hebrews is surely a 'text for our time'. 'Let us then go to him outside the camp and bear the abuse he endured' (Hebrews 13.13).

Inexplicably – or perhaps not inexplicably – our lectionary tells us to skip this verse.

Proper 18

The Sunday between 4 and 10 September

YEAR A

Ezekiel 33.7–1; Romans 13.8–14; Matthew 18.15–20

THE FAMILY GATHERED IN CHRIST'S NAME

The New Revised Standard Version of the Bible, in common with many other modern English versions of the Greek and Hebrew Scriptures, seeks to avoid 'linguistic sexism' in translating the original texts. Few would quarrel with that objective. Male bias misleads. But sometimes our translators, in their effort to eliminate this bias, come up with a wording that only makes matters worse. So it is with the passage from Matthew that we read on Sunday. We must notice what has happened. Nit-picking it is not.

The Greek text has: 'If your brother sins against you . . .' The NRSV reads: 'If another member of the church sins against you . . .' The surgery has been successful – the sexist language has been cut out – but the patient has died. The heart of the passage has stopped. An inclusive translation that does not miss the point would have to be: 'If your brother or sister sins against you . . .'

There is all the difference in the world between 'your brother or sister' and 'another member of the church'. If you are my 'brother' or my 'sister' there is an intimate personal relationship between us. 'Member of the church' has no suggestion of a personal relationship; it indicates no more than an impersonal affiliation. It sounds as if

Jesus is telling you what to do if someone on the electoral roll upsets you.

To be sure, in his little tract about Jesus, Matthew certainly has 'the church' in mind. He is the only Gospel writer to use the Greek word (*ekklesia*) which – for all its unhappy associations – we usually translate as 'church'. It is Matthew, only Matthew, who tells us that Jesus said that he would found his 'church' on Peter (Matthew 16.18). Matthew twice mentions 'the church' in our reading, although not in the unfortunate phrase 'member of the church', which the NRSV translators have made up.

Our Gospel prescribes what must be done as a last resort about the brother or sister who has behaved hurtfully. In the end, the offended party must 'tell it to the church'. If the one who has caused the pain refuses to listen to 'the church', then no one must have anything further to do with them.

It is impossible to say precisely what processes are contemplated, but the judgement ('bound in heaven') is one of uncompromising severity. 'Let him be to you as a Gentile and a tax-collector.' No amount of special pleading can stifle our suspicion that we might not be listening to Jesus here but to someone else.

Clearly by Matthew's time something called 'the church' exists and has some rudimentary organization, although it is still blessedly free of all the baggage which will later encumber it. What constitutes 'the church' for Matthew? Where is it to be found? From a first reading we might conclude that, for Matthew, 'the church' exists simply where two or three gather in the name of Jesus. From several more readings we might stay with the same conclusion.

Matthew notes the course of action that must be followed if someone offends a fellow Christian. What is prescribed is not a disciplinary procedure within an organization. It is *within the family* that injury has been done and it is *within the family* that reconciliation must take place. The memory has not been lost of all that Jesus taught about the intimate family relationship of those who trust and follow him (Mark 3.31–35). Those who walk the way of Jesus together are kith and kin – and more so than human siblings can ever be. Schism in the Church will always be much more serious than organizational breakdown.

Male bias misleads, both in the Bible's language and our own. So too do truncated readings. The lectionary tells us to stop where we should read on. Matthew, sounding rather like an archdeacon, has outlined the formal steps to be taken when a brother or sister says or does something injurious. (The scholars endorse our own misgivings, that there is more of Matthew than of Jesus in this passage.) Something is missing. What is missing is any mention of forgiveness.

That omission is at once repaired if we read on. We register what Jesus says – and now it is surely Jesus speaking and not Matthew – in response to Peter's question about forgiveness. How often, Peter wants to know, should he forgive a brother or sister who does him wrong? Peter has learned something from Jesus of the importance of forgiveness. (One day, through his own experience of being forgiven by his injured Lord, he will learn much more.) Peter's question shows that he understands that forgiveness must be generous. Jesus's response reveals what Peter – and the rest of us – have yet to grasp, that forgiveness must be uncalculating.

YEAR B

Isaiah 35.4–7a; James 2.1–10 (11–13) 14–17; Mark 7.24–37

SIGNS TO SING ABOUT

We're served too little for starters this Sunday. The Old Testament reading is just three and a bit verses. This is too thin a slice to carve from one of the meatiest chapters of the Bible. The surgery was no doubt well intended. We're meant to put two and two together. One day, Isaiah says, 'the ears of the deaf shall be unstopped' and 'the tongue of the speechless shall sing for joy'. We're meant to notice just these words and make the connection when we hear the Gospel. Those words come true, we are to conclude, when Jesus heals a demented child and – note especially – a deaf and dumb man. But Isaiah's prophecy that the disabled will be healed is only one detail of a much bigger picture, the prospect of a second exodus in which all God's imprisoned people will come at last – through a desert marvellously made a garden – to their promised land. *This* stupendous all-encompassing vision – not one fragment of it – '*this*,' we proclaim, 'is the Word of the Lord'.

It is this vision that the evangelists believe is fulfilled in the mission of Jesus, a mission, they boldly claim, which embraces the Gentiles. The deranged little girl and the deaf-mute are both foreigners. With that hindsight we go back to Isaiah 34 – to the whole chapter, not just the snippet we're served – and now we discover a new dimension to what the prophet foresees. The captives are coming home to God. The ransomed of the Lord are returning to Zion and – look who's there! Walking, dancing, and singing with them are the representatives of the nations, including a happy little girl from Tyre and a chap from Decapolis who, for some reason, seems to be talking to everybody.

There's much more to connect Isaiah 35 with our Gospel reading than the mention in both places of the mentally and physically impeded. Read the whole chapter this Sunday. Better still, if they're up to it, get the choir to sing Samuel Sebastian Wesley's setting of it, his glorious anthem 'The wilderness and the solitary place shall be glad for them.' It only lasts a quarter of an hour. Cut out the sermon if necessary.

Back to Tyre. Again Jesus tries to hide. His elusiveness is as much the truth about Jesus as all we affirm about him in our creeds. To make him obvious is to misrepresent him. Our little girl's feisty mother penetrates the veil of his secrecy. Jesus does not make it easy for her. Commentators try to tone down his apparently cruel words, the contrast he draws between the 'children' of Israel and the Gentile 'dogs'. 'Dogs', they tell us, doesn't mean big fierce dogs but friendly little ones. Whether it's more polite to call someone a Chihuahua than to call them a Rottweiler is a moot point.

According to Matthew, this distracted woman is treated still more harshly (Matthew 15.21–28). First, Jesus simply ignores her. The disciples then suggest he send her away because she's proving a nuisance. Then Jesus rebuffs her by saying that he is only looking for the lost of Israel. Finally we have the apparent put-down which Mark records.

This woman is one with every desperate mother who will go to any lengths to get help for her sick child. The word has got around that Jesus casts out demons. These exorcisms, he is saying, are signs of the Kingdom of God. If a cure for her daughter means making it into that kingdom she will stop at nothing to get in. She is one of 'the violent who take the Kingdom of God by force' (Matthew 11.12). So what about the snubs she receives? The disciples, who want her out of their hair, are simply being boorish. Jesus's comment about the Gentile dogs is in altogether different register. This is our witty, playful, ironic Lord speaking, and the mother is immediately in tune with him, as her equally teasing reply makes clear.

A conversation with the deaf-mute is impossible. Jesus himself is almost unable to speak. He 'sighs', as our versions feebly put it. The word used is far stronger. The man's plight makes Jesus howl. It is the word Paul uses of the cry of pain – could we but hear it – that all creation utters as it longs for its redemption (Romans 8.22). Later Jesus will cry out, in the same anguished bewilderment that things are as they are, 'My God, why?'

The deaf man doesn't forget the first word he hears. Its tongue-twisting sound is burned into his memory. That memory he must have shared, for we can hear the same word said to us. *Ephphatha* means more than 'be opened'. The 'cord of his tongue was loosed', says Mark. The image is of a prisoner released. The wonderful tongue-twisting Aramaic imperative – try saying it ten times quickly in succession – means 'Go free!'

YEAR C

Deuteronomy 30.15–20; Philemon 1–21; Luke 14.25–33

WHO COMES FIRST?

Luke's Jesus says that I cannot be his disciple without *hating*. Jesus begins to list those whom I must 'hate' – father and mother, spouse and children, brothers and sisters – but then he breaks off. For the list would be endless. I must, in his catch-all phrase, hate 'even life itself'. No one and nothing is to be excluded from this all-embracing 'hatred' required of me.

Commentators hasten to point out that to 'hate' would not have meant the same to those who first heard this shocking saying as it does to us. I 'love x' and 'hate y', so we are told, is the Semitic way of saying 'I prefer x to y' or 'I choose x over y'. We have the same extreme way of putting things in the saying of which Paul makes so much, 'Jacob I have loved, but Esau I have hated' (Malachi 1.2–3; Romans 9.13). On this view the sense of Jesus' words is captured in Matthew's more palatable paraphrase, 'Whoever loves father or mother more than me is not worthy of me' (Matthew 10.37). That said, we must be wary of interpretations which soften the impact of Jesus's hard words, even when it is another Gospel writer who tries to cushion the blow for us. Sometimes it is better to leave the difficult sayings of Jesus just as they are and to live with them as best we can. Why should we expect to grasp all he meant, the one at our side who is always beyond us?

'Whoever does not carry the cross . . .' Thus most of the modern versions translate Luke's Greek. These versions miss the emphasis

Luke adds to what has been said before about Christ's cross and ours (Mark 8.34, Matthew 16.24, Luke 9.23). All turns on Luke's precise choice of one word. As always, the 1881 Revised Version, for all its archaic and sexist language, gets it right. 'Whosoever doth not *bear* his own cross cannot be my disciple.' There is a world of difference between 'carrying' and 'bearing'. I carry a brief-case but I *bear* the cross.

The supreme commentary on Sunday's Gospel is Dietrich Bonhoeffer's *The Cost of Discipleship*. His chapter on 'Discipleship and the Cross' is an extended reflection on the 'bearing' that must be done if Christ is to have his way in us. 'For God is a God who *bears*. The Son of God bore our flesh; he bore our cross; he bore our sins, thus making atonement for us. In the same way his followers are called on to bear. That is precisely what it means to be a Christian.'

I must bear 'my brother's burden', says Bonhoeffer. That burden is not only 'his outward lot'. It is also 'quite literally his sin'. The Christian too has to bear the sins of others. 'He too must bear their shame and be driven like a scapegoat from the gate of the city.' Jesus bears the sin of others, but so must I. Any contradiction here was to be resolved at dawn on 9 April 1945 when Dietrich Bonhoeffer was hanged in the Flossenbürg concentration camp.

I cannot be a disciple without 'hating', without subordinating all else and everyone else to the prior claims of Christ and his kingdom. Nor can I be his disciple if I hang on to anything. I have to 'give up all my possessions'. We turn again, as we did last week, to Simone Weil. There are very few – though Bonhoeffer is among them – who have 'attended' (her word) as she did to Christ's call to renounce 'even life itself'. Crucially – the adverb must carry its full weight – I must renounce my supposed *rights*. To assert my rights, Weil taught, is to cease to love. I have no rights, none whatsoever. I have only duties. It is you, my brother, my sister, who alone has rights.

Christian discipleship is costly. That is the message of the twin parables – 'Don't start to build a tower you cannot afford to finish. Don't wage a war you do not have the resources to win.' So far my Christian allegiance has cost me little. Is there any sacrifice so small, I wonder, that I would not still be reluctant to make it?

The Cost of Discipleship was translated into English by the late R. H. Fuller. I have a copy on my desk as I write. I picked it up in a second-hand bookshop in York. It is signed by Fuller himself and beneath it – whether or not in his own hand is unclear – is a note saying 'translator's own copy'. Here on my desk is 'his' book. Now it is 'my' book, this book that teaches me that nothing is mine. Long ago, Fuller let his copy go. Do I have the grace to do the same?

Proper 19

The Sunday between 11 and 17 September

YEAR A

Genesis 50.15–21; Romans 14.1–12; Matthew 18.21–35

BEING FORGIVING AND BEING FORGIVEN

No sooner has it all begun than brother slaughters brother. Cain kills Abel. So begins the first book of the Bible. But Genesis closes on a different note. As we hear in our first reading, it ends not with bloodshed but with reconciliation. The shorter story rehearses the longer story. Genesis is the template of what is and what is to be, of fratricide finally quenched by grace. Certainly it will all end in tears, but the tears will be those of Reuben and the rest, the tears that wash away the last stains of our loathing of all we have been. We shall weep to find that we have been loved all along.

During dark nights, we dread that we are beyond forgiveness. John Donne did.

> Wilt thou forgive that sin where I begun,
> Which was my sin, though it were done before?

What he feared was altogether unforgivable was to have caused others to stumble.

> Wilt thou forgive that sin which I have won
> Others to sin, and made my sin their door?

He feared that, like Moses, he would glimpse the Promised Land, but never enter it.

I have a sin of fear, that when I have spun
My last thread, I shall perish on the shore.
('A Hymn to God the Father')

Peter too, it seems, had problems about forgiveness. He assumes that a ceiling must be set on the number of times a serial sinner should be forgiven. He wants to know at what level that ceiling should be fixed. Behind his question, perhaps, is his refusal to believe that he himself could be repeatedly forgiven. The night will fall when Peter will deny his Lord. Later, Jesus will have to work hard to persuade Peter that he has not thereby forfeited the role he has entrusted to him, to be pastor of his flock. Unable to forgive himself, Peter doubts whether Jesus still has a job for him (John 21). It is one of the wonderful ironies of Scripture that the keys of the Kingdom should be given to someone as unsure as Peter is about whether he himself deserves to be let in.

Jesus does not argue with Peter over numbers. The grace of God embodied in Christ knows no arbitrary limits, nor can the grace that characterizes the dynamics of Christian relationships be quantified. The context in which Matthew's Gospel was written was the Christian community. It is the context in which it is read this Sunday. In that context, each of us is to be as Joseph to his brethren. Each is to be as Christ to his friends – as, indeed, Christ to his enemies.

The Parable of the Unforgiving Servant, recorded only in Matthew, is disquieting. 'The kingdom of heaven' – the way God works – 'may be compared to a king who wished to settle accounts with his slaves.' Already we squirm. We are uneasy these days about calling God 'a king'. We are still more unhappy picturing him totting up figures in a dusty ledger, as we fidget in front of him. And, taught by Jesus, we certainly do not see ourselves as his slaves. The parable transports us to the court of a despot – a world to escape from, rather than to learn from. More problematic still is the parable's apparent contradiction of what Jesus has just said. The king in the story does not give the sinful servant a seventy-seventh chance. He does not give him even a second chance, before 'handing him over to be tortured' – a last touch to keep us squirming.

With this story, as with most of Jesus's parables, we must exorcize the demonic urge to allegorize, to squeeze meanings from every detail, like pips from a lemon. God is not an oriental despot, nor does he torture. The parable exaggerates, as many a good tale does. The debt owed by the unforgiving slave is inconceivably enormous. Had there been premier-league footballers in the ancient Near East, they would have not earned that much in a lifetime. The hyperbole serves to high-light the magnitude of God's mercy.

But the main point is not that. It is that there is an essential relation-ship between God's forgiveness and our readiness to forgive. There is more to this relationship than the fulfilment of a condition – God will forgive, if I forgive. The nature of that relationship is contained in the bidding of the Lord's Prayer, 'Forgive us our trespasses, as we forgive those who trespass against us.' 'As we forgive' rather than 'if we for-give'. As I forgive, I find that I am forgiven. As I am forgiven, I find that I forgive.

The circle of being forgiving and being forgiven is generated by love. Love is the well-spring of forgiveness. Neither the love nor the forgive-ness is a soft option or an expression of weakness. It was Martin Luther King who said, 'We must develop and maintain the capacity to forgive. He who is devoid of the power to forgive is devoid of the power to love.'

YEAR B

Isaiah 50.4–9a; James 3.1–12; Mark 8.27–38

THE GREAT GOD PAN IS DEAD

'The great god Pan is dead!' The rumour of Pan's passing sent shivers round the Roman world. Whether or not Pan is dead, certainly only fragments remain of the temple dedicated to him at Caesarea Philippi. Caesarea Philippi was called Paneas, 'the city of Pan', until Philip, son of Herod the Great, modestly renamed the place after himself. Pan's statue, which stood in a colossal cave above the city, has gone too. Pan's Cave, into which exhausted tourists now peer, was also known as 'the gateway to Hades'. Hermes – he was Pan's father and the Hermes of Mt Hermon which rises above Caesarea Philippi – was guardian of that gateway, as well as the messenger of the gods. He too was wor-shipped here. So were Caesar and sundry Syrian deities. In this holy hothouse, where so many divinities were revered and where most of them are dead and buried, the story of Jesus turns on its axis.

The great god Pan is dead. If he is, to whom shall we turn? To Jesus perhaps. And who might he be? It is the question which Jesus now puts to his disciples. 'Who do you say that I am?' It is the *disciples*, notice, those who have left their nets to follow him, who are asked this direct question. To be sure, it's interesting to hear what others think. But the personal question is not for those others. It's for Peter, James, John, and the rest. It's for us. 'Who do you – *you Christians* – say that I am?'

We do not have an answer to that question. Christians aren't people with answers, and those who claim to have them are not to be trusted. Christians are those who hear this question, who are dogged by it and will not drop it, and who wonder about it and work at it until the day dawns when no more questions will be needed.

To be sure, Peter has something to say by way of response. His brief reply, 'You are the Messiah', of which Matthew makes so much (Matthew 16.17–19) and some traditions in Christendom rather more, is a confession he does not begin to understand, as the sequel – 'Get behind me, Satan!' – makes plain. Jesus does not refuse the title of Messiah, but he is reluctant to use it of himself, so certain he is that it will be misunderstood. (Are there other such titles which, for the same reason, should be used of Jesus only with extreme caution? The appellation 'God' comes to mind.)

Yet again Jesus charges his disciples not to tell anyone about him. And yet again one wonders what shape the Church would take if we allowed the possibility that those words were not just for the Twelve. To shut up occasionally would certainly be a 'fresh expression of church'– not to say a refreshing one.

Now Jesus begins to speak more plainly of what must be. 'The Son of Man must suffer many things.' The title 'Son of Man' is deeply perplexing, but we can say something about it, a possibility to which ten thousand learned articles testify. Render Jesus's words as 'one must suffer', and we begin both to sense the title's baffling ambiguity and to catch some of its multiple meanings. I must suffer. We must suffer. He must suffer. 'One' meaning me, or 'one' meaning 'man' (that useful word which we mustn't use any more), or 'one' meaning the Messiah. The title, suggesting so much, concealing so much, is congruous with the essentially hidden character of Jesus's mission and reign.

'The Son of Man must suffer.' We could go on about 'the Son of Man', and the commentators do. The 'must' is much more mysterious. The necessity of redemptive suffering, hired wired into the order of things as much as the scientific regularities by which the universe subsists, is a mystery before which we can only fall silent. The same necessity shaped the role and destiny of the anonymous 'servant', about whom an unnamed poet wrote four centuries before the time of Jesus (Isaiah 52.13–53). That poet too found it beyond belief or comprehension.

'The Son of Man must suffer.' Explain that 'must' and you explain why Cordelia died.

At Caesarea Philippi Jesus asks his disciples to say who they think he is. The disciples might well have asked Jesus the same question. 'Who, Jesus, do you say *we* are?' Peter's confession – whatever he means by it – is a step forward on his journey to discover who Jesus is. Now the words of Jesus to the Twelve, his charge that they deny themselves, take up their cross, and follow him, disclose his estimate of them. I ask Jesus who he thinks I am – and he tells me what to do. He invites me to die with him. That's asking a lot, but just to be asked is the greatest possible assurance of my worth.

YEAR C

Exodus 32.7–14; 1 Timothy 1.12–17; Luke 15.1–10

COUNTING SHEEP

The picture on the front page of a recent *Times* supplement (*Times2*, 15 August, 2007) was of three sheep in a field. Or so it appeared. For when we turned the page we learned that the matter was not so simple. One of the sheep, we were told, was a lamb. Is a lamb a sheep? Another of the sheep, we were advised, was 'a pregnant ewe in advanced labour'. Is she one sheep, or two – or perhaps one and a half? A re-count, it seems, is called for. We shall come back to these sheep, however many of them there were, in a moment.

Jesus divides the house he is born to deliver. So Luke sees him from the start. The infant Jesus signifies to Simeon both salvation and schism. The child in his arms is both Israel's longed-for 'consolation' and 'a sign that will be opposed' (Luke 2.34–35). All the Gospel writers see Jesus as a divisive figure, but for Luke – as for John – the polarizing of opinion about Jesus is a leading theological theme.

Some welcome Jesus; others reject him. We meet both groups at the beginning of Sunday's Gospel. On the one side we have 'the tax collectors and sinners'. In Luke's Gospel they represent all those who have no standing in society – the misfits, the marginalized, the outcast – yet who hear Jesus gladly. We learn that they have drawn near to 'listen to him'. To 'listen' in the language of the Bible is to obey. These then are those who have responded to what was the last word of the last chapter – 'Anyone with ears, listen!' (Luke 14.35) Over against them are 'the Pharisees and the scribes', the custodians and authorized interpreters of the law. On that same side in Luke's thinking and Luke's Gospel are all who use their wealth and status to oppress the poor and powerless.

From the first singing of the Magnificat (Luke 1.46–55), this sharp schematic division runs deep through Luke's Gospel, the contrast between the mighty who, in God's good time and by God's good Son, will be brought down, and the lowly who will be lifted up.

Prophets cause people to take sides. They took sides over John the Baptist and now they are taking sides over one greater than John. It matters very much indeed what side we take, as Luke made clear by something he had said earlier in his Gospel, in an exceptionally important comment, which is often overlooked, as indeed it is in this year's lectionary readings from Luke. Luke tells us that those who took to heart what John said and were baptized by him 'justified God' – what an extraordinary expression! – but that the Pharisees and lawyers who refused his message and baptism 'rejected God's purpose for themselves' (Luke 7.29–30).

The parables of the lost sheep, the lost coin, and the lost children are Jesus's prophetic challenge to me to decide which side I am on. Wise teachers, from St Ignatius Loyola to Jerome Berryman, creator of 'Godly Play', advise us to ask a question about sacred stories. 'Where do you find yourself in the story?' So I ask myself this: for all my self-deprecation, am I at heart among those who are quietly proud of their status and probity? Or am I with those who can only echo Mark Antony's confession – 'I am so lated in the world that I have lost my way for ever'?

We read these familiar stories with too much detachment. We rightly see them as portraying Jesus's priorities – 'the poor' come first – and we correctly conclude that the Church should have the same priorities in its own mission. Much will be said along these lines from our pulpits this Sunday. But these stories have passed me by unless I recognize that they dramatize my own predicament. A useful exercise is to recall, as most of us can, some occasion in our own experience, possibly from childhood, when we have found ourselves lost, and to remind ourselves how devastating and desolating it was. There is no worse experience – even if my 'lost-ness' is a consequence of my own wilfulness and folly. The truth is that – baptized and confirmed, 'in good standing' with my church and nice to my neighbours – I never cease to be the lost sheep in desperate need of the good shepherd. That is where I am in the story. That is my desperate plight and my only hope.

Finally – back to them at last – those three sheep on the front page of *Times2*. After our recount, having noted that one of the sheep is a lamb and another is pregnant, we must adjust our reckoning. There are four sheep in the picture. For a sheep is no less a sheep for being little, nor is it less of a sheep for not yet having been born. The point is not wholly frivolous.

Proper 20

The Sunday between 18 and 24 September

YEAR A

Jonah 3.10–4.11; Philippians 1.21–30; Matthew 20.1–16

TELL ME THE OLD OLD STORY

Why should we listen to the tall tale of Jonah and the fish? For at least eight reasons – though there are many more.

First, we listen to it because it is a story. When my daughter was small, she would often ask at bedtime, 'Is there time for a story?' If we are in so much of a hurry that there is no time for a story, we imperil our humanity. It has been said, notwithstanding TV's endless 'soaps', that we suffer today from 'narrative deprivation'. 'The necessity for *homo sapiens* to tell and hear stories,' says the American novelist Reynolds Price, 'is second only to nourishment' (*A Palpable God*, Atheneum, 1978).

Stories begin with the most arresting words in our language: 'Once upon a time'. Stories end – and here is our second reason for listening to such a tale as Jonah's – with four more words. These are not the story-teller's words – 'they all lived happily ever afterwards', perhaps, but our words: 'Oh, now I see!' We listen to Jonah's adventures, so that we *see*.

The third reason for listening to Jonah's story is that Jesus told us to. Jesus said that no sign will be given to us 'except the sign of the prophet Jonah' (Matthew 12.38). This story, says Jesus, is uniquely significant. Why should that be? It is because there is a 'deep magic' to Jonah's story. It is the same divine magic that weaves the pattern of another story. We look through the 'dying' and 'rising' of Jonah to the death and resurrection of Jesus.

Hearing about Jonah – here's a fourth reason for doing so – reminds us that the story always comes first. All the clever meanings we milk from stories come later. Christian faith is driven by a story. That story, the story of Jesus, is 'the horse', if you like. Behind it comes 'the cart'. That 'cart' is overloaded. Its axles are buckled and close to breaking, under the weight of all our doctrines, our catechisms, our creeds, and our confessions. The horse and the cart need to be restored to their right order. Jonah is a tale – as once upon a time was the story of Jesus – largely unencumbered by dogmatic commentary. Space abounds for us to make of it what we will.

A fifth good reason for returning to the old, old story of Jonah and his fish is that it is a mirror. I look at the story and I see myself. Jonah nearly drowns twice. The first time is in the belly of the Leviathan that swallows him. That Leviathan was the beast of the deep the Hebrew people so dreaded, the primal chaos out of which God brought order, but which, they feared, might yet return to overwhelm them. The second time Jonah nearly drowns is in his fathomless self-pity. He sinks into a sulk, a pit, with whose contours I am all too familiar, excavated by resentment and anger.

Jonah is a man on the run. Again, I pick up the mirror. Again, I see myself. Facing this further truth about myself is a sixth reason for attending to Jonah's story. We are told that Jonah took a ship bound for somewhere far from Nineveh. At one level Jonah, sailing for Tarshish, was simply a deserter, refusing a dangerous job. Nineveh, famous for its violence, its corruption, and its 'countless debaucheries' (Nahum 3.4) was not likely to welcome a prophet announcing its doom.

But Jonah's flight is not really a flight from Nineveh. Jonah, we are told, 'set out to flee from the presence of the Lord'. Jonah is trying to escape the truth about God and the truth about himself. His complaint to God is bitter. 'I knew all along that you are a gracious God . . .' Jonah cannot bear that God should act so predictably, so exasperatingly in character, as to have mercy on this most wicked of cities. Jonah is in full flight from the truth that God loves Nineveh. The truth about himself that Jonah, to the last, refuses to recognize is that he has relished the prospect of Nineveh's destruction. He would have enjoyed every moment of it. So, I fear, would I.

A seventh reason for listening to this story is that Jonah is the only book in the Bible to end with a question mark. 'Should not I take pity on Nineveh,' God asks, 'where there are so many silly people and many animals as well?' ('And many animals': we are reminded – it is an eighth reason for hearing the story – of those who allow us to share their home.)

Jonah is left with the question, as we are, whether those who them- selves have shown little pity should be spared retribution. Hard choices must be made when the claims of mercy and justice clash. Our Gospel, the parable of the labourers in the vineyard, has the same stinging ques- tion in its tail, 'Are you envious,' asks the landowner, 'because I am generous?'

YEAR B

Wisdom of Solomon 1.16—2.1, 12–22 or Jeremiah 11.18–20; James 3.13—4.3, 7–8a; Mark 9.30–37

IF YOUR CHILD ASKS FOR BREAD . . .

Something strange will happen in a church near you this Sunday. A priest will read aloud a story from a big book about a teacher who put a child in the middle of his disciples. He will proclaim how this teacher embraced the child, how the teacher said that to welcome such a child was to welcome him – indeed, that to welcome a child was to welcome God. (If on Sunday the priest reads a little more than he's meant to, the people will hear that those who do not welcome children deserve to be drowned.) The reading of this story will be surrounded by pomp and circumstance. There will be a procession before it is read and an acolyte will bathe the book in incense. At the end of the reading, the book will be held high. The priest will tell the people that what they've heard is good news from God and they will respond with a shout of praise. You'll get the impression that this story is meant to be taken seriously.

This makes what will shortly follow so very peculiar. The priest will invite people to gather round a table to share in a simple meal of bread and wine in remembrance of this man who welcomed children. Timo- thy, just six years old, will be among those who come to the table. Timothy will hold up his cupped hands, looking forward to receiving a piece of bread like everybody else. But he'll be disappointed. The priest will ignore Timothy's request for bread. To be sure, the priest will have a blessing for him, but Timothy will know that this is second best.

Perhaps later the priest will explain to Timothy why he was missed out. If Timothy is a child of the Church of England, he may well be told that his exclusion was all because his name wasn't on a little list kept in the vestry, 'the register of children admitted to communion, to be available to be inspected by the Archdeacon at a parochial visitation'. Possibly the priest will explain to Timothy that he keeps this little list because the 'regulations', issued by the Archbishops' Council, tell him he must.

Timothy won't be quite old enough to ask why these regulations aren't processed and censed instead of the big book if, as it seems, they are more important.

Jesus silences his bickering disciples by setting a child in their midst. Of the historicity of this event there can be no doubt whatsoever. There is no precedent or parallel for what Jesus says about children. Children were precious to the community to which Jesus belonged as the Israel to be. Here is someone who, by contrast, placed infinite value on the child here and the child now.

Over the last fifty years there has been a wealth of theological reflection on the teaching of Jesus about children and the place of the child in church, but that reflection has yet to impact on the continuing marginalization of children at the Eucharist. The standard work on children in the Gospels – forgive the anorak – remains Légasse's *Jésus et L'Enfant* (Gabalda, 1969), still to be translated into English. Légasse showed that Jesus's estimate of children is not based on the qualities we like to attribute to them – their openness, trustfulness, spontaneity, insight, whatever – but on their helplessness. Like the poor, with whom Jesus also identified himself, children live by grace, human and divine. The disciples vie with each other for highest status in Christ's coming Kingdom. That status, Jesus teaches, belongs to those who have no status.

Jesus puts Timothy at the heart of his Church. His standing is emphatically not conditional on intellectual understanding. In this respect, Jesus's estimate of Timothy differs from that of the Archbishops' Council. Jesus does not expect from Timothy a precocious grasp of mysteries beyond mortal comprehending; he does not insist that Timothy 'appreciate the significance of the sacrament'.

We understand by grace and by the means of grace. We 'taste and see' – in that order. To insist on Timothy's prior instruction before admitting him to communion is like trying to teach him to read while refusing him books.

The child whom Jesus esteems so highly is any child, not the especially trusting, especially knowledgeable, or especially perceptive child. Recent studies on the child in the church, especially at the Eucharist, direct us to the role of the child in Judaism, notably at Passover. The importance of children at Passover has often been stressed. But there is one fact about the child at Passover which is often overlooked. It is precisely the child who does not yet understand, who does not yet, so to speak, 'appreciate the significance of the sacrament' whom Passover sets at the heart of the celebrating community. 'Why is this night different?' the child asks. The meal recalling their redemption can't even start without the child who doesn't know what's going on.

YEAR C

Amos 8.4–7; 1 Timothy 2.1–7; Luke 16.1–13

CRISIS MANAGEMENT

The parable of the dishonest steward is notoriously the most problematic of all the stories Jesus told. In trying to undo its knots scholars tie themselves in fresh ones. Commentators are bewildered by it. Those preaching on it long for the last hymn.

The scholars, the commentators and the preachers have all been in too much of a hurry to explain. They have forgotten what Jesus himself said about his parables – about all his parables, not just this one. Jesus did not tell us stories, so he said, to make things simple for us. If a parable such as this bewilders us, then it is doing its job (Mark 4.11–12). As with any good story, the only answer to the question 'What does the story mean?' is to tell it again.

The urge to explain the parables is natural enough. A parable explained is a parable contained. We have made it safe. It no longer threatens us. This anxiety to bring the disturbing teaching of Jesus under ecclesiastical control is there from the start. It is evident, for example, in the explanation of the parable of the sower that Jesus is said to have privately provided for his disciples when the crowds had gone away (Mark 4.13–20).

Our lust to explain leads us to interpret the parables simplistically and superficially. Turn back a page in Luke's Gospel and we have the story of 'the prodigal son' (Luke 15.11–32), the text for countless sermons about the readiness of a loving God to forgive. Such sermons speak truly, but they miss much that is strange and subversive in the familiar tale. The Methodist scholar Sheryl Anderson has pointed out that, while the son in the pig sty may have 'come to himself', there is no evidence that he was in the least repentant. His reasons for setting off home with his rehearsed speech were calculated and prudential. Much like the steward in our story, he had come to a crisis in his affairs and he had to act swiftly and shrewdly to avert disaster (*Children of God*, Angela Shier-Jones ed., Epworth, 2007).

The difficulties the parable poses are real enough, of course. It is hard to say where the story stops and where the 'moral' starts. Who is praising the steward in verse 8? Is it 'the master'? If so, we are still in the parable. Or is it 'the Lord'? If so, it could be that we have stepped outside the story and that it is Jesus who is now commending the rogue for his resourcefulness. (The New Revised Standard Version's '*his* master' is a mistranslation.) The jury is out on the issue of just how dishonest the dishonest steward in fact was. To determine his culpability would require a familiarity with the intricacies of Jewish laws of usury which few of us have the leisure to acquire.

What will resonate with many a modern reader in the frenzied western world – other times and other places may shed a different light on the story – is the fact that the steward faces catastrophe unless he acts fast. A growth industry in our own times is 'crisis management'. Organizations are advised to have a 'crisis management plan' in place and there are highly paid consultants eager to advise on the making of such plans. The *Journal of Contingencies and Crisis Management* is no doubt on every bishop's desk.

Our contemporary dread of imminent crisis, a fear as well-founded as it is all-pervasive, enables us to identify with the dishonest steward. We are all in his shoes. The fear we feel of what may well overtake us – the coming global flu epidemic, the act of terror that will overshadow 9/11, the enviromental catastrophe by which our abused planet will visit its retribution on us, irreversible financial melt-down – our terror of these imminent judgements should make us take this disconcerting tale to heart.

There are four stages to crisis management, so the experts tell us. The crisis must be identified, a response to it must be planned, the crisis must be confronted and then, and only then, can it be resolved. Our steward takes all these four steps. The man may have cheated and lied. That is not the point. What matters is that he is not unnerved by the dread of what threatens to befall him. He responds to the crisis speedily and effectively and for that – not for cooking the books – he is congratulated.

John the Baptist's cry, that the raised axe is about to fall (Luke 3.9), echoes through all the Gospels and across all the ages. We have no reason to suppose that out forbearing Lord will stay his hand much longer. If we have the horse sense of the 'dishonest steward', we too will 'flee from the wrath to come' (Luke 3.7). That flight is going to be difficult, so the closing verses of our Gospel suggest, if we are overloaded with this world's goods.

Proper 21

The Sunday between 25 September and 1 October

YEAR A

Ezekiel 18.1–4, 25–32; Philippians 2.1–13; Matthew 21.23–32

THE GASMAN, THE BISHOP, AND THE CHRIST OF GOD

Our readings this week are a range of summits, some lost in cloud. Ezekiel, pioneering the path that John Milton will follow, seeks 'to justify the ways of God to men'. Paul 'unfolds the mystery of the Incarnation'. Matthew requires us to reckon with the authority of Jesus – and not to play games with him. The peak Paul strives for – or rather the depths he sounds – must be left for another season.

Ezekiel's contemporaries have much in common with my grandson Alex. 'It's not fair,' says Alex. It is our earliest moral utterance. From infancy, we protest against injustice. To be sure, Alex is more alert to the injustices he thinks have been done to him than to those done to his younger brother Max. But as he grows older he will notice that Max too is sometimes hard done by. Then one day he will come to see that inequity is more widespread still. 'It's not fair!' Alex says today when refused an ice-cream. 'It's not fair!' he will say tomorrow when contemplating the moral order of the universe.

They say to Ezekiel, 'The way of the Lord is unfair!' Their complaint against God is that he permits children to suffer as a consequence of their parents' wrongdoing. What makes matters worse is that God has apparently decreed that that is how things should be. For generation after generation, God has punished children for their parents' sins

(Exodus 20.5). Ezekiel is bold enough to claim that God's command-ments – even the top ten – are not set in tablets of stone. From now on, he announces, individuals will suffer only for their own sins.

It will not be the last word that the Scriptures will say about God's justice. Ezekiel proclaimed that it was all going to be so very different, but Job, long after Ezekiel's day, noticed that little had changed. Job's anguished 'Why?' was a hammer blow on heaven's door. God's curi-ous response – 'Come child, look at my ostriches' – leads Job into a relationship which, fulfilled in the vision of God, silences his questions (Job 38–42).

Then one greater than Ezekiel, greater than Job, appears announcing God's just reign. And they ask him the question we all suspiciously ask: 'What's your authority?'

The gasman calls. From around his neck there dangles a laminated card confirming his authority to read your meter. The bishop emerges from the vestry. He is wearing a mitre, the sign of his authority to con-duct the service about to start. The gasman's authority and the bishop's have been conferred on them by others. They may or may not be in themselves authoritative figures. The gasman may be a coward and the bishop a wimp, but the former is no less entitled to inspect the dials under your stairs, nor the latter to confirm you.

The senior clergy we meet in Sunday's Gospel question Jesus's au-thority. They are not asking about his character. They want to be sure of his credentials. For 'the chief priests and the elders', Jesus is a mav-erick cleric whose orders are probably invalid and who anyway has no 'permission to officiate'. But the claim of Jesus is not subject to sup-porting paperwork. It needs no human endorsement or validation. The authority of Jesus is his own.

That authority was manifest from the start. The fishermen dropped their nets at his command and followed him. Mark, the earliest Gospel-writer, tells us that when Jesus began his public ministry everyone was astounded at his authority. 'For he taught as one having authority and not as the scribes' (Mark 1.22). Mark notes – though not all his readers do – that the authority of Jesus made its immediate impact before the miracles had begun.

Jesus declines to give the straight answer that those 'in authority', as they like to think they are, seek from him and by which they hope to condemn him. As is always his way, he returns their question with one of his own.

The authority of Jesus has always been questioned. The Jewish read-ers of Matthew's Gospel had their doubts about him, doubts which

Matthew seeks to settle by his frequent and ingenious appeals to the 'Old Testament', as we call it. The miracles Jesus works are seen as signs of his authority over all that challenges the reign of God. 'Who is this,' they ask, 'that even the wind and the sea obey him?' (Mark 4.41).

But we badly misunderstand the nature of Jesus's claim on us if we suppose that it stands or falls by this or that proof-text or by 'signs and wonders', however impressive. Jesus's authority is who he is. If, like Thomas, we insist on verification, all he will show us will be his wounds (John 20.27). He invites me to trust and follow him. If, in my pride, I ask what right he has to do so, his response will be what it was to the chief priests and the elders: 'Neither will I tell you.'

YEAR B

Numbers 11.4–6, 10–16, 24–29; James 5.13–20; Mark 9.38–50

NEUTRALITY NOT AN OPTION

'Whoever is not against us is for us.' I settle at my desk to compose my thoughts on these words. But not for long. I'm called out because of Warren. Warren is a 'street-drinker', well known to us. Warren has collapsed on the Rectory drive and is having a fit. There's a risk of his choking on his vomit. A passer-by, who has already dialled 999, is talking to him gently, reassuring him that help is on its way. A man appears with a bundle of tissues to clear up the mess. Soon the paramedics are there, then the ambulance, then the police. They are all as kind and as caring as they are competent – although in the end Warren refuses their assistance and weaves his unsteady way off.

I return to my desk and my text. I wonder about these good people who have been so attentive to Warren. I have no idea what they think about Jesus. But I do not suppose that they are not 'against' him. If so, to the mind of Jesus, infinitely more hospitable than that of his disciples, they are 'for' him. To be sure, Jesus also said, 'Whoever is not with me is against me' (Matthew 12.30). Perhaps there are critical times when neutrality is not an option, when not to confess Christ is to deny him. So it would be under some of the Caesars. So it has been under the various fearful Antichrists who have darkened history. So it may be in the last days. But, for the present, everyone else is my Christian brother or sister until they expressly disclaim that kinship.

Eldad and Medad are family too. We meet them, somewhere in the Sinai desert, in the Old Testament reading. Together with seventy others, they'd experienced one of those sudden strange ecstatic frenzies – enjoyed in our own time on the wilder shores of the charismatic movement – which the Bible describes as 'prophesying' (not to be confused with the rational and coherent utterances of an Amos, an Isaiah, or a Kenneth Leech). Eldad and Medad – about whom surely someone has made up a limerick – are in trouble because they had 'prophesied' without any authority to do so. They had neither the bishop's licence nor his 'permission to officiate'. But Moses – even Moses, the very embodiment of law and order – doesn't mind. Rules must bend before the wind blowing where it wills. It may be important to keep the house of God in order – those who manage our mainstream churches certainly think so – but not if it means keeping the doors and windows closed against God's supremely untidy Spirit.

I come to words about the giving of a cup of water. Again I am interrupted. It's Fred at the front door. Fred calls two or three times a day to ask for a drink of water. This time I give Fred a two-litre bottle of water, hoping that perhaps it will see him through the day. I return to the difficult Greek text of Mark 9.41, with all its tricky variant readings, and give myself a headache trying to sort it out. As usual, a footnote in the 1881 Revised Version provides the most accurate, if not the most felicitous, translation. 'Whosoever shall give you a cup of water to drink in name that ye are Christ's . . .' One thing is clear. If Fred calls again today asking for a drink of water I shall be Christianly obliged to give it to him.

'If your hand or foot causes you to stumble, cut it off.' 'If your eye is the problem, take it out.' I am struck by the distance between two discourses. There is, first, the discourse in which much is made of 'Christian values', 'the Christian ethos', and so on. Such terms are used, for example, by those wishing to build more and more church schools. When such enthusiasts are asked to say what they mean by those catch-phrases, it immediately becomes clear that what they have in mind are not distinctively Christian values but human values, principles upheld by all people of good-will.

The second discourse is the moral teaching of Jesus, the substance of Sunday's Gospel, what Jesus actually says we should do. 'Amputate or gouge out the bits of you which get you into trouble.' Whatever Jesus means by such utterances, so enigmatic and so characteristic of him, it is impossible to distil from them the kind of bland moral propositions, 'Christian values' and the rest, which everyone can sign up to.

Equally baffling are the observations which close the Gospel reading. These are assembled in domino fashion. 'Fire' and 'salt' are the connecting words, linking the disparate sayings. 'Everyone will be salted with fire.' 'How do you season salt that has lost its saltiness?' 'Have salt in yourselves.' These pithy utterances are like Zen koans, gnomic utterances intended to awaken the moribund mind. 'Koans don't make sense,' someone has said. 'They make *you*.'

YEAR C

Amos 6.1a, 4–7; 1 Timothy 6.6–19; Luke 16.19–31

TRIPPING OVER LAZARUS

I knew Lazarus. He slept on our doorstep when we lived on the corner of Trafalgar Square. Our doorstep was narrow and steep and he had to curl up awkwardly. He looked like a sack. I could have done more for him. I could have given him a blanket or directed him to a night-shelter. Better still, I could have invited him in for a bath and a meal. But usually I just stepped over him. Lazarus always had a dog with him, perhaps to lick his sores. When I had a lot of shopping, I would ask him to move. Generally he did – though I recollect his once saying, 'Why should I, you public-school dick-head?' Lazarus certainly looked as if he could have done with a few of the crumbs fallen from the table at which I feasted sumptuously every day.

One day, so Jesus teaches me, I shall see Lazarus again – though my glimpse of him, Jesus warns me, will be across a great gulf. By then Lazarus will be beyond any need of my help and there will be nothing he can do for me. I can only hope that Abraham will at least convey my apologies to him.

Lazarus sleeps on all our doorsteps, whether or not someone homeless is there in person for us to trip over each time we come home. Luke's story teems with fascinating but distracting details, so diverting that we may miss the point. Unless I treat Lazarus differently, I will find myself one day exchanging places with him.

The rich man in the story is unnamed. No matter, I am he and I have a name. His life-style is that denounced by Amos in our Old Testament reading – lamb for lunch, a glass or two of wine, a snooze on the sofa with some soothing music in the background. What the prophet condemns as unbridled extravagance is what many of us will settle for without a second thought after church this Sunday.

The parable vividly dramatizes the reversal of fortunes set out in the starkly opposed beatitudes and 'woes' at the outset of Luke's 'Sermon on the Plain' (Luke 6.20–25). The poor and hungry will not always be so, nor will the rich and full enjoy their affluence for ever. In God's coming Kingdom their situations will be reversed.

The rich man in Jesus's story is certainly pictured in a bad light. He is indifferent to the plight of the destitute. By refusing to share the abundance he has, he disregards his covenantal obligation to the poor of the land (Exodus 22.21–22; Deuteronomy 10.17–19). But the emphasis of the story is not on the moral contrast between its protagonists. Although Lazarus ends up in 'Abraham's bosom', nothing is said to suggest that he was especially pious. For all we know, it may have been his own fault that he ended up where he was.

The story turns on the material circumstances of Lazarus and the rich man, not on their morals. There are two 'great gulfs' in this parable – the gap between Heaven and Hades and the chasm between the haves and have-nots. What is 'obscene' as we say these days, is not the loose morals of your hedge-fund-manager – he is possibly on his PCC – but the fact that he earns more in a day than many do in a year. As the TUC General Secretary recently said, it is 'morally offensive' that the boss of Punch Taverns earns a thousand times as much as his barmen and barmaids.

Duncan Forrester has mounted what he calls 'a Christian vindication of equality' (*On Human Worth*, SCM Press, 2001). He tells us how he met someone much like Lazarus on a street in Madras, a beggar called Munuswamy. Munuswamy sent Professor Forrester back to his Bible. He found 'egalitarianism deeply rooted in the Judaeo-Christian tradition'. That principle is embedded in the Bible in the story of creation. All are created in the image of God. Made equal, they are to be treated equally. So it is that in Israel king and commoner are alike subject to the law of God. If Amos had survived to write a comment on Sunday's Gospel, he might have said that the economic structures that today separate ever more widely the richest and the poorest in our society are as heinously sinful as the moral faults of any individual, whether on the board or the breadline.

But the sting of the story is in its tail. 'If they do not listen to Moses and the prophets, neither will they be convinced even if someone rises from the dead.' For 'they' we must read 'we'. If we do not 'listen to' – that is to say, if we do not obey – the moral law long known to us that we must deal justly with one another, then much good will talk of an empty tomb do us.

Proper 22

Sunday between 2 and 8 October

YEAR A

Isaiah 5.1–7; Philippians 3.4b–14; Matthew 21.33–46

A JUST HARVEST

Like the Lord whom Isaiah loves and for whom he sings, my dear friend David 'hath a vineyard in a very fruitful hill'. When, years ago, David purchased his vineyard in the south of France, he too 'planted it with the choicest vine'. David too 'looked to his vineyard that it should bring forth grapes'. Happily, David's experience was different from that of the prophet's 'well-beloved'. David's expectations were abundantly fulfilled. His vineyard yielded good grapes. And so it has done year on year, his 2006 Château de Mazelières vintage winning the Paris gold medal for Buzet red wines.

I think of my friend David when I read Isaiah's love-song. I cannot imagine how devastated David would be if the vines he has tended so patiently and lovingly were to produce bad grapes. His bewilderment, grief – and anger too – would be boundless. How much more intense then – this is the thrust of Isaiah's parable – will be the divine bewilderment, the divine grief, and the divine anger when the 'harvest' of his people's deeds proves rotten!

The 'well-beloved' of the prophet's song – the intimate image is audacious – is God. The 'vineyard', God's 'pleasant planting', is his people. The familiar image (Isaiah 27.2–5; Jeremiah 2.21; 12.10–13) is pressed to far-fetched limits in Sunday's Psalm. 'You brought a vine out of Egypt,' we sing. According to the Psalmist, this vine is higher than the cedars – indeed it overshadows the mountains. In our Old Testament reading, the vineyard refers specifically to the eighth-century BCE kingdom of Judah. But we who have heard someone say 'I am the vine;

you are the branches' (John 15.5) will realize that Isaiah is singing to us too.

God chooses his people to be a beacon to humanity. The 'harvest' he seeks is a social order reflecting his character. In a word – and there is no more important word in the Hebrew Bible – he expects 'justice'. Isaiah has earlier made crystal clear what this word means: 'Rescue the oppressed, defend the orphan, plead for the widow' (Isaiah 1.17). He has made it equally clear that, in the absence of social justice, pious exercises are futile. 'Incense,' says the Lord through his prophet, 'is an abomination to me' (Isaiah 1.13).

The vintage God seeks is justice. But his vineyard yields a different fruit, its essence captured in two staccato words. There is a biting wordplay in the first of them. The Hebrew for 'bloodshed' (*mishpah*) sounds much the same as the word for justice (*mishpat*). The 'cry' the Lord hears is specifically the anguished cry of one who is wronged. The language of Isaiah's love-song makes plain just how bad those bad grapes are. Literally, they are *stinking* grapes. Such is the effluvia from the vineyard God has planted. And we must add – 'for the avoidance of confusion', as the solicitors say – that these oracles, uttered eight centuries before the time of Jesus, apply equally to the community meeting in his name twenty centuries after his time. For us, as for those who first heard Isaiah's strange love-song, there is no hiding from the God of justice beneath banks of incense.

The parable of the wicked tenants is in all three synoptic Gospels. It is much more of an allegory than most of the stories Jesus told. The vineyard is Israel and the landowner is Israel's Lord. The tenants are the religious hierarchy, the slaves are the maltreated prophets whom the hierarchy rejected. The slaughtered son is Jesus.

The trouble with allegories is that it is tempting to squeeze a meaning from every last detail. In this story, the landowner – that's to say, God – 'goes to another country'. Those who sometimes wonder where God is will ask whether that is something he is in the habit of doing.

Allegories also lend themselves to embroidery. Both Matthew and Luke add a significant stitch. According to Mark, the tenants first kill the landowner's son and then throw him out of the vineyard (Mark 12.8). Matthew and Luke, mindful that Jesus is crucified 'outside the city gate' (Hebrews 13.12), reverse Mark's order. The son of the landowner is first taken outside and then done to death. There, outside, is where we must meet him.

Matthew has disturbing words, found only here in his Gospel. 'The Kingdom of God will be taken away from you and given to a people that produces the fruits of the kingdom.' Much that has been made of this text has not improved Jewish–Christian relations. Those drawing such inferences, those who make simplistic pronouncements about 'the new Israel', fail to register where the weight of Matthew's words lies. Those now entrusted with the vineyard are those – it is immaterial whether they are Jews or Gentiles – who will ensure that it yields its intended harvest, those who – in that same one word – will see that God's *justice* is done.

YEAR B

Genesis 2.18–24; Hebrews 1.1–4; 2.5–12; Mark 10.2–16

GRACED VULNERABILITY

Jesus's teaching about marriage and divorce is not pastoral advice. He is not counselling a boy and girl who have fallen in love and who are wondering whether to wed. Nor is he talking to a man and wife who have fallen out of love and who are wondering whether to split up. Nor is he advising the middle-aged couple who come to see me – faithful partners for twenty years – and who want me to marry them, although somewhere out there a spouse survives from a previous marriage, a disastrous compact which lasted ten minutes.

The Pharisees are not after Jesus's advice. They are after his blood. They are, we read, 'testing' him, just as a certain unsavoury character had done in the wilderness shortly after his baptism. They want to convict him out of his own mouth, as they had tried to do over the issue of keeping the Sabbath (Mark 2.18 – 3.6), as one who dares set himself above Moses. They are casuists out to condemn him, determined to bind him with cords which, in their view, cannot be broken: the fine mesh of the Mosaic law, as they interpret it.

Jesus refuses to fight his opponents with their weapons – exchanging rule for rule – but recalls them to first principles. The divine intention in creation is that in marriage two should be one and be so for good. Jesus puts that principle to his disciples in such extreme terms that the response of many commentators, starting with Matthew (19.9), has been John McEnroe's, 'You cannot be serious!' But Jesus is being serious, just as serious as he is when he insists that his disciples give away all they have, or amputate offending limbs, or – *tout court* – 'be perfect' (Matthew 5.48). The pole star does not move. The principle stands.

Marriages, like dogs at Christmas, are for life. But I live in Hackney, not in Eden. Here marriages fail. Sometimes, miraculously, there is the hope of a new beginning. To wrench the words of Jesus from their polemical context, and to use them as a ligature to strangle that hope at birth is pastorally cruel, an abuse of Scripture, and a denial of the gospel.

Reasonably enough, Mark moves from marriage to children. 'Of such is the kingdom of God.' Here is another saying of Jesus which has met with the McEnroe response. It is, surely, an absurd idea that God's reign belongs to any and every child without qualification or exception. Certainly it is a notion which the western Church, whether Catholic or Protestant, has never really taken seriously. (The Eastern Orthodox churches have an altogether more Christian view of children.) 'Of such is the kingdom.' Jesus, we are told, is talking about the children whose parents have brought them to him. So they must be baptized children. Or they are children who have responded to his invitation to come to him. So they must be 'born again' children. (There are worrying signs in our own day of a revival of this 'beach-mission theology', with its enthusiasm for winning converts from the crèche.) It has even been argued by persons of otherwise sound mind that the story isn't really about children at all but about adult believers. The child, on this view, is a metaphor for the humble disciple.

We need to throw 'three anchors from the stern'. The first is the action of Jesus. He takes the children in his arms and blesses them. What Jesus *does* here, as when he sets a child 'in the midst' of his disciples (Mark 9.36), has few precedents or parallels and his words must be interpreted in the light of his deeds. Secondly, Mark's language is unequivocal. The 'of such' (the anorak, please, Jeeves) is, in the Greek, a correlative demonstrative pronoun of quality. The Kingdom belongs to *children*, as well as to those like them. Thirdly, the nearest equivalent in the Gospels to the word of Jesus here is the Lucan beatitude, 'Blessed are you poor, for yours is the kingdom of God' (Luke 6.20). Luke's text points to the significance of children for Jesus. Their title deeds to the highest place in God's kingdom are that, like the poor, they are helpless to help themselves.

Elsewhere Jesus does indeed imply that children have distinctive 'childlike' capacities. Unless we become like children (Matthew 18.3), or never quite grow up, those capacities usually die out as we turn into boring adults. But the grounds of Christ's estimate of childhood are not children's subjective qualities but – as a recent writer has put it in a book we have long needed – their 'graced vulnerability', the fact that left to themselves they will die (*Graced Vulnerability: a theology of childhood*, David H. Jensen, The Pilgrim Press, 2005).

YEAR C

Habakkuk 1.1–4; 2.1–4; 2 Timothy 1.1–14; Luke 17.5–10

HOW LONG, O LORD, HOW LONG?

The National Theatre's recent revival of George Bernard Shaw's *Saint Joan* played to packed houses. Shaw always provided detailed stage directions. He specifies how *St Joan's* last scene should be staged. '*The last remaining rays of light gather into a white radiance descending on Joan. The hour continues to strike.*' Then, before the curtain falls, Joan speaks for the last time. 'O God that madest this beautiful earth, when will it be ready to receive thy saints? How long, O Lord, how long?'

Joan's final words are the first words of Habakkuk. 'O Lord, how long shall I cry and you will not listen?' The same bitter prayer is heard again and again in the Psalms. 'How long wilt thou forget me, O Lord?' And the psalmist adds, screaming in the face turned away from him, '*For ever?*' (Psalm 13:1–2; see also Psalm 6.3; 35.17; 74.10; 79.5; 80.10; 89.46; 90.13; 94.3) Jeremiah, who bares his soul beyond any other prophet, demands, 'How long shall the land mourn, and the herbs of every field wither, for the wickedness of them that dwell therein?' (Jeremiah 12.1–4). Even the angels wonder how long the Lord intends earth's misery to last. 'Then the angel of the Lord answered and said, O Lord of hosts, how long wilt thou not have mercy on Jerusalem?' (Zechariah 1.12) The same prayer is even said in heaven. The martyred saints in glory cry, 'How long, O Lord, holy and true, dost thou not judge and avenge our blood on them that dwell on the earth?' (Revelation 6.9–10)

'How long, O Lord, how long?' So ends *Saint Joan*; so begins our Old Testament reading. The closing speech in *King Lear* affirms that that is a prayer we may properly utter, even though it calls God's goodwill in question. We must – so ends *Lear* – 'speak what we feel, not what we ought to say'. We must speak – and pray – what we *feel*. If 'the weight of this sad time' – the world's burdens and, such as they are, our own – are all too much for us and we long that God would call a halt to it all, then that longing must become our prayer. Any other prayer, however pious and proper, would be drowned out by the cry of our heart. Alone with the God who does not seem to be there, I ask when the whole sorry story will end. Such is my *felt* prayer and all the Scriptures and all the saints – as well as Shaw and Shakespeare – sanction my saying it.

In his book *The Intercessor's Guide* (Canterbury Press, 2007), Raymond Chapman has given us excellent advice about how to intercede publicly. Formal intercessions in church are 'what we *ought* to say'. In the presence of the congregation I do not pray aloud that the power-point presentation will work, though in the privacy of my heart I am probably desperately begging God that it will. I regularly ask God, as well as my wife, what I have done with my car keys. Such prayers too are *felt* prayers and most of us pray them, even if we exclude them from our liturgies and make no attempt to justify them theologically.

It is foolish to ask God to find your car keys. It would be still more foolish to walk up to a sycamore tree spoiling your view and to ask it to move. King George III talked to the trees in much this way and we know what happened to him. Yet Jesus tells his disciples that with the merest smidgeon of faith, they might do just that.

What is going on here? Is this preposterous suggestion, that we tell the trees to move, a further example of Jesus's taste for hyperbole? Or is it some sort of a joke? My friend Philip who is writing a book about the comedy of Jesus would say it is the latter. Jesus's response to the disciples' peremptory 'Increase our faith!' is teasing and playful. Jesus might have said, as he did once to James and John, 'You do not know what you are asking' (Mark 10.38). Here he is gentler with his naïve followers. If his reply baffles us, then all to the good. We might be moved to think a little more deeply about what it means – and what it costs – to believe.

The parable of the master and the slave reflects a society in which slavery is an institution that no one questions. Some translations mislead us by suggesting that the man told to do as he is told is a 'servant'. He is not a servant; he is a slave. The point of the parable is that a slave cannot earn. The master can never be beholden to the slave. God does not award any orders of merit. Even if we did our best, we would only have done our duty. It is a stern story and on its own would perhaps be disheartening. But Jesus had other tales to tell and in one of them there is the promise that, even if we have been faithful over only a very little, someone may still one day say to us, 'Well done' (Matthew 25.14–30).

Proper 23

The Sunday between 9 and 15 October

YEAR A

Isaiah 25.1–9; Philippians 4.1–9; Matthew 22.1–14

LOOK AT WHAT YOU'RE WEARING

Spiritual directors within the Ignatian tradition urge us to 'imagine our-selves into' the Bible stories we read. They invite us to identify ourselves with one or other character in the narrative or to give ourselves some walk-on part that lets us enter into what is going on. I sense what it means to feed on the Bread of Life if, in my imagination, I become one of that famished five thousand (John 6). I awake to the mercy of Jesus on the least deserving, myself among them, if I find a vantage point in the crowd waiting for Jesus beneath the sycamore tree in which Zac-chaeus is hiding (Luke 19.1–10). Sick in mind and body, I join the oth-ers around the Pool of Bethesda (John 5.1–17). With them, I wait for the waters to move, in the forlorn hope that – if I can crawl into the pool in time – those waters will work some wonder on my wasted body and weary spirit. Then I notice the stranger. And I hear his words to me, 'Take up your bed and walk.'

This method of studying the Bible works well with stories *about* Je-sus. It works less well with some of the stories *by* Jesus. To be sure, I can imagine myself as, say, the bemused inn-keeper in the parable of the good Samaritan (Luke 10.25–37), or as the jealous elder brother in the story of the prodigal son (Luke 15.11–24), or as the frustrated farmer in the tale of the wheat and the weeds (Matthew 13.24–30). But in other parables, such as the one we hear on Sunday, this Ignatian ap-proach only serves to highlight just how odd these tall tales are.

I can't see myself as one of the men in our story who murders the messengers. Nor can I imagine myself as the dictator who sends an army to sack the city that has defied him. And I certainly cannot en-ter into the feelings of the unfortunate wedding guest who is dragged straight off the streets into the wedding reception – and who is then im-mediately bound hand and foot and flung out because he is improperly dressed!

I can picture myself as part of the story as Luke tells it (Luke 14.15–24). Luke's version of our parable is a narrative with a coherent story-line. We are spared the extra details – the butchered messengers, the crazed king, the blood-thirsty talk of 'outer darkness' and 'weeping and teeth-gnashing' – that make for the problems in Matthew. We can enter into Luke's 'Parable of the Great Dinner' with little difficulty. But where the story is as cluttered with inconsistencies as Matthew's is, an Ignatian imagination is little help.

No doubt the main thrust of our parable, that God calls all and sundry to the heavenly father and mother of all parties, is clearer in Luke than in Matthew. (In our first reading we get a mouth-watering glimpse of the menu: 'A feast of rich food, a feast of well-matured wines, of rich food filled with marrow, of well-matured wines strained clear.')

Certainly Luke is easier reading. But that is no reason for giving Matthew a miss. His parable may be so overloaded with images that the thread of his story snaps, but each of those images has scriptural associations we need to explore. Some of those associations oblige us to modify what we might otherwise make of Matthew's parable. The conduct of the incensed monarch who puts a city to the sword is not the last the New Testament will have to say about divine sovereignty, nor should it determine our understanding of why Jerusalem fell in AD 70.

In Matthew, the party to end all parties is a wedding celebration. Marriage is the supreme scriptural metaphor for God's covenant relationship with his people. That covenant is, by corollary, a template for human marriage – a truth fast being lost on a society slipping all its Christian moorings.

Critics tell us that the parable as it stands in Matthew is not all of one piece. It is like an old car offered for sale that, on inspection, proves to be welded together from the wreckage of two or more vehicles. Or – a more felicitous analogy – it is a piecing together of fragments of stained glass that once belonged to more than one window. So the closing verses of our Gospel – for which there is no parallel in Luke – were once a separate parable. The extraordinary Pauline image of 'clothing oneself with Christ' (Galatians 3.27) suggests the key to its interpretation. In dressing for a wedding, I dress for the day. In 'dressing myself with Christ', I dress for eternity. There are overtones of another rite of passage here. 'The wedding garment' is apparel donned at baptism. That baptismal robe is a relationship to be constantly renewed. 'Love must be lived and realized afresh each day.'

For all its complications, one clear admonition emerges from our Gospel: 'Just look at what you're wearing.'

YEAR B

Amos 5.6–7, 10–15; Hebrews 4.12–16; Mark 10.17–31

BEATRICE AND THE BEATIFIC VISION

This week's paradox is posed by 'the rich young ruler'. I can sell all my possessions and give to the poor, as he is asked to, only if there is someone out there well-heeled enough to buy them. The reckless selfless ethic of Jesus is practicable just as long as most people are living by a more calculating and prudential ethic, within a stable and strong market economy in which such incautious conduct is not the norm.

The mistake is to suppose that we have here a 'higher' and 'lower' morality, to imagine that Smith who sells all he has and gives it away is necessarily a better man – and a better Christian – than Brown who buys Smith's goods and then resells them at a profit.

Behind this paradox, that radical obedience is only possible in a society living less heroically, lies a tormenting question: 'What is the Christian attitude to the material?' The question is not only about the importance to us of what money can buy. The issue is the value to us of everyone and everything, the worth to us of those we love as well as of the things we prize. Should Almighty God alone be dear to us?

The question is explored in *The Figure of Beatrice* (Faber, 1943), Charles Williams's study of Dante's *Divine Comedy*. Charles Williams shows that there have been two chief ways of approach to God in Christian thought. One has been 'the Way of Rejection', the renunciation of all affections except for God himself. This is Smith's way. Smith is a Carthusian monk living in a solitary cell in St Hugh's Charterhouse, Parkminster. The other way is 'the Way of Affirmation', to rejoice in our relationships and not to despise the things which human hands have made. The latter is Brown's way. Brown is a chartered accountant who lives with his wife and two children in a semi-detached house in Chipping Ongar.

Traditionally Christianity has honoured Smith above Brown, a mis-apprehension rooted in a misreading of the story of Mary and Martha (Luke 10.38–42). Most of us are perforce Marthas, but we feel vaguely guilty about our crippling attachments and we hanker to be Marys. Charles Williams speaks of 'the tangle of affirmation and rejection which is in each of us', the contradiction which Dante resolved in the image of Beatrice, the girl he fell for on a bridge in Florence. Dante came to understand that falling in love with a Beatrice cannot ultimately be dissociated from the Beatific Vision. Both are an experience of 'the eternal fountain'.

Smith sells all he has and gives to the poor. Brown buys Smith's things and resells them on eBay so he can convert the loft. As T. S. Eliot put it with such exquisite precision, 'Neither way is better. Both ways are necessary' (*The Cocktail Party*).

Of course it's hard for Brown to get to heaven. A camel has less of a problem in going through a needle's eye. Most of us were taught in Sunday school that the walled city of Jerusalem had a great big gate and that next to it was a much smaller gate – 'the eye of a needle'– which a sufficiently adroit and lissom camel might just squeeze through. So Brown, if he down-sizes sufficiently, might just make it through the pearly gates.

Such exegesis is misconceived. The thrust of Jesus's teaching is not the difficulty but the impossibility of entering the Kingdom of God – unless, of course, you are a child (Matthew 18.3). Yet 'all things are possible with God'. Entry, as much for Smith as for Brown, is, as St Paul will teach, by grace alone (Ephesians 2.8).

A nettle remains to be grasped. Jesus apparently denies that he is good or that he is one with God. Jesus's question 'Why do you call me good?' is a reminder to us of the importance of choosing our words carefully. After all, why *do* we call Jesus good? One answer is suggested in what is perhaps the greatest essay in moral philosophy of the twentieth century, Iris Murdoch's 1967 Leslie Stephen lecture, *The Sovereignty of Good* (Routledge, 1970). Iris Murdoch writes, 'Goodness is connected with the acceptance of real death and real chance and real transience.' Perhaps the story of Jesus is of the one life in which those conditions were fully accepted.

So two themes have come together in our story, the goodness of things and the goodness of God. It's good to have a family and a nice house and car – and it's good too to have nothing at all and to live in a monastery. We are saved neither by getting things nor by giving things, but only by the mercy of God. As for the goodness of God, if Iris Murdoch was right, the only God who could be called good would be one who lived our life and died our death.

YEAR C

2 Kings 5.1–3, 7–15c; 2 Timothy 2.8–15; Luke 17.11–19

THE HEALING WORK OF CHRIST AND HIS FRIENDS

There were ten of them altogether, all suffering from some dreadful skin disease. At least eleven points can be made about their story.

1 The ten stood 'at a distance'. As the law required, they were 'outside the camp' (Numbers 5.2–3). That is where we belong too, if we are disciples of Jesus (Hebrews 13.13). We are not asked to feel sorry for 'lepers' – or for Samaritans – but to join them.

2 The ten cried out to Jesus and so must we. Their prayer was the primal prayer – the Jesus Prayer – 'Lord Jesus Christ, Son of God, have mercy on me, a sinner.' No doubt they repeated it continually, as did the tax-collector who also 'stood far off' (Luke 18.9–14), as all of us must. The best little book about the prayer is *The Jesus Prayer* by Simon Barrington-Ward (The Bible Reading Fellowship, 1996).

3 Luke chooses three words carefully. On their way to the priests the ten are 'cleaned'. Yes, they are 'cleansed' or 'made clean', as our familiar versions say. The reason for their ceremonial impurity is removed. But there's more than a whiff of church and old Bibles about such expressions. Better to use a word people actually use if it is just as accurate, even if – especially if – it sounds a bit odd. Then the Samaritan saw that he was 'healed', that he was cured of his disease. But it is Jesus who, with Luke's third word, tells the full story of what has been done for him. 'Your faith has *saved* you.' 'God has made you all that you were meant to be.'

4 It does not belittle what has been done to the nine to note that the miracle has been only 10 per cent successful. The miracles of Jesus do not *reward* faith. They *invite* faith. Ten plead with Jesus, the Samaritan no less desperately but no more confidently than the rest. Ten are cured. The sign of God's coming Kingdom has been performed, the invitation extended. But only one of the ten reads the sign, hears the invitation, and accepts it. Only the Samaritan responds in faith.

5 The Samaritan 'turned back'. The vocabulary of 'turning' in the New Testament is extensive and significant. What matters is the

new direction – where we are now heading, not how far we have got. 'Turn' is the simpler word behind the more complicated word 'repent'.

6 'Turning' towards Jesus involves turning to work. The Gerasene demoniac was told to 'turn' home and to tell everyone what had been done for him (Luke 8.39). Each step of faith, including the first, is a step of obedience. Faith in Jesus is a moral response or it is not faith at all. We are not told that the Samaritan 'followed Jesus in the way', as Bartimaeus did (Mark 10.52). Jesus simply tells the Samaritan to get up and go. But wherever he goes, and whatever befalls him, he is now, and always will be, a disciple.

7 'Your faith has saved you' or 'made you whole'. The same words are said four times in Luke's Gospel. In each case, the one 'made whole' is an outcast (Luke 7.50; 8.48; 17.19; 18.42). If we are rejected, we disintegrate. We fall to bits and need someone to put us together again. That is the healing work of Christ and his friends.

8 A point that Luke hopes will not be lost on his readers is that the Samaritan who sets out to see the priests never arrives. There is no suggestion that the Samaritan, once on his way again, reports to a priest, either to one in Jerusalem or to one of his own persuasion. Priests are gatekeepers to social acceptance and to the presence of God. But one greater than the priests is here and it is to him the Samaritan turns. He will not be the last who, dispensing with institutional religion, turns to Jesus instead.

9 Jesus asks, 'Where are the other nine?' We ask the same question. Is it fanciful to suggest that those nine represent the great majority, at least in Western Europe, who may once have come under Christian influence in some way – at home, at school, at church – but for whom now the Christian faith means little or nothing? Some of those 'other nine' own to a sense of loss, others to a sense of liberation. 'Where are they?' Jesus asks. He has not forgotten them, it seems.

10 The Samaritan praised God and thanked Jesus. What may or may not have been in Luke's mind when he placed those statements so closely in parallel is immaterial. Luke does not identify Jesus with God. But the Samaritan, prostrate at Jesus's feet, comes close to doing so.

11 The eleventh point sums up the previous ten. In the words of the Scottish theologian Thomas Erskine, 'In New Testament, religion is grace and ethics is gratitude.'

Proper 24

The Sunday between 16 and 22 October

YEAR A

Isaiah 45.1–7; 1 Thessalonians 1.1–10; Matthew 22.15–22

CHRIST AND CAESAR

The bishop and the butcher meet in a bus queue. They fall into a discussion about the morality of gambling. The bishop says that gambling is bad. The butcher argues that there is nothing wrong with a little flutter. If the bishop then says we should put our faith in God and not in horses, then his new friend, who is not a Christian, will pooh-pooh his opinions. If, however, the bishop argues that gambling can become addictive and can lead to family breakdown, then the butcher may listen to him. By the same token, the bishop, if he is a humble man, will be rebuked when the butcher reminds him that it is only thanks to the National Lottery that the great west window of the bishop's cathedral survives.

The issue of whether gambling is right or wrong is a moral question. The point of the fanciful anecdote is to suggest that consecration as a bishop does not confer privileged access to the answer to such questions any more than elevation to the management of a butcher's shop.

The spectacle of church leaders 'speaking out' – often in the House of Lords – on social, economic, moral, and political questions on which they have no special expertise is a familiar but extremely peculiar feature of the ecclesiastical landscape.

Whether or not what a noble prelate pronounces on, say, euthanasia, is judicious, the nagging questions remain. Why should a bishop's word on the issue of the hour carry more weight than that of a butcher? What relevance can moral judgements, made on Christian premises, hold for a society long adrift from its Christian anchorage? If policies have to be made to work in a pluralist society, should not the common moral ground shared by all people of good will be their basis, rather than the presuppositions – inevitably divisive – of those of religious conviction?

This tangled web of questions radiates from one central one. What is the relationship of Church and society? Or, to put the question in

New Testament terms: What has Christ to do with Caesar? We turn hungrily to Sunday's Gospel reading for light.

The conflict between this eccentric exorcist, Jesus of Nazareth, with his wild claims about the imminence of God's Kingdom, and the religious establishment is now coming to a head. That establishment, desperate to silence him, tries to trick him into condemning himself out of his own mouth.

'Is it lawful to pay taxes to the emperor?' they ask. The Pharisees anticipate that, however Jesus answers their question, he will impale himself. The question is specifically about the *census*, the poll tax loathed by all the Jews as a sign of their subjection to Rome. If Jesus advocates refusal to pay the tax, he can be immediately denounced to the Romans. If he says that the tax must be paid, then he will be seen as collaborating with the hated occupying power. Either way, he's skewered.

Jesus's reply, the Roman *denarius* in his hand, is as enigmatic as it is famous. We owe our fealty, it seems, to both God and Caesar. Each, in his realm, commands our obedience. But how do those realms relate? Are they completely separate? Martin Luther argued in his 'doctrine of the two kingdoms' that God rules in two ways. There is his 'left-hand kingdom', that of the state and his 'right–hand kingdom', that of the Church. These two spheres, the civil and the spiritual, are completely distinct. Or do these realms coincide? There have been those, notably Leo Tolstoy, who have believed that societies should order their common life according to the Semon on the Mount.

Or do the two realms partly overlap? This is the messy reality experienced by most Christians who struggle to live by the light of the gospel in a complicated world. The Bible does not tell us how to run the National Health Service. But equally, for the Christan believer, it is surely incontestable that the witness of the prophets, Jesus of Nazareth among them, should be brought to bear on such an issue.

Perhaps the 'middle axioms', for which the late Professor Ronald Preston pleaded, would help. 'Middle axioms' are moral principles drawn from biblical insights and shared by as wide a Christian constituency as possible. These axioms, neither bland truisms, nor detailed blueprints, offer a basis, Preston suggested, on which Christians can enter into dialogue with those who have to make tough decisions on complex issues.

One such 'middle axiom' might be that policies for the vulnerable and marginalized must never be shaped by considerations of how much that constituency contributes to society's prosperity. Another might be that every child should find itself a member of a family. A third axiom –

pertinent to the matter of whether we need more betting shops – might be that greed is socially as well as individually corruptive.

YEAR B

Isaiah 53.4–12; Hebrews 5.1–10; Mark 10.35–45

THE TASTE OF DEATH AND THE LIFE OF GRACE

We are on firm ground. James and John ask Jesus for the most conspicuous places in his Kingdom. Mark is not going to make up a story which reflects so badly on them. Matthew is embarrassed by the story and claims that it is their ambitious mother who pesters Jesus on behalf of her sons (Matthew 20.20–28). Jesus insists that it is not for him to say who will have the top places at his table. Again Mark can't have invented a saying in which Jesus seems anxious not to be confused with God. Furthermore, according to Mark, Jesus implies that both brothers will be martyred. James was put to the sword (Acts 12.2), but John, from all the best accounts, survived to a ripe old age. These are not words put into the mouth of Jesus in the light of later events. Mark's account rings true.

Jesus does not directly condemn his disciples' lust for preferment. But neither does he collude with it, as one day his Church will, by giving them advice on how to construct impressive CVs or how to shine in interviews. He simply asks them whether they understand – to use an anachronism – what it means to be a Christian. To be a Christian is to drink and drown, to taste Christ's bitter cup and to suffer his baptism.

We must stay with these terrible images.

> In the hand of the Lord there is a cup,
> with foaming wine, well mixed;
> and he will pour a draught from it,
> and all the wicked of the earth
> shall drain it down to the dregs.
> (Psalm 75.8)

As we sip wine this Sunday, such a text – and there are many others like it – may not come to mind. 'The cup' in the Hebrew Bible is the cup of God's wrath against sin. In the Christian 'New Testament' Jesus both drinks this cup so that we shall not have to – and hands it to us.

He spares us the chalice that he presses to our lips. He dies in our place, but we must carry his cross. This is the most painful of all the many paradoxes Christian theology must wrestle with.

In a largely forgotten, altogether extraordinary, and exceedingly scarce little book, *The Taste of Death and the Life of Grace* (1901), the Congregationalist theologian P. T. Forsyth wrote of the flavour of the wine Christ alone drank from the cup we too must drink. What does that fatally poisoned chalice taste like? 'Death in its lees is bitter and ashy,' writes Forsyth. 'It is nauseous and sordid when we really taste its last touch on life. The more we live and the greater our vitality the more acrid and squalid is that subtle stealthy death which thwarts, poisons, corrodes and erases life. It is grey, leprous, and slow.' This is Christ's cup and ours and the only preferment he offers.

To be baptized with Christ's baptism is to go down for the third time with no more assurance of surfacing than Christ felt of being rescued on the third day. Again, the tap-roots of the Christian image are deep in the Hebrew Bible. The psalmist, his soul cast down within him, 'drowning not waving', cries, 'All thy waves and thy billows have gone over me' (Psalm 42.7).

The Church that encourages me to carve out my career has capitulated to the world's culture. Christ's counter-cultural judgement is terse. 'Not so with you.' Occasionally, of course, we meet someone who takes Jesus at his word. Such encounters are unnerving. I recall an experience at an airport somewhere in Africa. A scruffy and clearly impoverished porter seized my heavy and expensive suitcases and staggered off towards a row of clapped-out taxis. I hurried after him, fuming that there was no one to meet me. Then my scruffy porter introduced himself. He was the diocesan bishop.

The death Jesus tasted was 'a ransom for many'. Who are 'the many'? Strict Calvinists point out that 'many' is not the same as 'all' and that some, such is the sovereignty of the potter over our poor clay, remain unransomed. P. T. Forsyth, believing that God must be at least as good as Jesus, rejected this appalling doctrine. He saw 'the many' as the untold millions, those far too exhausted to grasp the finer points of the theology of the atonement. It was their death Jesus tasted – 'death by sickly candlelight in a little house in a back street among miles of them'.

'A ransom *for* many.' The preposition *anti*, innocently translated in our English versions as 'for', is another semantic battleground soaked in vitriol. Is the force of the language that Christ died as my 'representative' or as my 'substitute'? I recall with shame that I once thought I knew the mind of God well enough to tell.

YEAR C

Genesis 32.22–31; 2 Timothy 3.14—4.5; Luke 18.1–8

WHEN MERCY LONG DELAYS

Jesus tells the comic story of the feisty widow and the grumpy judge so that we should keep praying and never despair. We should never *despair*. 'Lose heart' (NEB and RSV) is too weak. We need the weightier word so that we can bring the light of the gospel to bear on a darker place than any region to which loss of heart can lead us. Despair is not the loneliness and desolation of 'the dark night of the soul'. The darkness of the soul is the darkness before the dawn. Nor is it 'accidie', the torpor that overtakes us when the sun is high, the listlessness that has been identified with the 'noonday demon' of the ninety-first psalm (Psalm 91.6). Nor is it 'spiritual distress', the condition that, in all its many unhappy manifestations, has been the subject of much valuable research in recent years, notably by those working among the hospitalized.

As traditionally understood, despair is far worse than any anxiety of spirit, however acute. It is it is the deliberate and wilful abandonment of all hope of salvation. It is deadlier than any deadly sin. Some have claimed that it is the 'unforgivable sin'. And yet, paradoxically, it is those closest to God who are most tempted to commit it.

Benedictine monks and nuns are wholehearted in their search for God. To equip them for that quest, St Benedict presents them in his Rule with no less than seventy-three 'instruments of good works', seventy-three rungs on 'the ladder of perfection'. The seventy-second 'good work' is 'to make peace with an adversary before the setting of the sun'. Benedict, knowing what by now his brothers and sisters must be feeling, adds a final seventy-third admonition: 'Never despair of God's mercy.'

Despair can be an easy and attractive option. That is why it is so dangerous. Giving up the struggle comes as a great relief. The mountaineer lost in the snows is tempted simply to lie down and to surrender to whatever will be. Gerard Manley Hopkins understood the seductive appeal of despair.

Not, I'll not, carrion comfort, Despair, not feast on thee;
Not untwist — slack they may be — these last strands of man
In me ór, most weary, cry 'I can no more'. I can;
Can something, hope, wish, day come, not choose not to be.
('Carrion Comfort')

Luke emphasizes what it is that drives Jesus's disciples to despair.
It is that he takes such a long time coming. Luke understands history,
particularly that there is an awful lot of it left. Luke, and only Luke,
records Jesus's warning, 'The days are coming when you will long to
see one of the days of the Son of Man and you will not see it' (Luke
17.22). Two millennia later, that is where we are. The Kingdom of God
seems as distant as ever. Apart perhaps from dentistry and Sellotape,
the world seems no better a place than when the first friends of Jesus set
out with such a spring in their step. Surely there is reason to despair.

Back to our story. The judge ignores the widow. We must remember
that in the Old Testament judges, whatever else they were there for,
were appointed to defend the rights of 'widows and orphans' (Deuteronomy 10.18 and many texts besides.) So this judge is shockingly –
comically – negligent. Luke has fun reading his mind. Luke hears him
saying to himself, 'This tiresome woman will end up giving me a black
eye!' The image is from the language of prize-fighting. Paul, something
of a bruiser himself, uses the same figure of speech (1 Corinthians 9.27).
(This really was once a funny story. It's just that jokes tend to be less
funny when they are told every three years on the twentieth Sunday
after Trinity.)

Here then is a 'how much more' story. If this grossly neglectful judge
in the end yields to the persistent widow, how much more willing will
God be to vindicate his people! And, Jesus adds, he will do so 'quickly'.

We are inclined to ask, 'How quickly is "quickly"?' Jesus does not say.
Instead he puts a question of his own. 'Will the Son of Man find faith
on earth when he comes?' That plaintive enquiry confirms the context in
which this story is to be understood. It is the memory and prospect of history unfolding, age on age, which causes faith to falter. To abandon hope –
hope having so often been dashed – would be to find peace of mind.

Jesus fears that many of us will take that easy way out. But in our
way stands this doughty widow who refuses to despair and who teaches
us how to pray. So, Lord, grant us,

Patience to watch, and wait, and weep,
Though mercy long delay;

Courage, our fainting souls to keep,
And trust thee though thou slay.
(James Montgomery)

Proper 25

The Sunday between 23 and 29 October

YEAR A

Leviticus 19.1–2, 15–18; I Thessalonians 2.1–8; Matthew 22.34–46

THE FOUR STEPS OF LOVE

We are picky people in our reading of Leviticus. Those who disapprove of same-sex relationships, for example, steer us to the texts in
Leviticus that support their opinions, not to the texts defending notions
or advocating conduct that, presumably, they would not agree with.
So they will often refer us to Leviticus 18.22, which calls homosexual
behaviour an 'abomination'. They draw our attention less often to the
verses in the previous chapter which, arguably, forbid the consumption
of rare steaks (Leviticus 17.10–13).

The lectionary is just as choosy. Our reading from Leviticus this Sunday is just six verses from a lengthy chapter. But our lectionary editors
have a better reason for choosing the verses they do than a desire to
cherry-pick texts that support their views on this or that issue of the
hour.

They have chosen a text that Jesus chooses. If the lectionary is selective in its use of Leviticus, that is because Jesus is selective too. It is a
matter of some interest and importance that, when Jesus quotes Leviticus, it is a text about loving one's neighbour he cites, not one about
going to bed with someone of the same sex. A basic principle about
how the Church uses the Bible emerges. A Christian reading of what we
call the Old Testament is necessarily an interpretation of those texts in
the light of what we call the New Testament. That does not mean that
a reading of the Old Testament on other premises is wrong. Christians
need the light that Jewish interpretations of Holy Scripture shed. But

what we make of Scripture depends on where we are. That place, by our baptism, is 'in Christ'.

Jesus does not turn only to Leviticus. He sets the Levitical injunction to love one's neighbour alongside 'the greatest and the first commandment' from Deuteronomy that we should love God wholeheartedly (Deuteronomy 6.5).

Which is easily said. But many of us are not much good at loving God. We are not sure how to go about it. Indeed, we are not entirely clear what the idea of loving God means. We need the help of those who have fallen in love – and who have stayed in love – with God. St Bernard of Clairvaux was one such. Bernard taught that loving God, like everything else we try to do that is difficult, is a step-by-step process. According to Bernard, there are 'four steps of love'. The first step, says St Bernard is to love ourselves for ourselves. Then we must learn to love God. We love God – this is the second step – initially for what he gives us. But if we are true to this path we shall come to love God for himself, the third step. Finally, we love ourselves for God's sake. For some, that last step is the hardest of all.

This step-by-step approach to loving God has been explored in a helpful little book by Fiona Gardner, *The Four Steps of Love* (Darton, Longman and Todd, 2007). She makes it clear that these four steps are not rungs of a ladder that I set up inside my head, shutting out the rest of the world. For those who are single minded in their search for God, other people are not a distraction. Far from it. The journey from self-love to the love of God never by-passes my neighbour.

For Fiona Gardner, to love God and to love one's neighbour in God is the only way to break free from the 'hamster-wheel' character of the lives so many of us lead. Such lives – however frenetically busy they are – are ultimately futile. Gardner would not agree with Shakespeare that love is 'frantic-mad with evermore unrest' (*Sonnet* 147). On the contrary, love – Christianly understood – traces the one steady path through life's shifting sands. In his great 'hymn to love' in 1 Corinthians 13, Paul catalogues the multiple attributes of love. Had he been writing in the twenty-first century, he might have added one more: 'Love is sane.'

'Love God.' 'Love your neighbour.' Jesus was not the first, as is often suggested, to link these two commands together. But the more we read the Gospels, the plainer it becomes that for Jesus the two commandments are virtually one. That loving God and loving one's neighbour are a single love is the message of the mighty 'inasmuch' of the parable of the sheep and the goats (Matthew 25.31–46).

'Love God.' 'Love your neighbour.' For Jesus, these two mandates are the heart of the revealed will of God. These twin loves are to shape the life of the community of his disciples in every age. 'There is to be no retreat from the world. There is no passivity induced by vast human needs . . . Love is lived faithfulness and active compassion' (Warren Carter, *Matthew and the Margins*, Orbis, 2005). *Ubi caritas Deus ibi est.*

YEAR B

Jeremiah 31.7–9; Hebrews 7.23–28; Mark 10.46–52

TELL THE TRUTH BUT TELL IT SLANT

Mark's stories are not bits of washing pegged on the clothes line in whatever order they came out of the tub. Mark arranges his material. In his Gospel Jesus does not say directly who he is. Instead, he drops hints and scatters clues. These are the half-hidden 'miracles', as they're sometimes called, which Jesus is so anxious to keep hushed-up. These cryptic events function as signs – to any who have the faith and insight to read them aright – that the reign of God is imminent. Mark's central chapters are the carefully structured record of how the significance of Jesus's words and works slowly dawns on his disciples. It is an agonizingly slow process. The sign of the multiplication of the loaves and fish is repeated, but still they don't twig. 'Do you still not perceive or understand? Do you have eyes and fail to see? Do you have ears and fail to hear?' (Mark 8.17). The impatience of Jesus is palpable.

The disciples see and they don't see. The disciples' fitful stumbling progress to the point where all becomes clear is illustrated by the story of the healing of the blind man at Bethsaida (Mark 8.22–26). At first, all the man sees are 'men as trees walking'. Jesus's apparent struggle to restore the man's sight dramatizes the difficulties he has with his disciples, who continually fail to put two and two together. Even when the light seems to break with Peter's confession at Caesarea Philippi it proves a false dawn (Mark 8.27–3).

A year or two ago Canon Stephen Chivers, then at Westminster Abbey, pointed us to a poem by Emily Dickinson which exactly captures how Mark tells his story:

Tell all the Truth but tell it slant
Success in Circuit lies

Too bright for our infirm Delight
The Truth's superb surprise
As Lightning to the Children eased
With explanation kind:
The truth must dazzle gradually
Or every man be blind –

Mark's good news, as much as is John's Gospel, is an account of light
shining in darkness. Such truth 'must dazzle gradually'. The disciples
could not bear all the light at once, any more than we can. But at last
someone sees, not a privileged disciple but a blind beggar.

Three features of his story highlight its crucial importance. First, we
know Bartimaeus by name. Possibly he was a member of the Christian community in which this Gospel originally circulated. Secondly,
whether or not Bartimaeus was known to Mark's first readers, we
know that he became a disciple. Mark leaves us in no doubt. Bartimaeus addresses Jesus not only as 'son of David', but also as *Rabboni* –
'my master'. The latter title, used elsewhere only by Mary Magdalene
when she recognizes her risen Lord (John 20.16), speaks powerfully of
his personal faith. Mark adds that Bartimaeus 'followed Jesus in the
way', a choice of words meaning much more than that he literally fell
in step behind Jesus as he left Jericho. Thirdly, there is the placing of the
story as the prelude to Holy Week. The healing of blind Bartimaeus, his
'superb surprise', is the climax of Mark's meticulously crafted account
of Jesus's journey to Jerusalem. What is there now left for Jesus to do?
Only, the next day, to ride on to die.

Details in this story fascinate me. Bartimaeus shouts at Jesus. They
tell him to shut up, but he cries out even more loudly. I think of the
chronically intoxicated character who hangs around the bus stop at the
end of our drive and who greets me several times a day with his 'Hey!
Vic!' I think of another of my Hackney friends, a legless inebriate who
propels his wheelchair down the middle of the road, bellowing profani-
ties at oncoming buses. Perhaps Bartimaeus had an alcohol problem, as
well as being blind. We picture those whom Jesus healed, apart perhaps
from the demoniacs, as meek, inoffensive and deferential. We are seeing these stories through a pious filter. In the resultant dim religious
light we may not be getting the whole picture. Bartimaeus may not have
been at all a cuddly character.

When Bartimaeus called, Jesus 'stood still'. Around him is the clamour-
ing crowd; above its noise the blind man redoubles his cries; no doubt
the disciples are loudly volunteering their views on what should be

done. None of this touches Jesus's deep stillness. I think of the noisiest place in Asia, the Arrivals hall at Calcutta airport, and of a quiet, diminutive, wholly recollected figure I once noticed there. Like Jesus, Mother Teresa 'stood still'.

Bartimaeus 'throws off his cloak'. I think of the filthy sleeping-bags in which my homeless neighbours in Hackney doss down by night and with which they swathe themselves by day. It is all they have, some of them. For Bartimaeus, to let his probably verminous cloak go is as reckless an act of abandonment to Christ as that of Francis of Assisi stepping naked from his all his finery.

YEAR C

Ecclesiasticus 35.12–17 or Jeremiah 14.7–10, 19–22; 2 Timothy 4.6–8, 16–18; Luke 18.9–14

A GOD WITH EXPLAINING TO DO

Jeremiah's description of 'the drought', immediately preceding our reading from him, is as vivid and harrowing as any of the pictures familiar to us from OXFAM publicity or from televised reports from the parched places of the earth. The women return from the wells, their water-pots empty. The farmers, contemplating their dry fields, are in despair. 'Even the doe in the field forsakes her newborn fawn.' The images are enough to break our hearts.

'Enough to break *our* hearts', certainly – but not enough, apparently, to break God's heart. He alone remains unmoved, impervious to the plight of the newborn fawn, not to speak of the people whom he has called his own.

Jeremiah is one with Job in calling God to account. Like Job, he wants to know what is going on in the mind of his maker. To be sure, they have all sinned. Their iniquities cry to heaven. (If Jeremiah wonders what the doe and her fawn have done to deserve their suffering, he keeps that thought to himself.) But even allowing for the heinousness of his people's transgressions, there is still a compelling reason for God to act. 'If, Lord, you will not take pity on us for our sake, if indeed we are beyond pity, then for *your* sake, for the good of your own name, do something.'

The Almighty has some explaining to do. In one respect, Jeremiah probes the mind of God even more sharply than Job does. He invites

God to offer some reason for the sheer *strangeness* of his conduct, for his acting so out of character. Bitterly, ironically, Jeremiah rehearses the titles that God has been given. He is – or has been – 'the hope of Israel, its saviour in time of trouble'. Now he is like 'someone confused'.

'Someone *confused*.' The RSV's translation of a word our different versions render variously is striking and suggestive. Is God's problem, not so much that he is deaf to the feeble cries of little children and baby fawns dying of thirst, nor that there are limits to what even an almighty God can do, but that – omniscient as he is – he simply does not know what to do? Here is a very human God, much like the one we meet in the Gospels who is torn two ways about what his mission and destiny should be.

Jeremiah's searching prayer exposes the vulnerability of the God to whom he appeals. It is to that crucified God we turn.

Jeremiah pours his heart out. So does Paul. In an astonishing image, he says that he is 'already being poured out as a libation'. Paul has said the same before. He told the Christians at Philippi that he was 'being poured out as a libation over the sacrifice and offering of your faith' (Philippians 2.17). The sacrificial metaphors are very bold, but are they more than metaphors? Some commentators insist that there is no thought of atoning sacrifice present. That insistence is not wholly persuasive when we recall another Pauline testimony, his claim to be 'completing what is lacking in Christ's afflictions' (Colossians 1.24).

Jeremiah, like Job, teaches us how to pray. So does Jesus. In the parable of the Pharisee and the tax-collector, we have two patterns of prayer. The first pattern is self-satisfied and self-congratulatory. It is the prayer of the Sunday School teacher who, having told her charges this story, said, 'Now, children, let's close our eyes and put our hands together and thank God that we are not like that nasty Pharisee.'

Professor Aviad Kleinberg of Tel Aviv University believes that there is an eighth deadly sins more lethal than the other seven (*Seven Deadly Sins*, Harvard University Press, 2008). That eighth super-sin is self-righteousness. It is indulged in by the kind of people who like to think – or who at least like other people to think – that they are innocent of the other seven. Those who belong to religious elites – priests, rabbis, mullahs and the like – are most prone to it. Some Pharisees, such as the one in our story, succumbed to this sin, though it would be wrong to suppose that the Pharisees generally were any more self-righteous than any other religious grouping then or later. The self-righteous suppose that they know better than simple believers. These, the professionally pious, Kleinberg maintains, are careful not to air their doubts or to disseminate ideas that might prove unsettling. When a religious leader does not collude with this conspiracy – one thinks of David Jenkins, the former Bishop of Durham – everyone gets very upset.

The second pattern of prayer is the tax-collector's cry for mercy. In this cry is the seed of 'the Jesus Prayer' which, across the centuries, Eastern saints have said in their hearts with every breath on their lips. 'Lord Jesus Christ, Son of God, have mercy on me, a sinner.'

This prayer for Eastern saints is a prayer for Western sinners too.

The Fourth Sunday before Advent

The Sunday between 30 October and 5 November

YEAR A

Micah 3.5–12; 1 Thessalonians 2.9–13; Matthew 24.1–14

LOVE WILL COME AGAIN

Hidden in our Gospel are perhaps the saddest words in the Bible. Jesus says that, towards the end, 'the love of many will grow cold'. Only Matthew has this poignant saying. Much said in the Bible about the last things concerns the cosmic and the catastrophic, the apocalyptic convulsions that will tear the created order apart. There will be the famines, the floods, the falling stars, and the rest. In contemplating the end times, we tend to focus on these immense upheavals which the Bible predicts and to forget the less dramatic signs of things coming to an end. That obsession can become morbid and addictive. There are those who positively welcome the latest natural disaster – with however many thousand dead – as additional evidence that the end is nigh.

Jesus's sad words suggest that we adopt a humbler and more sober perspective on what will be. It would be better for us to speculate less about the cataclysms that threaten the fabric of the universe and to think instead of what tears apart the fabric of our relationships, our failure to love.

'The love of many will grow cold'. Matthew depicts a church under persecution. So far from bringing the Church together, the effect of adversity will be to set Christians against each other. Brothers and sisters in the one Christian family will betray one another. Many will be 'caused to stumble' – and we recall the judgement reserved for those whose fault that is (Matthew 18.6). Those taught to love will come to hate.

Jesus foresees what will happen. As night falls, he sees us turning on one another. We recall the question, recorded but once, but which Jesus must have asked himself many times. 'When the Son of Man comes, will he find faith on the earth?' (Luke 18.8).

Not that we need to be persecuted to become lukewarm in our Christian affections. There is no evidence that the Laodiceans were being thrown to the lions (Revelation 3.14–22). Nor do the Christians now at war with one another – about the role of women in the ministry, say, or some issue over sexuality – need external adversity to fuel their belligerence. And if we steer clear of such conflicts, it will not necessarily be because we love our enemies too much to do battle with them. The world works on us and we become weary. Lethargy saps both the will to fight under Christ's banner and the heart to love our neighbours.

The loss of love, love of our Lord, love for one another, is a far more serious matter than the sun turning to sackcloth or the moon becoming blood (Revelation 6.12). We should pray that it will not come to that, but we rarely do. Just as rarely does our generally upbeat hymnody contemplate the possibility that love fails. An exception is Henry Twells' great hymn, 'At even, ere the sun was set . . .'

> O Savior Christ, our woes dispel;
> For some are sick, and some are sad;
> And some have never loved Thee well,
> And some have lost the love they had.

Can that lost love be retrieved? Taught by our Gospel, we are emboldened to hope that it can be. For some, it is already 'the sad hour of Compline' of life's little day. For all of us, history's darkness gathers. But it is not too late to love again. If we do not know how to ask for the love we have lost, Twells's hymn comes to our aid.

> Thy touch has still its ancient power.
> No word from Thee can fruitless fall;
> Hear, in this solemn evening hour,
> And in Thy mercy heal us all.

W. B. Yeats doubted whether it were possible that love could come again. The best we can do, he believed, was to

Murmur, a little sadly, how Love fled
And paced upon the mountains overhead
('When you are Old')

We dare to believe that the poet was wrong, that we can love once more. That hope is not grounded in an optimism that our love can grow again like a lost finger-nail. We have no such faith in our unaided powers of self-recovery. Our hope rests in God's love, not ours, a love that, unlike ours, does not grow cold.

Now the green blade riseth from the buried grain.
Wheat that in dark earth many days has lain.
Love lives again, that with the dead has been,
Love is come again
Like wheat that springeth green . . .

When our hearts are wintry, grieving or in pain,
Your touch can call us back to life again,
Fields of our hearts that dead and bare have been,
Love is come again
Like wheat that springeth green.
(John Macleod Campbell Crum)

Love is come again. This is the gospel of Christ.

YEAR B

Deuteronomy 6.1–9; Hebrews 9.11–14; Mark 12.28–34

CHRISTIAN NURTURE

This Sunday we read the most important words in the Hebrew Bible: 'Hear, O Israel: the Lord our God is one Lord.' The text is known by its first word, the imperative *Shema*. For the observant Jew, this pledge of allegiance to the one God is the first prayer to be said on waking and the final prayer before falling asleep. It is the first prayer that a Jewish child is taught. It is the last words a Jew says prior to death. Throughout the ages, the *Shema* has been the ultimate cry of faith at the darkest hour. With the *Shema* on their lips, Jews accepted martyrdom at the inquisitor's stake and in the Nazi gas chambers.

The *Shema* must be taught. Deuteronomy is throughout an educational text. It is about what to teach and how to teach. The form of education commended by Deuteronomy is nurture. Education and nurture are not the same. All nurture is education, but not all education is nurture, nor should it be. In religious education lessons in schools children learn about different faiths. They may learn about Sikhism, for example. It is to be hoped that they learn *from* Sikhism, as well as *about* Sikhism. But they do not necessarily subscribe to Sikhism, or to any other religion they study, and it would be wrong to pressurize them to do so.

Nurture, such as is advocated by Deuteronomy, is certainly 'learning about' and 'learning from', but it is above all 'learning within'. The child is brought up within the community of faith. That community, in the child's earliest years, is the family home. Nurture takes place at home where the faith by which the family lives is seen as a natural talking point. Here we must glance ahead in our reading, otherwise it might seem that it's Mum and Dad alone who do any talking. Nurture must not be an unceasing parental monologue. Tell your children about the Exodus, 'when your children ask' (Deuteronomy 6.20). The qualifying clause is important. Moses might have added, 'And wait until they do.'

The command to keep the words of the *Shema* close to one's heart, to bind them to one's forehead and to put them up by one's front door are obeyed outwardly as well as inwardly by orthodox Jews. The use of these artefacts, the *tefillin* and the *mezuzah*, recognizes the educative power of things we touch and handle. 'I wonder what they're for', the child will ask. In our own time the Godly Play approach to Christian education has shown how beautifully made objects can help us explore the stories which make us wonder.

Godly Play notwithstanding, Christianity has yet to absorb into its bloodstream the Jewish understanding of nurture as it is classically presented in Deuteronomy. In Deuteronomy the obligation to nurture children belongs to the body of what is believed. To fear Yahweh and to teach one's children are not two separate religious duties, the second following from the first, but a single response of loving obedience to God. Faith and nurture are inseparable. For all the emphasis Christianity has laid on teaching, it has rarely given to the nurture of the children that central role. We worship in the church, while the Sunday School goes on in the church hall.

All this sends us back to Horace Bushnell's *Christian Nurture*, first published in 1847. Bushnell confronted the Calvinistic orthodoxy of his own day – that children were old enough to go to hell, but too young to go to heaven – with the claim that the child is to grow up as Christian and never know himself or herself as being otherwise. Bushnell believed that children belong long before they understand.

Jesus knew and loved Deuteronomy. Sunday's Gospel records how he combined the *Shema* with the Levitical injunction, that I must love my neighbour as myself (Leviticus 19.18), to give us the greatest commandment. Jesus repelled temptation by quoting Deuteronomy (Matthew 4.1–11). There is deep compassion in this book for the poor (Deuteronomy 24.10–22), as indeed for animals (22.1–4; 6—7; 25.4).

But Deuteronomy remains a disturbing text. The book is not good news if you are a Girgashite (Deuteronomy 7.1–6). Nor is it good news if you convert to another faith (6.13). And it certainly is not good news if you have suffered a painful injury to your private parts (23.1). Most problematical is Deuteronomy's consistent teaching that the reward of piety is material prosperity (28.11). That doctrine is widely preached in poor neighbourhoods. Some who preach it certainly seem to be doing very nicely.

Deuteronomy is a profoundly important educational manifesto. There is a tenderness to much of its teaching. Jesus confronted the world, the flesh and the devil armed with this text. But as we read it, we hear Jesus's words, 'You have heard that it was said . . . But I say to you . . .'

YEAR C

Isaiah 1.10–18; 2 Thessalonians 1.1–12; Luke 19.1–10

SEARCHING FOR EACH OTHER

'Zacchaeus was a very little man, and a very little man was he.' Probably we should stop singing that rollicking chorus. For two good reasons. First, short people are not figures of fun. Secondly, Zacchaeus is not just an entertaining story for the Sunday School. We are told about Zacchaeus in his sycamore tree because we need to hear what it costs to repent, especially to repent of the kind of deliberate, committed and sustained sinning that only we grown-ups are good at. Tell the children the story, by all means. If they enjoy it, fine. But it is not children whom Luke has in his sights, but us iniquitous adults. And we shouldn't be laughing but squirming.

Zacchaeus was 'of small stature'. In Luke's Greek, as in every language, the adjective 'small' can have a pejorative suggestion. Luke does not expect us to rid our minds of that suggestion. Zacchaeus would still have been a mean little man had he been two metres tall. To his victims, his diminutive physique simply made him the more despicable.

We have to remember that the first-century citizens of Jericho would not have backed our legislation on equal access for the disabled. Those 'differently abled' had to keep their distance. 'For any man who has a defect shall not approach: a man blind or lame, who has a marred face or any limb too long, a man who has a broken foot or broken hand, or is a hunchback or a dwarf, or a man who has a defect in his eye, or eczema or scab, or is a eunuch' (Leviticus 2.17–20). Zacchaeus, the dwarf, climbs his tree so he can see Jesus, but also because he knows that many in the crowd below would have regarded contact with him as contaminating. So we have here someone doubly offensive and doubly detested. He is shunned because of what is perceived as his disfigurement and loathed because of his cooperation with the occupying powers.

'I must stay at your house today', says Jesus to Zacchaeus. Luke's 'musts' matter. For Luke, it is divine necessity that drives Jesus to Jerusalem. 'I must keep going today and tomorrow and the next day—for surely no prophet can die outside Jerusalem' (Luke 13.33). That imperative determines what will transpire there. 'The Son of Man must be delivered into the hands of sinful men, be crucified and on the third day be raised again' (Luke 24.7). The same necessity – written from the foundation of the world, written for the salvation of the world – requires Jesus to enter the house of Zacchaeus and dwell there.

It is no light thing to have Jesus move in. When he does, he takes possession. Zacchaeus himself will have done some 'taking possession' in his time, invading the homes of those who had defaulted in their payments and distraining their goods – or, as the 'chief tax-collector', getting his heavies to do so. Now the invader has been invaded. Such is grace, freely given but infinitely demanding.

Remarkably, one of the best recent commentaries on this story has come from 10 Downing Street. In the 2007 BBC Lent talks, Cherie Booth QC, wife of the then Prime Minister, suggested that what Jesus required of a repentant Zacchaeus was that he should submit to a process of 'restorative justice' – the approach to the righting of wrongs that has proved so powerful in post-apartheid South Africa. Zacchaeus's victims needed the chance to tell him what had been the impact of his extortionate treatment of them. Zacchaeus himself had to understand the real consequences of his rapacity, to express true contrition, and, so far as possible, to make amends. That was the repenting he had to do – and extremely uncomfortable it must have been.

Why did Zacchaeus want a good view of Jesus? All Luke tells us is that he sought to see who Jesus was – as we all do. (The Revised English Bible's 'he was eager to see what Jesus looked like' is bathos.) Luke presents Zacchaeus's encounter with Jesus as the culmination of two quests. Zacchaeus was looking for Jesus. Jesus was looking for Zacchaeus. Beneath the sycamore tree they find each other. Luke uses the same word for Zacchaeus's search ('he *sought* to see who Jesus was') as he does for Jesus's search ('the Son of Man came to *seek* and to save the lost'). The artistry and depth of Luke's telling of the story is in this deliberate use of the same verb.

There is not just one 'long search'. There are two. We seek him who seeks us. The promise of the story is that one day we shall fall into each other's arms. In all our old versions, the translators carefully use the same English word for the two quests, ours and his. None of our modern translators do so. We are bound to wonder whether they have noticed what the story is about.

The Third Sunday before Advent

The Sunday between 6 and 12 November

YEAR A

Amos 5.18–24; 1 Thessalonians 4.13–18; Matthew 25.1–13

A WAITING GAME

The Baptist church of my boyhood did not have an altar. It was furnished simply with a plain wooden table. Save for a bunch of flowers, the table was unadorned – except, that is, for three words carved along the front. Because there was little else to catch the eye, my gaze kept returning to these words. Even as a boy, I brooded on them. I still do. 'Till he come.' When we break bread and share wine, says St Paul, 'We show forth the Lord's death till he come' (1 Corinthians 11.26).

We await the day of the Lord's coming – of his 'second coming', as we sometimes say, although that precise phrase is not scriptural. My boyhood Baptist church took the promise of the Lord's return seriously. When we broke bread together, we half expected that Jesus would be back before the meal was done. Naïve or not, that expectation was very close to that of the New Testament church. The night is far spent. The day is at hand. Such was the faith of the first Christians. Such was the faith of Coney Hall Baptist Church in the 1950s.

All three of our readings on Sunday are about 'the day of the Lord', the day when our prayer is answered and his Kingdom comes. All three readings, too, emphasize that we should live now in the light of what will happen then. What will be must shape what we are. Christianity is a waiting game. What matters is how we wait.

The contemporaries of the prophet Amos were confidently awaiting the day of the Lord, the day when God would crush their ancient enemies – the Edomites, the Ammonites, the Moabites, and the rest. Their way of waiting was to participate in ever more frequent and extravagant festivals, to slaughter more and more sacrificial beasts, to sing still more 'worship songs', and to indulge in any and every form of observance that, they hoped, would confirm the Almighty's good opinion of them and encourage him to intervene decisively on their behalf. In a word, they resorted to religion.

In my Baptist boyhood, 'winsomeness' was held to be a virtue. ('If you're winsome, you'll win some.') Winsome Amos wasn't. He was brutal. He had to be. Some misconceptions are worse than life-threatening. To cherish them is to imperil one's eternal destiny. If violent words are needed to demolish them, so be it. One such misconception is the belief that God is impressed by industrial quantities of religion.

So the prophet tells the people what they must hear, that the day they so desire will be 'darkness, not light', that there will be no escaping the judgement that the day will visit on them, that the Lord loathes the liturgies they love – and that he simply can't stand their singing.

A debating point used to be whether there can be morality without religion. It is not an issue Amos cares to discuss. What appals him is there should be religion without morality, that religion should flourish – to use his great word – without *righteousness*.

We too need to hear Amos. The world's inequities are still with us. The poor are still trampled in the dust; the afflicted are still bundled out of the way (Amos 2.7). We too 'desire the day of the Lord'. At least, we say we do each time we pray 'Your kingdom come.' We believe that the day we desire will be all sweetness and light. On All Saints' Day we sing, 'But lo there breaks a yet more glorious day.' So there will. But by the light of that day we shall know what we have done and – more pertinently – what we have left undone. We may wonder then whether our Sundays were entirely well spent.

Paul, too, addresses those who wait for the day of the Lord. There is an undertow of bewilderment and sadness about their waiting, for some of the community have died – something they had no business to do before the Lord's return. Paul tells the young church at Thessalonica what they must do while they wait. The dead now rest, but they shall rise. So those who remain – 'we who are left', as we say on Remembrance Sunday – must not grieve. And while we wait we are to encourage each other.

So to our Gospel, to 'the parable of the ten bridesmaids'. They too had to wait. Half of them were better at waiting than the others. Unlike the contemporaries of Amos, the foolish bridesmaids do not pass the time engaging in religious exercises. They simply sleep. Lovers of T. S. Eliot's light verse will recall his lines about the hippopotamus who sleeps by day and hunts by night. Eliot dryly observes that the Church, by contrast, can sleep and feed at the same time.

Our Gospel is a wake-up call. If we do not rouse ourselves, someone else will. Pray God, his first words to us will not be, 'Sorry, do I know you?'

YEAR B

Jonah 3.1–5, 10; Hebrews 9.24–28; Mark 1.14–20

REPENTANT CATTLE

Jonah's mission to Nineveh recalls George Fox's to Lichfield. Fox's first words as he rode into the city were 'Woe to the bloody city of Lichfield!' Fox was, of course, quoting from the Bible, citing that inflammatory little tract Nahum: 'Woe to the bloody city!' (Nahum 3.1) The prophet gloats over the imminent downfall of Nineveh and the proud Assyrian empire of which it was the capital. Jonah relished the prospect of Nineveh's destruction as much as did Nahum. Nineveh was more than a dreaded imperial power, the Reich that had obliterated the northern kingdom of Israel and had imposed a reign of terror over the ancient Near-East. Already in the Hebrew Bible, Nineveh belongs to myth as much as to history. Nineveh is the hated other, the enemy on whom we project all our fear and anger and urge to destroy. The possibility that God loves Nineveh is unthinkable.

Jonah does not invite the people of Nineveh to repent. All he says is that they are doomed. They are, after all, irredeemable. But then the story departs from the script. It does so in two remarkable ways. First, the people 'turn from their evil way'. They certainly weren't supposed to do that. Secondly, God 'repents of the evil which he had said he would do'. Nineveh is spared. The same vocabulary of turning and repenting from evil is used of God as is used of the people. Squeamish translators make a distinction here where there is none in the Hebrew text. According to the NIV, God doesn't 'repent'; he 'relents'. God doesn't threaten Nineveh with 'evil', but with 'destruction', as if God can be let off the hook – or the cross. Here, as nearly everywhere else, the most reliable English translation is the 1881 Revised Version. The people turn and repent – and so does God.

Well, *does* God repent? Not if – as some believe – his mind is made up. Not if, as some Calvinists claim, God has determined once and for all what will happen to us both here and hereafter. Not if – as a Church in love with long words likes to argue – God is 'immutable'.

You can't believe that God repents if you sing with conviction,

Great is thy faithfulness, O God my Father;
There is no shadow of turning with thee;
Thou changest not, thy compassions, they fail not;
As thou hast been, thou forever will be.
(Thomas Chisholm)

Perhaps the children of Nineveh are now singing these words in heaven. If so, perhaps the angels will point out to them that they are where they are only because some of the words they're singing aren't true. They are there in heaven because God changed his mind about what was going to happen to them. 'Process theology', with its claim that God is changeable, seems to be out of fashion. If Jonah were more widely read, it might be taken seriously again.

The editors of our lectionary, anxious that we should not have too much fun in church, leave out some of the most delightful verses in the Bible (Jonah 3.6–9). The king of Nineveh calls on his people to fast, to don sackcloth and ashes, and 'to cry mightily to God'. And so too, he insists, must all the animals. We find the notion that animals have a moral life eccentric. Earlier ages did not find the idea strange. Pigs were regularly hanged for infanticide. (My brief research in this field leaves me baffled, however, as to why, in 1596, the judiciary of Marseilles brought proceedings against a group of dolphins.) The universalism of the book of Jonah lies not only in its recognition that God loves Nineveh. The vision of this marvellous tale is larger still. God loves the animals too. The life which we enjoy, and for which we must answer, is the life we share with all sentient beings. Hence the astonishing last words to Jonah. 'Shouldn't I care for Nineveh,' God asks, 'where there are 120,000 silly people – *and also much cattle?*' (Jonah 4.11). (Robert Graves wrote a delightful poem about Jonah suggesting that the whale – or, if you insist, 'the large fish' – was just as disappointed as Jonah was that Nineveh was spared.)

Jonah calls on Nineveh to repent. In the Gospel we hear how one greater than Jonah comes to Galilee with the same summons. That call to repentance is addressed to us too. But we can't repent – not properly. So, according to the writer to the Hebrews, Christ himself becomes on our behalf 'the perfect penitent', yielding in his broken flesh the contrition we could never offer. It is all in R. C. Moberley's *Atonement and Personality* (John Murray, 1901).

The author of Hebrews would not have been as embarrassed as our translators are with that naïve story of an anthropophagous fish and a penitent deity.

YEAR C

Job 19.23–27a; 2 Thessalonians 2.1–5, 13–17; Luke 20.27–38

DARKNESS PIERCED BY A GREAT LIGHT

'I know that my redeemer liveth.' We cannot be as sure as Handel was who this 'redeemer' is. Strictly speaking, my 'redeemer' is a near relative who is obliged to come to my defence, to act as my vindicator or avenger, if some grave injustice has been done me (Leviticus 25.47–55). In his affliction Job had longed for an 'umpire', a go-between, to plead his case before God (Job 9.32). The text is difficult, but we can make this much out, that Job now believes that there is indeed someone who will speak for him, an unknown arbiter who will ensure that his case is heard.

Does it dawn on Job that 'the umpire' he seeks is 'the go-between God' himself? All depends on what we make of the words that follow. Here we approach one of the Himalayan summits of Holy Scripture, but it is a summit wrapped in cloud. The Hebrew Bible can be read as a long ascent to this lonely peak, to an utterance that soars above anything else said in the Old Testament. Job had every reason to curse God and die. Yet his exultant cry is that beyond the living death of his tormented days he will be granted the vision of God. If, that is, that is what he said. For at this point impenetrable mists embrace the mountain top. The Hebrew text seems to collapse under the weight of what it is asked to carry. The footnotes to our English versions say it all: 'The meaning of the Hebrew of this verse (Job 19.26) is uncertain'; 'Hebrew obscure', or simply and despairingly, 'Hebrew unintelligible'.

Why should the text suddenly break down at this critical point? Is it a case of a scribe's lapse of attention or of his exhaustion leading to a drift into gibberish? Or has the text been tampered with, as some scholars think, by a copyist who disapproved of the novel notion of a bodily resurrection? Or was there once a historical figure, a man of flesh and blood and mighty spirit, whose Calvary becomes the subject of the poem that bears the name of Job? And was that man's darkness pierced by a great light, a vision of an end of sorrows beyond words to describe? Did Job glimpse that of which – so said Thomas Traherne – even the angels dare not speak?

Perhaps what we have in Job 19.26 is not a 'corrupt text' but someone speaking in tongues.

That there was a life beyond this one was indeed a novel idea and the Sadducees would have none of it. Their question to Jesus was intended to tie him in knots over a matter on which their minds were made up. Their debate with Jesus turns on the intricacies of the 'levirate law' which allowed a man to marry his deceased brother's widow, if the brother had died childless. So what happens, they ask, if seven brothers in turn marry the same woman? Who is her husband in heaven?

Behind the preposterous question, intended only to flummox Jesus, is an issue that is far from absurd. Unless we can make some sense of the concept of the resurrection of the dead, the question of whether the notion is true or false does not arise. So Jesus takes their silly question seriously. We may well find the convolutions of his argument unpersuasive, even if we can concentrate closely enough to follow it. (The prospect of ending up like angels will not appeal to everyone.) All turns on the tenses. If, generations after Abraham's death, God still *is* – present tense – the God of Abraham, then Abraham too *is* as well. We may not be won over by this reasoning, but that was how the rabbis liked to argue and in such an exchange Jesus could hold his own with the best of them. Indeed Luke tells us that they congratulated him on how well he did so.

The story is in Matthew and Mark as well, but there are four intensely significant words only in Luke. 'For all live to him', or as the Revised English Bible has it: 'in his sight all are alive'. With these words we move way beyond word-play. God's relationship with those he loves is not severed by death. What we believe about the resurrection of the dead depends on how we understand our relationship with God. If the God made known in Jesus is essentially a God who does not break off relationships then we have reason to hope.

I have had another window open on my PC as I have been preparing these notes on our Sunday readings. The email I have just received tells me that a young mother in my family has died, 'her face a mask of fear'. What do I say? Words fail, as they did for Job. But then Job never got an answer to his questions. Perhaps answers are not the answer, but, as for Job, a relationship in which questions are no longer necessary.

The Second Sunday before Advent

The Sunday between 13 and 19 November

YEAR A

Zephaniah 1.7, 12–18; 1 Thessalonians 5.1–11; Matthew 25.14–30

THE LAST INTERRUPTION

Last week we trembled – or we should have done – when we heard Amos's warning that the day of the Lord is 'darkness, not light' (Amos 5.18). Zephaniah, if possible, is even fiercer than Amos. This Sunday we hear a brief extract from the blistering diatribe that bears his name. Zephaniah catalogues the calamities that the fast-approaching 'day of wrath' will bring. We must not let the metaphor mislead us. When the prophet says that these woes are what '*the day*' will bring, he means, of course, that these are the woes that *God* will inflict. We'll return to the important matter of metaphors and other figures of speech in a moment.

Zephaniah tells us why such a terrifying divine judgement looms over Jerusalem. Its citizens, we read, have been dangerously complacent.

They are 'like wine left on its lees'. (Easy-reading translations, such as the Good News Bible, recognizing that some are less acquainted with the bottle than others, avoid the image.) People have said to themselves, 'The Lord will do nothing, neither good nor bad.' It is a kind of atheism. A god who doesn't do anything is effectively not there. It is the atheism of most of our contemporaries, even if they tell the pollsters that they believe in God.

God will not do nothing. 'In the day of his wrath, in the fire of his passion, the whole earth shall be consumed.' This is strong language. Two points must be made. It is not Zephaniah's last word on God's purpose for his people. His last word is love. 'The Lord will show you his love once more' (Zephaniah 3.17) – such is a typical modern translation of a line from the exultant conclusion to this extraordinary but neglected little book. Literally, the Hebrew reads: 'He will be silent in his love.' He will be silent in his love. Some things begin to be explained if this is not a mangled chunk of Hebrew but the inspired word of God.

The second point concerns both the incandescence of Zephaniah and talk of the wrath of God generally. Moral complacency – we think of the story of the Pharisee and the publican (Luke 18.9–14) – is so perilous that the strongest measures, including the strongest language, are justified in confronting it. That does not mean I should use such language. It means I must listen to it.

That is why I must hear the reading from the first letter of Paul to the Thessalonians and the Gospel of our Lord Jesus Christ according to Matthew. Paul and Matthew speak with Zephaniah's prophetic voice. The day of the Lord – that is to say, the Lord himself – will come suddenly. We do not know when he will come or how he will come, and it is an absurd misreading of such apocalyptic texts as the book of Revelation to suppose that they provide such information. But this we may surely say: the coming of the Lord will be the Last Interruption.

General Synod is in session. The remuneration of archdeacons is being discussed. A rural dean is moving an important amendment. But synod is not listening. It is late in the day, yet the light in the sky is increasing. Soon the light is greater than any in the chamber can bear. The sound of a trumpet and of people singing is heard. The chairman hastily gathers his papers and whispers into the microphone, 'Synod is adjourned.'

The prophets of both testaments use bold images to impress on us the suddenness of the Lord's return. The day – that is, the Lord – will come 'like a thief in the night', says St Paul. Jesus himself had used the same shocking language. A householder who knows when a thief intends to break in will take all necessary steps to apprehend him (Matthew 24.43).

It is not entirely needless to say – back to the Bible's figurative language – that when Jesus compares his coming to that of thief he is not lending his blessing to burglary. The same common-sense distinction between sign and significance must be made when we turn to 'the Parable of the Talents'. We must make the best use of the brief space left to us before the Lord comes. The zealous disciple will be like the enterprising slaves who use the money their master has entrusted to them to make a lot more money.

Nothing is said about how this massively increased wealth will be used. So does the parable tacitly endorse the kind of financial activity – and the greed which drives it – that has had such calamitous consequences in recent years? Not at all, any more than the parable sanctions the institution of slavery – or the brutal treatment of the 'worthless slave' whose comeuppance is the parable's conclusion. Indeed, when Jesus addresses directly those who create wealth for wealth's sake, he leaves us in little doubt about where he stands (Luke 12.13–34).

YEAR B

Daniel 12.1–3; Hebrews 10.11–14 (15–18) 19–25; Mark 13.1–8

THE BEST YET TO BE – THE WORST YET TO COME

'Not one stone will be left on another.' Jesus uses hyperbole. Some stones are still in place – just as, for a little longer, some of our own ecclesiastical structures survive. The vast retaining walls, supporting the platform on which Herod built Jerusalem's Second Temple, still stand. The masonry of the lower courses is the original Herodian work. As we say our prayers at 'the Western Wall', alongside our Jewish sisters and brothers, we are moved to wonder by these colossal stones, as were the disciples.

With those disciples, we cross the Kidron and climb to the top of the Mount of Olives. With them, we survey the city spread beneath us and with them we ask the question Jerusalem always makes us ask. When will it all end? The disciples ask 'When?' and so do we, for we feel that we've had enough. The first Christian prayer was 'Come, Lord Jesus!'(Revelation 22.20). Two millennia later we ask, 'How long, O Lord? How long?' And so we search the Bible for whatever hints and clues it offers about what is to be and when it is to be. In Mark 13, the so-called 'Little Apocalypse', Jesus addresses these longings directly. (We need to read the whole chapter, not just the first eight verses.)

Jesus's teaching about the end is characterized by two paradoxes. The first paradox is that he appears to speak in some detail about events of which he says he knows nothing. He claims that he has told his disciples everything that is going to happen. Yet he says that these things are hidden from him.

This first paradox is eased, though not eliminated, when we take account of the character of Jesus's 'eschatological' teaching. Jesus's purpose is not to provide a timetable, some kind of countdown to Armageddon, a series of predictions capable of being ticked off one by one as they are fulfilled. Such 'apocalypses', purporting to reveal esoteric information about the last days, abounded in the period 'between the Testaments' and many a head was addled by them.

Jesus's aim was not to publish a programme of the end of history. The focus of his teaching is the here and now. His words about tomorrow are about how to live today. The disciples' question, and ours, is factual: 'When is it going to be?' But Jesus's answer is moral. Our queries about the future are met with instructions about the present. 'Make sure no one leads you astray.'

The second paradox in Jesus's teaching about what is to come is more troubling. The paradox is stark. Jesus teaches that things will get much better – and that they will get far worse. He urges us to pray and work for the coming of God's Kingdom on earth. In this conviction Christians run night-shelters in church halls, dig wells in dry places, persuade rich countries to write off the debts owed them by poor ones. These are bridgeheads of the approaching Kingdom. God's reign of justice and peace is brought that much nearer as each is established. According to this scenario, things here get better, however slowly and painfully, and evangelism is primarily social and political action to make it happen.

But then we turn to Mark 13, with its talk of wars, earthquakes, and famines. And these are just for starters. God will say 'Let there be darkness' and there will be darkness. Things will go from bad to worse. It is the scenario described in one of the great passages of modern theological literature, written in Germany as Hitler was seizing power.

All the calamities which meet and have met us are but the menacing heralds of a final, fearful visitation which God has appointed for the end of history. When that time comes the avalanche of sin, sorrow, and death, which ever since man's first sin has been sliding down history with unremitting, increasing and overpowering momentum, will finally come to rest in one mighty roll of thunder. (E. Stauffer, *New Testament Theology*, Macmillan, 1941)

Those who believe that this is all the future holds will see social action as a dangerous distraction from the Church's proper task. The business of evangelism, they'll say, is the saving of souls, the plucking of brands from the burning, and nothing else.

Can we resolve these conflicting prospects, that the best is yet to be but the worst is still to come? No, nor should we try to. The same principle applies to the doctrine of the last things as to every other Christian doctrine: 'They who will to do his will shall know of the doctrine' (John 7.17). The only path to understanding is the next thing to be done.

And suppose the cosmologists are right, that one by one the stars will go out, that we are all for the dark? We'll still dig those wells and share our story. Rearranging the deck chairs on the Titanic never was a silly thing to do. On the contrary, it is the courtesy of the Kingdom to do just that.

YEAR C

Malachi 4.1–2a; 2 Thessalonians 3.6–13; Luke 21.5–19

THE BEGINNING OF THE END

Now the outward face of the temple wanted nothing that was likely to surprise either men's minds or their eyes; for it was covered all over with plates of gold of great weight, and, at the first rising of the sun, reflected back a very fiery splendour, and made those who forced themselves to look upon it to turn their eyes away, just as they would have done at the sun's own rays.

Such, according to the Jewish historian Josephus, was the glory of the mightiest of the building projects of Herod the Great. But Josephus also tells us what the High Priest of the Temple wore when he went to work.

When he officiated, he had on a pair of breeches that reached beneath his privy parts to his thighs, and had on an inner garment of linen, together with a blue garment, round, without seam, with fringe work, and reaching to the feet. There were also golden bells that hung upon the fringes, and pomegranates intermixed among them. The bells signified thunder and the pomegranates lightning.

Why did the Temple have to go? It was, after all, a Grade 1 listed building of outstanding architectural importance. No Diocesan Advisory Committee would have tolerated the relocation of one of its candlesticks, let alone its demolition.

For Jesus of Nazareth – his mind on these matters later to be reflected in the letter to the Hebrews – the reason the Temple had to go was that it hallowed and perpetuated a way of relating to God that required both elaborate ceremonial and a hierarchy of intermediaries. Jesus spoke witheringly of those who went about 'wearing broad phylacteries and with large tassels on their robes' (Matthew 23.5). He had in mind the scribes and Pharisees, who in our terms were laymen. The staff of the Temple – those 'ordained', if you like – were stricter still about the proper ordering of the liturgy and the correct seasonal vestments. The Temple institutionalized an extremely complicated and burdensome system of what was required to approach one's maker. In a word, the Temple made *religion* the way to God. No wonder Jesus turned up there one day with a whip.

The fall of Jerusalem and the destruction of the Temple are seen by Jesus as a prelude to the end of history, the end that will be both history's conclusion and its consummation. When Luke's Gospel was being studied by its first readers, those portentous events had already taken place. Jesus had shown himself a prophet to be trusted. We live in the same period of 'salvation-history'. The first of 'the last things' has already taken place. The Temple is no more, even if, sadly, many of our subsequent Church structures – not to speak of clerical wardrobe – can be seen as pathetic attempts to rebuild it. Now we live in the interval between the first and the final of those 'last things'.

This is the era on which the second half of our Gospel reading focuses. It is the age when believers are betrayed by family and friends, when they are arrested and persecuted, when they are put on trial, imprisoned and executed. Jesus's predictions are literally fulfilled in the events Luke records in the second of his two volumes about the beginnings of Christianity, in the book known to us as the Acts of the Apostles. Again his first readers will have registered, as we do, how clearly Jesus saw what was coming.

Betrayal, arrest, imprisonment, and execution. Such trials have not overtaken the present writer since his moving from Hackney to Hove.

Nor will they be the experience of most readers. But we are not Filipino Christians working in Saudi Arabia; nor are we among the thousands of believers reportedly enduring torture and starvation in North Korean labour camps; nor are we Pentecostal pastors locked in shipping containers in Eritrea; nor do we run Christian bookshops in Gaza.

Nor does Jesus speak of the times when Christians have been the perpetrators rather than the victims of persecution – even if the horrors they have inflicted have been on each other. But whether the Church is persecuted or persecuting it is always the Church at the cross. There we are either sharing Christ's sufferings or inflicting them. We carry his cross or nail him to it.

The first of the last things was the destruction of the Temple. No longer do those golden walls blaze with the light of the rising sun. Now we must wait and pray for grace to bear what may be required of us. If the days are dark, it is the darkness before dawn. As George MacDonald used to say, 'The light is only the other side of the hill.' That promised light is greater than the light that touched the Temple with fire. Our Old Testament reading tells us to look east. There – soon – 'the sun of righteousness shall rise with healing in its wings'.

Christ the King

The Sunday between 20 and 26 November

YEAR A

Ezekiel 34.11–16, 20–24; Ephesians 1.15–23; Matthew 25.31–46

THE LAST JUDGEMENT

On the south wall of the nave of the church of St Nicholas, Portslade, in the Diocese of Chichester, there was once a wall-painting depicting the Last Judgement. Traces of it were last seen in 1847 when the wall was being repaired. All evidence of it is now lost. Examples of such paintings, though rare, are better preserved and still to be seen in other churches. I mention Portslade because it is in that parish that we tend our allotment. It is a stubborn plot, abounding in weeds and prompting fearful thoughts of how the angels will dispose of the tares, when God comes to take his harvest home.

The Last Judgement is not much on our minds these days. But there was a time when you could never forget it. There it was, on the walls of your church. There, Sunday by Sunday, you saw Christ in Majesty – often above the chancel arch – weighing souls, some of whom were seen ascending the steps of heaven, while others were being dragged to the mouth of hell.

On this last Sunday of the church year, we are one with the medieval parishioners of Portslade. On the insistence of St Matthew, we contemplate the Last Judgement.

Like Islam, Matthew's Gospel has five pillars. These are the five separate extended discourses in which Matthew presents much of the teaching of Jesus. Our Gospel readings for 'the Sundays before Advent' have come from the last of these great discourses. The Gospel for 'the Sunday next before Advent' and the Feast of Christ the King is its conclusion. Jesus has spoken of the severity of the trials that will beset his disciples before the end. He has warned of the suddenness of the coming of the Son of Man. He has emphasized the need for watchfulness and for the right use of God's gifts – including that most precious gift of all, the little time left before the 'unexpected hour'.

Now Jesus has a last word. To be sure, he will have more to say to his disciples, at Bethany, in the upper room, in Gethsemane, and, after his resurrection, in Galilee. But there is dreadful finality about what he says now. The next thing we hear from Matthew will be that the conspiracy to arrest and kill Jesus is under way. Before all draws to its appointed end, he has one thing more to say to his disciples and, in history's twilight, to his Church.

It is my Lord's final warning to me. If I fail to feed him when he is hungry or to give him something to drink when he is thirsty, if I do not provide shelter for him when he is homeless, or warm clothes for him when he is shivering, if I do not visit him when he is ill or imprisoned, then my doom is the eternal fire. Confronted with this warning, what matters are not my opinions about hell – if it is, what it is, where it is, or how long it lasts. What matters is whether I recognize Jesus in 'the least, the last, and the lost' and reach out to him.

Periodically there is a debate on TV about whether you should give money to beggars. The major TV channels keep a list of clergy to contact when they want to wheel out a parson to pontificate on the folly of doing so. For a year or two I was on that list. That list is not the same as the Lamb's Book of Life (Revelation 21.27).

'Inasmuch as you did it to one of the least of these my brothers and sisters, you did it to me.' Here, as in the Sermon on the Mount, I am faced with the distinctive characteristic of the moral teaching of Jesus. That distinctive characteristic is its impossibility. It is impossible for me, not only because I am not Mother Teresa of Calcutta. It is impossible, too, because I meet Jesus in the needy and the vulnerable every time I step out of my front door or switch on the news. How am I supposed to feed every hungry Jesus who begs me to spare some change or whose wasted figure appears briefly on a screen in the corner of my lounge?

In bewilderment and despair, we turn to our Saviour and return to the text. The Lord's last warning to me should force me to my knees, crying for mercy. Such repentance is the first turning we must take. Like all turnings, it opens for us a new direction. In Christian discipleship, the direction we are going is much more important than how far we have got.

And we turn back to the text. I notice what I'd missed in too hasty a reading. 'Inasmuch,' says Jesus, 'as you did it to *one* of the least . . .' Not all of the least, but *one* of the least. Each of us – for himself, herself – will know who that is.

YEAR B

Daniel 7.9–10, 13–14; Revelation 1.4b–8; John 18.33–37

POWER EMBODIED – TRUTH MADE FLESH

The Gospel readings for the year close with a scene from John's account of the trial of Jesus. Jesus stands before Pilate. The drama unfolding is the clash of empires, the confrontation of Christ and Caesar.

Composers of lectionaries are interpreters. They pick and choose bits from the Bible on the basis of which scriptural passages they think are the most important. Unfortunately, they sometimes go further. They decide what we should read on the grounds of what they think is good for us. So it is with this Sunday's Gospel reading. The lectionary stipulates that we break off at verse 37, with Jesus's claim that he is testifying to the truth. That provides a neat and satisfying ending as we come to the close of the church year. But where we're told to stop isn't where John stops. The last line of this little scene as John tells the story is Pilate's famous question, 'What is truth?' The lectionary reading leaves us with an assertion. It is both the artistry and the wisdom of John to leave us with a question. To omit Pilate's wistful enquiry is to ignore the integrity of what John writes and, once again, to treat a book which invites the right questions as a manual of right answers.

It is vital that we read that extra verse as we conclude this year's cycle of readings. The theme of the exchange between Jesus and Pilate is the relationship of power and truth. We'll not get very far with that subject without hearing Pilate's question.

It has sometimes been suggested that 'truth' is no more than victorious opinion. On this view, religious 'truth', Christian orthodoxy included, is simply the belief of those who happened to win. 'Heresy', then, is defeated opinion. The doctrines defined by the early councils of the Church were the points of view of those there – all men, of course – with the most muscle. We don't have to be quite that cynical to be uneasily aware that struggles for power have played a big part in shaping Christian belief. Manifestly the debates threatening to tear the Anglican communion apart are more about power than truth.

When John describes the meeting of Pilate and Jesus, it as is he is contemplating two incarnations, power embodied ranged against truth made flesh. Both Pilate and Jesus claim to rule but their understandings of sovereignty are utterly opposed. Pilate's incredulity is manifest. 'Are *you* the king of the Jews?' His contempt for the absurd parody of a monarch brought before him is memorably voiced by the Pontius Pilate of *Jesus Christ Superstar*. 'Who is this broken man cluttering up my hallway? Who is this unfortunate?' Pilate cannot understand that strength is made perfect in weakness.

Jesus claims that his Kingdom is 'not of this world'. It is always difficult to capture exactly what Jesus means by his 'kingdom'. That kingdom is neither a place nor an era. It is not 'from here', says Jesus, a strangely elusive phrase. It is 'elsewhere', as the Revised English Bible opaquely puts it. If his Kingdom is not 'from here' then presumably it is 'from there', but we do not know where 'there' might be. That his Kingdom is not of 'this world' perhaps implies that it belongs to the world to come. But the context of Jesus's comments is the immediate crisis of his arrest and trial. The response of his disciples to that crisis, the fact that they have kept its rules by not resorting to violence to save him, is a sign that his Kingdom is already present.

I used to tell the teenagers I taught that 'the Kingdom of God' means 'the way God works'. I still think that this simple paraphrase gets close to what Jesus means. These days we are used to discussions about models of monarchy and alternative royal life-styles. The Kingdom of God is the divine model of monarchy, God's way of doing things. Jesus's

Kingdom, needless to say, is not some other kingdom. It is his way too.

There are circumstances in which the followers of Jesus must not fight. That aspect of the way of Jesus is made very clear by what he says to Pilate. Jesus's words no doubt raise the whole issue of Christian pacifism, but the point he makes here is more specific and it is important, in focusing on this text, not to be immediately swept away into that wider debate. Jesus forbids his disciples to try to stop him being handed over to his accusers. His disciples are expressly forbidden to fly to his defence.

As we still are. The way of Jesus prohibits the exercise of power to assert or to defend the truth, as we see it, of who he is. In a word, we may not resort to violence in the cause of Christ. And of course there are more ways than one of throwing your weight around. The 'religious right' have got it wrong.

YEAR C

Jeremiah 23.1–6; Colossians 1.11–20; Luke 23.33–43

CHRIST THE KING AND THE SLAUGHTERED OF SHARPEVILLE

Sunday's feast recalls me to the Diocese of Christ the King in the Anglican Church of Southern Africa. The diocese was formed in 1990 in the last days of the apartheid era. The area the diocese covers, south of Johannesburg, was at that time virtually a war-zone. Place names on the map of the diocese – Sharpeville, Boipotong, Sebokeng – memorialize the barbarity of the apartheid regime and the affliction and courage of those who rose against it.

The diocese was named as it was as a defiant assertion of Christ's kingship in the face of all that contradicted his just and gentle rule. The Rt Revd Peter Lee, the first bishop of the diocese, chose to be 'enthroned' (needless to say, not the word he used) in Sharpeville where, ten years before, sixty-nine were killed and over one hundred and eighty injured, shot – mostly in the back – by the South African Police.

We affirm Christ's kingship in defiance of all that denies it. We affirm his kingship in Sharpeville. We affirm his kingship at Calvary, where Luke sends us this Sunday.

We have been walking with Luke for the best part of a year. Our companion next year will be Matthew who, as we shall see, has his own understanding of the kingship of Christ. We leave Luke before he ends his story, but for Luke, as for all the Gospel writers, Jesus 'reigns from a tree'. Only in the shadow of that tree can we speak of Christ's kingship without capitulating to triumphalism. Just as Bishop Peter Lee affirmed the sovereignty of Christ on the ground where the slaughtered innocents fell, so we celebrate Christ's kingship beneath the cross. To be sure, Easter and Ascension proclaim Christ's victory and reign. 'Hail the day that sees him rise, glorious to his native skies!' and all that. But it is better for us this Sunday that we stay with our feet firmly planted on the cruel earth where the cross stood and where, for the time being, we have to serve his Kingdom.

Here at the cross Luke touches on themes dear to his heart. Three may be mentioned – the paradoxical nature of Christ's kingship, the priority of the poor, and the cost of salvation.

Luke underscores more sharply than do Matthew or Mark the absurdity of claiming that someone crucified might also be a king. Notice the contemptuous 'ifs'. The rulers sneer, 'If this is the Christ of God, the chosen one . . .' The soldiers are equally mocking, 'If you are the king of the Jews . . .'

Luke learned from his Lord a love of those counted for little. These are 'the poor' to whom the good news is announced (Luke 4.18) and to whom the Kingdom is promised (Luke 6.20). We meet them again here at the cross. Luke is careful to distinguish them – if only by the lightest of touches – from those with clout. It is the *rulers* who sneer, the *soldiers* who mock. The common people just watched and, when it was all over, turned broken-heartedly away (Luke 23.48). The distinction is suggested, not forced on our attention. But, like any good teacher, Luke prefers to drop quiet hints rather than to shout.

As we have seen across the year now closing, Luke's Jesus came 'to seek and to save the lost' (Luke 19.10). In all three synoptic Gospels Jesus is ridiculed for having repeatedly claimed the power to save when now, strung up on a cross, he is manifestly helpless even to help himself. But it is Luke who adds the bitter voice of 'the impenitent thief' to this chorus of misunderstanding about what it means to be saved. So he drives home the truth that the salvation offered by this utterly atypical King does not deliver us from experiences such as crucifixion. So far from being spared the cross, we are promised it.

If Christ is king, where does he reign? In our Old Testament reading, Jeremiah speaks of 'the once and future king', of David long ago and of one greater than David who will be born of David's line. This promised king will contrast with petty demagogues and puppet monarchs of Jeremiah's own day. The king whom Jeremiah awaits will reign wisely and will ensure 'justice and righteousness in the land'. The juxtaposition of Sunday's readings invites us to see Jeremiah's hope fulfilled in Jesus. If that interpretation is correct, we should look for an answer to the question 'Where does he reign?' in places where – here as well as in heaven – wisdom, justice and righteousness prevail. Few earthly kingdoms, or republics either, meet those criteria. But there are the odd corners, some very odd, where they do things differently, where the topsy-turvy world of 'the Kingdom of our God and of his Christ' is already functioning. Churches – Lord, have mercy on us – are meant to be such places.